TEN COMMENDATIONS
BY GLOBAL CHURCH LEADERS

Listed alphabetically

"I appreciate and thank Rev. Shibu Cherian for the systematic study of the word of God on a daily basis by covering the entire bible in 365 days. Studying and meditating the word of God early in the morning gives the right thought pattern for the day, and you will be green, fresh and whatever you do will prosper (Psalm 1:3). You create your own environment with the attitude you develop, and the right attitude (physical, psychological, emotional, spiritual) can be developed by studying the word of God through this devotional book. I have personally studied the book of Job from this blog in 2011 that has helped me to understand why God allows suffering in my life. I congratulate Rev. Shibu Cherian for this effort in bringing biblical thought pattern into the minds of people through his writings and pray that many more theological books will follow."

Dr. Rev. Abraham Varghese
Executive Director, Lucknow Teen Challenge
Drug Rehabilitation Ministry, India

"It is very important to read the Bible systematically through daily devotion and scripture reflection that will help people to refocus their thoughts on the Lord Jesus Christ. Reading the entire Bible helps further your spiritual walk, because the whole Bible shows us how we should think, talk, walk, act, and live. If we neglect certain parts of the Bible we may miss out on some of the practical life lessons the Bible teaches us. This devotional book "United in The WORD" written by Rev. Shibu Cherian serves the purpose of assisting people journey through reading the whole Bible in a year. I salute Rev. Cherian for his dedication and publishing the daily devotions as a collective writing. I hope and pray that this will encourage many to read the Bible, and be able to live out what they are reading. May God bless you!"

Rev. Dr. C. V. Andrews
Senior Pastor, Atlanta Church of God, USA

7

"A healthy diet and regular exercise are essential for the balanced growth and development. The systematic daily intake of God's Word in its entirety and digesting the same is crucial in the life of a Christian. Our families, churches, communities and the world at large are in need of men and women/boys and girls who would feed on the Word for daily spiritual strength, reflection and positive and healthy life style that is rooted in the principles and standards of the Bible. "United in The WORD" is an excellent tool and guide that would take the reader and student of the Word to deeper depths and higher heights for a year-long experience through the Holy Scriptures. I commend this devotional book by my good friend and colleague in the ministry, Rev. Shibu Cherian, and wish God's blessings and favours upon all that would take advantage of this journey and experience through the Word of God."

Rev. Dr. Joe Kurian
Director, UK Church of God Cross Cultural Ministries, London

"At the start of the year 2012, I give a clarion call to the young and the old to be blessed from the continuous and systematic reading of the Bible. When the Word is read, studied, and lived by, it transforms individuals, families and the whole society. The world would become heaven on earth. This day-by-day Devotional that Rev. Shibu Cherian compiled from his daily blogs is an exceptionally great tool to promote the strengthening of the Christian youth. May God bless him abundantly in his labor of love for the Kingdom! MARANATHA!"

Rev. Joseph Mathew
Overseer, Church of God, Central West Region, India

"Anyone who desires to grow and get intimate with God cannot ignore or neglect the Word of God, which is given to us as light to our path and lamp to our feet and help us to progress in our walk with God. Without God's Word to guide us, we will stumble and be lost. God's Word is also the "Sword of the Spirit" to protect us as well as to destroy our enemy. God's Word is like pure milk given to us to get stronger until we reach the full stature of Jesus Christ. God's Word produces faith in our spiritual walk as well. This daily devotional will surely capture your imagination and stir you up to grow intimate with God. May this devotional produce the desired results is my hope and prayer!"

Rev. Pappy Mathai
Senior Pastor, Assemblies of God, Lucknow, India
Superintendent, Northern District of Assemblies of God of North India

8

United In
The Word

365 Daily Devotions To Assist Your Journey Through
The Bible In One Year
The First Journey

Pastor Shibu Cherian is an Ordained Minister with the Church of God (www.churchofgod.org), and currently serves as an Associate Pastor of Atlanta Church of God (www.atlantachurchofgod.org) in Lawrenceville, Georgia, USA. He is a certified Chaplain, a Bible Teacher & has a passion for teaching and mentoring. He is also a Premarital Counselor and is certified as a PREPARE-ENRICH Facilitator. He authors a daily Bible reading-meditation blog called 'United in The WORD' (http://unitedintheword.blogspot.com). He resides in Lilburn, Georgia, USA with his wife Nissy (who is a Nursing Instructor) and three daughters Priscila, Pheba & Persis. You can follow Pastor Shibu on Twitter @Shibunissy.

UNITED IN THE WORD

365 Daily Devotions To Assist Your Journey Through
The Bible In One Year
The First Journey

SHIBU CHERIAN
MS, MBA, DMIN-Pastoral Counseling (Cand.)

RHEMA PUBLISHERS INTERNATIONAL
P.O. Box 69, Thiruvalla - 689 101, Kerala, India
E-mail: rhemabookhouse@yahoo.com

(English)
UNITED IN THE WORD
THE BIBLE IN ONE YEAR

Author: Shibu Cherian
© Reserved
First Impression: February 2012
Cover: Pheba Shibu
Layout: Global, Tiruvalla Ph: 0469-263355
Printed at: Anaswara Offset Pvt Ltd., Ernakulam
Published by : Rhema Publishers International,
P.O. Box 69, Thiruvalla - 689 101
Ph: 0469-2731484

Price **US$ 19.95**

ISBN 978-1475055320

01995 >

9 781475 055320

Contents

PUBLISHERS NOTE

This Book, 'United in THE WORD', a 365 days devotional with a Bible Reading Guide will assist your journey through the Bible in one year. Pastor Shibu Cherian is a prolific writer and a church pastor who has devoted his life in ministry. He has done an excellent job in exposing different passages in the Bible as wonderful devotions. We are certain that this book will no doubt benefit the people of God to meditate and learn the word of God, and furnish their duties effectively. We are so privileged to bring out this book in a simple and easy reading style. May the insights and inspiration gathered in this book be a source of deeper understanding for all the readers on their responsibilities as effective gospel witnesses! We are grateful to Almighty God for enabling us to offer this exposition to enrich people in their study of God's Word. We hope that the reading of this book will inspire many to work sincerely and wholeheartedly for advancing the Kingdom of God.

Sali Monai, M.Sc., JD(PhD)

"Pastor Shibu Cherian writes well in a technical/scholarly style as well as in a devotional style. This book is a collection of devotional/ meditational reflections concerning Christ's glory. He strives to apply Scripture to our place and time in history. As such, his works, both scholarly and devotional, are accessible, relevant, enjoyable, and powerful. It comforts, encourages and supports those on a spiritual journey seeking a closer walk with God. This book is 'Soul Food' for the spiritual traveller."

Rev. Shibu K. Mathew
Registrar, Mount Zion Bible College, Church of God, Kerala State, India

"It gives me much pleasure to know that Rev. Shibu Cherian is publishing his collective writings of his devotional blog 'United in The WORD'. It is written in the Bible that "Man does not live by bread alone but by every word that comes out of the mouth of the God". The spiritual food that he prepared for the people of God will really be a blessing from the beginning of the year till its end. Let this endeavour bring spiritual growth and encouragement to every reader day by day and find out hidden treasures of the Word of God. I wish all success to this new endeavour!"

Rev. K M Thankachan
Regional Overseer, Church of God in India,
Central Eastern Region, Calcutta, India

"United in The WORD is a wonderful collection of daily Bible Devotions, designed to be used as a 365-day devotional reading. Not only is this an excellent devotional, but also an excellent Bible study resource for teens and young adults. As a pastor and a counselor, I highly recommend this book to every committed Christian."

Dr. Thomas Idiculla, PhD
President, Agape Partners International
Director, Mental Health Services Evaluation, McLean Hospital, USA
Instructor in Psychiatry, Harvard Medical School, USA

"With marvellously insightful words and very thoughtful commentary on each daily portion, this book has made an impact on individuals and will continue on to ripple out to other Christians. It's an encouraging and inspiring start to God's people each morning."

Rev. Thomas Mathew, Ph. D.
Assistant Pastor, Atlanta Church of God, Lawrenceville, USA

"I take this opportunity to thank Pastor Shibu Cherian a great man of God who is being used in a powerful way for the kingdom purpose. It is through him that God allowed having a wealth of information through the daily devotional reading made possible for all of us. The purpose of it is that we must be Kingdom minded people. "The kingdom of God is at hand" (Mark 1:14-15) and "Seek first the kingdom of God, His righteousness, and all these things shall be added to you" (Matthew 6:33). The dynamic of Christian life and the power of the Word can be experienced only be reading and making the word of God into practice by understanding the principles. Further in Luke 16:16, the kingdom of God is advanced through reading the word daily, preaching, impassioned prayer, confrontation with the demonic, a flaming heart to reach the unreached then do the miraculous with God's anointing and His power that is working in all of us."

Rev. Wilson Varghese,
World Missionary Evangelist, Louisiana, USA

ACKNOWLEDGEMENT

First and foremost, I wish to acknowledge my Lord and Savior Jesus Christ who has enabled me to frame the devotions that you will read in this book. It was the Holy Spirit who injected this thought into my mind in October 2010 that I should start writing devotions based on my daily Bible reading and meditation. We have many devotional books in the market, but none of them encourage the readers to have a systematic reading of the Bible on a daily basis. How much better it would have been if the readers would be able to read through the Bible in one year using a daily Bible reading guide! Keeping all this in mind, God allowed me to launch a group Bible devotion blog entitled *United in The WORD* (http:// unitedintheword.blogspot.com) on January 1, 2011. Thus began my first journey through the Bible in 2011, and by God's grace, I was able to complete my journey through the Bible on December 31, 2011. What you read in this book are the thoughts/devotion that God has spoken to me through the pages of His Word as they became both real and relevant to my personal growth and spiritual discernment. It is my earnest prayer that God will speak to you as well through His Word as he has spoken to me every day in 2011.

I would like to acknowledge many people in my life who have supported me with encouraging words and prayers. On the top of my list is my dearest wife of 20+ years - Nissy - who has been my soul mate and my prayer partner through the many challenges I have faced during 2011. My three dearest daughters Priscila, Pheba and Persis have always stood by me to encourage and commend many of my devotions when I have shared with them during our family prayer time. My parents (V. C. & Aminikutty Cherian), Nissy's Mom (Mary

Chacko), my sisters (Shirley & Sheeba), their spouses (Pastor Joseph Mathew & Shaji John), Nissy's sister (Jolly), her spouse (Johnson), my nephews (Nelvin, Jasper, Steve, Edwin, Sam) and my nieces (Christine, Sharon) have all prayed for God to use me to bless others through His Word. All the Pastors, brothers, sisters, youth and children of my church (Atlanta Church of God) have encouraged my effort to promote daily Bible reading for which I am grateful. Lastly, a few of my dearest friends and well-wishers from my Covenant and Bible Study Groups have all played a role in getting me to successfully complete my first devotional journey through the Bible so far.

All glory be to God alone!

Lilburn, GA

January, 2012

FOREWORD

The iconic figure of protestant reformation, a German priest, and world-renowned theologian, Martin Luther (1483-1546) insisted the importance of reading the Word (Bible) and understanding the truth when he said, *"God is everywhere. However, He does not want you to reach out for Him everywhere but only in the Word. Reach out for it and you will grasp Him aright. Otherwise you are tempting God and setting up idolatry. That is why He has established a certain method for us. This teaches us how and where we are to look for Him and find Him, namely, in the Word."* God has given us a great treasure, Bible in this world to find answers for every challenge we face today. Former president of the Unites Sates of America, Ronald Reagan (1911-2004) once said, *"Within the covers of one single book, the Bible, are all the answers to all the problems that face us today—if only we would read and believe."*

The Word of God primarily teach two most important truths: 1.What man is to believe about God and 2, What God requires of man. As God is the author of mankind, these words are authoritative because these are inspired by God. We read in 2 Timothy 3:16, 17 – *"All Scripture is God-breathed and is useful for teaching, rebuking, correcting and training in righteousness, so that the man of God may be thoroughly equipped for every good work".* Because of the sinful nature, man's biggest problem is his inability to carry out good things in life. That is why the Word of God is so important in the process of transformation from one's old-self to newness. The Scripture is authoritative because the inspiration that lead to the Word is verbal (as God communicated to Jeremiah), organic (through the research of Godly men) and complete in all respects. The Word of God is both "inerrant" and "infallible". The word, "inerrant" means "exempted from errors" and the other word "infallible" means "incapable of error". "Inerrancy" emphasizes the truthfulness of Scripture (Psalm 119:160: *"All your words are True"*) and "Infallible" emphasizes the trustworthiness of the Scripture (John 17:17: *"Sanctify them by the truth; your word is truth"*).

In this day and age, amidst roller-coaster life-style, where believers find hard to give enough time to read the Word of God and pray, the daily devotional, "United in The WORD" by our enthusiastic, highly-motivated, and knowledgeable in the Word exposition, Rev. Shibu Cherian comes handy to enable a quality time in the presence of our Lord and Savior Jesus Christ.

To understand the Word of God with clarity, the daily devotional, "United in The WORD" would be of immense value and help to the believers as an additional supplemental guidance to the Bible. Pastor Cherian's God-given vision is to reach a wide variety of audience who are interested in learning the Word and equip them with the Word of God through clear understanding of the truth to face the life challenges of today. The daily devotional reveals the deeper understanding of Pastor Cherian in the biblical truth and is very clearly written to help believers without theological training to understand the greater truths of the Bible. A regular reading of the Word and a devotional to help understand the Word of God better, are critical to maintain a spiritually disciplined life. The other important aspect of the devotional, "United in The WORD" is the brief historical background based on the need written to make the devotional very interesting. For those who want to read through the Bible at least once in a life time, the daily Bible reading schedule in the devotional enables the reader if followed regularly, to read the Bible through in one year.

I enthusiastically and strongly recommend, the daily devotional book, "United in The WORD" to the believers who are serious about learning and applying the Word of God in their day-to-day living.

Dr. Paul J. Joseph, PhD
Senior Scientist, Georgia Institute of Technology, GA, USA
Ordained Ruling Elder, Christ Church Presbyterian (PCA), Atlanta, GA, USA

United In
the Word

January

JANUARY 1   *Bible Reading: Genesis Chapters 1-3*

THE POWER OF THE 'SPOKEN WORD'

Genesis chapter 1 speaks to me about the power of the SPOKEN word. In Gen 1:2 the Spirit of God was hovering over the face of the waters, but it was only when God spoke (Gen 1:3, 6, 9, 11, 14, 20, 24, 26) that everything came into existence. The word of God has power to heal us even today (Ps. 107:20; Mathew 8:16). Remember that death and life are in the power of the tongue (Prov. 18:21), so let us pray that God will give us a wholesome tongue (Prov. 15:4a) and we will only speak positive things and thereby bless others (Luke 6:28).

In Genesis 3:6 we see that Adam willfully disobeyed God's direct commandment to him (see Gen 2:16, 17) even though he lacked nothing in the Garden of Eden – including food (unlimited provision of fruits from the garden) and companionship (Eve). The last Adam, Jesus Christ overcame temptations even though He did not have any food for 40 days/nights neither did He have any companionship as He was alone in the wilderness (Matt. 4:1-11). Both temptations were similar and involved the lust of the flesh, the lust of the eyes and the pride of life (1 John 2:16) – compare Gen. 3:6 with Matt. 4:3, 6, 9. The lesson learnt here is that it is only our relationship and proximity with God (James 1:12-16; 1 Cor. 10:13) and His Word (Psalms 119:11) that can enable us to overcome temptations. Let's pray the Lord's Prayer today (Matt. 6:13) – "Do not lead us into temptation but deliver us from the evil one"!

JANUARY 2   *Bible Reading: Genesis Chapters 4-6*

HOW CAN WE WALK WITH GOD 'DAILY'?

In God's counsel to Cain in Genesis 4:7, God says that if Cain did well he would have been accepted as well. However, Cain did not do well as sin lay at the door of his life. Cain was entrapped by sin's desire (James 1:14-15), which resulted that he offered to God a sacrifice that was not pleasing to God. So, the core problem in Cain's life was the sin which controlled him. Even God's final counsel to Cain that he should rule over sin (Gen 4:7b) was in vain and Cain killed his brother Abel in a fit of anger and jealousy. The tragedy in Cain's life was his ultimate separation from God (Gen 4:16), and his disappearance from the pages of history. Let's examine our hearts today if there is any sin in our lives that is not pleasing to God.

As a stark contrast, we see in Genesis 5:24 that Enoch walked with God, and he was not (found) as God took him (to His abode). His spiritual walk with God was so close that God took him directly into heaven. Due to his lifelong commitment, his great grandson Noah also walked with God (Gen 6:9b), found grace in God's eyes (Gen 6:8) and was spared along with family from God's judgment. How can we walk with God daily? By daily reading & meditating on God's word (hearing from God), by constant prayer (talking to God), by obeying God's word literally and completely, by looking for God's dealings in our life activities, by paying close attention to the Holy Spirit who guides us daily and through regular fellowship and worship with God's people.

JANUARY 3   *Bible Reading: Genesis Chapters 7-9*

7 *IMPORTANT* THINGS TO REMEMBER:

Genesis 8:1 tells us that God *remembered* Noah, his family and all the animals who were held up with him in the ark. As a result, God caused a wind to pass over the earth to evaporate the waters, and the same time closed the fountains of the deep, the windows of heaven and stopped the rain (8:2). God's purpose was to ease Noah's situation, and allow him to get out of the ark. In Exodus 2:24-25, we read that God heard the groaning of the children of Israel, He *remembered* His covenant with Abraham; He looked upon the children of Israel and acknowledged them. God then assigned Moses with the task of liberating the children of Israel (Exodus 3). Another time God *remembered* Hannah who prayed for a child earnestly (1 Samuel 1:19b) and granted her desire. Our Lord Jesus *remembered* the thief on the cross upon his request while he was dying (Luke 23:42-43). God has *remembered* us in our lowly state (Psalms 136:23) & He alone has brought us this far in our life.

What about us? Is there anything that we need to *remember* this year? Yesterday morning, I had the privilege of reminding our church family about **7 important things that we need to *remember* in 2011** - based out of Psalms 27:

1. *Remember* to have confidence in God alone (v. 1)
2. *Remember* to live near to God's presence (v. 4)
3. *Remember* to lean on to God in times of trouble (v. 5)
4. *Remember* to seek God's face for every need (v. 8, 9)
5. *Remember* to learn from God daily through His Word (v. 11)
6. *Remember* to hope in the goodness of God (v. 13)
7. *Remember* to wait on God for strength and renewal (v. 14)

JANUARY 4   *Bible Reading: Genesis Chapters 10-12*

WITHOUT GOD WE CAN DO 'NOTHING'

The unfinished tower and city of Babel (Genesis 11:1-9) stands out as a dire testimony that God hates every effort of man to make a name for himself *apart from God*. Their plans to build the city and tower were harmless, but they were conceived out of selfishness, inflated egos and pride – just to <u>make a name for themselves</u> (Gen. 11:4). God's principle in this matter is specified in Psalms 127:1 - *"Unless the Lord builds a house (or tower or city) they labor in vain who build it..."* With their building projects unfinished and having serious communication issues, God scattered these workers everywhere on the earth into oblivion.

Compare this incident with God's call to Abram in Gen. 12:1-3, where God unilaterally promised Abram to make him a great nation, <u>make his name great</u> and make all the families of the earth to be blessed in him if he only obeyed His word. Abram, whose name was later changed to Abraham - the father of many nations (Gen. 17:5) truly became great as God promised and his children (descendents of Israel & Ishmael) still influence our world today. The lesson to be learned here is that when we obey God's word and humble ourselves under the mighty hand of God, He will exalt us in due time (1 Peter 5:6). Without God we can do <u>NOTHING</u> in our lives (John 15:5b).

JANUARY 5   *Bible Reading: Genesis Chapters 13-15*

RESOLVING A FAMILY PROBLEM 'AMICABLY'

Today's reading in Genesis chapter 13 gives us an interesting perspective about how a family problem was resolved amicably. The problem occurred because of a quarrel between the servants of Abraham and Lot due to their inability to live together. Jesus has taught us a spiritual principle that I believe Abraham also understood that a *"...house divided against itself shall not stand"* (Matt 12:25), therefore the time had come for him and Lot to separate as families. Abraham had understood the root of the problem: *"the land was not able to support them that they might dwell together, for their possessions were so great that they could not dwell together"* (Gen 13:6).

The steps that Abraham took to resolve this problem (Gen. 13: 8-9) were as follows:

1. He took the initiative to speak directly to his nephew *(taking charge of resolving the problem)*

2. He expressed his desire to end the quarrel immediately explaining to Lot in Gen. 13:8: "for we are brethren" *(showing clear and direct communication)*. He must have been distinctly aware that Canaanites and Perizzites lived in their neighborhood (Gen. 13:7b) and he did not want his neighbors to know about their family quarrel.

3. His suggestion was that he and Lot should separate immediately *(offering a win-win solution)*

4. He offered the choice of the land to Lot *(displaying humility).* Philippians 2:3 says: *"Let nothing be done through selfish ambition or conceit, but in lowliness of mind let each esteem others better than himself."*

Lot chose the best land for himself, but Abraham was not troubled or sad in this matter as God had prepared for him something better (Gen. 13:14) for him. Hebrews 11:10 tell us that Abraham actually waited for a city which had foundations, whose builder and maker was God *(reflecting clear life's perspective).* Let us follow Abraham's example in solving our personal problems as well.

JANUARY 6   *Bible Reading: Genesis Chapters 16-18*

GOD'S PROMISES <u>MAY BE</u> DELAYED BUT <u>NEVER</u> DENIED

When God promises us something, He will surely keep his promise no matter how long the delay is. God's delays are not denials. *"God is not a man, that He should lie…"* (Numbers 23:19a). God had told Abraham specifically that his own son will be his heir and his descendants will be as numerous as the stars in the sky (Gen. 15: 4, 5). However, Abraham listened to his wife Sarah and obtained a child Ishmael through Hagar, his wife's maidservant. This hasty decision bears repercussions that are still affecting us today. We now know that God had delayed His blessing until Abraham was very old and Sarah had passed the age of childbearing (Gen. 18:11) in order to prove that there was <u>nothing</u> too hard for Him (Gen. 18:14). Let us wait patiently that God will fulfill His purposes in our lives in His time.

In Genesis 18:19, God testifies about Abraham that He has known him *"in order that he may command his children and his household after him, that they keep the way of the Lord, to do righteousness and justice…"* Here God singled out Abraham to direct his family to keep the way of the Lord. I believe that there is a message to all fathers/husbands here. As the 'spiritual leaders' of our homes it is our responsibility to actively promote family altar, Bible reading, prayer and holy living among family members. Ultimately the 'buck stops here'. Fathers/Husbands, let us not shirk our responsibility to lead and direct our family in godly ways.

Bible Reading: Genesis Chapters 19-21

GOD HEARS OUR CRIES – EVEN TODAY!

After serving her mistress Sarah faithfully all her life, Hagar and her young son gets expelled from her master's home with just some bread and water into the wilderness of Beersheba (Gen. 21:14). When her water was used up and she could not move on in the hot desert any longer, she left her son under one of the shrubs (v. 15), went a little distance, and started weeping loudly and uncontrollably about her current dire situation (v. 16). However, what caught my attention was verse 17: *"And God heard the voice of the lad…"* In order to confirm this earlier statement, the angel of the Lord who called out to Hagar speaks out: *"Fear not, for God has heard the voice of the lad where he is."*

How did God hear the voice of a child when it was his mother who was crying loudly at a distance? The answer is that the child must have cried out to God for help at the same time and God could not shut off His ears from the desperate cry of a child. Psalms 34:6 says that *"The poor man (or child) cried out, and the Lord heard him, and saved him out of all his troubles"*. Luke 18: 7, 8a tells us: *"And shall God not avenge His own elect who cry out day and night to Him…I tell you that He will avenge them speedily…"*

Let us be assured that when we cry out to God in our distress – even today - He will surely hear us & deliver us speedily!

Bible Reading: Genesis Chapters 22-24

GOD ORCHESTRATES EVERYTHING IF WE OBEY AND TRUST HIM COMPLETELY

In our reading from Genesis 24 which details the selection of a bride for Isaac, we can understand that *God orchestrates everything in our lives if we obey God and trust in his provisions.* God had commanded Abraham to take a wife for his son Isaac only from his parental home, and had promised him prosperity and angelic guidance (Gen. 24: 7, 40) in fulfilling his objective.

1. Abraham obeyed God by delegating this task to his oldest servant giving him precise instructions about how to achieve his task.
2. This servant prayed for God's will using a conditional clause for selecting the bride.
3. Rebekah acted exactly to meet the conditions of selection.
4. Rebekah's family met all the conditions put forward by Abraham, and this was in line with God's directives.
5. Finally, Rebekah was herself willing to leave her father's home to be Isaac's wife (Gen. 24: 57) thus fulfilling God's perfect plan for Isaac.

What a wonderful real life example of Romans 8:28: *"And we know that all things work together for good to those who love God, to those who are the called according to His purpose"*!

JANUARY 9   *Bible Reading: Genesis Chapters 25-27*

GOD'S PLAN IN OUR LIVES WILL PREVAIL EVENTUALLY EVEN IF WE FAIL UP TO LIVE UP TO HIS DIRECTIONS:

God's plan in our lives will prevail eventually even if we fail up to live up to His directions. We have a good example of this in the case of Esau and Jacob. Even before they were born, God had clearly spoken to Rebekah that *"the older shall serve the younger"* (Gen. 25: 23b).

However, as the boys grew up, Isaac loved his older son Esau *"because he ate of his game"* (Gen. 25: 28a). Eventually, Isaac decided to bless Isaac before he died as a token of his love for his firstborn son. However, God allowed Rebekah to overhear the conversation of Isaac and Esau, and with quick action got Jacob to present himself to his father as Esau. The blessings that Isaac had reserved for Esau was received by Jacob through deception: *"...Be master over your brethren, and let your mother's sons bow down to you..."* (Gen. 27: 29b). This blessing was reconfirmed to Esau again by Isaac: *"...and you shall serve your brother..."* (Gen. 27: 40b).

Let us understand clearly that God will fulfill His plans in our lives eventually in His time even though others may try to thwart it time and again. *"Therefore humble yourselves under the mighty hand of God, that He may exalt you in due time"* (1 Peter 5: 6)

JANUARY 10   *Bible Reading: Genesis Chapters 28-30*

DO NOT BE UNEQUALLY YOKED TOGETHER WITH UNBELIEVERS:

"Do not be unequally yoked together with unbelievers. For what fellowship has righteousness with lawlessness? And what communion has light with darkness?" (2 Cor. 6:14) This is the message that we receive through the final instructions that Isaac gives his son Jacob before sending him off to his brother-in-law Laban (Gen. 28:1-5). They were living in Canaan territory and there were plenty of beautiful eligible daughters of Canaan for marriage. However, Isaac follows his father Abraham's example and directs Jacob to choose a wife from his own kindred. We see that Jacob obeys his father and starts on a 400-mile trip to Padan Aram, a place north of Haran, in search of a wife for himself. As part of his customary dowry for Rachel, Jacob pledges seven years' labor (which becomes seven more years, thanks to Laban's deception). On obeying his father's directive, Jacob receives all the blessings of Abraham (Gen. 28: 3-4). On the other hand, Esau marries a Canaanite girl knowing full well that this will not please his father (Gen. 28: 6-9). In doing so, Esau further forfeits all the blessings that he would have inherited through descent.

God demands that we hate sin but love the sinner. When it comes to marriage, we have clear instructions from God's Word that we should only marry a child of God. When we obey God's commandment in this regard, we will also receive all that blessings that God reserves for His children as described in Psalms 128.

Bible Reading: Genesis Chapters 31-33

THE STEPS OF A 'GOOD MAN' ARE ORDERED BY THE LORD

"The steps of a good man are ordered by the LORD, and He delights in his way. Though he falls, he shall not be utterly cast down; for the LORD upholds him with His hand" (Psalms 37:23-24)

After serving his father-in-law for 20 years, Jacob has now reached a place of personal desperation. His life was going nowhere. Even though Jacob had faithfully served Laban by shepherding his flock spending sleepless nights and through rough weather – drought during day and frost during night – bearing all the loss on his own account (Gen. 31:38-40), Laban and his sons were antagonistic towards Jacob. In fact they were now accusing Jacob of becoming rich at Laban's expense (Gen. 31:1-2) even though it was God who had made Jacob rich (Gen. 31:9). Jacob had now reached a complete life cycle having now served Laban twenty years (fourteen years for Rachel and six years for the flock) during which time Laban had changed Jacob's wages ten times (Gen. 31:41). God directed Jacob's steps as He told him that it was time now to relocate back to the land of his fathers and his family (Gen. 31:3). We need to understand that working for an employer will have limits, but it is God alone who will show us *"the path of life"* (Psalms 16:11a) and lead us to our final destination.

Another lesson to learn through this passage - when we make a major change in our life, we should definitely get our family (spouse, children, etc) on board with our plans just as Jacob confirmed his plans to relocate only after consulting with his two wives Rachel and Leah (Gen. 31:4-16). Even though it was obvious that the living conditions were untenable for Jacob continue serving Laban, and even after getting the directive from God to return, Jacob displayed consultative leadership skills by discussing his situation with his family. As we make a critical move in our life, let us remember the words of Proverbs 4:25-26: *"Let your eyes look straight ahead, and your eyelids look right before you. Ponder the path of your feet, and let all your ways be established"*.

JANUARY 12   *Bible Reading: Genesis Chapters 34-36*

RENEWING OF PERSONAL LIFE THROUGH A 'RADICAL' CHANGE:

In Genesis 35:1, we read that Jacob heard the voice of God asking him to return to Bethel – the place where he had made his initial commitment to serve God. Even today, God has not stopped speaking to us, but it is possible that we have stopped listening to Him. He may be talking to us through a still small voice or, shouting to us through unpleasant situations in our lives. In Gen. 35:2 we read that Jacob put away all hindrances that stood between him and God. Hindrances in our lives are anything that competes with us having quality time with God. Earlier, Jacob had already made restitution with God (Gen. 32:22-30) and with Esau (Gen. 33:10) thus clearing his pathway to the place where he had first encountered God. Jacob's return to Bethel was to recapture his vision and to reaffirm his commitment with God (Gen. 35:5, 6).

Jacob now built an altar and called it *El-Bethel*, which means *'God of the House of God'*. After 20 years of 'growing up' Jacob's perspective has changed and what was more important for him now was *his God alone*. When Jacob does everything required of him, God renews his covenant by changing his name to *Israel* (Gen. 35:10), blessing him personally (v. 11), and gifting him the land that He had promised to Abraham and Isaac (v. 12). Psalms 105: 7-11 describes this beautifully as follows: *He is the LORD our God; His judgments are in all the earth. He remembers His covenant forever, the word which He commanded, for a thousand generations, the covenant which He made with Abraham, and His oath to Isaac, and confirmed it to Jacob for a statute, to Israel as an everlasting covenant, saying, "To you I will give the land of Canaan as the allotment of your inheritance"*

God wants us to renew our commitment with Him as well by offering our bodies as *"...a living sacrifice, holy, acceptable to God..."* (Rom. 12:1), and is waiting for us to go back to *'our Bethel'* – the place where we started our intimate relationship with God. Won't you do that today?

Bible Reading: Genesis Chapters 37-39

STEPS TO 'REAL' GODLY SUCCESS

When he was only seventeen years old, Joseph had two different dreams that he will achieve success in his life to that extent that his entire family (including his parents) will bow down and acknowledge his honor and authority (Genesis 37: 5-11). This is wonderful for Joseph, but little did he know that during the next thirteen years God would develop him in the crucible of prolonged suffering, pain and rejection. It is a close reading of Genesis 39 that teaches us the steps to success in Joseph's life.

1. The Lord was with Joseph in his daily secular work (vv. 2, 21a, 23b).

2. Joseph was faithful to God and his position even during the time his supervisor was not around (vv. 8, 9).

3. Joseph's supervisor could see the quality of his work, and discern that God was with him to prosper him (v. 3).

4. Finally, God gave favor to Joseph in the sight of his supervisors (vv. 4, 21b).

Joseph became very successful in life even as he had dreamed as a young boy, and his dreams were literally fulfilled and confirmed three times after 13 years (See Gen. 42:6; 44:14; 50:18). God will grant us success in our lives as well when we are true to our calling and status as His child, and if we would be faithful in what has been committed to us. Philippians 1:6 exhorts us that we should be "*...confident of this very thing, that He who has begun a good work in you will complete it until the day of Jesus Christ*".

Bible Reading: Genesis Chapters 40-42

IT IS BETTER 'ALWAYS' TO TRUST GOD FOR OUR NEEDS

Due to his past experience of betrayal and rejection by his own brothers and Potiphar's wife, Joseph should have understood the futility of putting his faith in any human being. However, he was convinced that the chief butler would be restored into his former position of authority/influence in just three days and may be able to help him out of his misery. So, he opened out his heart and explained himself to the chief butler as follows: *"But remember me when it is well with you, and please show kindness to me; make mention of me to Pharaoh, and get me out of this house. For indeed I was stolen away from the land of the Hebrews; and also I have done nothing here that they should put me into the dungeon"* (Gen. 40:14-15). However, we read in Gen. 40:23 what actually happened: *"Yet the chief butler did not remember Joseph, but forgot him"*. A teaching point for us through this incident is that we should NEVER put our confidence in humans, but in God alone. The central verse of the Bible gives us a similar message as well: *"It is better to trust in the LORD than to put confidence in man"* (Psalms 118:8). Our Lord Jesus Christ was very much aware of this fact early on in life, and this is what we read about Him in St. John 2:24-25: *"But Jesus did not commit Himself to them, because He knew all men, and had no need that anyone should testify of man, for He knew what was in man"*. It is always better to trust God for our needs, and we can always express our desires to Him openly through prayer.

We also realize that it was the plan of God to exalt Joseph to a position of great authority, so it was not time for him to leave the prison yet. After two complete years (Gen. 41:1), God gave two dreams to Pharaoh and the ensuing events brought Joseph to the limelight and into the position of authority that God had intended for him. Let us always remember the words of Habakkuk 2:3 *"For the vision is yet for an appointed time; but at the end it will speak, and it will not lie. Though it tarries, wait for it; because it will surely come, it will not tarry"*.

JANUARY 15   *Bible Reading: Genesis Chapters 43-45*

GOD HAS A 'GREATER' PURPOSE IN OUR LIVES!

When Joseph finally reveals himself to his brothers, he speaks profound words of revelation as he explains the reason why he came to Egypt earlier through this very painful process. In Genesis 45:4-5 he exposes his true identity with the following words: *"I am your brother Joseph, the one you sold into Egypt! And now, do not be distressed and do not be angry with yourselves for selling me here, because <u>it was</u>*

to save lives that God sent me ahead of you". Joseph clarifies his statement further in verse 7: "*But God sent me ahead of you to preserve for you a remnant on earth and to save your lives by a great deliverance*". Joseph was convinced that he was fulfilling God's greater plan in his life all these years. For this he had to travel the pathway of pain, rejection and suffering which God allowed in order to save his family alive through the terrible famine and to preserve a remnant on earth (out of which one day would be born our Savior Jesus Christ).

The story of Joseph reminds us so much about Jesus Christ, whom God sent into this world to save lives of humanity. Just like Joseph, our Lord Jesus was totally innocent of all the crimes he was accused of, and was sold off by someone He considered his very own. Just like in the case of Joseph, it was God's eternal plan that He would send His only begotten Son Jesus ahead of time for us to suffer and pay the penalty of our sin so that we might be saved from eternal destruction. Thank you Lord, for all your unseen provisions in our lives!

JANUARY 16   *Bible Reading: Genesis Chapters 46-48*

THE SIGNIFICANCE OF 'BLESSING' OUR CHILDREN

In Genesis 48 we see that the aged Jacob is sick, so Joseph brings his two sons Manasseh and Ephraim to Jacob so that he may bless his grandchildren before he dies. Joseph knows the significance of a patriarchal blessing as he has seen the effects of the blessings in the life of his father Jacob, who had deceitfully snatched away the blessings of a firstborn from his elder brother Esau. Jacob actually blesses Joseph (Gen. 48:15a) even though his hands are laid on the heads of his children. *So he blessed them that day, saying, "By you Israel will bless, saying, 'May God make you as Ephraim and as Manasseh!'"* (Gen. 48:20a).

In their book 'The Blessing', Gary Smalley and John Trent writes that the above blessing (Gen. 48:20a) is still used by Rabbis to bless Jewish children during Sabbath services and is a favorite of Jewish parents to bless their children. Even today, a family blessing is considered as an important vehicle to communicate a sense of identity, love and acceptance in the Jewish community. In many Jewish homes, a weekly blessing is given by the father to each of his children. This action models how Christian parents should appreciate their children today and communicate their high value and special strength that God has bestowed on them. We know from the Gospels that Jesus laid his hands on little children and blessed them (Matt. 19:13-15). As Joseph mentioned in Gen. 48:9, God is the one who gives us children, which is also found in Psalms 127:3: *"Behold, children are a heritage from the LORD, the fruit of the womb is a reward"*. As parents, can we also extend His blessings to our children so that they grow up convinced of God's amazing love?

JANUARY 17   *Bible Reading: Genesis Chapters 49-50*

THERE IS 'TRUE' POWER IN FORGIVENESS

After Jacob died and was buried, there was no one now to stand before Joseph if he had wanted to take revenge on his brothers. The way Joseph's brothers had behaved to him earlier had been like *"the archers who bitterly grieved him, shot at him and hated him"* (Gen. 49:23) according to the last prophetical words of his father Jacob. His brothers had hated him, plotted to murder him, and then sold him to Egypt where he was separated from all his loved ones. As the master of Egypt Joseph had all the reasons along with the political power/ authority and now also the opportunity to repay his brothers for their hatred and betrayal towards him. That is why his brothers pleaded for mercy and declared their servitude to him. What was Joseph's reaction when the messengers sent by his brothers requested his clemency? Gen. 50:17b says that *"Joseph **wept** when they spoke to him"*. We can visualize the tender heart of Joseph as he becomes very emotional. After this, Joseph spoke something profound to his brothers: *"Do not be afraid, for **am I in the place of God?** But as for you, you meant evil against me; but **God meant it for good**, in order to bring it about as it is this day, **to save many people alive**. Now therefore, **do not be afraid; I will provide for you and your little ones.**" And **he comforted them** and **spoke kindly to them**"*. (Gen. 50:19-20)

Based on Joseph's response to his brothers, let's look to Romans 12:19-21: *"Beloved, do not avenge yourselves, but rather give place to wrath; for it is written, "Vengeance is Mine, I will repay," says the Lord. Therefore "If your enemy is hungry, feed him; if he is thirsty, give him a drink; for in so doing you will heap coals of fire on his head." Do not be overcome by evil, but overcome evil with good".* Below are some learning points for us:

1. We should not replace God's role at any time when it comes to striking back at others who have harmed us.

2. We need to love and forgive our enemies as Christ has taught us (Matt. 5:43-44; 6:14-15)

3. We need to move beyond forgiveness and show our love in action by providing for the needs of our enemies as Joseph had done for his brothers.

There is **true power in forgiveness** that we should exercise in our daily lives and relationships!

JANUARY 18   *Bible Reading: Exodus Chapters 1-3*

GOD WILL NOT ABANDON US DURING TOUGH TIMES

The children of Israel living in Egypt were enslaved and afflicted by Pharaoh and the Egyptian taskmasters, and their lives became bitter due to the hard bondage set upon them (Exodus 1:8-14). Unable to bear any longer, they groaned and cried to God because of the bondage (Exodus 2:23b). Exodus 2:24-25 takes us through the steps how God answered their prayers and still answers our prayers today. God _heard_ their groaning and cries. Even today, His ears are always inclined to hear our cry. *"For the eyes of the LORD are on the righteous, and His ears are open to their prayers"* (1 Peter 3:12a). God _remembered_ His covenant with Abraham, Isaac and Jacob. In our case, God always remembers that we are His children, and He remembers His promises to answer us when we call upon His name. He has promised us in Jer. 33:3: *"Call to Me, and I will answer you, and show you great and mighty things, which you do not know".* Jesus has promised us in John 14:14: *"If you ask anything in My name, I will do it"* God _looked_ upon the children of Israel. We have a similar promise in 2 Chron. 16:9a: *"For the eyes of the LORD run to and fro throughout the whole earth, to show Himself strong on behalf of those whose heart is loyal to Him"* Finally, God _acknowledged_ the children of Israel. When we cry unto the Lord, he will acknowledge us and answer our prayers.

In Exodus 3, we see that God came down to a mountain called Horeb, appeared to Moses in a burning bush and commissioned him to lead the children of Israel out of Egypt as an answer to their prayer. God revealed Himself as 'I AM WHO I AM' – as a God who is there in the midst of their current need.

Remember, God hears our prayers and fulfills our needs as He did for the children of Israel. Let us go to our heavenly Father by faith today and petition to Him our pressing needs. He will not abandon us during tough times. *"But without faith it is impossible to please Him, for he who comes to God must believe that He is, and that He is a rewarder of those who diligently seek Him"* (Hebrews 11:6)

JANUARY 19   *Bible Reading: Exodus Chapters 4-6*

GOD CAN USE US WHERE WE ARE AND WITH WHAT WE HAVE

When God revealed to Moses about His master plan of delivering the children of Israel from the clutches of Pharaoh in Egypt through him, Moses was reluctant to move forward. In Exodus 4:1, we read the following: *Then Moses answered and said, "But suppose they will not believe me or listen to my voice; suppose they say, 'The LORD has not appeared to you.'"* This response is typical to that given by a modern day believer who has to convey the gospel to his/her unbelieving friends. From this passage (Exodus 4:1-5) we can distill some important truths that should help us in our personal witnessing of the gospel:

1. God asks Moses what he has in his hand (v. 2). Through the last 40 years, Moses had a rod that he carried as a shepherd. This rod signifies the past experiences in the life of Moses. *When we witness the gospel to others, we can just use our past experience as the context to communicate the gospel with others.*

2. God asks Moses to throw the rod down into the ground (v. 3). This denotes giving up the control of our lives to God at His word. God caused a dead piece of wood to turn into a living snake. Remember, *God can do a miracle through our ordinary everyday life experiences if we surrender everything to God.* When Moses caught the snake by the tail at the word of God, it turned

back into a rod (v. 4). *The miracles that God will perform will not harm us, but will cause others to believe in the power of God (v. 5).*

3. After Moses threw the rod down, the ownership of the rod transferred from Moses to God. From that moment onwards, the rod is referred to as the "rod of God". (Exodus 4:20). *"I have been crucified with Christ; it is no longer I who live, but Christ lives in me; and the life which I now live in the flesh I live by faith in the Son of God, who loved me and gave Himself for me"* (Gal. 2:20)

4. Moses used this "rod of God" to perform most of the miracles in the process of delivering the children of Israel and during their wilderness journey (Exodus 4:17; 7:12, 15; 8:5, 16; 9:23; 10:13; 14:16; 17:9). *This tells me that God will use our experiences as a wonderful testimony to attract many people to Jesus Christ during our spiritual journey.*

Let us surrender ourselves into the mighty hand of God that He will use us as effective witnesses of the saving knowledge of Christ. *"Now thanks be to God who always leads us in triumph in Christ, and through us diffuses the fragrance of His knowledge in every place. For we are to God the fragrance of Christ among those who are being saved and among those who are perishing. To the one we are the aroma of death leading to death, and to the other the aroma of life leading to life"* (2 Cor. 2:14-16)

JANUARY 20   *Bible Reading: Exodus Chapters 7-9*

PRIDE GOES BEFORE A FALL

God had raised Pharaoh in Egypt in order to display His power in him which would result in God's name be declared in all the earth. Yet, Pharaoh exalted himself against God and the children of Israel and would not let them go to worship God (Exodus 9:16-17). That is the reason why God hardened Pharaoh's heart, and multiplied His signs and wonders in the land of Egypt (Exodus 7:3) so that the Egyptians would realize the power of the true God (v. 5). With the passing of each miracle or plague, we read that Pharaoh hardened his heart (Exodus 7:13, 22; 8:15, 19, 32; 9:7, 12, 35).

In his book *'In the Name of Jesus'* Henri Nouwen asks this question: *What makes the temptation of power so seemingly irresistible?* He goes on to answer that maybe it is that power offers an easy substitute to the hard task of love. It seems easier to *be* God than to *love* God, easier to *control people* than to *love people*, easier to *own life* than to *love life*. Jesus asks us, *"Do you love me?"*, and we ask him back, *"Can we sit at your right hand and your left hand in your kingdom?"* (Matt. 20:21). Ever since Eve made a choice in the Garden of Eden to become *"like gods knowing good from evil"* (Gen. 3:5), we have been tempted to *replace love with power, choose control over the cross* and to *become a leader over being led.*

Let us not be like Pharaoh whose hardened his heart and exalted himself – he ended up in the bottom of the Red Sea eventually. Let us always remember that *"pride goes before destruction and a haughty spirit before a fall"* (Proverbs 16:18). Let us today *"humble ourselves under the mighty hand of God, that He may exalt us in due time"* (1 Peter 5:6)

JANUARY 21   *Bible Reading: Exodus Chapters 10-12*

THERE IS DELIVERANCE ONLY THROUGH THE BLOOD OF CHRIST!

What God had foretold to Abraham while sealing His covenant back in Genesis 15:13-14 was now literally being fulfilled for the children of Israel in Egypt. After serving Pharaoh and the Egyptians for 430 years (Exodus 12:40-41), it was now time for God to deliver His people from bondage. This deliverance will not come without a price being paid. For every household of the children of Israel, a lamb without blemish had to be killed (Exodus 12:3-6; 21) and the blood of that lamb had to be smeared on the two doorposts and on the lintel of their homes (vv. 7, 22). At night God would pass through the land of Egypt and will strike dead all the firstborns of every home, both man and beast (vv. 12, 23a). However, when God sees the blood on the doorposts of the homes of the children of Israel, He would *pass over* them without executing any judgment (vv. 13, 23b), since a lamb had already paid the ultimate price for the lives of the firstborn.

To apply this incident in our lives, Pharaoh and Egypt is comparable to Satan and his kingdom. Like the children of Israel, we were under bondage of Satan and his evil powers (Eph. 2:1-3). Just as the blood of an innocent lamb was smeared on the doorposts of the homes belonging to the children of Israel, the innocent blood of the Lamb of God (Isaiah 53:7; John 1:29) was smeared on another post that we know as the cross of Calvary. It was God himself who paid the ultimate price to make us free from death and eternal darkness. We have now been brought near to God through the blood that was shed for us (Eph. 2:13), redeemed (1 Peter 1:18-19) and have peace with God (Col. 1:20). This blood can cleanse us from all our sins if we only confess our sins to Him (1 John 1:9).

If you have not got cleansed from your sins through the blood of Christ, please know that you are headed to an eternal death and separation from God (like the firstborn of the Egyptians). Now is your day of salvation (2 Cor. 6:2). Accept Christ in your heart and confess all your sins (Rom. 10:8) and you will receive the true freedom that only God can give. *Know this for a fact - there is deliverance ONLY through the blood of Christ!*

JANUARY 22   *Bible Reading: Exodus Chapters 13-15*

TRUSTING GOD IN THE WILDERNESS

When God led the children of Israel out of Egypt through Moses, the journey was meticulously planned by God beforehand. Even though the children of Israel was not a fighting force but consisted of 600,000 men on foot besides women, children and a mixed multitude (Exodus 12:37-38), they were referred to as *"the armies of the Lord"* (Exodus 12:41b, 51b) and they went up in *"orderly ranks"* out of Egypt (Exodus 13:18b). God did not allow the Israelites to go by the land of the Philistines even though it was a shorter way, for God said *"Lest perhaps the people change their minds when they see war, and return to Egypt." So God led the people around by way of the wilderness of the Red Sea.* (Exodus 13:17-18a). There were many obstacles to be encountered in the wilderness journey starting with the Red Sea (Exodus 14) and the bitter waters at Marah (Exodus 15:22-25). However, God went before them by day in a pillar of cloud to lead the way, and by night in a pillar of fire to give them light (Exodus 13:21-22). We also read that the Angel of God was their navigator and their protector as well (Exodus 14:19).

Just like God chose to lead the Israelites through a longer route that protected, trained and tested them, at times God also leads us through a longer route of trails and difficulties. Do you feel impatient and discouraged when things don't happen the way *we* plan in our lives? Just accept the path that God has placed us in, and be content with God's purpose in our lives. As Hebrews 12:1-2 exhorts us, *"let us lay aside every weight, and the sin which so easily ensnares us, and **let us run with endurance the race that is set before us**, looking unto Jesus, the author and finisher of our faith, who for the joy that was set before Him endured the cross, despising the shame, and has sat down at the right hand of the throne of God".* **Let us trust in God to lead us through in our wilderness journey into the Promised Land!**

JANUARY 23   *Bible Reading: Exodus Chapters 16-18*

DO NOT COMPLAIN AGAINST GOD

For over 400 years, the Israelites had been living in the fertile land of Goshen in Egypt. Now they were gloriously delivered from bondage, but were traveling through the wilderness. Instead of focusing on their glorious redemption from slavery, they soon started complaining against Moses and Aaron in the wilderness, which were actually complaints against God (Exodus 16:7-8). They focused on their physical needs little knowing that God was teaching them to trust in God's provisions alone. *Then the whole congregation of the children of Israel complained against Moses and Aaron in the wilderness. And the children of Israel said to them, "Oh, that we had died by the hand of the LORD in the land of Egypt, when we sat by the pots of meat and when we ate bread to the full! For you have brought us out into this wilderness to kill this whole assembly with hunger"* (Exodus 16:2-3). God heard their complaints and provided them bread in the morning and meat in the evening daily. *And the LORD spoke to Moses, saying, "I have heard the complaints of the children of Israel. Speak to them, saying, 'At twilight you shall eat meat, and in the morning you shall be filled with bread. And you shall know that I am the LORD your God'"* (Exodus 16:11-12). After a while they started complaining for water (Exodus 17:3), and God provided them plentiful water to satisfy their thirst from the rock (Exodus 17:5-6).

This complaining continued all the way throughout the wilderness journey even until the Israelites reached the outskirts of Canaan. Eventually God became very angry at the endless complaints of the Israelites and consumed many of them through fire (see Numbers 11:1-15), and finally decided that none of the people who complained would enter the Promised Land except for Joshua and Caleb (see Numbers 14:26-35). *Such a tragic ending to the people of God who could not reach their destination because they were constantly complaining and not trusting in God!*

Apostle Paul taking examples from the Old Testament exhorts us clearly that **we should not** *"complain, as some of them also complained, and were destroyed by the destroyer. Now all these things happened to them as examples, and they were written for our admonition, upon whom the ends of the ages have come"* (1 Cor. 10:10-11). Again in Philippians 2:14-15 he warns us: *"Do all things without complaining and disputing, that you may become blameless and harmless, children of God without fault in the midst of a crooked and perverse generation, among whom you shine as lights in the world"* **Let us never complain against God – no matter what adversities come in our lives!**

JANUARY 24   *Bible Reading: Exodus Chapters 19-21*

WE ARE TO GOD A KINGDOM OF PRIESTS AND A HOLY NATION

In the third month after the children of Israel had left Egypt, they have now reached the Wilderness of Sinai (Exodus 19:1). God had fulfilled the first part of His original plan that He had revealed to Moses from the burning bush (Exodus 3:12) that they would serve God on Mount Sinai. As part of the preamble of God's expectations from His people, He called Moses up to the mountain top and told Moses to convey to the children of Israel a few things that they should never forget, which we read in Exodus 19:3-6. Let us check out what God's plan was for the children of Israel then, and what His plan are for us now as the 'new' spiritual Israel:

1. They were to never forget what God did to the Egyptians (v. 4a) – how He trouble Pharaoh and the Egyptians with the ten plagues

(including death of their firstborn during the last plague), and finally destroyed Pharaoh and his choice army in the Red Sea. *We should never forget that God has already destroyed the powers of Satan through His death on the cross* (Hebrews 2:14-15).

2. They were to always remember that God bore them on eagles' wings (v. 4b) – protecting them from the attack of the Egyptian army and providing them bread, meat and water in the wilderness. *We should always remember that God both protects us and provides for us daily in more ways than we can count* (Psalms 68:19).

3. They were to reflect how God brought them to Himself (v. 4c) – by allowing them to visualize His glory and grandeur on Mount Sinai (v. 10-20). God wanted the children of Israel to be drawn to Him in worship. *Jesus Christ has broken the middle wall of separation* (Ephesians 2:14) *and has drawn us to the throne of grace so that we can obtain mercy and find grace to help in time of need* (Hebrews 4:16).

4. They were to always understand their newly obtained status with God – a special treasure, a kingdom of priests and a holy nation (v. 5-6). This is how Apostle Peter describes our status in Christ: *"But you are a chosen generation, a royal priesthood, a holy nation, His own special people, that you may proclaim the praises of Him who called you out of darkness into His marvelous light; who once were not a people but are now the people of God, who had not obtained mercy but now have obtained mercy"* (1Peter 2:9-10).

As we live in this world, let us *never forget* what God has done for us in the past, *always remember* what God is doing for us today, and *always understand* our position in God's kingdom. **We are to God a kingdom of priests and a holy nation!**

JANUARY 25   *Bible Reading: Exodus Chapters 22-24*

GOD PROMISES TO GUIDE US ALL THE WAY

After providing the Ten Commandments as the foundation of the rule of law, God gave various guidelines to the Israelites which would serve them in their relationships with one another. These guidelines set apart the Israelites from all the other surrounding nations. In the midst of the guidelines, God gives His people a wonderful promise that we read in Exodus 23:20: *"Behold, I send an Angel before you to keep you in the way and to bring you into the place which I have prepared"*. If we examine the Old Testament, we can read about the Angel of God in many places: Exodus 3:2; 14:19; 32:34; 33:2; Numbers 20:16; Joshua 5:13-14; Isaiah 63:9. As we see the continuing verses (21-26) of Exodus 20, this Angel of God will go before them and protect them from their enemies (vv. 22-24) and lead them safely to the Promised Land. Further, if the Israelites would sincerely serve God, He will cater for their daily physical needs (v. 25a – food and water), take away sickness from their midst (v. 25b), give them children (v. 26a) and none will die a premature death (v. 26b).

As the 'New Testament Israelites', we too have precious God's promises to guide us all the way. Let's rest on these promises and ask God to give us guidance (Psalm 25:4-5) for He will surely guide us (Psalm 32:8) in our daily life. At times God will guide us through His Word (Psalm 119:133), and He will direct ours path when we put our trust in Him alone (Proverbs 3:5-6). *"For this is God, Our God forever and ever; He will be our guide even to death"* (Psalms 48:14).

Let's rest assured that God will finally take us to the place He is preparing for us for this is the promise our Lord Jesus has given us: *"Let not your heart be troubled; you believe in God, believe also in Me. In My Father's house are many mansions; if it were not so, I would have told you. I go to prepare a place for you. And if I go and prepare a place for you, I will come again and receive you to Myself; that where I am, there you may be also"* (John 14:1-3).

JANUARY 26   *Bible Reading: Exodus Chapters 25-27*

ALLOW GOD TO BE AT THE CENTER OF OUR LIVES

After giving various guidelines to the Israelites, God expressed His desire for fellowship with His people. *"...let them make Me a sanctuary, that I may dwell among them"* (Exodus 25:8). God now wanted to reinstate back the fellowship with His children that got lost in the Garden of Eden as a result of sin and disobedience. Apart from dwelling among His redeemed children, God also wanted to meet, speak and give His laws and commandments in the sanctuary called the Tabernacle. *"And **there I will meet with you, and I will speak with you** from above the mercy seat, from between the two cherubim which are on the ark of the Testimony, about everything which I will give you in commandment to the children of Israel"* (Exodus 25:22)

This has been God's intention through the passage of time. About 2000 years ago, God came down to this earth in the form of a man, and in the words of Apostle John *"...**the Word became flesh and dwelt among us**..."* (John 1:14). *So all this was done that it might be fulfilled which was spoken by the Lord through the prophet, saying: "Behold, the virgin shall be with child, and bear a Son, and they shall call His name **Immanuel**," which is translated, "**God with us**"* (Mathew 1:22-23). After spending thirty-three and half years in this earth, our Lord Jesus went back to heaven, but not before promising us the ever abiding presence of the Holy Spirit in our lives. In fact, God decided to use our earthly bodies as His sanctuary, as we became the temple of God. *"Do you not know that **you are the temple of God** and that **the Spirit of God dwells in you?**"* (1 Cor. 3:16). In 1 Cor. 6:19, Apostle Paul asks us *"...do you not know that **your body is the temple of the Holy Spirit who is in you**, whom you have from God, and you are not your own?"* Again in 2 Cor. 6:16, Apostle Paul reminds us: *For **you are the temple of the living God** as God has said: "I will dwell in them and walk among them. I will be their God, and they shall be My people."*

Can we allow God to dwell in us and be at the center of our lives so that we may please Him during our earthly existence?

JANUARY 27   *Bible Reading: Exodus Chapters 28-30*

CONSIDER OUR HIGH PRIEST, CHRIST JESUS

Exodus chapters 28 and 29 describe the priestly garments of the High Priest, Aaron, which served three purposes:

1. **Decorative** — They were to give Aaron glory and beauty (Exodus 28:2), which would display the beauty and authority that belonged to God himself.

2. **Functional** — Each item of the garments had a functional role. The breastplate served as a pouch to contain the sacred lot, Urim

and Thummim (Exodus 28:30) while the linen trousers were for the sake of modesty (Exodus 28:42)

3. **Symbolic** – There was symbolic elements to these garments as well. The two onyx stones on the ephod bearing the names of the twelve tribes of Israel were a memorial gesture (Exodus 28:9-12). The twelve precious stones of the breastplate representing the twelve tribes of Israel symbolized the High Priest bearing the judgment of the children of Israel before God continually (Exodus 28:29-30). The clothing of the High Priest was to provide a measure of realization of his task in representing Israel to God.

All of the high priestly garments have a wonderful significance for us too. Once we understand what these tell us about our heavenly High Priest, Jesus, we will find a deep-seated thankfulness rising up from within our spirit, and an encouragement to draw near to God with a purified heart in full assurance of faith (Hebrews 13:15; 10:22).

Hebrews 3:1 exhorts us to *"consider the Apostle and High Priest of our confession, Christ Jesus"*. Jesus Christ is now our High Priest who sits at the right hand of God the Father and continually makes intervention for us. Romans 8:34 tells us *"It is Christ who died, and furthermore is also risen, who is even at the right hand of God, who also makes intercession for us"*.

Today let us go boldly to the throne room of God in prayer as we consider our High Priest Jesus Christ. *"Seeing we have such a great High Priest who has passed through the heavens, Jesus the Son of God, a High Priest who can sympathize with our weaknesses (being tempted in all points as we are, yet without sin), let us therefore come boldly to the throne of grace, that we may obtain mercy and find grace to help in time of need"* (Hebrews 4:14-16).

JANUARY 28   *Bible Reading: Exodus Chapters 31-33*

EXPERIENCE THE GLORY OF GOD

After the children of Israel were punished for worshipping the golden calf through the death of three thousand men (Exodus 32:28), we read in the ensuing chapter that Moses has an intimate encounter with God. In the tabernacle of meeting, *God speaks to Moses face to face as a man speaks to his friend* (Exodus 33:9-11). During this conversation, **Moses asks God for two very important things that we also need to ask God everyday in our life:**

First, Moses asks God to show him the way to the Promised Land (Exodus 33:13). God should be the navigator for the onward journey. In reply, God promises His presence to go with Moses and the children of Israel (Exodus 33:14-17). We are also traveling on a spiritual journey to our Promised Land called Heaven, which is behind the veil. **Let us ask God to show us the way everyday so that we do not get distracted or get diverted or get lost in the way.** We can hold on to a similar promise from God in Mathew 28:20 "*...I am with you always, even to the end of the age*". This is reiterated in Hebrews 13:5: *For He Himself has said, "I will never leave you nor forsake you."*

Second, Moses asks God to show him His glory (Exodus 33:18). In reply, this is what God tells Moses: "*Here is a place by Me, and you shall stand on the rock. So it shall be, while My glory passes by, that I will put you in the cleft of the rock, and will cover you with My hand while I pass by. Then I will take away My hand, and you shall see My back; but My face shall not be seen.*" (Exodus 33:21-23). There is something so wonderful we see here. All Moses did was to ask. God did the rest. God gave Moses a place to stand, and placed him in a cleft. God covered Moses with His hand. God passed by in front of Moses, and God revealed Himself.

Here's a spiritual application for us. When we ask, we receive (Mathew 7:7). God has placed us on the Rock of Ages, Jesus Christ (Psalms 40:2), and has given us a cleft, His grace. He has covered us with His pierced Hand, and equipped us for an eternal relationship with Him. **Let us join with the Psalmist in seeking Him and thirsting for His presence and glory.** "*O God, You are my God; early will I seek You; my soul thirsts for You; my flesh longs for You in a dry and thirsty land where there is no water. So I have looked for You in the sanctuary, to see Your power and Your glory*" (Psalms 63:1-2). **Let us experience the glory of God, even today!**

JANUARY 29   *Bible Reading: Exodus Chapters 34-36*

WORKING TOGETHER TO BUILD THE CHURCH OF JESUS CHRIST

Exodus chapters 35 & 36 give us a beautiful picture of how God wants to build His Church, the universal body of Jesus Christ. Without any doubt, God, the Master Architect and Designer, designed every detail of the Tabernacle, and verbally conveyed the details to Moses (Exodus 25:1 – 31:18). God also renewed His covenant with the children of Israel (Exodus 34:10-26), and makes Moses to write down all the words of the covenant including the Ten Commandments (Exodus 34:27-28). Moses gave the instructions to the children of Israel as to what is required from them in building the Tabernacle, which is to willingly and cheerfully bring offerings to the Lord of articles that are required to build the Tabernacle (Exodus 35:1-19). The people gave offerings freely and in abundance (Exodus 35:20-29; 36:3-7). God called out Bezalel and Aholiab and gifted them with wisdom, understanding, design and work expertise and teaching skills to provide technical leadership to all the other gifted artisans and craftsmen in this building project (Exodus 35:30-36:2). Based on very specific design instructions (Exodus 36:8-38) the Tabernacle building project started in full swing.

When we apply on a spiritual basis, Jesus Christ is building His Church even today. He declared in Matthew 16:18b *"...I will build My church, and the gates of Hades shall not prevail against it"*. The Church of Jesus Christ is being built with Jesus Christ being the foundation stone (Matthew 16:18a, 1 Cor. 3:11; 10:4). We are the living stones of the Church (1 Peter 2:5), as well as God's fellow workers (1 Cor. 3:9a). God has given us different intrinsic abilities that we should use to build His church. As the children of Israel under the leadership of Moses build the Tabernacle, **let us realize what our abilities are these days, rise up and work together to build the Church of Jesus Christ.**

JANUARY 30   *Bible Reading: Exodus Chapters 37-40*

BLESSINGS FOR FOLLOWING GOD'S INSTRUCTIONS COMPLETELY

After about eight months' labor, the Tabernacle, with all its equipments, was completed and erected on the first day of the first month (Nisan) of the second year after the departure from Egypt (Exod. 40:17). This included the Ark of the Testimony (Exodus 37:1-9), the Table for the Showbread (vv. 10-16), the God Lampstand (vv. 17-24), the Altar of Incense (vv. 25-28), the Anointing Oil and the Incense (v. 29), the Altar of Burnt Offering (Exodus 38:1-7), the

Bronze Laver (v. 8), the Court of the Tabernacle (vv. 9-31) and the Garments of the Priesthood (Exodus 39:1-31). Let us see the evidence from God's word about the people involved in building the Tabernacle:

Bezalel and Aholiab: *"Bezalel the son of Uri, the son of Hur, of the tribe of Judah, made ALL that the Lord had commanded Moses. And with him was Aholiab the son of Ahisamach, of the tribe of Dan, an engraver and designer, a weaver of blue, purple, and scarlet thread, and of fine linen".* (Exodus 38:22-23)

Children of Israel: *"Thus all the work of the tabernacle of the tent of meeting was finished. And the children of Israel did according to ALL that the Lord had commanded Moses; so they did".* (Exodus 39:32)

Moses: *"Thus Moses did; according to ALL that the Lord had commanded him, so he did"* (Exodus 40:16)

What was the reward for following God's instructions completely?

Blessings from God's servant: *"According to ALL that the Lord had commanded Moses, so the children of Israel did all the work. Then Moses looked over all the work, and indeed they had done it; as the Lord had commanded, just so they had done it.* ***And Moses blessed them".*** (Exodus 39:42-43)

The Cloud and the Glory of God Almighty: *"Then the cloud covered the tabernacle of meeting, and the glory of the Lord filled the tabernacle. And Moses was not able to enter the tabernacle of meeting, because the cloud rested above it, and the glory of the Lord filled the tabernacle"* (Exodus 40:34-35)

The continuing abiding presence of God throughout the onward journey: *"Whenever the cloud was taken up from above the tabernacle, the children of Israel would go onward in all their journeys. But if the cloud was not taken up, then they did not journey till the day that it was taken up. For the cloud of the Lord was above the tabernacle by day, and fire was over it by night, in the sight of all the house of Israel, throughout all their journeys"* (Exodus 40:36-38)

Let us follow God's instructions COMPLETELY as there are great blessings from God that will follow us throughout our earthly journey!

JANUARY 31   *Bible Reading: Leviticus Chapters 1-3*

JESUS CHRIST IS OUR ULTIMATE BURNT OFFERING

Leviticus chapters 1-3 describes three offerings that the children of Israel had to offer to God – the Burnt Offering, the Grain Offering and the Peace Offering. Of the three, the Burnt Offering is the most relevant to our lives as they offer three valuable insights for us:

This offering is a shadow of Jesus Christ, the **sinless** Son of God, offering Himself **without spot** to God **in delight** to do His Father's will even in death. *"If his offering is a burnt sacrifice of the herd, let him offer a **male without blemish**; he shall offer it **of his own free will** at the door of the tabernacle of meeting before the Lord"* (Lev 1:3)

This offering of Jesus Christ is **substitutionary**, because He offered His own body as our substitute. *"Then **he shall put his hand on the head of the burnt offering**…"* (Lev 1:4a). See also Hebrews 9:11-14; 10:5-7; Psalms 40:6-8 and Philippians 2:8.

This offering by Jesus Christ is **atoning** as He reconciled us back to God by offering Himself as a punishment for our sins. *"…and it will be accepted on his behalf **to make atonement for him**"* (Lev 1:4b)

Let us sincerely thank God today as He suffered and died in our place. Jesus Christ has become our ultimate burnt offering. *"For when we were still without strength, in due time Christ died for the ungodly. For scarcely for a righteous man will one die; yet perhaps for a good man someone would even dare to die. But God demonstrates His own love toward us, in that while we were still sinners, Christ died for us. Much more then, having now been justified by His blood, we shall be saved from wrath through Him".* (Romans 5:6-9)

February

Bible Reading: Leviticus Chapters 4-6

'DO NOT TREAT GOD'S FORGIVENESS LIGHTLY'

Leviticus chapters 4-6 mainly describe two offerings that the children of Israel had to offer to God: the sin offering (4:1-35) and the trespass offering (5:1-6:7). It is to be noted that **these offerings are only for sins that are committed unintentionally**. See the different examples mentioned below:

1. **When any person sins**: *'If a **person sins unintentionally** against any of the commandments of the Lord in anything which ought not to be done, and does any of them'* (Lev 4:2)

2. **When the whole congregation sins**: *'Now if the **whole congregation** of Israel **sins unintentionally**, and the thing is hidden from the eyes of the assembly, and they have done something against any of the commandments of the Lord in anything which should not be done, and are guilty'* (Lev 4:13)

3. **When the ruler sins**: *'When a **ruler** has sinned, and done something **unintentionally** against any of the commandments of the Lord his God in anything which should not be done, and is guilty'* (Lev 4:22)

4. **When common people sin**: *'If anyone of the **common people** sins **unintentionally** by doing something against any of the commandments of the Lord in anything which ought not to be done, and is guilty'* (Lev 4:27)

5. **When a person commits a trespass:** *'If a **person commits a trespass, and sins unintentionally** in regard to the holy things of the Lord...'* (Lev 5:15)

Once the offering is made, we read in Lev 4:35b: *'So the priest shall make atonement for his sin that he has committed, and **it shall be forgiven him***'.

There is a spiritual application for us: *we can receive the same forgiveness of our sins through the blood of Christ.* *'For if the blood of bulls and goats and the ashes of a heifer, sprinkling the unclean, sanctifies for the purifying of the flesh, **how much more shall the blood of Christ**, who through the eternal Spirit offered Himself without spot to God, **cleanse your conscience from dead works to serve the living God?'** (Heb 9:13-14). 'But if we walk in the light as He is in the light, we have fellowship with one another, and **the blood of Jesus Christ His Son cleanses us from all sin. If we confess our sins, He is faithful and just to forgive us our sins and to cleanse us from all unrighteousness'.* (1 John 1:7, 9)

However, we need to understand that we cannot keep on sinning intentionally again and again and expect forgiveness from God. *'He who covers his sins will not prosper, but **whoever confesses and forsakes them will have mercy'** (Proverbs 28:13). Our Lord Jesus Christ made it clear that we should not keep on sinning and expect forgiveness from God, as he told the man whom he had healed by the pool of Bethesda: *"See, you have been made well. **Sin no more, lest a worse thing come upon you**"* (John 5:14). This is what Jesus also told the woman caught in the act of adultery: *"Neither do I condemn you; **go and sin no more**"* (John 8:11). **Let us be careful that we do not treat God's forgiveness lightly!**

FEBRUARY 2   *Bible Reading: Leviticus Chapters 7-9*

OUR RESPONSIBILITIES AS GOD'S 'HOLY & ROYAL PRIESTS'

The Bible is clear that we are **now** both the *'holy priesthood'* (1 Peter 2:5) and the *'royal priesthood'* (1 Peter 2:9) of God. We will continue in this role as *"...priests of God and of Christ, and shall reign with Him a thousand years"* (Rev 20:6). Our reading today highlights the consecration and the start of the priestly ministry of Aaron and his sons, and there are some learning points for us as we reflect on Leviticus chapters 8 & 9:

1. In Leviticus 8:7-9, we read that Aaron and his sons were dressed up with the priestly garments consisting of the tunic, sash, robe, ephod, breastplate, turban and crown. *As the 'royal priests' of God fighting the 'good fight of faith' (1 Tim. 6:12; 2 Tim. 4:7), we also have an armor of God to wear, which include the belt of truth, the breastplate of righteousness, the sandals of the preparation of the gospel of peace, the shield of faith, the helmet of salvation and the sword of the Spirit, which is the word of God* (Eph. 6:11-17).

2. In Leviticus 9:7-14, we see that Aaron *first* offered the sin and burnt offerings *for himself*, and *thereafter* he presented the offerings *for the other people* (Lev 9:15-21). Our role as priests unto God is also to *"...offer up spiritual sacrifices acceptable to God through Jesus Christ"* (1 Peter 2:5), which are praises to God. *"Therefore by Him let us continually offer the sacrifice of praise to God, that is, the fruit of our lips, giving thanks to His name"* (Heb 13:15).

3. In Leviticus 9:22-23a, we see that Aaron blessed the children of Israel after offering the sin, burnt and peace offerings on their behalf. *We are also instructed as 'priests of God' to bless others irrespective of their behavior towards us* (Luke 6:28; Romans 12:14; 1 Cor. 4:12).

After Aaron had done all that was required of him, we see in Leviticus 9:23b-24 that (1) the glory of God appeared to all people; (2) the fire of God consumed the burnt offerings and the fat on the altar, and (3) the people shouted and fell on their faces acknowledging the greatness of God. **When we faithfully carry out our responsibilities as God's 'Holy & Royal Priests', God is pleased with us, God's name is glorified, acknowledged and revered by others around us.**

FEBRUARY 3   *Bible Reading: Leviticus Chapters 10-12*

OUR GOD IS A 'CONSUMING FIRE'

As we begin reading Leviticus chapter 10, we are startled by the sudden turn of events that has happened among the priestly leadership of Israel. Immediately after assuming the priestly ministry, Nadab and

Abihu - the two sons of Aaron the High Priest – each took his censer, put fire and incense in it, and offered 'profane' fire before the Lord **which God had NOT commanded them**. Immediately, there was a swift punishment from God through fire which 'devoured them and they died before the Lord' (Lev. 10:1-2).

This incident reminds me about the swift judgment of God against Ananias and Sapphira in Acts 5:1-11 due to which they died too suddenly for *'lying to God'* (v. 4b). This was shortly after the glorious experience of the 120 disciples through the baptism of the Holy Spirit who came down as 'divided tongues of fire' (Acts 2:3). In the case of Nadab and Abihu, God told very clearly through Moses the **three reasons** why He imposed the 'death penalty' upon the priests of God:

1. They offered 'profane' fire before the Lord which God had NOT commanded them. (Lev. 10:1)

2. They did NOT regard God and His Tabernacle as 'holy' (Lev. 10:3a)

3. They did NOT give glory to God before the people (Lev. 10:3b)

Hebrews 10:31 warns us: *"It is a fearful thing to fall into the hands of the living God"*. If God had imposed swift judgment on Nadab/Abihu and Ananias/Sapphira, He will not hesitate to judge us (God's ministers) as well today if we cross the line in our ministry. This refers to all those *'Preachers'* who stretch the word of God to preach their own ideas, or those *'Prophets'* who prophesy falsely about things that God never told them to speak, or those *'Faith Healers'* who try to showcase healings that never happened, or those *'Worship Leaders'* whose songs do not give glory to God, or even those *'Bible Teachers'* who are twisting God's word to teach false doctrines in order to satisfy their church traditions.

Let's always remember this: **Our God is a 'Consuming Fire' (Hebrews 12:29)**

FEBRUARY 4   *Bible Reading: Leviticus Chapters 13-15*

GOD DID NOT CALL US TO UNCLEANNESS

In our reading portion today, we see the laws concerning leprosy that included leprous people, garments, houses, bodily discharges and the rituals for cleansing them. Holy living encompassed every part of the life in the children of Israel, and God instituted these laws with a purpose.

"Now the leper on whom the sore is, his clothes shall be torn and his head bare; and he shall cover his mustache, and cry, 'Unclean! Unclean!' He shall be unclean. All the days he has the sore he shall be unclean. He is unclean, and he shall dwell alone; his dwelling shall be outside the camp" (Lev 13:45-46).

"Thus you shall separate the children of Israel from their uncleanness, lest they die in their uncleanness when they defile My tabernacle that is among them" (Lev 15:31)

As we draw a spiritual application in our lives, let us examine the some scripture passages that speak about our uncleanness.

How does uncleanness enter into our lives? Romans 1:21-24 gives us the answer" *"...because, although they knew God, they did not glorify Him as God, nor were thankful, but became futile in their thoughts, and their foolish hearts were darkened. Professing to be wise, they became fools, and changed the glory of the incorruptible God into an image made like corruptible man—and birds and four-footed animals and creeping things. **Therefore God also gave them up to uncleanness,** in the lusts of their hearts, to dishonor their bodies among themselves"*

What does God require from us?

Colossians 3:5-6 instructs us: *"Therefore **put to death your members which are on the earth**: fornication, **uncleanness**, passion, evil desire, and covetousness, which is idolatry. Because of these things the wrath of God is coming upon the sons of disobedience"*

Ephesians 5:3-7 further tells us: *"But fornication and **all uncleanness** or covetousness, let it not even be named among you, as is fitting for saints; neither filthiness, nor foolish talking, nor coarse jesting, which are not fitting, but rather giving of thanks. For this you know, that no fornicator, **unclean person**, nor covetous man, who is an idolater, has any inheritance in the kingdom of Christ and God. Let no one deceive you with empty words, for because of these things the wrath of God comes upon the sons of disobedience. Therefore do not be partakers with them"*.

Let us always remember: *"**...God did not call us to uncleanness, but in holiness**"* (1 Thess. 4:7)

JESUS CHRIST <u>ALONE</u> IS THE 'PERFECT ATONEMENT' FOR OUR SINS

After the death of the two sons of Aaron, God restricted access for any priest to enter the Holy Place inside the veil and come into God's presence (Lev. 16:2). On the tenth day of the seventh month called the Day of Atonement (Lev. 16:29), the High Priest enters the most Holy Place with one bull for himself as a sin offering (Lev. 16:6, 11-14), two goat kids of goats as sin offering for the people (Lev. 16:5, 7-10, 15-22), and one ram as a burnt offering for himself and the people of Israel (Lev. 16:5b, 24). It is interesting to note that of the two goats presented to God as a sin offering for the people, only one goat kid shall be killed and offered as a sin offering to God, while the other goat kid is set free into the wilderness (Lev. 16:7-10; 15-22). *Jesus Christ became the 'sin goat' for us as the death sentence fell on Him, while we became the 'goat set free' by the grace of God.*

By way of spiritual application, we can consider other things as well:

·   **Sin requires that a sacrifice be made** (Hebrews 9:22)

·   **The blood alone makes atonement for us** (Lev 17:11)

·   **Jesus paid for all of our sins** (Isaiah 53:3-12)

·   **Jesus' sacrifice was perfect** (1 Peter 1:18-19)

·   **Jesus took our punishment** (1 Peter 2:21-24)

·   **Jesus willingly died for our sins** (John 10:17; 1 Corinthians 15:3)

·   **Jesus secured salvation through His blood** (Acts 20:28)

·   **Jesus provided the atonement for our sins** (Romans 3:23-25)

·   **Jesus' death purchased forgiveness** (1 Corinthians 7:23)

·   **We cannot improve Jesus' sacrifice** (1 Peter 3:18)

·   **Our atonement allows us to know God** (Ephesians 2:13)

·   **Jesus' death rescues us from eternal punishment** (Colossians 1:13)

Knowing that we can *"...come boldly to the throne of grace, that we may obtain mercy and find grace to help in time of need"* (Heb 4:16),

let us reach out to God today through the shed blood of Jesus on the cross, for **Jesus Christ <u>alone</u> is the 'Perfect Atonement' for our sins.**

FEBRUARY 6   *Bible Reading: Leviticus Chapters 19-21*

HONORING OUR PARENTS

We need to realize that God was leading the Israelites from one pagan culture (Egypt) to another pagan culture (Canaan). While among these pagan cultures, God wanted His people to keep various moral and ceremonial laws (Leviticus 19), and God instituted penalties for breaking these laws (Leviticus 20). Among these laws, we see that honoring parents ranked very high in the list, and keeping this law shows their adherence to holiness that God required from the children of Israel. *'You shall be holy, for I the Lord your God am holy. **Every one of you shall revere his mother and his father**...I am the Lord your God"* (Lev 19:2-3). The penalty for breaking this law was mentioned in Lev. 20:7-9: *'Consecrate yourselves therefore, and be holy, for I am the Lord your God. And you shall keep My statutes, and perform them: I am the Lord who sanctifies you. **For everyone who curses his father or his mother shall surely be put to death. He has cursed his father or his mother. His blood shall be upon him'**.*

God instituted this law as part of the Ten Commandments and this was the first commandment with a promise: *'**Honor your father and your mother** that your days may be long upon the land which the Lord your God is giving you'* (Ex 20:12). **So, how do you honor your parents?**

- Listen to your parents what they tell you (Proverbs 1:8-9; 13:1; 23:22)
- Obey your parents for this is well pleasing to God (Proverbs 6:20-21; Ephesians 6:1; Colossians 3:20)
- Honor your parents (Lev. 19:3; Deut. 5:16; Eph. 6:2)
- Do not despise your parents when they are old (Proverbs 23:22b)

Let us remember today and always to honor our parents - for this is well pleasing to God!

FEBRUARY 7   *Bible Reading: Leviticus Chapters 22-24*

PRINCIPLES FOR GOD'S ACCEPTABLE FREEWILL OFFERINGS:

In our readings today in Leviticus 22:17-33, we can get a clear understanding about the kind of freewill offerings that God will accept from us.

- **Our offerings must be 'voluntary':** *"You shall offer of your own free will..."* (v. 19a)
- **Our offerings must be 'perfect'** - without having any blemish or defects (v. 19b-24)
- **Our offerings must 'not be borrowed from others'** but should be our very own (v. 25)

What are the principles for our freewill offerings to be accepted by God?

1. Our offering should be the best we can give to God - even our own bodies (Rom. 12:1-2)
2. God is honored by our gifts (Exodus 35:22)
3. Generous giving honors God (Ezra 2:68-69)
4. God will reward us for giving to others (Mark 9:41)
5. Giving helps others live (Acts 2:44-45)
6. We should support Christian workers (Acts 28:10)
7. We should give generously and cheerfully (2 Cor. 9:6-9)
8. Wealthy people should give more generously (1 Timothy 6:17-19)
9. God is pleased with our gifts (Hebrews 13:16)
10. Giving reflects God's love (1 John 3:17)

Our Lord Jesus has instructed us clearly: ***"Freely you have received, freely give"*** (Matt 10:8). May God open up our hearts and wallets, and enable us to sow good seeds and give generously to His kingdom, even today!

FEBRUARY 8   *Bible Reading: Leviticus Chapters 25-27*

GOD'S SABBATH PRINCIPLE AND PROVISION FOR OBEDIENCE

In Leviticus 25:1-22, we read about God's Sabbath principle, which occurred every seventh day of the week and every seventh year in the life of the Israelites. *"...in the seventh year there shall be a Sabbath of solemn rest for the land, a Sabbath to the Lord. You shall neither sow your field nor prune your vineyard"* (Lev 25:4).

We note that Sabbath was instituted by God (Gen 2:3), blessed by God (Exodus 20:11) and sanctified by God (Exodus 31:15). It was made for the Israelites (Mark 2:27) as a sign of the covenant with God (Exodus 31:13, 17), and they were commanded to keep it and sanctify it (Ex 20:8; Lev 19:3, 30). During the Sabbath everyone (including servants and cattle) were allowed to rest (Exodus 20:10; Deut 5:14), and no work was allowed to be done during Sabbath (Lev 23:3).

This was a type of the heavenly rest (Heb 4:4, 9) for worship (Ezek 46:3; Acts 16:13), scripture reading (Acts 13:27; 15:21), and preaching of God's word (Acts 13:14-15, 44; 17:2; 18:4). Even though Jesus was the Lord of Sabbath (Mark 2:28), He was accustomed to observe it (Luke 4:16) and taught others on this day (Luke 4:31; 6:6). The New Testament Church observed it on the first day of the week (Acts 20:7; 1 Cor. 16:2), as it was commanded to be a perpetual observance (Exodus 31:16-17; Matt 5:17-18).

God's Sabbath principle for us is to cease from our daily work activities one day per week and offer it to God for worship, Bible meditation, Bible Study, prayer, fasting and fellowship with the saints of God. As in the Old Testament where God promised to provide for the daily needs of the Israelites for observing the Sabbath (see Leviticus 25:20-22), **God will provide for all our basic needs if we dedicate one day a week to Him and His kingdom.** *"But seek first the kingdom of God and His righteousness, and all these things (what to eat, drink, wear, etc.) shall be added to you"* (Matt 6:33).

FEBRUARY 9   *Bible Reading: Numbers Chapters 1-3*

TEAM EFFORT AND SYNERGY

As we start reading the book of Numbers, we see that God directs Moses and Aaron to take a census of the Israelites. *"Take a census of all the congregation of the children of Israel, by their families, by their fathers' houses, according to the number of names, every male individually, from twenty years old and above—all who are able to go to war in Israel. **You and Aaron shall number them by their armies"***

(Num 1:2-3). However, this was a gigantic task that both Moses and Aaron could not do by themselves. So, God told them: *"And with you there shall be a man from every tribe, each one the head of his father's house"* (Num 1:4b). These twelve men *"...were chosen from the congregation, leaders of their fathers' tribes, heads of the divisions in Israel"* (Num 1:16).

So, Moses, Aaron and the twelve tribe leaders assembled all the people, and the census was taken by each head of family orally reciting their family ancestry on their father's side from twenty year old and above individually (Num 1:17-18). The mammoth task of taking the census was done in order exactly as the Lord commanded (Num 1:19, 54). All the Israelites (except the tribe of Levi) numbered to 603,550 (Num 1:46) and the tribe of Levi were later numbered to 22,000 (Lev 3:39).

This task teaches us about team effort and synergy. A **team** is defined as *"a small number of people with complementary skills who are committed to a common purpose and performance goals for which they hold themselves mutually accountable"*. It is commonly seen that a team effort enables results that are far beyond its combined capabilities as individuals. *This may be the reason* why our Lord Jesus Christ chose for himself a team of twelve disciples for the great task of propagating the Kingdom of God and send them in teams initially (Luke 9:1-6). After this, Jesus appointed seventy other disciples and send them in teams of two to every city and place where He Himself was about to go (Luke 10:1). *This may be the reason* why the church today should be a team of believers working as many parts of one body (1 Corinthians 12) to spread the gospel all over the world. **There is great synergy when people combine their efforts and work together as a team.** *"The harvest truly is plentiful, but the laborers are few"* (Matt 9:37). **Let us join in the efforts of others to achieve great things for the kingdom of God!**

FEBRUARY 10   *Bible Reading: Numbers Chapters 4-6*

GOD'S PRINCIPLE OF SEPARATION

In Numbers 6:1-21, we read about the law of the Nazirite. God established the Nazirite rule to form a small group who would separate themselves from others in total service to God (Num 6:2). They would follow special rules to be closer in mind and spirit to God. There are two kinds of Nazirites mentioned in the Bible:

1. Those who were separated from the womb - like Samson (Judges 13:5) and John the Baptist (Luke 1:15)
2. Those who were separated by a particular vow (Num 6:2)

The Nazirites were required to be holy (Num 6:8) and were esteemed pure by others (Lam 4:7). Due to this, they were prohibited from wine or strong drink (Num 6:3, Luke 1:15) and also from grapes or anything made from the vine (Num 6:3-4, Judges 13:14). They were also prohibited from cutting hair or shaving the head (Num 6:5, Judges 13:5; 16:17) and from defiling themselves by the dead (Num 6:6-7). They were raised by God for the good of the nation (Amos 2:11).

However, we find a bad example in the case of Samson who disregarded two of the three main prohibitions of the Nazirite: touching the dead (Judges 14:8-9) and cutting hair (Judges 16:19). Due to this, he had a tragic end in his life and is a warning to us as well.

God has also set up a principle of separation for us. We should not be unequally yoked with unbelievers through marriage, and we should stay away from everything that is unclean. **Our bodies are the temples of the living God** (2 Cor. 6:14-16). *Therefore "Come out from among them and be separate, says the Lord. Do not touch what is unclean, and I will receive you. I will be a Father to you, and you shall be My sons and daughters, says the LORD Almighty."* (2 Cor. 6:17-18)

FEBRUARY 11   *Bible Reading: Numbers Chapters 7-9*

EXPERIENCING GOD'S GUIDANCE EVERY DAY

In Numbers 9:15-23, we read in great detail about how God guided the Israelites in the wilderness as a cloud by day and a pillar of fire by night. The cloud and the fire moved according to God's will. When they moved, the people moved; where they stopped, the people stopped. *"At the command of the LORD they remained encamped, and at the command of the LORD they journeyed; they kept the charge of the LORD, at the command of the LORD by the hand of Moses"* (Num 9:23).

This cloud and fire was appointed to be the visible sign and symbol of God's presence with Israel. Thus we (the spiritual Israel) are taught to see God always near us, both night and day. As long as the cloud rested on the tabernacle, so long the Israelites continued in the same place. There is no time lost while we are waiting on God's time. When the cloud was taken up, the Israelites moved as well, however comfortably they were settled there. When we follow God's guidance, we please Him. Although His plans may not always be clear to us, we must follow Him. In Psalm 73:24 we are assured that God will guide us with His counsel and afterward receive us to glory. In Psalms 48:14, this is what we learn: *"For this is God, our God forever and ever; He will be our guide even to death"*. We are kept at uncertainty even concerning the time of our putting off the earthly house of this tabernacle *so that we may be always ready to move beyond the veil at the command of the Lord* (2 Cor. 5:1-5).

As children of God, let us be daily led by the Spirit of God (Rom. 8:14). Like a Good Shepherd, He will lead us to green pastures and still waters every day (Psalms 23:1-2). If we acknowledge Him on our every step, He will direct our paths (Proverbs 3:6). **Let us follow the pillar of the cloud and fire, and experience God's guidance every day of our lives!**

FEBRUARY 12   *Bible Reading: Numbers Chapters 10-12*

FIVE LEADERSHIP QUALITIES FROM THE LIFE OF MOSES:

Approximately two years has passed since the departure of the Israelites from Egypt under the leadership of Moses. There have been definite instances of *frustration* for Moses when the Israelites complained regarding lack of food (Num 11:1), cried out in despair (v. 2) and wept in anguish (v. 10), *Moses vented his own frustration to God* (v. 11-15). When God promised to provide meat for a whole month for over 600,000+ people, *Moses was doubtful and expressed it to God as well* (v. 21-22). This showed that Moses was very human, but **we can see five wonderful leadership qualities from the life of Moses that all spiritual leaders should adopt in their lives as well.**

1. <u>Moses was a man of prayer:</u> When the people complained and cried out to Moses, we see that Moses takes this matter in prayer before God. *"Then the people cried out to Moses, and when **Moses prayed to the LORD**, the fire was quenched"* (Num 11:2). Also,

when his sister Miriam was punished by God with leprosy, we see that Moses prayed for her. *So **Moses cried out to the LORD**, saying, "Please heal her, O God, I pray!"* (Num 12:13).

2. <u>**Moses invoked God's presence with every move**</u>: In Num 10:35-36, we read that whenever the ark of God started a journey or stopped, Moses called upon God's presence. *So it was **whenever the ark set out, that Moses said**: "Rise up, O LORD! Let Your enemies be scattered, and let those who hate You flee before You." **And when it rested, he said**: "Return, O LORD, to the many thousands of Israel".*

3. <u>**Moses was unselfish with his anointing**</u>: Due to the tremendous burden upon Moses, God decided to take the Spirit of anointing that was upon Moses and transfer this anointing upon the seventy elders of Israel (Num 11:16-17; 24-25). When Joshua was upset when two of the elders prophesied in the camp (vv. 26-28) and expressed it to Moses, **Moses replies with words that show that he was truly unselfish with his anointing**: *Then Moses said to him (Joshua), "Are you zealous for my sake? **Oh, that all the LORD's people were prophets and that the LORD would put His Spirit upon them!**"* (v. 29).

4. <u>**Moses was a very humble man**</u>: Check out the character report about Moses in Num 12:3: ***(Now the man Moses was very humble, more than all men who were on the face of the earth.)***

5. <u>**Moses was faithful in the work of God**</u>: This is what God had to testify about Moses, which is true: ***"Not so with My servant Moses; He is faithful in all My house."***

With all these wonderful leadership qualities, it is not surprising that God interacted so closely with His servant-prophet-leader Moses and made Himself know through visions, dreams and even face-to-face and even allowed Moses to see the form of God as well (Num 12:6-88). **Let us adopt these five leadership qualities of Moses in our lives as well in order to have a closer encounter with God.**

FEBRUARY 13   *Bible Reading: Numbers Chapters 13-15*

FAITH IN GOD AND HIS WORD IS THE KEY TO OUR SPIRITUAL VICTORY

The Israelites had now reached the border of Canaan, which God had promised to give to their great grandfather Abraham back in

Genesis 12:1. **This was God's gift to them as a reward for Abraham obeying the call of God.** *And the Lord spoke to Moses, saying, "Send men to spy out* **the land of Canaan, which I am giving to the children of Israel;** *from each tribe of their fathers you shall send a man, everyone a leader among them"* (Num 13:1-2).

So, Moses chose twelve leaders to spy out and report about the Promised Land that no one had seen before, and send them with an encouragement: *"**Be of good courage**...and bring some of the fruit of the land"* (v. 20). The spies found that the land they were to inherit truly flowed with milk and honey because of the abundance of grapes, figs, dates, pomegranates and nuts, and they brought a sample of one cluster of grapes that had to be carried by two men in a pole (v. 23). However, ten of the twelve spies also exaggerated the strength of the inhabitants of the land, and brought a 'bad' report in which they saw themselves as grasshoppers in their own sight and in the sight of their enemies (vv. 31-33).

One of the prime reasons why God had brought the Israelites out of Egypt with great signs and wonders is that they would trust God in all their future encounters – like conquering Canaan. However, they refused to believe in God and have faith in His abilities to help them achieve their goals. God expresses His frustrations to Moses: *Then the Lord said to Moses: "How long will these people* **reject Me?** *And how long will* **they not believe Me, with all the signs which I have performed among them?** (Num 14:11). This unbelief in God resulted in the death of all the ten spies who brought the evil report (v. 37), the wanderings of the Israelites in the wilderness for 40 years (v. 33-34) and the death of all the older generation Israelites (v. 32) who had refused to have faith in God and His word. *What a tragic ending to God's own people who were redeemed from Egypt so gloriously?*

This brings home a very important lesson for us – our faith in God and His Word is our key for Spiritual Victory. *"But without faith it is impossible to please Him, for he who comes to God must believe that He is, and that He is a rewarder of those who diligently seek Him"* (Heb 11:6)

FEBRUARY 14   *Bible Reading: Numbers Chapters 16-18*

THE CONSEQUENCES OF REBELLING AGAINST GOD'S LEADERS

After God directed the Israelites back to the wilderness for forty years because of their unbelief, disobedience and lack of trust in God, we see that a group of Israelites resisted this tough directive. Some of the Levites became disgruntled with Moses' leadership. Korah, one of the Levites, led a disastrous insurrection along with two-hundred and fifty leaders and representatives of the congregation who all died when the earth parted itself and swallowed them up (Num 16:1-40).

The lesson learned through this incident is that there are dire consequences for rebelling against God's anointed leaders. Our leaders deserve our respect and support, even during trying times. We must not take part in a rebellion or gossip slander against God's anointed leaders. Rather, we should follow the footsteps of Jesus Christ (Mark 14:36; Luke 22:42; Heb 5:8) and Apostle Paul (1Co 16:7) and consider them as our examples of submission to authority. Jesus Christ is our best example of submission to God the Father's will (Matthew 26:39, 42), and following Christ requires our submission to Him (Luke 14:27). **It is God who has created lines of authority for harmonious relationships** (1 Corinthians 11:2-16), **and ultimately we all need to submit to God alone** (James 4:7-10).

FEBRUARY 15   *Bible Reading: Numbers Chapters 19-21*

MISSING GOD'S BEST THROUGH DISOBEDIENCE

After thirty-eight years at Kadesh Barnea, the Israelites prepared to resume the journey to Canaan but this time by following a route south of the Dead Sea and through Edom (20:14). Before this took place several incidents occurred in rapid succession. Miriam died and was buried at Kadesh (20:1); the people ran out of water and Moses, *enraged by their incessant complaining, struck the rock twice from which God promised water if Moses only spoke the word* (20:2–13); and Moses tried without success to get permission from the king of Edom to pass through his land on the so-called King's Highway (20:14–21).

Though understandable, Moses' loss of temper displeased the Lord and **resulted in his being unable to enter the Promised Land** (Num. 20:12; 27:14; Deut. 3:26–27). Moses' disobedience as Israel's leader had damaged not only his own reputation in the eyes of the people but the Lord's reputation as well. We note that God continued to be in control as He led His people even by denying Moses and Aaron entry into the Promised Land.

Such punishment for what might seem to be a relatively minor offense underscores the principle that **God expects more of those to whom He entrusts responsibility than He does from others.** Jesus said, *"From everyone who has been given much shall much be required"* (Luke 12:48). Through this incident it is clear that **God's work and power only depends on those dynamic leaders who are willing to take instructions from Him always and glorify Him through their ministry.**

Unlike Moses and Aaron, let us not miss God's BEST through disobedience! Let us remain faithful and obedient to God even until death in order to receive the 'crown of life' that our Lord has promised us (Rev 2:10).

FEBRUARY 16   *Bible Reading: Numbers Chapters 22-24*

THE TRAGEDY OF FOLLOWING GOD'S PERMISSIVE WILL

Today's reading of Numbers 22-24 tells us the story of Balaam, the son of Beor, who originated from Mesopotamia (Deut 23:4). He was a soothsayer by profession (Joshua 13:22) and used sorcery (Num 24:1) to bewitch others. He is referred to as a prophet as well (2 Peter 2:15, 16) because God was pleased to inspire and direct him to speak prophecies towards Israel (Num 24:2-9). In fact many of the Jewish writers say that Balaam had been a great prophet, who for the accomplishment of his predictions, and the answers of his prayers, had been looked upon justly as a man of great interest with God.

When Balak the king of Moabites saw the Israelites camped in the plains of Moab, he knew that his people's fate (Num 22:1-4) would be similar to that of Sihon, the king of Amorites (Num 21:21-32) and Og the king of Bashan (Num 21:33-35). He sends for Balaam to curse Israel with large sums of money (Num 22:5-7, Joshua 24:9, Nehemiah

13:2, Micah 6:5). When Balaam talked to God regarding cursing the Israelites (Deut 23:5), God revealed His PERFECT WILL in this matter to Balaam in Num 22:12: *And God said to Balaam,* **"You shall <u>not</u> go with them; you shall not curse the people, for they are blessed."** However, when Balaam persisted with his request, we see that God revealed His PERMISSIVE WILL in this matter in Num 22:20: *And God came to Balaam at night and said to him, "If the men come to call you, rise and go with them; but only the word which I speak to you— that you shall do."*

Following God's PERMISSIVE WILL, Balaam almost lost his life being rebuked by a donkey and the Angel of God (Num 22:22-35, 2 Peter 2:16). Balaam was covetous, and desired to become rich quickly through unrighteousness (2 Peter 2:15). The apostle Jude describes Balaam's sin that he *'ran greedily into an error for profit'* (Jude 1:11). When Balaam could not curse the Israelites because of God's favor, he gave wrong counsel to Balak that caused Israel's corruption with the Midianites (Num 25:1-3; 31:16; Rev 2:14, 15). However it is certain, that afterwards for his covetousness, God departed from him. He wished to die the death of a righteous (Num 23:10b), but his end was tragic to say the least (Num 31:8; Joshua 13:22).

What is the lesson for us through this real life story of Balaam? If we follow God's PERMISSIVE WILL instead of His PERFECT WILL, our life will end in tragedy. We have to draw near to God (James 4:8) and seek His PERFECT WILL through total consecration of ourselves. **"I beseech you therefore, brethren, by the mercies of God, that you present your bodies a living sacrifice, holy, acceptable to God, which is your reasonable service. And do not be conformed to this world, but be transformed by the renewing of your mind, that you may prove what is that good and acceptable and PERFECT WILL of God"** (Romans 12:1-2).

FEBRUARY 17   *Bible Reading: Numbers Chapters 25-27*

GOD'S ORDER IN LEADERSHIP SUCCESSION

Just as the Israelites were preparing to enter the Promised Land, they needed a new census because everyone over the age of 20 who were counted in the previous census had died in the wilderness. The need to take a new census was paramount as God was keeping His people united and organized. Another reason for knowing the exact count was to assist in dividing the land of Canaan by lot among the 12 tribes according to their number and size (Num 26:52-56).

Moses was the greatest leader that the Israelites had ever known, and he followed the directions of God consistently throughout the last 40 years of the journey from Egypt. However due to one error, Moses was not permitted to enter Canaan, but could only view the land from the top of Mount Pisgah (Num 27:12-14). The time had now come for an orderly leadership succession, and his long-time faithful servant Joshua was chosen as his successor (Num 27:22, 23). Joshua was the son of Nun (Num 13:8) who was intimately associated with Moses as his assistant (Exodus 24:13; 32:17; 33:11). He was a religious zealot (Num 11:28) who was sent with others to view the Promised Land (Num 13:8) many years ago. He made a favorable report of the land with Caleb (Num 14:6-10) due to which his life was miraculously preserved when others perished (Num 14:10). Due to this, he was rewarded for his courage and fidelity (Num 14:30, 38; 32:12). In Num 27:18 we read that he was divinely inspired and had the anointing of the Holy Spirit. As per God's command, Joshua was commissioned, ordained, and charged with the responsibilities of Moses' office (Num 27:18-23). *"So Moses did as the Lord commanded him. He took Joshua and set him before Eleazar the priest and before all the congregation. **And he laid his hands on him and inaugurated him, just as the Lord commanded by the hand of Moses"*** (Num 27:22-23).

This incident displays God's order of leadership succession. No leader *(however great he or she may be)* is supposed to last forever. *"To everything there is a season, a time for every purpose under heaven"*(Eccl 3:1). There will come a time when they have to transfer the authority and power of their position to a worthwhile successor. *How much better would it be if our spiritual leaders understood this fact, and would groom and mentor able disciples to take over the leadership in due course of time!* Even our Lord Jesus Christ groomed and mentored His twelve disciples to take over the leadership of the Church after His physical ascension to heaven. We also see Apostle Paul also groomed young Timothy to a leadership role.

Let all leaders understand this basic fact: *"For exaltation comes neither from the east nor from the west nor from the south. But God is the Judge: He puts down one, and exalts another"* (Psalms 75:6-7).

GOD'S LAW CONCERNING TAKING VOWS AND OATHS

In Num 30:1-2, we read the following: *"Then Moses spoke to the heads of the tribes concerning the children of Israel, saying, **"This is the thing which the Lord has commanded: If a man makes a vow to the Lord, or swears an oath to bind himself by some agreement, he shall not break his word; he shall do according to all that proceeds out of his mouth"***. It is evident that God takes vows and oaths very seriously. A vow (*"neder"*) is a pledge to do something. On the other hand, by means of an oath (*"shavua"*) one may either prohibit or require oneself to perform a particular act.

Vows and oaths were solemn promises made to God in reference to devoting oneself to God (Num 6:2), dedicating children to God (1 Sam 1:11), devoting property to God (Gen 28:22), offering sacrifices (Lev 7:16; Num 15:3) and afflicting our soul (Num 30:13). Vows and oaths were meant to be voluntary (Deut 23:21-22), and were required to be performed faithfully (Num 30:2) and without any delay (Deut 23:23). There were many instances of vows and oaths recorded in scripture: Jacob (Gen 28:20-22; 31:13), Israelites (Num 21:2), Jephthah (Judges 11:30-31), Hannah (1 Sam 1:11), David (Psalms 132:2-5), Jonah (Jonah 2:9) and Paul (Acts 18:18).

There are predominantly two aspects of God's law concerning vows and oaths:

If you make a vow or oath, DO NOT break it under any circumstances. *"When you make a vow to the Lord your God, **you shall not delay to pay it**; for the Lord your God will surely require it of you, and it would be sin to you. But if you abstain from vowing, it shall not be sin to you. That which has gone from your lips **you shall keep and perform**, for you voluntarily vowed to the Lord your God what you have promised with your mouth"* (Deut 23:21-23). *"Make vows to the Lord your God, and **pay them**..."* (Psalms 76:11)

It is however BETTER NOT to take a vow or oath at all. *"When you make a vow to God, do not delay to pay it; for He has no pleasure in fools. Pay what you have vowed. **Better not to vow than to vow and not pay.** Do not let your mouth cause your flesh to sin, nor say before the messenger of God that it was an error. Why should God be angry at* *your excuse and destroy the work of your hands?"* (Eccl 5:4-6). *"Again you have heard that it was said to those of old, 'You shall not swear falsely, but shall perform your oaths to the Lord.'* **But I say to you, do not swear at all:** *neither by heaven, for it is God's throne; nor by the earth, for it is His footstool; nor by Jerusalem, for it is the city of the great King. Nor shall you swear by your head, because you cannot make one hair white or black. But let your 'Yes' be 'Yes,' and your 'No,' 'No.' For whatever is more than these is from the evil one"* (Matt 5:33-37). *"But above all, my brethren,* **do not swear,** *either by heaven or by earth or with any other oath. But let your "Yes," be "Yes," and your "No," "No," lest you fall into judgment"* (James 5:12).

FEBRUARY 19   *Bible Reading: Numbers Chapters 31-33*

Settling for LESS than God's BEST

In Numbers 32, we read about the tribes of Reuben, Gad and the half tribe of Manasseh wanting to settle down in the land of Jazer and Gilead, which is east of the Jordan River, as they had a great multitude of livestock and this region was a place of livestock. (Num 32:1). They came to Moses and expressed their desire: *"If we have found favor in your sight, let this land be given to your servants as a possession. Do not take us over the Jordan"* (Num 32:5). This proposal showed disregard to the land of Canaan, distrust of the Lord's promise, and unwillingness to encounter the difficulties and dangers of conquering and driving out the inhabitants of that land. Moses warns them of their foolish desire in Num 32:6-15.

Two things common in the world might lead these tribes to make this choice: **the lust of the eye,** and **the pride of life.** They considered their own convenience more than the plan of God for their future, which was to settle down in the Promised Land. Even today, many seek their own convenience more than God's ultimate plan for them. They are led by worldly interests and temporal advantages that fall short of the heavenly Canaan that God is preparing for them. The Reubenites, Gadites, and half-tribe of Manasseh, who chose their inheritance just outside the Promised Land, are types of world-bordering carnal Christians.

These tribes propose that their men of war will go armed before the children of Israel into the land of Canaan, and that they will not return until the conquest of Canaan was ended (Num 32:16-32). Moses then grants their request, which clearly was less than what God had intended for them. *"So Moses gave to the children of Gad, to the children of Reuben, and to half the tribe of Manasseh the son of Joseph, the kingdom of Sihon king of the Amorites and the kingdom of Og king of Bashan, the land with its cities within the borders, the cities of the surrounding country"* (Num 32:33) . This was **clearly a wrong choice** and history tells us that **this compromise led to their captivity** by Assyria much sooner than all the other tribes of Israel. *"And **they were unfaithful to the God of their fathers**, and played the harlot after the gods of the peoples of the land, whom God had destroyed before them. So the God of Israel stirred up the spirit of Pul king of Assyria, that is, Tiglath-Pileser king of Assyria. **He carried the Reubenites, the Gadites, and the half-tribe of Manasseh into captivity.** He took them to Halah, Habor, Hara, and the river of Gozan to this day"* (1 Chron 5:25-26)

We should never settle for anything less than God's best for us. We should never compromise our convictions (1 Kings 11:4) as compromise can keep us from doing what is right and weaken our faith (2 Corinthians 6:14-18), **which will ultimately lead to our downfall**.

FEBRUARY 20   *Bible Reading: Numbers Chapters 34-36*

JESUS CHRIST IS OUR ULTIMATE "CITY OF REFUGE"

In Numbers 35:9-34, God commands Moses to appoint **six cities of refuge <u>to run in and hide</u>,** which would serve as interim shelters for murderers who commit crime by accident until they are brought to trial. They should not leave the vicinity of the cities of refuge until the death of the High Priest, and it is only then that they are free to go back to their homes (v. 28).

In **both the Old and New Testament, our Lord Jesus Christ is alluded to as our "City of Refuge":**

· <u>Old Testament</u>: *"Return to the **stronghold**, you prisoners of hope. Even today I declare that I will restore double to you"* (Zech 9:12)

· <u>New Testament:</u>*"Thus God, determining to show more abundantly to the heirs of promise the immutability of His counsel, confirmed it by an oath, that by two immutable things, in which it is impossible for God to lie, **we might have strong consolation, who have fled for refuge to lay hold of the hope set before us**"* (Heb 6:17-18)

These cities of refuge are a shadow of the rich mercies of salvation that we have obtained through Jesus Christ:

1. These cities of refuge **rear their towers of safety on high** – *similar to Christ raised up on the cross* (John 3:14-15) *and then exalted to the right hand of God the Father after His ascension* (Philippians 2:9).
2. The highway of salvation resembles **the smooth and plain paths** to the cities of refuge – *similar to the path that leads to our Redeemer Jesus* (John 14:6).
3. **Road signs were set up pointing to the cities of refuge** – *similar to the ministers of the gospel who direct sinners to Christ* (Ephesians 4:11-13).
4. The **gates of the cities of refuge stood open night and day** – *similar to Christ who will not cast anyone who goes to Him. Him* (John 6:37).
5. The cities of refuge **afforded support to everyone who entered its walls** – *similar to Christ who promises support for us when we abide in Him* (John 15:4-5).
6. Finally, the cities of refuge **were a protection for all** – *similar to Christ who promises us divine protection from the wrath of God* (Romans 8:1).

It is therefore clear that **Jesus Christ is our ULTIMATE "City of Refuge"!** <u>God is our refuge</u> and strength, <u>a very present help in trouble</u> (Psalms 46:1). Let us <u>run to Him alone</u> for help in the time of need. *"Let us therefore come boldly to the throne of grace that we may obtain mercy and find grace to help in time of need"* (Heb 4:16).

FEBRUARY 21   *Bible Reading: Deuteronomy Chapters 1-3*

DELEGATION – GOD'S ANSWER FOR SHARING THE BURDEN:

In Deut 1:9-18, Moses reiterates one of the most important decisions that he took early on during the wilderness journey of the Israelites. Through the wise counsel of his father-in-law Jethro (see Exodus

18:13-26), Moses quickly realized his inability to bear the burden of all the people even though he was a mighty leader with God's power and abilities at his disposal. In his own words: *"And I spoke to you at that time, saying: 'I alone am not able to bear you...How can I alone bear your problems and your burdens and your complaints? "* (Deut 1:9, 12). So, he chose **'wise, understanding and knowledgeable men'** as leaders/officers over thousands, hundreds, fifties and tens (vv. 13-15), and instructed them to judge impartially over the matters brought to them (v. 17a). Moses only took those matters to judge that could not be adjudicated by the officers under him (v. 17b). This is the pattern of judicial matters were followed smoothly for the Israelites throughout the forty years of the wilderness journey.

In the New Testament - in **Acts 6:1-6**, we see the same **principle of delegation** working out in matters concerning food distribution in the first century church. The Apostles rightly decided to concentrate on spiritual matters like prayer and the ministry of the Word (vv. 2, 4). *"Therefore, brethren, seek out from among you **seven men of good reputation, full of the Holy Spirit and wisdom**, whom we may appoint over this business"* (Acts 6:3). They then chose seven godly men (including Stephen, who became the first Christian martyr), prayed with the laying on of hands, and commissioned them for the 'secular' administrative tasks. Everyone did their part in the ministry of the Church and no more complaints were heard among the believers.

This **principle of delegation** is **evident in the functioning of today's church as well**. *"And He Himself gave some to be apostles, some prophets, some evangelists, and some pastors and teachers, for the equipping of the saints for the work of ministry, for the edifying of the body of Christ..."* (Eph 4:11-16). The great tasks of the church can only be effectively fulfilled if the leaders are willing to delegate the tasks among godly people who meet the biblical standards mentioned above. **Let's always remember that delegation is God's answer for sharing the burden!**

FEBRUARY 22   *Bible Reading: Deuteronomy Chapters 4-6*

THE GREATEST COMMANDMENT IN THE BIBLE

After 40 years of wandering in the desert, Moses dutifully carried out God's instructions to reiterate and remind the Israelites about their journey so far, and teach them God's law as their preparation to enter the Promised Land. Obedience to God's law should be a priority, as in the words of Moses: *"For the Lord your God is a consuming fire, a jealous God"* (Deut 4:24). After introducing God's law (Deut 4:44-49), Moses reviews the Ten Commandments with the Israelites (Deut 5:1-22). By way of concluding his teaching of God's commandments, Moses then proclaims the GREATEST commandment ever mentioned in the Bible: ***"Hear, O Israel: The Lord our God, the Lord is one! You shall love the Lord your God with all your heart, with all your soul, and with all your strength"*** (Deut 6:4-5)

The first and greatest commandment of God's law is that we love God with ALL our heart, soul, mind and strength. This love should include <u>four crucial components</u>:

1. **Sincere** – we must love God from our hearts and not in lip service and empty words.

2. **Strong** – we must love God passionately surpassing all our other emotions.

3. **Shrewd** – we must love God with all of our understanding and reasoning power.

4. **Superlative** – we must love God above anybody or anything else in our lives.

In the New Testament, our Lord Jesus Christ confirmed this fact: *Then one of them, a lawyer, asked Him a question, testing Him, and saying, "Teacher, which is the great commandment in the law?" Jesus said to him, "'**You shall love the Lord your God with all your heart, with all your soul, and with all your mind.'** This is the first and great commandment. And the second is like it: '**You shall love your neighbor as yourself.'** On these two commandments hang all the Law and the Prophets"* (Matt 22:35-40).

In order to please God, let us focus all our energy in loving God truly in all areas our lives - reflected by fearing God, obeying all that He has commanded us and by loving others. If we do that, we will fulfill God's longing for us mentioned in Deut 5:29: *"Oh, that they had such a heart in them that they would fear Me and always keep all My commandments, that it might be well with them and with their children forever!"* (Deut 5:29)

INTERCESSION –
A KEY TO OUR SURVIVAL

As Moses reviews the rebellious acts of the Israelites during their wilderness journey, he reveals an important role that he played in their survival. When we read Deut 9:4-6 closely, we can understand that God did not give the Promised Land to the Israelites because of their righteousness for they were a stiff-necked people. The real two reasons why God gave them the land were: (a) to fulfill His word that he had promised to their forefathers Abraham, Isaac and Jacob, and (b) because of the wickedness of the seven nations whose land they were preparing to occupy (Deut 7:1).

There were many instances that the Israelites provoked the Lord to anger. *"Remember. Do not forget how you provoked the Lord your God to wrath in the wilderness. From the day that you departed from the land of Egypt until you came to this place, you have been rebellious against the Lord. Also in Horeb you provoked the Lord to wrath, so that the Lord was angry enough with you to have destroyed you"* (Deut 9:7-8). The Lord was so angry with the Israelites that He wanted destroy all of them and start a new nation through Moses. This is what God said to Moses: *'I have seen this people, and indeed they are a stiff-necked people. Let Me alone, that I may destroy them and blot out their name from under heaven; and I will make of you a nation mightier and greater than they'* (Deut 9:13-14). However, we see Moses interceding and pleading for His people and His brother Aaron time and time again (see Deut 9:18-29). We need to understand that it was only through Moses interceding for the Israelites that their lives were spared many times.

We now have our Lord Jesus Christ seated at the right hand of God the Father, who is greater than Moses, interceding on our behalf in the throne room of God. *"...and He was numbered with the transgressors, and He bore the sin of many, and **made intercession** for the transgressors"* (Isaiah 53:12b). *"Now He who searches the hearts knows what the mind of the Spirit is, **because He makes intercession for the saints according to the will of God"** (Romans 8:27). **"It is Christ who died, and furthermore is also risen, who is even at the right hand of God, who also **makes intercession** for us"** (Romans 8:34).

*"Therefore He is also able to save to the uttermost those who come to God through Him, since **He always lives <u>to make intercession</u> for them**"* (Heb 7:25).

Even through **<u>intercession is the key to our survival</u>,** let us not take advantage during this age of grace and provoke God to anger by sinning deliberately and consistently. Even though Moses interceded for the Israelites many times, however due to their consistent rebellion they lost their rite of passage into the Promised Land. In 1 Corinthians 10:1-11, Apostle Paul quoted many examples concerning the Israelites, and finally gave us an advice that we must always remember in our spiritual journey: *"**Therefore let him who thinks he stands take heed lest he fall**"* (1 Cor 10:12)

FEBRUARY 24   *Bible Reading: Deuteronomy Chapters 10-12*

EDUCATING OUR CHILDREN IN GODLY WAYS IS OUR RESPONSIBILITY

In our reading passage today, Moses continued to emphasize the requirements of a personal relationship with God, and reminded the moral laws that God had provided. Obedience to God's word and submission to His will result in spiritual prosperity. *"Therefore you shall lay up these words of mine in your heart and in your soul, and bind them as a sign on your hand, and they shall be as frontlets between your eyes. You shall teach them to your children, speaking of them when you sit in your house, when you walk by the way, when you lie down, and when you rise up"* (Deut 11:18-19). There are **three rules to be observed** here:

1. **Let our hearts be filled with the word of God** - through regular reading and reflection.
2. **Let our eyes be fixed upon the word of God** – through visible unavoidable signs that we carry around with us.
3. **Let our tongues be used to teach our children the word of God** – through our words and godly lifestyle

We can see **<u>six instances</u>** in the book of Deuteronomy itself that Moses refers to educating our children, and **we can distill from these verses <u>WHAT we should teach our children</u>:**

1. **Deut 4:9-10**: *Teach about your own salvation experience and especially the events that led you to the feet of Jesus.*

2. **Deut 4:14**: *Teach Godly principles and rules for living an exemplary godly life.*

3. **Deut 6:1-9**: *Teach how to love God passionately and sincerely.*

4. **Deut 6:20-25**: *Teach about your spiritual journey so far and the miracles you have experienced during various times of trials in your life.*

5. **Deut 11:13-21**: *Teach about the blessings that will follow if we obey God wholeheartedly.*

6. **Deut 32:45-46**: *Teach about being "careful to observe the entire Scripture" in daily living.*

As parents, let us clearly understand one simple fact: "educating OUR children in godly ways is OUR responsibility". Let's take to heart all of God's truth ourselves, and share them with our children as a way of life. **Let us also understand that the richest legacy that we can leave our children behind is a godly example that they can emulate!**

FEBRUARY 25   *Bible Reading: Deuteronomy Chapters 13-15*

THE TRUE MEANING OF 'IDOLATRY'

*"If there arises among you a **prophet** or a **dreamer of dreams**, and he gives you a **sign or a wonder**, and the sign or the wonder comes to pass, of which he spoke to you, saying, 'Let us go after other gods'—which you have not known—'and let us serve them,' **you shall not listen to the words of that prophet or that dreamer of dreams, for the Lord your God is testing you to know whether you love the Lord your God with all your heart and with all your soul"** (Deut 13:1-3)*

Moses cautioned the Israelites against idolatry that may arise from the Canaanites. We should be aware of the truths and precepts of the Bible; for we may expect to be proved by temptations of evil under the appearance of good, and of error in the guise of truth. This would be a proof of our sincere allegiance for God that we should not forsake God and follow other hobbies/things/people that take the first place meant for God in our lives. Deut 13 speaks clearly about the ultimate punishment that should be given for apostates as **God desired that the Israelites worship of God must be free from idolatry**. Deut 13:1-5 speaks about the enticers to idolatry must be put to death; Deut 13:6-11 speaks about relations who entice to idolatry not be spared, and Deut 13:12-18 tells us that idolatrous cities must be not be spared either.

What is idolatry in our context? 1 Chronicles 16:26 and Psalms 96:5 tell us that *"all the __gods of the peoples__ are idols"*. 1 Sam 15:23 warns us that *"...rebellion is as the sin of witchcraft, and __stubbornness__ is as iniquity and idolatry"*. Colossians 3:4-5 reminds us that **covetousness is idolatry**. *"When Christ who is our life appears, then you also will appear with Him in glory. Therefore put to death your members which are on the earth: fornication, uncleanness, passion, evil desire, **and covetousness, which is idolatry**"*.

Beware of idolatry, which is really 'covetousness' in our lives. *"For this you know, that no fornicator, unclean person, __nor covetous man, who is an idolater, has any inheritance in the kingdom of Christ and God__"* (Eph 5:5)

FEBRUARY 26   *Bible Reading: Deuteronomy Chapters 16-18*

JESUS CHRIST IS THE GREAT PROPHET LIKE MOSES

In our readings today from Deut 18, we see that Moses prophesies that God will raise up a great Prophet like him in the future. *"**The Lord your God will raise up for you a Prophet like me from your midst, from your brethren.** Him you shall hear... And the Lord said to me: 'What they have spoken is good. **I will raise up for them a Prophet like you from among their brethren, and will put My words in His mouth, and He shall speak to them all that I command Him.** And it shall be that whoever will not hear My words, which He speaks in My name, I will require it of him"* (Deut 18:15, 17-19).

This prediction was literally fulfilled fifteen hundred years later in our Lord Jesus Christ who was referred to by Apostle Peter (Acts 3:22, 23) and by Stephen, the first Christian martyr (Acts 7:37). Jesus Christ is The Prophet, great above all other prophets; by whom God would make known Himself and His will to the children of men, more fully and clearly than he had ever done before. Jesus Christ is the Light of the world (John 8:12), and He would reveal the hidden mysteries of God. He is The Word by whom God speaks to us (John 1:1; Heb 1:2). He should be like unto Moses, only above him. Whoever refuses to listen to Jesus Christ today, shall find out one day that this Prophet will be his/her Judge in the future (John 12:48).

Let us pay careful attention to all that our Lord Jesus Christ has told us to do which are clearly written in the four gospels. **Let us always remember that Jesus Christ is truly the GREAT Prophet like Moses whose words we need to hear and obey!**

FEBRUARY 27   *Bible Reading: Deuteronomy Chapters 19-21*

IS OUR GOD A 'SELECTIVE CONSERVATIONIST'?

In the midst of expounding the principles governing warfare and the military rules for the Israelites, Moses expounds an intriguing piece of ecological planning from God in Deut 20:19-20: *"When you besiege a city for a long time, while making war against it to take it, **you shall not destroy its trees by wielding an ax against them; if you can eat of them**, do not cut them down to use in the siege, for the tree of the field is man's food. **Only the trees which you know are not trees for food you may destroy and cut down**, to build siegeworks against the city that makes war with you, until it is subdued.*

In other words, **God did not want the Israelites to cut down any trees that bore fruit.** So, fruit-bearing trees were to be carefully spared. We see that trees are mentioned in many places in the Bible. Trees provide food (Deut 24:20-21), serve as memorials (Gen 21:33), supply building materials (1 Chronicles 14:1), offer shade (Zech 3:10; John 1:48), and even stand as landmarks (Gen 12:6). There are definite rules about planting and cultivation (Lev 19:23-25). However, in a protracted siege, wood would be required for various purposes, both for military works and for fuel and **so the trees that did not bear fruit were to be cut down without mercy.**

So, to answer the question - **Is our God a 'Selective Conservationist'?** - We can definitely say 'YES'. How does this relate to our lives? In

74

Psalms 1:3, it is God's desire that we should *"...be like trees planted by the rivers of water, that brings forth its fruit in its season"*. Jeremiah 17:7-8 tells us the following: *"Blessed is the man who trusts in the Lord, and whose hope is the Lord. For he shall be like a tree planted by the waters, which spreads out its roots by the river, and will not fear when heat comes; but its leaf will be green, and will not be anxious in the year of drought, **nor will cease from yielding fruit"**.* **We have been planted for bearing fruit**. There are dire consequences for not bearing fruit as we are supposed to do. *"And even now the ax is laid to the root of the trees. **Therefore every tree which does not bear good fruit is cut down and thrown into the fire"*** (Matt 3:10)

Let us be fruit-bearing in our lives for we will be known by the fruits we produce. In the words of Jesus: *"You will know them by their fruits. Do men gather grapes from thornbushes or figs from thistles? Even so, **every good tree bears good fruit, but a bad tree bears bad fruit**. A good tree cannot bear bad fruit, nor can a bad tree bear good fruit. **Every tree that does not bear good fruit is cut down and thrown into the fire.**"* (Matt 7:16-19) Let us bear **much fruit** (John 15:8), **fruit that remain** (John 15:16) and **let the *fruit of the Spirit* be evident in our lives.** *"But the fruit of the Spirit is love, joy, peace, longsuffering, kindness, goodness, faithfulness, gentleness, self-control. Against such there is no law"* (Gal 5:22-23).

FEBRUARY 28   *Bible Reading: Deuteronomy Chapters 22-24*

DO NOT BE UNEQUALLY YOKED TOGETHER WITH UNBELIEVERS:

As Moses continued to reiterate the various miscellaneous laws to the Israelites, he says the following in Deut 22:10: *"You shall not plow with an ox and a donkey together"*.

While the ox was a clean beast, the donkey was unclean. God wanted Israelites to avoid polluting themselves with unclean persons or things. Further, the ox and donkey, being different cannot associate comfortably in pulling a plough together. The donkey being much smaller and able to take shorter steps would not be able to synergize with the ox.

In the New Testament, we have the following directive from Apostle Paul: *"Do not be unequally yoked together with unbelievers"* (2 Cor.

6:14). The yoke is a very clear symbol of marriage. The picture is of two oxen pulling a plough together - symbolizing a husband and a wife united and working together for the Lord. A believer is a child of God as per John 1:12 while an unbeliever is the child of the devil (John 8:44; 1 John 3:10). It is NEVER good for any believer to have the devil related as a father-in-law! **Further, if a believer marries an unbeliever, this is in clear violation of the command of Scripture.**

Let us understand clearly that God *cannot,* **under any circumstances, sanction the marriage of His child with an unbeliever.** Always remember this statement: "**DO NOT be unequally yoked together with unbelievers**".

March

MARCH 1 *Bible Reading: Deuteronomy Chapters 25-27*

"BY HIS STRIPES, WE ARE HEALED"

During the process of explaining the miscellaneous laws to the Israelites, Moses speaks about God's ruling concerning punishment: *"...if the wicked man deserves to be beaten, that the judge will cause him to lie down and be beaten in his presence, according to his guilt, with a certain number of blows. Forty blows he may give him and no more, lest he should exceed this and beat him with many blows above these and your brother be humiliated in your sight"* (Deut 25:2-3).

In judicial sentences, which awarded punishment short of capital, **scourging** was the most common form in which they were executed. The Mosaic Law, however, introduced **two important restrictions**; namely:

The punishment should be inflicted in presence of the judge instead of being inflicted in private by some heartless official; and The maximum amount of it should be limited to forty stripes, instead of being awarded according to the decision of the magistrate.

The Egyptian, like Turkish and Chinese rulers, often applied the stick till they caused death or lameness for life. The scourge used in Israel was formed of three cords, terminating in leathern thongs, and thirteen strokes of this counted as thirty-nine stripes (2Co 11:24). Thus, the corporal punishment by stripes was prescribed in the Mosaic Law for committing the sin of fornication (Lev 19:20; Deut 22:18), and also for other wicked offenses (Deut 25:2). Forty stripes was the maximum number (Deut 25:3), which sometimes was even fatal (Job 9:23, Exodus 21:20).

Our Lord Jesus Christ allowed himself to be scourged (Matthew 20:19; 27:26; Mark 15:15; John 19:1), not because he was wicked or deserved this heinous punishment, but he wanted to take our place for our sins. God's justice required that He "*...will punish their transgression with the rod and their iniquity with stripes*" (Psalms 89:32). "*And that servant who knew his master's will, and did not prepare himself or do according to his will, shall be beaten with many stripes*" (Luke 12:47).

Let us remember that our Lord Jesus took stripes upon himself for a reason. "*But He was wounded for our transgressions, He was bruised for our iniquities; the chastisement for our peace was upon Him, and by His stripes we are healed*" (Isaiah 53:5). **Jesus took the stripes and scourging upon Himself so that WE could be FORGIVEN, HEALED and DELIVERED from our SINS and SICKNESS!**

MARCH 2   *Bible Reading: Deuteronomy Chapters 28-30*

"IT IS ALL A MATTER OF CHOICE"

As Moses summarizes God's guidance and provision for the Israelites during the last forty years; he invites the people of God to take part in God's covenant, and reiterates that **only those who choose to obey the covenant will receive the blessings from God**. "*See, I have set before you today life and good, death and evil, in that I command you today to love the Lord your God, to walk in His ways, and to keep His commandments, His statutes, and His judgments, that you may live and multiply; and the Lord your God will bless you in the land which you go to possess*" (Deut 30:15-16). Finally, Moses ends his long discourse with the following: "*I call heaven and earth as witnesses today against you, that I have set before you life and death, blessing and cursing; therefore choose life, that both you and your descendants may live; that you may love the Lord your God, that you may obey His voice, and that you may cling to Him, for He is your life and the length of your days; and that you may dwell in the land which the Lord swore to your fathers, to Abraham, Isaac, and Jacob, to give them*" (Deut 30:19-20)

The Apostle Paul in Romans 10:6-8 has applied this passage to the Gospel - for the law of Christ is substantially the same as that of Moses, only more clear and accompanied with the advantages of Gospel grace. The alternative of a good and happy life is a disobedient and miserable life. **Loving God and obeying His Word are the only ways of securing God's blessings.** Paul warned the elders of Ephesus in the same manner: *"Therefore I testify to you this day that I am innocent of the blood of all men. For I have not shunned to declare to you the whole counsel of God"* (Acts 20:26, 27).

Dr. Pierce Harris, a former pastor of the First Methodist Church of Atlanta, Georgia, preached to some prisoners. One of the prisoners got up and introduced him to the others with these words: *"Several years ago, two boys lived in a town in north Georgia. They went to the same school, played together and attended the same Sunday school. One dropped out of Sunday school and said that it was 'sissy stuff' the other boy kept on going. One rejected Christ; the other accepted Him. The boy who rejected Christ is making this introduction today. The boy who accepted Christ is the honored preacher who will speak to us today!"*

It is ALL a matter of CHOICE! You too have a choice to serve sin or serve God. To choose against God brings emptiness and pain and results in death and eternal separation from God. **To choose God brings blessings and fulfillment. If you accept Jesus Christ as your Lord and Savior and make Him your Master and live a life of obedience to His Word, you will live forever. Make the right choice TODAY!**

MARCH 3   *Bible Reading: Deuteronomy Chapters 31-34*

KEEPING DEATH AS A REALITY IN OUR DAILY LIVING

As we come to the closing chapters of Deuteronomy, God clarifies what will happen to Moses now: **Then the Lord said to Moses, "Behold, the days approach when you must die; call Joshua, and present yourselves in the tabernacle of meeting, that I may inaugurate him"** (Deut 31:14). Moses was to *"rest with his fathers"* in a short time (v. 16a). However, there were certain things that Moses was to accomplish on earth before he died:

1. Moses had to **write down the law and deliver it to the priests** so that they will safeguard it in the Ark of the Covenant. This law

was to be read to the Israelites once in every seven years at the Feast of the Tabernacles (Deut 31:9-13)

2. Moses was to **hand over the leadership to Joshua** and inaugurate him in the sight of the Israelites (Deut 31:7-8, 14)

3. Moses was to **write down a song and teach it to the children of Israel** so that this song would be a witness for God against the children of Israel. *"Now therefore, write down this song for yourselves, and teach it to the children of Israel; put it in their mouths, that this song may be a witness for Me against the children of Israel"* (Deut 31:19). This 'Song of Moses' is recorded for our benefit in Deut 32:1-43.

4. Moses had to **give his final blessings to the children of Israel** according to their tribes, which is recorded in Deut 33:1-29.

5. Finally, Moses had to **view the land of Israel from a distance** standing on top of Mount Nebo and see for himself The Promised Land that he had lead the Israelites the past forty years to inherit (Deut 32:48-52; 34:1-5).

When Moses saw death as a reality in his life, he could accomplish a lot of things in a short time. This is what God requires from us as well, which is explicitly mentioned as part of the 'Song of Moses': *"Oh, that they were wise, that they understood this, that they would consider their latter end!"* (Deut 32:29). We need to understand the brevity of our life, and **keep death as a reality in our daily living**.

I recently came across a website called 'The Death Clock' that would allow us to use their *'advanced life expectancy calculator'* to predict the date of our death depending on where and how we live. *I know it sounds morbid, and we **cannot** predict the date of our death – for only God knows when we will die or when our Lord Jesus Christ is coming back.* However, being aware of our own death in the near future will allow us to have the right perspective towards life, and prioritize the things that really have eternal value, significance and lasting rewards.

Let us join with Moses in praying the following: *"So teach us to number our days that we may gain a heart of wisdom"* (Psalms 90:12). **Let us live as if today was the last day of our lives!**

THE RECIPE FOR TRUE SUCCESS IN OUR LIVES:

The story of the Israelites continues after the death of Moses when God appoints Joshua to govern instead of Moses, and gives him instructions and encouragement (Josh 1:1-9) to cross over the Jordan River into the land of Canaan. The time has come for the new leadership to continue the work under God's direction. A wise leader does not completely abandon the past, but builds on the work already accomplished and progresses towards the future. Moses was mentioned fifty-seven times in the book of Joshua, which is a good indication that his leadership was still revered and emulated. Just like Moses was mentioned twice as *'the servant of God'* in Josh 1:1-2, Joshua was also mentioned as *'the servant of God'* in Josh 24:29. We should note that the important person in the story is <u>not</u> the servant but the Master.

During the course of giving instructions and encouragement to Joshua, God also gives **the recipe for true success**, which is also very much meaningful for our lives:

1. **God's favor and presence should be with us in everything we do.** God told Joshua: *"...as I was with Moses, so I will be with you. I will not leave you nor forsake you"* (Josh 1:5b). Our Lord Jesus has also promised to be with us always, no matter what: *"...I am with you always, even to the end of the age"* (Matt 28:20b). *For He (Jesus) Himself has said, "I will never leave you nor forsake you"* (Heb 13:5b).

2. **We should be strong and of good courage.** God told Joshua: *"Be strong and of good courage, for to this people you shall divide as an inheritance the land which I swore to their fathers to give them. Only be strong and very courageous, that you may observe to do according to all the law which Moses My servant commanded you"* (Josh 1:6-7a). We have also received a similar exhortation: *"Finally, my brethren, be strong in the Lord and in the power of His might"* (Eph 6:10). To aid in that attitude, we are told to put on the *whole armor of God* and supplement with watchful prayer at all times (Eph 6:11-18).

3. **We should read and continually meditate on God's Word.** God told Joshua: *"This Book of the Law shall not depart from your mouth, but you shall meditate in it day and night..."* (Josh 1:8a). Bible reading and meditation is an integral part of God's recipe for true success.

4. **We should do everything that God's Word tells us to do.** God further told Joshua: *"...that you may observe to do according to all that is written in it. For then you will make your way prosperous, and then you will have good success"* (Josh 1:8b). The Book of the Law can be equated to God's Word for us. Total obedience to God's Word will give us lasting and real success.

We should note that Joshua was one of the few leaders of Israel who had an unblemished and successful leadership. God did truly great miracles through Joshua, like parting the Jordan River, toppling the walls of Jericho and making the sun stand still. He was able to *'walk wisely'* as and when He followed God's instructions completely. God wants us also to obey His Word completely and follow **the recipe for true success**. Then we will be able to *'walk wisely'* as well. *"See then that you walk circumspectly, not as fools but as wise"* (Eph 5:15).

MARCH 5 *Bible Reading: Joshua Chapters 4-6*

Our FAITH and TRUST in God will DELIVER us from Future Judgment

It is through a great miracle from God that the Israelites under the leadership of Joshua crossed the Jordan River. However, the Israelites faced an impenetrable city Jericho, which was doomed for destruction. However, we read about something very remarkable – God spared a prostitute and her family alive from death. *"Now the city shall be doomed by the Lord to destruction, it and all who are in it. **Only Rahab the harlot shall live, she and all who are with her in the house,** because she hid the messengers that we sent"* (Josh 6:17). *"**And Joshua spared Rahab the harlot, her father's household, and all that she had**"* (Josh 6:25a).

Why was Rahab the harlot and her family spared when all other Jericho inhabitants were killed? By birth, Rahab was an Amorite who was condemned for God's judgment (Deut 20:17-18). By profession, Rahab was a prostitute and condemned for judgment. **However, Rahab is commended for her faith in God.** *"I will make mention of Rahab ... to those who know Me..."* (Psalms 87:4a) *"By faith the harlot Rahab did not perish with those who did not believe, when she had received the spies with peace"* (Heb 11:31). What was Rahab's faith confession? In her own words to the two Jewish spies: *"And as soon as we heard these things, our hearts melted; neither did there remain any more courage in anyone because of you, for the Lord your God, He is God in heaven above and on earth beneath"* (Josh 2:11). **Rahab's faith in God caused her to receive the spies in peace and even hide them from the King of Jericho even risking her own life.** *"Likewise, was not Rahab the harlot also justified by works when she received the messengers and sent them out another way?"* (James 2:25).

Rahab expressed her faith in God and God honored that in sparing her life along with her family in the midst of God's judgment against Jericho. We know that she got absorbed in the Jewish community: *"So she dwells in Israel to this day, because she hid the messengers whom Joshua sent to spy out Jericho"* (Josh 6:25b). Finally, she ended up in the genealogy of our Lord Jesus Christ as the great grandmother of the Messiah (Matt 1:5). **Let us always remember that it is our faith and trust in God's redeeming grace will deliver us from God's future judgment as well..!!!**

MARCH 6   *Bible Reading: Joshua Chapters 7-9*

THE IMPORTANCE OF DAILY SELF-EXAMINATION

After tasting a resounding victory over Jericho under the leadership of Joshua, the Israelites were confident to continue their conquest over Canaan. The next target was a small city of Ai (Gen 12:8; 13:3) that was located in the hill country. Accordingly, spies went up the mountain pass to view this city and they returned brimming with confidence. *"Do not let all the people go up but let about two or three thousand men go up and attack Ai. Do not weary all the people there, for the people of Ai are few. So about three thousand men went up there from the people, but they fled before the men of Ai"* (Josh 7:3, 4). In reality, the population of Ai amounted to twelve thousand men and women (Josh 8:25), but to the spies this city may have appeared small in comparison to Jericho and this may have been the reason for their confidence. **However, the Israelites tasted defeat for the first time in their Canaan conquest!**

The first mistake was that the Israelites had grossly underestimated the enemy's strength. Our Lord Jesus describes a scenario of the dire need to count the cost before we initiate war against another country: *"Or what king, going to make war against another king, does not sit down first and consider whether he is able with ten thousand to meet him who comes against him with twenty thousand? Or else, while the other is still a great way off, he sends a delegation and asks conditions of peace"* (Luke 14:28-32). How could the Israelites expect to defeat twelve thousand people with just three thousand soldiers?

The second and bigger mistake that the Israelites committed was the lack of self-examination. They did not check with God to see if He was with them in battle! Actually Israel had sinned and transgressed God's covenant through Achan (Josh 7:1, 11). So, God had left them because there was sin in the camp. **The sin of Achan and its results teach the great truth of the oneness of the people of God.** *"Israel hath sinned"* (Josh 7:11). **We are one body in Christ** (1 Corinthians 5:1-7; 12:12-14: 26), **and the church is adversely affected by the sin, neglect, or un-spirituality of ONE believer.**

So as individual believers, we have a responsibility to examine ourselves daily. We are constantly engaged in a spiritual battle with the enemy (Satan) having put on the whole armor of God (Eph. 6:10-18). If there is sin in our lives, there are serious dents and gaps in the armor and the enemy will wound us severely. Let us join with Job and ask God: *"How many are my iniquities and sins? **Make me know my transgression and my sin"*** (Job 13:23). Let us join with the Psalmist and plead to God: *"Who can understand his errors? **Cleanse me from secret faults"*** (Psalms 19:12). *"**Examine me, O Lord, and prove me; try my mind and my heart"*** (Psalms 26:2). *"**Search me, O God, and know my heart; try me, and know my anxieties; and see if there is any wicked way in me, and lead me in the way everlasting"*** (Psalms 139:23-24)

GOD WILL FIGHT OUR BATTLES IF WE LET HIM

When Joshua had assumed the charge of leading the Israelites to conquer Canaan, there was a definite assurance from God: *"No man shall be able to stand before you all the days of your life; as I was with Moses, so I will be with you. I will not leave you nor forsake you"* (Josh 1:5). God had promised the land of Canaan to the Israelites with the underlying assurance that He would give them the strength to conquer it and also if needed, He would fight the battles for them.

So, when the five kings of Canaan joined forces to defeat the Israelites (Josh 10:1-5), it was evident that Joshua and the Israelites would need God's help to win the battle. In keeping with His promise, God assures Joshua: *"Do not fear them, for I have delivered them into your hand; not a man of them shall stand before you"* (Josh 10:8). **God did indeed fight the battle for Joshua**: *"So **the Lord routed them** before Israel, **killed them** with a great slaughter at Gibeon, **chased them** along the road that goes to Beth Horon, and **struck them down** as far as Azekah and Makkedah. And it happened, as they fled before Israel and were on the descent of Beth Horon, that **the Lord cast down large hailstones from heaven on them** as far as Azekah, and they died. **There were more who died from the hailstones than the children of Israel killed with the sword"** (Josh 10:10-11).

We can see a greater monumental miracle in Josh 10:12-14 that is also referred in Job 9:7 and Habakkuk 3:11. Joshua, moved by the Lord's will, commanded the sun to delay (Heb., *'be still, silent, leave off'*). The earth actually stopped revolving or, more likely, the sun moved in the same way to keep perfect pace with the battlefield. **There are <u>five things</u> we can note from this miracle:**

1. Something miraculous took place that day that enabled them to have a wonderful victory.

2. This miracle came about because of Joshua's prayer.

3. This miracle had something to do with the sun and moon, with which only God could affect.

4. This victory had to do with an extended time to fight the enemy before they scattered back to their cities.

5. Truly God was fighting for Israel.

The main point is that God not only gave them a great victory, but the victory came about in such a manner that made a great impression on the Israelites and the enemies about them. *"And there was no day like that before it or after it, when the LORD listened to the voice of a man; for the LORD fought for Israel"* (Josh 10:14)

Remember, God will fight our battles too if we let Him! It is interesting to note that when Christ conquered our enemies upon the cross, the miracle that happened in connection with the sun was the reverse of what happened at Joshua's time. It was then darkened, as if going down at noon. Christ did not need the light of the sun to complete His victory, so He made darkness His pavilion. **Let us understand that** *without Christ we can do nothing* (John 15:5b). He [Christ] who is in us is greater than he [Satan] who is in the world (1 John 4:4). **Let us surrender completely to Him so that He can fight our battles for us!**

MARCH 8   *Bible Reading: Joshua Chapters 13-15*

CLAIMING GOD'S PROMISES BY FAITH

"Now Joshua was old, advanced in years. And the Lord said to him: "You are old, advanced in years, and there remains very much land yet to be possessed" (Josh 13:1). Joshua was probably a hundred years old now, and his advanced age necessitated the allocating of Canaan among the tribes of Israel — not only the land already possessed but those also which were still left to be conquered.

"Then the children of Judah came to Joshua in Gilgal. And Caleb the son of Jephunneh the Kenizzite..." (Josh 14:6a). This incident is recorded here because it occurred while the preparations were being made for casting the lots in Gilgal. Caleb was one of the two survivors of the Israelites permitted to enter the land of promise (Num 14:30, 38; 32:11-13; Deut 1:34-36) because he was sent to Canaan as a spy (Num 13:6) and brought a favorable report (Num 13:26-30; 14:6-9) in line with God's plan. The claim of Caleb to the mountains of Hebron as his personal and family possessions was founded on a solemn promise

of Moses forty-five years before (Num 14:24; Deut 1:36), to give him that land on account of his loyalty towards God.

Caleb's request was: *"Give me this mountain"* or Hebron (Deut 14:12) because it was God's promise to him and he valued that promise. Those who live by faith value God's promises far above what is obtained by God's providence only. The name Caleb means *"all heart"*. During the last eighty-five years of his life Caleb was singular in his devotion *to God's will, and "wholly followed the Lord God of Israel"* (Deut 14:8b, 14b). Hebron was now occupied by Anakims' but Caleb did not fear his enemy as he considered himself still strong and able to do mighty exploits. In his own words: *"As yet I am as strong this day as on the day that Moses sent me; just as my strength was then, so now is my strength for war, both for going out and for coming in. Now therefore, give me this mountain of which the Lord spoke in that day; for you heard in that day how the Anakim were there, and that the cities were great and fortified. **It may be that the Lord will be with me, and I shall be able to drive them out as the Lord said**"* (Josh 14:11-12). **Eventually, Caleb did possess his inheritance and claimed his promises by faith** (Josh 15:13-19).

Like Caleb, we too have lots of promises in God's Word that we need to claim by faith. We have been given *"...exceedingly great and precious promises that through these we may be partakers of the divine nature, having escaped the corruption that is in the world through lust"* (2 Peter 1:4). **We should not become sluggish, but imitate those (like Caleb) who through faith and patience inherited the promises** (Heb 6:12). *Therefore do not cast away your confidence, which has great reward. For you have need of endurance, so that after you have done the will of God, you may receive the promise: "For yet a little while, and He who is coming will come and will not tarry"* (Heb 10:35-37)

MARCH 9   *Bible Reading: Joshua Chapters 16-18*

ALLOWING GOD COMPLETE OWNERSHIP OVER OUR LIVES

The twelve tribes of Israel received the Promised Land as their inheritance, which was divided among them according to God's plan administered through Joshua. *"Then Joshua cast lots for them in Shiloh before the Lord, and there Joshua divided the land to the children of Israel according to their divisions"* (Josh 18:10). However, we read again and again that the Israelites could not exercise full dominion over the land as the new owners, and drive out the Canaanite inhabitants from the land property. With each of the tribes of Israel, the same sad story was repeated again and again (Josh 13:13; 15:63; 16:10; 17:12). Even though they were convinced that they were a great people due to God's blessings, they feared the strength of the Canaanites and their weaponry like iron chariots (Josh 17:14-18) and were not brave enough to drive out the enemy from their territory. Sadly, due to this compromise they slowly drifted away from God's laws, intermingled with the heathen and adopted their religious practices including worshipping idols which ultimately brought their destruction.

It is the will of God that we, as God's children, should be aware of our rights, privileges and responsibilities. The writer of the book of Hebrews reminds us: *But one testified in a certain place, saying: "What is man that You are mindful of him, or the son of man that You take care of him? You have made him a little lower than the angels;* **You have crowned him with glory and honor, and set him over the works of Your hands. You have put all things in subjection under his feet." For in that He put all in subjection under him, He left nothing that is not put under him.** (Heb 2:6-8).

Our Lord Jesus Christ is a type of Joshua, who has not only conquered the gates of hell for us but has opened to us the gates of heaven, and having purchased for us the eternal inheritance so that we should take possession of it by faith and trust in Him. It was God's plan from the very beginning of creation that man should have dominion (Gen 1:27-28). However, since Satan has usurped our godly inheritance, God wants us to recapture the dominion that man held from the very beginning. This is only possible when we allow God to have complete ownership over our lives.

Let us look deep within us and check if there is any area of our lives that we have not given complete ownership to God. It is our act of total surrender and our willingness to resist the enemy that will allow us to exercise full dominion over our lives – the way God had planned from the very beginning. **Today, let us allow God to have complete ownership over our lives!**

Bible Reading: Joshua Chapters 19-21

GOD WILL ULTIMATELY FULFILL ALL HIS PROMISES:

"So the Lord gave to Israel all the land of which He had sworn to give to their fathers and they took possession of it and dwelt in it. The Lord gave them rest all around, according to all that He had sworn to their fathers. And not a man of all their enemies stood against them; the Lord delivered all their enemies into their hand. Not a word failed of any good thing which the Lord had spoken to the house of Israel. All came to pass." (Josh 21:43-45)

God promised to give to the seed of Abraham the land of Canaan for a possession, and now they possessed it and made it their home. The above passage is a general winding up of the history from Deut chapter 13, which narrates the occupation of the land by the Israelites. All the promises made by God, whether to the Israelites or to Joshua (Josh 1:5) had been, or were in the course of being fulfilled. **The above passage speaks about the fulfillment of three great promises of God:**

1. **God will give the Promised Land to Abraham's children.** Prophecy: *Then the LORD appeared to Abram and said, "To your descendants I will give this land."* (Gen 12:7). Fulfillment: *"So the Lord gave to Israel all the land of which He had sworn to give to their fathers and they took possession of it and dwelt in it."* (Josh 21:43)

2. **God will give rest to the Israelites when they inherit the Promised Land.** Prophecy: *"But when you cross over the Jordan and dwell in the land which the Lord your God is giving you to inherit, and He gives you rest from all your enemies round about, so that you dwell in safety"* (Deut 12:10). Fulfillment: *"The Lord gave them rest all around, according to all that He had sworn to their fathers"* (Josh 21:44a)

3. **God will deliver the Israelites from all their enemies in the Promised Land.** Prophecy: *"When the Lord your God brings you into the land which you go to possess, and has cast out many nations before you...and when the Lord your God delivers them over to you, you shall conquer them and utterly destroy them"* (Deut 7:1-

2) <u>Fulfillment</u>: *"And not a man of all their enemies stood against them; the Lord delivered all their enemies into their hand"* (Josh 21:44b)

ALL the promises made by God towards Israel were literally fulfilled and recorded in the Old Testament. Later, King Solomon confirms this matter in his prayer: *"Blessed be the Lord, who has given rest to His people Israel, according to all that He promised. There has not failed one word of all His good promise, which He promised through His servant Moses"* (1 Kings 8:56)

Let us be rest assured that God will ultimately fulfill ALL His promises concerning our heavenly Canaan to us - His spiritual Israel. This recorded experience of the Israelites (Josh 21:45) is a reason for hope and confidence to God's people in every period of history that all other promises made to the Church will, in due time, be accomplished. **Let us be careful how we lead our lives here on earth.** *"Therefore, since a promise remains of entering His rest, let us fear lest any of you seem to have come short of it"* (Heb 4:1)

MARCH 11   *Bible Reading: Joshua Chapters 22-24*

MAKING THE RIGHT CHOICES IN OUR LIVES

After having served as the leader of Israel for many years, Joshua is old and knows that he is going to die shortly (Josh 23:1, 14). So, he gathers all the Israelites together to give his 'farewell address' in Shechem (Josh 23:2; 24:1). He reminds everyone of God's bountiful grace and mercy, how God has led them through all these past years and how God has given them rest from all their enemies. As he concludes his speech, Joshua issues the following challenge to the Israelites: *"Now therefore, **fear the Lord, serve Him in sincerity and in truth**, and put away the gods which your fathers served on the other side of the River and in Egypt. **Serve the Lord!** And if it seems evil to you to serve the Lord, <u>**choose for yourselves this day whom you will serve**</u>, whether the gods which your fathers served that were on the other side of the River, or the gods of the Amorites, in whose land you dwell. **But as for me and my house, we will serve the Lord.**"* (Josh 24:14-15).

The Israelites respond to Joshua's challenge with these words: *"The Lord our God we will serve, and His voice we will obey!"* (Josh 24:24). The book of Joshua concludes like this: *"Israel served the Lord all the days of Joshua, and all the days of the elders who outlived Joshua, who had known all the works of the Lord which He had done for Israel"* (Josh 24:31).

Every day we are confronted with making choices. Some choices are easy or have very less consequence. However, some choices are hard and the decisions have lasting impact throughout our lives and beyond. The destiny of future generations is in our hands. The choices we make with our family today will determine the quality of life in our family tree for generations to come. That is why our choices, especially concerning matters of eternal value, are so important for us. Joshua made the right choice to serve God with his family. We need to choose life and all the blessings associated with it by loving God, obeying His voice, clinging to Him and serving Him (Deut 30:19, 20). **Let's be careful to make the right choices daily in our lives! Like Joshua, let us boldly say: "As for me and my house, we will serve the Lord".**

MARCH 12   *Bible Reading: Judges Chapters 1-3*

HANDING DOWN OUR FAITH TO OUR CHILDREN

The book of Judges begins with an account of the *incomplete conquest* of the land of Canaan by each of the individual tribes (Judges 1:19, 21, 27, 29, 30, 31, 33, 34) due to *compromise of their values*. To add injury to insult, the Israelites *disobeyed* the voice of God, which the Angel of the Lord clearly voiced out: *"But you have not obeyed My voice"* (Judges 2:2).

However, the greatest mistake that the Israelites did concerning their faith was that after the Joshua generation was dead and gone, **the next generation did not hand down their faith to their children.** *"When all that generation had been gathered to their fathers, another generation arose after them who did not know the Lord nor the work which He had done for Israel"* (Judges 2:10). The new generation neglected their relationship with God, and they could not visualize God's hand at work for them like their parents did. They bowed down and worshipped the idols of Canaan (Judges 2:12, 13, 17), disobeyed God's commandments and did not pay attention to God's voice (Judges 2:17b, 20), and intermarried with the foreigners of the land (Judges 3:5-6). God purposely left foreign nations to oppress the Israelites as He wanted to '*test*' them to see if they would obey the commandments of God or not, if they would keep the ways of God or not, and if they would walk in the ways of their fathers or not (Judges 2:20 -3:4). They had to now grapple the bondage of their enemies as the hand of the Lord was against them for calamity, and they were '*greatly distressed*' (Judges 2:15).

One of the greatest responsibilities that God has given to us (parents) is to hand down our faith and godly values to our children. Through us, our children should know God more intimately, and should be aware of the great things that God has done in our past. We should hand down our faith, our sense of moral values, and our understanding of the principles of Scripture. We should love our children deeply enough to listen to them concerning their hurts and troubles. Through those periods of interaction we should leave with our children the strong foundation of faith in the faithfulness of God that they can sustain and overcome every difficulty and trial that will come in their life.

MARCH 13   *Bible Reading: Judges Chapters 4-6*

GOD'S CALL TO AN EXTRAORDINARY LEADERSHIP

"Now Deborah, a prophetess, the wife of Lapidoth, was judging Israel at that time. And she would sit under the palm tree of Deborah between Ramah and Bethel in the mountains of Ephraim. And the children of Israel came up to her for judgment" (Judges 4:4-5).

As there were men-prophets mentioned in the Bible, there were also women-prophetesses like Miriam (Exodus 15:20), Huldah (2Kings 22:14), and the four daughters of Philip the Evangelist (Acts 21:9). Deborah was a prophetess who was instructed in divine knowledge by the inspiration of the Spirit of God. She judged Israel as God's mouth to them; correcting abuses, and redressing grievances. She was a woman of eminent holiness, and knowledge of the Holy Scriptures, by which she was singularly qualified for judging the people according to the laws of God. Further, she was a woman of extraordinary wisdom, instructed in divine knowledge by the Spirit and accustomed to interpret His will. She had extensive influence, and was held in respect as she discharged all the special duties of a judge.

By God's direction, she ordered Barak to raise an army and engage Sisera's forces. When Barak insisted much upon her presence, Deborah went with him to the battlefield. This is extraordinary as she is one of the first women leaders who lead an army to fight against the enemy. She was a **wife** (Judges 4:4a) and *"a mother in Israel"* (Judges 5:7). But she arose to **God's call to an extraordinary leadership** & won a great battle against the enemy forces.

Like Deborah, we also need to arise to God's call to leadership as sometimes God chooses the person with the strongest character to lead His people to victory at crucial times. The key elements of such leadership are faith, trust and worship. We also need to understand that with the call, God will also expand our abilities and resources to accomplish His will successfully.

MARCH 14   *Bible Reading: Judges Chapters 7-9*

DEPENDING ON GOD ALONE FOR OUR SPIRITUAL BATTLES

When Gideon prepared himself to make war with the Midianites, God told him bluntly that he had too many people in his army. *And the Lord said to Gideon, "The people who are with you are too many for Me to give the Midianites into their hands, lest Israel claim glory for itself against Me, saying, 'My own hand has saved me'* (Judges 7:2). However, in fact the enemy strength was formidable on the natural. *"Now the Midianites and Amalekites, all the people of the East, were lying in the valley as numerous as locusts; and their camels were without number, as the sand by the seashore in multitude"* (Judges 7:12). Although Gideon could muster *only* thirty-two thousand (or one-sixth of the Midianite army), this number was too great by God's standards, for it was God's purpose to teach Israel a memorable lesson of dependence on Him. God wanted that the praise of Israel's victory may be totally directed to Him alone, and no one should claim the glory that He alone deserves. This way the Israelites will be more strongly obliged to serve God. With three hundred committed soldiers, a great attack strategy and God's help, Israel won a decisive victory through Gideon's leadership.

This incident teaches us a valuable lesson: **we need to depend on God ALONE for our spiritual battles**. *"For we do not wrestle against flesh and blood, but against principalities, against powers, against the rulers of the darkness of this age, against spiritual hosts of wickedness in the heavenly places"* (Eph 6:12). We have an unseen enemy – an enemy that we cannot see with our natural vision. God is Spirit (John 4:24a), and He alone can help us win our spiritual battles. We need to *"take up the whole armor of God that we may be able to withstand in the evil day"* (Eph 6:13) using the *"the sword of the Spirit, which is the word of God"* (Eph 6:17) and *"praying always with all prayer and supplication in the Spirit"* (Eph 6:18). We have an enemy who has already been defeated on the cross by our Lord Jesus Christ, so we may boldly declare: ***"I can do all things through Christ who strengthens me"*** (Phil 4:13)

March 15   *Bible Reading: Judges Chapters 10-12*

THE TERRIBLE TRAGEDY OF MAKING RASH VOWS TO GOD

Jephthah the Gileadite stands condemned in history as someone who made a rash and foolish vow to God even though he was a mighty man who led the Israelites to win a decisive battle against the enemy. We read in Judges 11:30-31 like this: *And Jephthah made a vow to the Lord, and said, "If You will indeed deliver the people of Ammon into my hands, then it will be that **whatever comes out of the doors of my house to meet me**, when I return in peace from the people of Ammon, **shall surely be the Lord's, and I will offer it up as a burnt offering.".*
By the very wordings of this vow, it is clear that Jephthah expected an animal at his door when he returned back victoriously from battle. Jephthah's vow however turned out to be rash and cruel as his only daughter was the one who greeted him at the door and he had to ultimately consecrate her as a sacrifice to God (Judges 11:32-40).

In ancient Israel, vows were solemn promises made to God (Psalms 76:11) in reference with devoting a person (Num 6:2) or dedicating children (1 Sam 1:11) or devoting property to God (Gen 28:22). Vows needed to be voluntary (Deut 23:21-22), and performed faithfully (Num 30:2) without any delay (Deut 23:21, 23). However there was danger of inconsiderately making vows. *"It is a snare for a man to devote rashly something as holy, and afterward to reconsider his vows"* (Prov 20:25)

Several important lessons are to be learned from Jephthah's rash vow:

1. There may be doubts in our hearts concerning our future but that should not drive us to make foolish vows to God.

2. We should never make vows to God as a purchase of a favor we desire but only to express gratitude to Him.

3. We need to carefully consider the consequences before making a vow, and the golden rule is: "we should only make vows that we can keep".

4. Finally, what we have solemnly vowed to God, we must perform even though it is hard – this is the least that God expects from us.

The **BEST advice** that we can receive from God's word concerning making vows is found in Eccl 5:4-7: *"**When you make a vow to God, do not delay to pay it**; for He has no pleasure in fools. **Pay what you have vowed— better not to vow than to vow and not pay.** Do not let your mouth cause your flesh to sin, nor say before the messenger of God that it was an error. Why should God be angry at your excuse and destroy the work of your hands? **For in the multitude of dreams and many words there is also vanity…but fear God**".*

MARCH 16   *Bible Reading: Judges Chapters 13-15*

Never let your guard down like Samson

The story of Israel is repeated again and again. Israel did evil: then God delivered them again into the hands of the Philistines. When Israel was in this distress, Samson was born to Manoah and his wife who had been childless. The Angel of the Lord declared that Samson would be special, and therefore had to follow some restrictions. *"Now therefore, please be careful **not to drink wine or similar drink**, and **not to eat anything unclean**. For behold, you shall conceive and bear a* *son. And **no razor shall come upon his head**, for the child shall be a Nazirite to God from the womb; and he shall begin to deliver Israel out of the hand of the Philistines"* (Judges 13:4-5).

There were three restrictions that the Angel of the Lord had imposed on Samson and his mother (while she was carrying him in her womb):

1. Should not drink wine or similar drink (that is intoxicating)
2. Should not eat anything that is unclean
3. Should not get a haircut with a razor

God's purposes were clear as He appeared to Samson's parents two times to repeat the rules. However, as Samson grew up it appears that he had a weakness for foreign women and did not hesitate to marry a Philistine. This was the *first instance* of letting his guard down. However, God used this relationship to trouble the Philistines through Samson. The *second instance* when Samson let his guard was when *he took and ate honey that was in the carcass of a lion* that he had killed with his bare hands (Judges 14:8-9). This was directly against God's ruling that he should not eat anything that is unclean. The *third instance* when Samson let his guard down was when he succumbed to the crying and pleading of his Philistine wife to explain the riddle. He had a weakness that would prove detrimental to his ultimate downfall. However, the Spirit of God came mightily upon Samson (Judges 14:6, 19; 15:14) when it was time to confront the enemy, and equipped him to do great exploits on behalf of Israel.

We should be careful that we never let our guard down like Samson. We should always operate under strict boundaries that are given to us in God's word, and should shy away even from those things that may appear to be improper and lead us away from God. Let us pay close attention to the following verses that will guide us in our daily living: *"All things are lawful for me, but all things are not helpful. All things are lawful for me, but I will not be brought under the power of any"* (1 Cor 6:12). *"Or do you not know that your body is the temple of the Holy Spirit who is in you, whom you have from God, and you are not your own? For you were bought at a price; therefore glorify God in your body and in your spirit, which are God's"* (1 Cor 6:19-20)

THE IMPORTANCE OF GOD'S ANOINTING IN OUR LIVES:

*"So he awoke from his sleep, and said, "I will go out as before, at other times, and shake myself free!" **But he did not know that the Lord had departed from him***" (Judges 16:20)

Samson had fallen into trouble and danger many times before by his love of foreign women, but he did not take these warnings seriously. His blind love for Delilah (Judges 16:4) and her constant daily pestering made him blurt out the truth: *"No razor has ever come upon my head, for I have been a Nazirite to God from my mother's womb. If I am shaven, then my strength will leave me, and I shall become weak, and be like any other man"* (Judges 16:17). We should note that Samson's herculean powers did not arise from his hair, but from his peculiar relation to God as a Nazarene. His unshorn locks were a sign that he was a Nazarene, and a pledge on the part of God to endow him with supernatural strength. Samson's hair in itself was not the cause of his strength but since it was the chief condition of God's covenant, God withdrew His presence and anointing when the covenant was violated. We see that the anguish of Samson's suffering was so much greater than all the pleasures of sin he had got so far: *"Then the Philistines took him and put out his eyes, and brought him down to Gaza. They bound him with bronze fetters, and he became a grinder in the prison"* (Judges 16:21)

It was God's anointing through the presence of the Holy Spirit alone that enabled Samson to fight his battles and judge Israel. That anointing alone can help us today as well. We may be born again and that is certainly the work of the Holy Spirit. But we must still know the Spirit of the Lord coming upon us and empowering us to serve the Lord. We should never be satisfied to do God's work without the power of the Holy Spirit. We can never do God's work without the power of the Holy Spirit. Even Jesus who lived a perfect life for 30 years - Who was born of the Spirit, and Who had lived in obedience to the Holy Spirit for 30 years – had to be anointed by the Holy Spirit before He went out to serve His Father. As He prayed in the river Jordan, the Spirit of God came upon Him. We need to follow His example. Any amount of knowledge or natural gifts can never be a substitute for this anointing from God. We need to live under this anointing constantly. *Samson's example is a tragic reminder to us how we can be anointed at one time, and then lose it later due to our willful sins.*

"But those who wait on the Lord shall renew their strength; they shall mount up with wings like eagles, they shall run and not be weary, they shall walk and not faint" (Isaiah 40:31)

MARCH 18   *Bible Reading: Judges Chapters 19-21*

THE TRUE VALUE OF SPIRITUAL DISCIPLINES

The book of Judges chronicles the dark ages in the history of Israel, as it sums up the three hundred years of the Israelites in Canaan after the death of Joshua with these words: *"In those days there was no king in Israel; everyone did what was right in his own eyes"* (Judges 21:25). This whole episode of the vile abuse of the Levite priest's concubine by the wicked men of Gibeah from Benjamin, and the resulting war between the tribe of Benjamin and the other eleven tribes of Israel took place as a result of one major factor – **the lack of any leadership in Israel**. *"And it came to pass in those days, when there was no king in Israel..."* (Judges 19:1a). There was **anarchy** and the **prevailing disorder** in Israel as **there was no one to implement God's rules and set boundaries for the Israelites**. This further set to a **disappearance of spiritual values** that are inherent in a godly society. *"Where there is no counsel, the people fall; but in the multitude of counselors there is safety"* (Prov 11:14).

There is a true value of having spiritual disciplines in our lives. In order to implement spiritual disciplines in the lives of the believers, God has appointed spiritual leadership in the church and given them set responsibilities. *"Preach the word! Be ready in season and out of season. Convince, rebuke, exhort, with all longsuffering and teaching"* (2 Tim 4:2). Every believer is required to submit under the spiritual leadership and God's word. *"Obey those who rule over you, and be submissive, for they watch out for your souls, as those who must give account. Let them do so with joy and not with grief, for that would be unprofitable for you"* (Heb 13:17).

Let us strictly follow Apostle Paul's example in our daily living: ***"But I discipline my body and bring it into subjection, lest, when I have preached to others, I myself should become disqualified"*** (1 Cor 9:27)

OUR ULTIMATE REFUGE SHOULD BE GOD ALONE

The story of Ruth took place sometime during the rule of the Judges (Ruth 1:1a) when there was anarchy and total disregard for God's law, and *"...everyone did what was right in his own eyes"* (Judges 17:6). One family left their ancestral property and went to the land of Moab to live among foreigners in a strange culture. This resulted in the two sons getting married to Moabite women, and the death of the three men of the family leaving behind an old Jewish widow and two young Moabite widows. However, the story of Ruth hinges on a **crucial decision** that Ruth took when it was time to make a choice between returning back to her heathen parent's home and slipping into oblivion like her sister-in-law Orpah or adopting the God of Israel as her God and the people of Israel as her people. *But Ruth said: "Entreat me not to leave you, or to turn back from following after you; for wherever you go, I will go; and wherever you lodge, I will lodge; **your people shall be my people, and your God, my God**. Where you die, I will die, and there will I be buried. The Lord do so to me, and more also, if anything but death parts you and me."* (Ruth 1:16-17)

Ruth was a Moabite, a descendent of Lot (Gen 19:37) who was excluded from the congregation of Israel forever (see Deut 23:3-4; Neh 13:1-2). However, what we see here is that Ruth left her parents (earthly ties), her people (societal ties), and the land of her birth (territorial ties) to adopt and live among the people of Israel she never knew before. Her Kinsman-Redeemer Boaz recognized what she had done. *And Boaz answered and said to her, "It has been fully reported to me, all that you have done for your mother-in-law since the death of your husband, and **how you have left your father and your mother and the land of your birth, and have come to a people whom you did not know before. The Lord repay your work and a full reward be given you by the Lord God of Israel, <u>under whose wings you have come for refuge</u>**."* (Ruth 2:11-12). **In reality, Ruth had taken refuge**

under the wings of the Lord God of Israel Himself. Due to this one act, she became the great grandmother of King David and was listed in the genealogy of our Lord Jesus Christ (Matt 1:5) and also had the wonderful privilege of having a book in the Bible named after her.

Let us be clear about one thing: <u>our ultimate refuge should be God alone</u>. If we take refuge in God, He will surely take care of us. He will be our safety zone in the times of trouble. *"God is <u>our refuge</u> and strength, a very present help in trouble."* (Psalms 46:1)

MARCH 20   *Bible Reading: 1 Samuel Chapters 1-3*

RAISING UP GODLY CHILDREN

As the book of 1 Samuel opens, judges had ruled Israel for more than two hundred years. In the midst of the gross wickedness committed by the High Priest's sons, God prepared a woman from the tribe of Ephraim called Hannah to offer her child Samuel for God's services. Samuel became the last judge and priest as well as the first *official* prophet for Israel. He took the place of the two sons of Eli the High Priest, who were corrupt and did not know God (1 Sam 2:12). They sinned against God greatly by despising the meat offerings brought to the Tabernacle (v. 17), committing sexual acts with the women who came to the door of the Tabernacle (v. 22), and disobeying the instructions of their father Eli (v. 25). In contrast, the boy Samuel ministered to the Lord before Eli the priest (1 Sam 2:11b, 18; 3:1a), grew in stature before the Lord and men (1 Sam 2:21b, 26), and was a recipient of God's revelation concerning the future of Israel (1 Sam 3:1-18, 21). The Lord was with Samuel and did not allow any of his words *"fall to the ground"* (be in vain), as he became established as a prophet of God all over Israel (1 Sam 3:20).

In the midst of the prophecy against the house of Eli (1 Sam 2:35-36), mercy was promised to Israel. God's work shall be done by faithful people that He will raise up like prophet Samuel. Jesus Christ is that merciful and faithful High Priest, whom God raised up when the Levitical priesthood was thrown off. *"Then I will raise up for Myself a faithful priest who shall do according to what is in My heart and in My mind. I will build him a sure house, and he shall walk before My anointed forever"* (1 Sam 2:35)

The sad story of Eli and his sons tell us how important it is for us to raise godly children. We should never allow our children to continue in any evil way but use our authority to restrain, correct and train them in godly ways. Let Eli's example lead all parents earnestly to look out for any ungodly habits in their children, and take a real effort to train them up in the nurture and admonition of the Lord.

MARCH 21   *Bible Reading: 1 Samuel Chapters 4-6*

TASTING DEFEAT WITH GOD'S SYMBOLIC PRESENCE

When the Israelites went out to battle against the Philistines, they were defeated and about 4000 Israelites were killed. Then the elders of Israel reasoned among themselves: *"Why has the Lord defeated us today before the Philistines? Let us bring the ark of the covenant of the Lord from Shiloh to us, that when it comes among us it may save us from the hand of our enemies"* (1 Sam 4:3). Nobody had bothered to consult with Samuel who was by now an established prophet in Israel. (1 Sam 4:1a). The Israelites assumed that if they could carry with them the Ark of God into battle, they would win the battle. The Ark of God - the visible symbol of God's presence and help - was like the straw that the Israelites tried to grab to prevent from drowning. Instead of humbling themselves, turning away from their sins and getting right with God, the Israelites took an easier course as they wrongly assumed that God would help them to defeat their enemy.

However, God did not operate on Israel's terms in the battle, and we see the sad account of what happened: *"So the Philistines fought, and Israel was defeated, and every man fled to his tent. There was a very great slaughter, and there fell of Israel thirty thousand foot soldiers. Also the ark of God was captured; and the two sons of Eli, Hophni and Phinehas, died"* (1 Sam 4:10-11). While 4000 soldiers were killed earlier, now with the symbolic presence of God 30,000 soldiers were killed and the Ark of God was captured by the enemy. On hearing this horrific news, the High Priest Eli fell backwards on his seat, broke his neck and died instantly. These were the dark days of Israel indeed!

This incident teaches us that we can taste defeat in our lives with just having a superficial relationship with God. We may have all the outward manifestations of being a spiritual person – attend church regularly, take part in church activities, pay our monetary dues to Church, etc – but if our hearts are far away from God we will taste defeat as well. Our Lord Jesus asks us a direct question in this regard: *"But why do you call Me 'Lord, Lord,' and do not do the things which I say?"* (Luke 6:46). In the very words of Jesus, this will be fate of those who are satisfied with God's symbolic presence in their daily lives: *"Not everyone who says to Me, 'Lord, Lord,' shall enter the kingdom of heaven, but he who does the will of My Father in heaven. Many will say to Me in that day, 'Lord, Lord, have we not prophesied in Your name, cast out demons in Your name, and done many wonders in Your name?' And then I will declare to them, 'I never knew you; depart from Me, you who practice lawlessness!'* (Matt 7:21-23)

MARCH 22   *Bible Reading: 1 Samuel Chapters 7-9*

ACKNOWLEDGE THE CROSS OF CALVARY AS OUR "EBENEZER"

*"Then Samuel took a stone and set it up between Mizpah and Shen, and called its name **Ebenezer**, saying, **"Thus far the Lord has helped us"*** (1 Sam 7:12).

The Ark of God was away for over twenty years and *"all the house of Israel lamented after the Lord"* (1 Sam 7:2) as they longed for God's intervention. Samuel urged the Israelites to return to God with all their hearts, put away their foreign idols, prepare their hearts and serve God only and God will deliver them from the Philistines (v. 3). In response, the Israelites put away all foreign gods and decided to serve God only (v. 4). They gathered in Mizpah, fasted the whole day and acknowledged their sins to God (v. 6). Samuel offered a lamb as a burnt offering as a restitution for the sins of Israel and cried to God on their behalf (v. 9). God answered the prayers of Samuel miraculously: *"But the Lord thundered with a loud thunder upon the Philistines that day, and so confused them that they were overcome before Israel"* (1 Sam 7:10). The Israelites won a great victory <u>only</u> because God intervened for them and fought on their behalf. *The reason why God helped the Israelites to win a great victory was because they followed the pathway of repentance and were justified through the sacrifice of the innocent lamb on their behalf.* This victory enabled the

Israelites to subdue the Philistines in such a way that they never encroached into Israel's land, and the hand of God was against the Philistines from that point forward (v. 13). Also, Israel recovered all the territory back from the Philistines that was stolen from them (v. 14).

This victory should remind us about our Lord Jesus Christ - the Lamb of God (John 1:29) - who died on our behalf on the cross of Calvary. He thundered at Satan "It is FINISHED" (John 19:30), thus breaking Satan's hold on humankind forever. Just like the Philistines, Satan does not have dominion over God's children any more. God has indeed helped us and has fought our battle against the enemy. **Today, let us acknowledge the cross of Calvary as our "Ebenezer" – thus far the Lord has helped us.** *"There is therefore now **no condemnation to those who are in Christ Jesus,** who do not walk according to the flesh, but according to the Spirit. For the law of the Spirit of life in Christ Jesus has made me free from the law of sin and death."* (Romans 8:1-2)

MARCH 23   *Bible Reading: 1 Samuel Chapters 10-12*

QUALITIES OF A GOD -APPOINTED LEADER

Samuel had been an exceptional judge over Israel but he was old now (1 Sam 8:1). He had failed to mentor and raise up godly sons to take his place when it was time for him to retire. His sons were corrupt and inadequate for leading the nation (1 Sam 8:4). On the other hand, the Israelites failed to recognize that God ALONE was their king, and their disobedience to God was the reason of their problems. Now, they wanted a king as they wanted to be like other nations and they relied more on human strength and leadership. **It is important to note here that seeking God's will and being obedient to Him will alone lead us to victory.**

So, God appointed Saul through Samuel as the first king of Israel. There are many good qualities in Saul that God saw in him, which we can emulate in our lives:

1. **Physical Qualities**: Saul was a choice and handsome young man and taller than everyone else in Israel (1 Sam 9:2; 10:23-24). *However, physical appearance is not important as other qualities.*

Our Lord Jesus had no (physical) beauty that we should desire Him (Isaiah 53:2).

2. **Obedient to Parents/Elders**: When Saul was asked by his father Kish to go and look for the missing donkeys, he obeyed without any hesitation (1 Sam 9:3-4). He was obedient and respectful to Samuel as we read in his encounter narrative with the prophet.

3. **Honoring God's servants**: Saul wanted to honor Samuel with a gift when he asks for his counsel. This must have been a good trait that he learned from his parents.

4. **Humility**: Saul was a humble person, and we can see this trait in his reply to Samuel who had told him that on him was the desire of Israel. *And Saul answered and said, "Am I not a Benjamite, of the smallest of the tribes of Israel, and my family the least of all the families of the tribe of Benjamin? Why then do you speak like this to me?"* (1 Sam 9:21)

5. **Lack of self-promotion**: Saul was not willing to reveal the prophecy of Samuel that he was chosen as the King of Israel (1 Sam 10:14-16). Also, when the selections for the king was being made, Saul was hiding among the equipment (1 Sam 10:22). Saul was not willing to promote himself in any manner.

6. **Restraint in his reactions**: When some rebels questioned his ability to be the king, Saul kept silent. *But some rebels said, "How can this man save us?" So they despised him, and brought him no presents. But he held his peace.* (1 Sam 10:27)

7. **Willing to take risks**: When the time came to rescue Jabesh Gilead from the Ammonites, Saul stepped out and took a risk to fulfill God's plan. He exemplifies that God protects us as we take intelligent risks to accomplish His will.

8. **Magnanimous**: After the victory against the Ammonites, some people urged Saul to bring out the people who doubted his ability to be the king of Israel and execute them. It is here that we see the magnanimity of Saul: *But Saul said, "Not a man shall be put to death this day, for today the Lord has accomplished salvation in Israel."* (1 Sam 11:13)

With all the above qualities of Saul, God had made the right selection. After Saul was anointed by Samuel to be the first king of Israel (1 Sam 10:1), **God gave Saul another heart** (v. 9). The Spirit of God empowered Saul to take over the leadership of Israel during times of crisis (1 Sam 11:6). All Saul had to do now was to **fear God, serve God with all his heart**, and **obey God's commandments** (1 Sam 12:14, 20-25) and his leadership would have been secured. Let us ensure that we have the same qualities that Saul had when he was selected for leadership over Israel. God will then choose us for leadership assignments as well.

MARCH 24   *Bible Reading: 1 Samuel Chapters 13-15*

OBEDIENCE IS THE KEY FOR LASTING SUCCESS:

"Has the Lord as great delight in burnt offerings and sacrifices, as in obeying the voice of the Lord? Behold, to obey is better than sacrifice, and to heed than the fat of rams. For rebellion is as the sin of witchcraft, and stubbornness is as iniquity and idolatry. Because you have rejected the word of the Lord, He also has rejected you from being king." (1 Sam 15:22-23)

King Saul started out well, but when the Philistines gathered to attack Israel at Geba, the Israelites were badly outnumbered. Samuel delayed in coming as promised as Saul waited for him to come and offer sacrifices. As the Israelites started to desert, Saul grew tired of waiting for Samuel and made a fatal error as he offered the burnt offering instead of Samuel.

In the second instance, God through Samuel commanded Saul to attack and destroy Amalekites completely and not spare anyone. *Thus says the Lord of hosts: 'I will punish Amalek for what he did to Israel, how he ambushed him on the way when he came up from Egypt. Now go and attack Amalek, and utterly destroy all that they have, and do not spare them. But kill both man and woman, infant and nursing child, ox and sheep, camel and donkey.'* "(1 Sam 15:2-3) The Amalekites had defeated the Israelites earlier (Num 14:45, Judges 3:13), so Israel was commanded to destroy them (Deut 25:17-19, 1 Sam 28:18). There were various prophecies against Amalekites as well (Exodus 17:14, 16; Num 24:20). However, Saul did not obey God as he was supposed to do. *"But Saul and the people spared Agag and the best of the sheep, the oxen, the fatlings, the lambs, and all that was good, and were unwilling to utterly destroy them. But everything despised and worthless, that they utterly destroyed."* (1 Sam 15:9)

We should note that obedience is the key for our lasting success. Obedience to God is our moral duty and an absolute necessity. God is not pleased with anything else that we do for Him at the cost of obedience. We need to obey God's commandments under all circumstances. Saul lost his kingdom because he disobeyed God. It is easy to compromise when people are waiting for us to act quickly. We should determine that no matter the pressure, no matter the cost, no matter the delay, we will act only when our response honors God. We should never compromise our integrity to satisfy others.

MARCH 25   *Bible Reading: 1 Samuel Chapters 16-18*

OUR BATTLES BELONG TO GOD ALONE

Then David said to the Philistine, "You come to me with a sword, with a spear, and with a javelin. **But I come to you in the name of the Lord of hosts**, *the God of the armies of Israel, whom you have defied.* **This day the Lord will deliver you into my hand**, *and I will strike you and take your head from you. And this day I will give the carcasses of the camp of the Philistines to the birds of the air and the wild beasts of the earth, that all the earth may know that there is a God in Israel.* **Then all this assembly shall know** *that the Lord does not save with sword and spear;* **for the battle is the Lord's**, *and He will give you into our hands."* (1 Sam 17:45-47)

When Saul disobeyed the commandments of God and acted presumptuously, God chose David to be the next king of Israel as He was a man after His own heart. This is what Samuel prophetically spoke to King Saul: **"The Lord has sought for Himself a man after His own heart**, *and the Lord has commanded him to be commander over His people, because you have not kept what the Lord commanded you."* (1 Sam 13:14). Even though Samuel erred in assuming one of the elder sons of Jesse as a likely candidate for the throne, God looked at the heart of David and chose him among his more 'worthy' elder brothers. *"For the Lord does not see as man sees; for man looks at the outward appearance, but* **the Lord looks at the heart**." (1 Sam 16:7b)

106

When David volunteered to fight Goliath, there were **seven specific reasons** for him to enter into this battle alone:

David was anointed by God's Spirit: After David was anointed with oil by Samuel, the Spirit of the Lord came upon him to empower him for all future battles. *"Then Samuel took the horn of oil and anointed him in the midst of his brothers; and the Spirit of the Lord came upon David from that day forward."* (1 Sam 16:13)

1. **David was courageous and skilled in warfare:** This was the testimony of one of Saul's servants about David: "Look, I have seen a son of Jesse the Bethlehemite, who is skillful in playing, **a mighty man of valor, a man of war**, prudent in speech, and a handsome person; and the Lord is with him." (1 Sam 16:18)

2. **David had righteous anger against God's enemy:** In his reaction to the challenge of Goliath, David displayed his righteous anger against God's enemy. *"For who is this uncircumcised Philistine, that he should defy the armies of the living God?"* (1 Sam 17:26)

3. **David had a testimony about past victories:** David had wonderful experience of past victories during the time that he was a shepherd boy that he described to King Saul: *"Your servant has killed both lion and bear; and this uncircumcised Philistine will be like one of them, seeing he has defied the armies of the living God."* (1 Sam 17:36)

4. **David was confident in God's ability to deliver:** David was very confident that his God who delivered him from ferocious animals that were stronger than him would deliver him from Goliath. This is what he said to King Saul: *"The Lord, who delivered me from the paw of the lion and from the paw of the bear, He will deliver me from the hand of this Philistine."* (1 Sam 17:37)

5. **David fought the battle in God's mighty name:** It is striking to note that David fought the battle in the almighty name of Jehovah, the Lord of Hosts. This was his challenge to Goliath: *Then David said to the Philistine, "You come to me with a sword, with a spear, and with a javelin. But I come to you in the name of the Lord of hosts, the God of the armies of Israel, whom you have defied."* (1 Sam 17:45)

6. **David had faith in God fighting his battle:** David knew in his heart that God did not save by the sword or the spear, but **the battle belonged to God alone**. This was what he spoke finally to

Goliath:*"Then all this assembly shall know that the Lord does not save with sword and spear; **for the battle is the Lord's**, and He will give you into our hands."* (1 Sam 17:47)

The Israelites had totally forgotten about God's promises that He would fight their battles for them, as all they could fear about was losing to Goliath. The Israelites had seen God fight many of their previous battles and win great victories for them, but they neglected to trust God with this battle. However, David's focus was not on the size of the enemy, but on God. **David was convinced that his battles belonged to God alone – truly he was a man after God's own heart!**

MARCH 26   *Bible Reading: 1 Samuel Chapters 19-21*

GODLINESS WITH CONTENTMENT IS GREAT GAIN

Even though Saul was the king of Israel and Jonathan was his heir-apparent in line with succeeding him on the throne, God had already appointed David as the next king of Israel. Instead of the Spirit of the Lord, now *"the distressing spirit from the Lord came upon Saul"* (1 Sam 19:9) that provoked him to jealousy against David. Saul was convinced that as long as David was alive, neither his throne nor his kingdom would be established (1 Sam 20:31). Even though David was good towards Saul risking his own life to fight Goliath on behalf of Israel, Saul was bent upon killing David as he was afraid of David (1 Sam 18:12). Saul told his son Jonathan and his servants that they should kill David (1 Sam 19:1), sent messengers to David's house to kill him (1 Sam 19:11), and even threw a spear at David in order to kill him (1 Sam 18:10-11). Saul's goal was to guard his throne and power at any cost.

Saul chose jealousy against God's will, while his son Jonathan chose obedience to God's plan and friendship with David over jealousy. Though Jonathan did not take over the throne from his father, **he was content with his situation as he had peace in his heart and had his priorities straight**.

In Phil 4:11-12, Apostle Paul says that he has learned the secret of remaining content despite either plenty or poverty. His secret was that *he was ready for anything through the strength of the One who lived inside him.* Contentment is not found in circumstances, wealth, pleasures or fame. Contentment is found in a person, the Lord Jesus Christ.

In her book *Diamonds in the Dust*, Joni Eareckson Tada has mentioned the following: *'It requires a special act of grace to accommodate ourselves to every condition of life, to carry an equal temper of mind through every circumstance. On the one hand, only in Christ can we face poverty contentedly, that is, without losing our comfort in God. On the other hand, only in Christ can we face plenty and not be filled with pride'.* She has recorded a beautiful prayer in this subject as well: *'Lord, there are many things I desire, but I really don't need. Subtract my desires and keep me from adding my own wants. Help me to find satisfaction in You, for only then will I find real and lasting contentment.'*

Let us clearly understand that **"godliness with contentment is great gain"** (1 Tim 6:6). *"A little that a righteous man has is better than the riches of many wicked"* (Psalms 37:16). **Let our conduct be without covetousness - let us be content with the things we have - for He Himself has said, "I will never leave you nor forsake you"** (Heb 13:5)

MARCH 27   *Bible Reading: 1 Samuel Chapters 22-24*

CARING FOR PARENTS IS OUR DUTY AND PRIVILEGE

"Then David went from there to Mizpah of Moab; and he said to the king of Moab, "Please let my father and mother come here with you, till I know what God will do for me." So he brought them before the king of Moab, and they dwelt with him all the time that David was in the stronghold" (1 Sam 22:3-4)

David is being chased around the country side like a dog by King Saul. During the course of his travels he reaches Mizpah in the country of Moab. "Mizpah" signifies a watchtower or fort (1Sam 22:4). The king of Moab was an enemy of Saul (1Sam 14:47), whereas David being the great-grandson of Ruth was related to Moab. David was willing to seek an asylum in Moab as the Moabites had no grounds for entertaining vindictive feelings against him. Their enmity with Saul made them more willing to receive an illustrious refugee from Israel.

We can observe with what tender concern David provided for his aged parents. The first thing he does is to find them a quiet habitation and keep them from harm no matter whatever happened to him. As children we need to honor our parents and provide for their needs, especially when they are old. In the Bible, we see many examples of saints taking care of their parents. In the Old Testament, Joseph took care of his parents and provided for them when they were old. In the New Testament, our Lord Jesus is the best example of someone who had concern for his mother during his dying moments. In John 19:26-27, Jesus entrusts John with the responsibility of taking care of his earthly mother Mary when he would depart from the earth.

Caring for parents is both our duty and our privilege. One of the Ten Commandments tells us: *"Honor your father and your mother that your days may be long upon the land which the Lord your God is giving you"* (Ex 20:12). *"But if any widow has children or grandchildren, let them first learn to show piety at home and to repay their parents; for this is good and acceptable before God"* (1 Tim 5:4). **Let us obey, honor and care for our parents - for this is well pleasing to God!**

MARCH 28   *Bible Reading: 1 Samuel Chapters 25-27*

GIVE RESPECT TO GET RESPECT

So David received from her hand what she had brought him, and said to her, "Go up in peace to your house. See, I have heeded your voice and respected your person." (1 Sam 25:35)

As an outcast, David struggled for his daily existence out in the wilderness. During this period, he requested for help from a very rich man called Nabal whom he had helped in the past by protecting his sheep day and night. However, Nabal was a scoundrel and a fool (1 Sam 25:17b, 25) as well as harsh and evil in his doings (v. 3b). Due to his evil nature he refused to even recognize David and help him (v. 10-11). *"To do evil is like sport to a fool"* (Prov 10:23). When Nabal refused to provide provisions for David, matters turned from bad to worse. David took 400 men to destroy all the males in the household of Nabal (v. 12-13). *"The mouth of the foolish is near destruction"* (Prov 10:14).

In contrast, Nabal had a beautiful wife called Abigail who was a woman of understanding and wisdom. When Abigail came to know about how Nabal had responded to David's request, she took immediate action. She gathered food for David and his men (v. 18) and through that act atoned for Nabal's denial of David's request. Her behavior was very submissive. Yielding pacifies great offences. She put herself in the place of a penitent, and of a petitioner. She could not excuse her husband's conduct. She depended not upon her own reasoning, but on God's grace, to soften David, so that grace would work powerfully. She told David that it was below him to take vengeance on so weak and despicable an enemy as Nabal, who, as he would do him no kindness, so he could do him no hurt. She also foretold the glorious end of David's present troubles and requested him to remember her when he was exalted in due time (v. 23-31).

When Abigail gave respect to David by falling on her face at his feet bowing to the ground (v. 23), David accepted her apologies and in turn respected her as a person (v. 35b). We need to understand this universal truth: *"The fear of the Lord is the instruction of wisdom, and* **before honor is humility***."* (Prov 15:33) *"A man (or woman) will be commended according to his (or her) wisdom, but he (or she) who is of a perverse heart will be despised."* (Prov 12:8). In ten days time, the Lord struck Nabal and he died for his wickedness (v. 38). *"The lips of the righteous feed many, but fools die for lack of wisdom"* (Prov 10:21)

As it says in Prov 3:35 *"The wise shall inherit glory, but shame shall be the legacy of fools"*, Abigail became David's wife shortly and a queen of Israel in due time. All this happened because she was willing to give respect to David and not be proud like her husband Nabal. *'All of you* **be submissive to one another***, and* **be clothed with humility***, for "God resists the proud, but gives grace to the humble." Therefore* **humble yourselves** *under the mighty hand of God, that He may exalt you in due time'* (1 Peter 5:5-6). **Let us give respect to others to get respect as well.**

MARCH 29   *Bible Reading: 1 Samuel Chapters 28-31*

FINDING STRENGTH IN GOD ALONE

"But David strengthened himself in the Lord his God" (1 Sam 30:6b)

David was in a great distress (1 Sam 30:6a). While he was gone to fight with the Philistines, he had left his city unguarded and the

Amalekites (whom Saul did not destroy completely as per God's command) had attacked Ziklag. David had received Ziklag as a gift from Achish, the king of Gath (1 Sam 27:6). Now the Amalekites had not only destroyed Ziklag by burning it with fire, they had taken their wives and children as captives (1 Sam 30:3). Unable to bear the loss, David and his men wept in anguish until they did not have any power to weep any more (v. 4). To add to David's distress, his own men out of their personal grief spoke of stoning David to death for allowing this incident to happen (v. 6a). Instead of giving in to his current tragedy, David did something unusual – he found strength in God alone and encouraged himself by relying on God's strength (v. 6b). This is what distinguished David from all the others – including Saul. Unlike David, Saul became afraid after seeing how strong his enemy was (1 Sam 28:5), and in a struggle to solve his problem turned away from God to alternate sources (1 Sam 28:6-7). **When David put his trust and strengthened himself in God alone, God directed him to pursue the Amalekites and recover everything that he had lost so far** (1 Sam 30:8, 18-19).

Let us remember this important fact - **God has to strip us before He can strengthen us**, humble us before He honors us, crush us before He crowns us, crucify us before He credentials us, empty us before He empowers us, and prepare us before He promotes us. *"No matter how tough life gets, if you can see the shore [of heaven] and draw your strength from Christ, you'll make it"* (Randy Alcor). **When we are in distress and despair, let us find strength in God alone!**

"God is our refuge and strength, a very present help in trouble. Therefore we will not fear, even though the earth be removed, and though the mountains be carried into the midst of the sea; Though its waters roar and be troubled, though the mountains shake with its swelling." (Psalms 46:1-3)

MARCH 30   *Bible Reading: 2 Samuel Chapters 1-3*

IS IT WORTH DYING LIKE A FOOL?

And the king sang a lament over Abner and said: "Should Abner die as a fool dies? Your hands were not bound nor your feet put into fetters; as a man falls before wicked men, so you fell." Then all the people wept over him again. (2 Sam 3:33-34)

This brief eulogy from King David was an outpouring of indignation as much as of sorrow. David was willing to make a covenant with Abner (2 Sam 3:13), having already feasted with him (v. 20) and had sent him away in peace (v. 21) so that he could gather all the Israelites in order to make a covenant and make David the king of Israel. David's army commander Joab was not happy with this arrangement, and had an old score to settle with Abner for killing his brother Asahel. Through deceit, Joab called Abner back to Hebron and cunningly stabbed him in the stomach while making pretence of speaking with him privately (v. 26-27).

The question is – **how did Abner die like a fool?** The answer lies in the context of how Abner was killed. 1 Sam 3:37 clarifies that Abner died at the gate of the city called Hebron. **Hebron** was a city of the tribe of Judah, south of Jerusalem, and **was designated as a city of refuge for the Israelites in Canaan** (Josh 20:7; 21:11, 13). If Abner had stayed within the gates of Hebron, Joab would not have been able to kill Abner by Israelite law until Abner was tried and convicted publicly. Abner ventured out of the gates of the city of refuge, and was murdered in cold blood by his enemy in deceit. *If only Abner had stayed within Hebron!* That is why King David laments about Abner - why he died as a fool since his hands were not bound nor his feet put into fetters! **Just a few steps inside the city of refuge and Abner would have been safe!**

There is a spiritual lesson for us through this incident. Hebron, the city of refuge symbolizes our Lord Jesus Christ. If we believe in Christ and accept Him as our Lord and Savior, we have eternal life. *The fool has said in his heart, "There is no God."* (Psalms 14:1). If our life is only focused in amassing riches and achieving worldly success, we will die a fool's death like the rich fool mentioned in Luke 12:16-20. *But God said to him, 'Fool! This night your soul will be required of you; then whose will those things be which you have provided?' So is he who lays up treasure for himself, and is not rich toward God."* (Luke 12:20-21). *For what profit is it to a man if he gains the whole world, and loses his own soul?* (Matt 16:26).

Tillotson has made the following statement that is so relevant even today- *"He who provides for this life, but takes no care for eternity is wise for a moment, but a fool forever"*. Let us focus on eternal values and live a life hidden in Jesus Christ who is our City of Refuge! **It is not worth dying like a FOOL...!!!**

WAITING ON GOD'S PERFECT TIME

*"Therefore all the elders of Israel came to the king at Hebron, and King David made a covenant with them at Hebron before the Lord. **And they anointed David king over Israel. David was thirty years old when he began to reign and he reigned forty years.** In Hebron he reigned over Judah seven years and six months, and in Jerusalem he reigned thirty-three years over all Israel and Judah."* (2 Sam 5:3-5) "**So David <u>knew</u> that the Lord had established him as king over Israel, and that He had exalted His kingdom for the sake of His people Israel"** (2 Sam 5:12)

David was anointed as a future king of Israel when he was a young shepherd boy (1 Sam 16:11-13), perhaps when he was 12-15 years old. He was anointed as King of Israel when he was thirty years old. (2 Sam. 5:3) This means that David had to wait for at least 15 years before he became the king of Israel. In fact, this was the third time David was anointed, the one before was when he was anointed king over the house of Judah (2 Sam 2:4).

There were so many instances in David's life when he could have murdered Saul and taken over the leadership of Israel. David must have understood that before God blesses someone or gives them authority of any kind, He tests them over a period of time to see if they will be worthy of the blessing or calling. God looks on the heart of man and not on the outward appearance as people generally do (1 Samuel 16:7).

Though David continued to have many trials during his lifetime, he became the greatest king of Israel ruling for forty years. **There are many lessons we can learn from the delay that happened for David to become Israel's second king:**

1. David became the king of Israel only after encountering a great deal of adversity, which was typical of God's training through hardship and maturing before handing over the enormous task of ruling over Israel. **Let's understand that delays may be God's training period in our lives.**

2. The delay in David is typical of the way God brings about His promises and purposes. God is not in a hurry but has all the time in the world. In fact, God is bigger than time and certainly not limited by time. **Let's understand that God has a perfect time for anything substantial that happens in our lives.**

3. It is in times of waiting for God that many have failed in their obedience. Waiting is one of the forms of adversity, a test of our endurance to check if we remain true to God. **Let's understand that our obedience through perseverance is tested during our waiting period.**

4. Satan often attacks us by trying to capitalize on divine delays as he tries to put our mind at ease by pointing to divine delays as proof God either does not know, or does not care, when we sin. **Let's be careful as not to slack off from our divine calling while we wait on God.**

5. Lastly, the times of waiting on the Lord are designed to be those times when our faith is stretched and our intimacy with Him is enhanced. **Let's remain strong in our faith in God's promises and draw closer to Him during our waiting period.**

Let us learn from David that waiting is a part of our calling when God wants to achieve great things through us. We will be tempted to short-cut this waiting, but this would be sin. There may be others who are willing to help us with such short-cuts. **But let us resolve in our hearts to be like David, and to wait upon the Lord to fulfill His purposes and promises in His perfect time. Let us be assured that while we wait, God is working in us to prepare us for the good things that lie ahead.** Let us not doubt that we shall see them, and instead devote ourselves to doing the good we know to do and that we are able to do, while we wait.

"Wait on the Lord and keep His way, and He shall exalt you to inherit the land; when the wicked are cut off, you shall see it" (Psalms 37:34)

April

Bible Reading: 2 Samuel Chapters 7-9

GOD HAS NOT FORGOTTEN YOU

*Now David said, **"Is there still anyone who is left of the house of Saul, that I may show him kindness for Jonathan's sake?"** (2 Sam 9:1) **"Is there not still someone of the house of Saul, to whom I may show the kindness of God?"** (2 Sam 9:3)*

After David had settled down and established his throne of Israel, *"for the Lord preserved David wherever he went"* (2 Sam 8:6b, 14b), David remembered the covenant that he had made with his beloved friend Jonathan many years ago, and what Jonathan had specifically told him: *"And you shall not only show me the kindness of the Lord while I still live, that I may not die; **but you shall not cut off your kindness from my house forever, no, not when the Lord has cut off every one of the enemies of David from the face of the earth."** So Jonathan made a covenant with the house of David, saying, "Let the Lord require it at the hand of David's enemies." Now Jonathan again caused David to vow, because he loved him; for he loved him as he loved his own soul.* (1 Sam 20:14-17)

David made some specific inquiries and found out that Mephibosheth, Jonathan's son, who was lame in both his feet still survived. According to 2 Sam 4:4, he was five years old at his father's death and David had never seen him as he was hidden in *Lo-debar*, which in Hebrew means, *"a place of no pasture"*. Being of the house of Saul, the enemy of David, he was possibly concealed by his friends to prevent David from killing him as was the general custom of monarchy in those days. *"Then King David sent and brought him out..."* (2 Sam. 9:5). Mephibosheth had done nothing to merit this kindness, but was indeed lame and not able to act on his own accord. David brought Mephibosheth out of obscurity to a place of prominence. This is what David said to him, *"Do not fear, for **I will surely show you kindness** for Jonathan your father's sake, and **will restore to you all the land of Saul your grandfather; and you shall eat bread at my table continually."** (2 Sam 9:7) Mephibosheth was invited to stay continually at David's royal palace and was bestowed a permanent seat at David's royal table. Saul's family estate, which had fallen to David in right of his wife (Num 27:8) and forfeited to the crown by Ishbosheth's rebellion (2Sam 12:8), was also provided to Mephibosheth to enable him to maintain an establishment suitable to his rank (2Sam 9:11; 19:28). This is how this incident is described later on: *"But the king spared Mephibosheth the son of Jonathan, the son of Saul, because of the Lord's oath that was between them, between David and Jonathan the son of Saul"* (2 Sam 21:7).

This incident speaks to us a very important message – **God has not forgotten us!** Just like King David who brought Mephibosheth from *"a place of no pasture"* to a secure place of care and providence, God has *"...brought us up out of a horrible pit and out of the miry clay and set our feet upon a rock, and established my steps. He has put a new song in my mouth— praise to our God; many will see it and fear, and will trust in the Lord"*(Psalms 40:2-3). This act speaks volumes about the grace of God, *the unmerited favor* that He has bestowed upon us. God is always looking out for us. Let us always rest on His wonderful promise that God will NEVER forget us. ***"Can a woman forget her nursing child, and not have compassion on the son of her womb? Surely they may forget, yet I will not forget you. See, I have inscribed you on the palms of My hands; your walls are continually before Me."*** (Isaiah 49:15-16)

APRIL 2   *Bible Reading: 2 Samuel Chapters 10-12*

ALERTNESS AND PRAYER PREVENTS TEMPTATION

In the first ten chapters of Second Samuel, we see a king who could do no wrong. David was a man truly after God's own heart, victorious in his battles, making the correct judgments and was even magnanimous to Saul's family. He begins his reign in prayer (2 Sam 2:1), and advances in faith. However, when we arrive at chapter eleven, King David falls down from his lofty pedestal into sin that was so egregious that this chapter ends with these words: *"But the thing that David had done displeased the Lord"* (2 Sam 11:27).

How did things go so wrong in David's life? We can note the four steps that led David down the slippery slope of sin:

1. *David neglected his duty.* David was supposed to go to the battlefield during the spring time, but he stayed back in Jerusalem (2 Sam 11:1). When we are out of place where we should be, we fall into temptation.
2. *David desired for idleness and comfort* as he got up from his bed and wandered on the roof of his house (v. 2). Idleness usually gives way to temptation.
3. *David's eyes wandered to forbidden places.* He committed adultery in his heart first before committing the act of adultery (Matt 5:28).
4. *David frantically tried to cover up his sin* by murdering an innocent man who was much more honorable that him.

David sinned against God - *having broken at least three of the Ten Commandments* - and thought that he had managed to build an effective cover-up plan. He only overlooked one small detail: *he could not hide his sins from God.* God sent his servant Nathan to confront and condemn David, which was God's way of restoring His servant. The penitent David confessed readily of his sin: *So David said to Nathan, "I have sinned against the Lord"* (2 Sam 12:13) and wrote about this in one of his psalms: *"For I acknowledge my transgressions and my sin is always before me. Against You, You only, have I sinned, and done this evil in Your sight"* (Psalms 51:3-4).

In the event we are tempted, like David let us be honest with God and with ourselves. We should stop trying to hide our sins behind cheap excuses and lies. We should be willing to deal with and accept the consequences of our sin. We should totally surrender ourselves to God. We should allow Jesus to come into our hearts, forgive our sin by accepting His free gift of salvation and let Him start the process of rebuilding our lives on His firm, eternal foundation.

Let us also remember that alertness and prayer prevents temptations in our lives. *"Watch and pray, lest you enter into temptation. The spirit indeed is willing, but the flesh is weak"* (Matt 26:41; Mark 14:38; Luke 22:40, 46). **We succumb to temptation when**

we neglect our intimacy with God and wander off to forbidden places. *Let no one say when he is tempted, "I am tempted by God"; for God cannot be tempted by evil, nor does He Himself tempt anyone. But each one is tempted when he is drawn away by his own desires and enticed. Then, when desire has conceived, it gives birth to sin; and sin, when it is full-grown, brings forth death* (James 1:13-15).

A final word of wisdom: *"Therefore let him who thinks he stands take heed lest he fall"* (1 Cor 10:12).

APRIL 3   *Bible Reading: 2 Samuel Chapters 13-15*

"SOW THE WIND AND REAP THE WHIRLWIND"

This is a passage taken from Hosea 8:7, but it aptly describes what happens in King David's life and his family as a direct consequence of his sinful actions. Prophet Nathan had prophesied this dire warning earlier: *"Now therefore, the sword shall never depart from your house, because you have despised Me..."* (2 Sam 12:10). King David's family is now embroiled in conflicts that started coming in like waves on the seashore. David's eldest son Amnon rapes his own half-sister Tamar, who was Absalom's sister. Absalom schemes and murders Amnon to take revenge for defiling his sister. Absalom then flees to Geshur, but returns back to Jerusalem after three years and finally is forgiven by his father. Absalom then deceitfully charms the people of Israel, and through his charisma plots a coup against David. This treason by his own son forces King David to escape from Jerusalem after many of his trusted people including his trusted friend Ahithophel defects with Absalom.

Even though God had forgiven David, his sins brought him painful consequences. Even today, this is true – God forgives and even forgets, people may forgive but some never forgets. Our sins will find us out and they forever remain a blot and stain in the perception of others about us. According to *'God Guides Your Tomorrows'* by Roger C. Palms, there are three aspects that we can consider with regards to messing up our lives:

1. We don't have to yield to temptation. God has made a way of escape for us. *"No temptation has overtaken you except such as is*

common to man; but God is faithful, who will not allow you to be tempted beyond what you are able, but with the temptation will also make the way of escape, that you may be able to bear it." (1 Cor 10:13)

2. **If we do slip, we don't have to wallow in our mistakes. There is deliverance when we cry unto God for help.** Let's join with Psalmist David as he considers his deliverance: *"I waited patiently for the Lord; and He inclined to me, and heard my cry. He also brought me up out of a horrible pit, out of the miry clay, and set my feet upon a rock, and established my steps. He has put a new song in my mouth— praise to our God; many will see it and fear, and will trust in the Lord"* (Psalms 40:1-3)

3. **We can use the lesson learned from falling not only to avoid falling again, but to help some other person who is facing similar pressures.** Let's follow Apostle Paul's instruction in this matter: *"Brethren, if anyone is overtaken in any trespass, you who are spiritual restore such a one in a spirit of gentleness, considering yourself lest you also be tempted. Bear one another's burdens, and so fulfill the law of Christ"* (Gal 6:1-2)

Let us never forget what happened to King David when he sinned against God – there are lasting repercussions when we break God's commandment. When we *"sow the wind, we will reap the whirlwind"*. Just like Apostle Paul, let us also *"...discipline our bodies and bring it into subjection, otherwise after we have preached to others we ourselves will be disqualified"* (1 Cor 9:27)

APRIL 4   *Bible Reading: 2 Samuel Chapters 16-18*

BEWARE! – THE SOURCE OF OUR PRIDE CAN BE OUR DOWNFALL

"Absalom rode on a mule. The mule went under the thick boughs of a great terebinth tree, and his head caught in the terebinth; so he was left hanging between heaven and earth. And the mule which was under him went on" (2 Sam 18:9)

Absalom rebelled against his father, and attempted to take over the leadership of Israel by deception. Using his charm, he stole the hearts of the men of Israel (2 Sam 15:6b). This was not acceptable because until now God had chosen the person who would rule over Israel by confirming this selection through His prophet Samuel who anointed the future king by pouring oil on his head – as was in the case of both Saul (1 Sam 10:1) and David (1 Sam 16:13). Absalom should have just looked into the history of Israel, and have known that God selects the future king of Israel. Any attempts to thwart the purposes of God will only end up in defeat and disaster!

Absalom had good looks and a lot of hair that was the source of his pride. *"Now in all Israel there was no one who was praised as much as Absalom for his good looks. From the sole of his foot to the crown of his head there was no blemish in him. And when he cut the hair of his head—at the end of every year he cut it because it was heavy on him— when he cut it, he weighed the hair of his head at two hundred shekels according to the king's standard"* (2 Sam 14:25-26). We see that the source of his pride resulted in his downfall and death later.

In 2 Sam 18:9 we see Absalom hanging from a tree cursed by God and forsaken by heaven and earth, and understand God's abhorrence of children rebelling against their own parents. Absalom was probably entangled by the hair of his head, which being very long and thick might easily catch hold of a bough, especially when God directed it. Some however think that the head of Absalom, which being caught while running between two branches, was enclosed so firmly that he could not disengage himself from the hold, nor make use of his hands while the mule that was under him went away. Thus the matter of his pride was the instrument of his ruin.

Pride is sin (Prov 21:4) and hateful to God (Prov 6:16-17; Prov 16:5). It often originates in self-righteousness (Luke 18:11-12) and defiles us internally (Mark 7:20, 22) while hardening our minds (Dan 5:20). Let us understand that pride is a hindrance to us seeking God (Psalms 10:4; Hosea 7:10) as well as being a hindrance to our improvement (Prov 26:12) Pride is the characteristic of the devil (1Tim 3:6) and the world (1 John 2:16). **Let us beware and learn from the sad story of Absalom– the source of our pride can be our downfall as well…!!!**

APRIL 5   *Bible Reading: 2 Samuel Chapters 19-21*

WHY GOD DOES NOT ANSWER SOME OF OUR PRAYERS?

*Now there was a **famine** in the days of David for three years, year after year; and David inquired of the Lord. And the Lord answered, "It is because of Saul and his bloodthirsty house, because he killed the Gibeonites."* (2 Sam 21:1)

The cause for famine during David's time was Saul and his bloody house, because he slew the Gibeonites. Some think that they were sufferers in the atrocity perpetrated by Saul at Nob (1Sam 22:19) where many of them may have resided as attendants of the priests. This famine would continue until David took definite steps of restitution, and God would answer their prayers as soon as His requirements of justice are satisfied. *"So they performed all that the king commanded. And after that God heeded the prayer for the land"* (2 Sam 21:14)

Why does not God answer some of our prayers as well? The Bible gives us *many* reasons why God does not answer some of our prayers, especially if our motives are wrong (James 4:3), if we regard iniquity in the heart (Psalms 66:18), if we live in sin (Isaiah 59:2; John 9:31), if we offer unworthy service to God (Mal 1:7-9), if we forsake God (Jer 14:10, 12), if we reject the call of God (Prov 1:24-25, 28), and if we do not hear and obey God's word (Prov 28:9; Zech 7:11-13). Our prayers will also not be answered if we are wavering (James 1:6-7), hypocrites (Job 27:8-9), proud (Job 35:12-13) or self-righteous (Luke 18:11-12, 14).

Thus there are many reasons for unanswered prayer and when we see our prayers not answered we should seek God to address the problem. When afflictions come into our lives, like David, we should sincerely ask God for the reasons behind them and God will answer us in some way. Many troubles are sent our way to bring our sin to remembrance, and are meant to lead us to repentance and to humble ourselves before God.

Today, let us boldly approach the throne room of God and understand the specific reasons for our troubles and why our prayers are not being answered. *"Let us therefore come boldly to the throne of grace, that we may obtain mercy and find grace to help in time of need"* (Heb 4:16)

ADMITTING OUR MISTAKES BEFORE GOD BRINGS DELIVERENCE

*And David's heart condemned him after he had numbered the people. So David said to the Lord, "**I have sinned greatly in what I have done**; but now, I pray, O Lord, take away the iniquity of Your servant, for I have done very foolishly."* (2 Sam 24:10) *Then David spoke to the Lord when he saw the angel who was striking the people, and said, "**Surely I have sinned, and I have done wickedly**; but these sheep, what have they done? Let Your hand, I pray, be against me and against my father's house."* (2 Sam 24:17)

The act of numbering the people was not in itself sinful; for Moses had done it earlier under God's command and direction not once but twice that we read in Numbers chapters 1 and 26. However, King David ordered a census without God's express permission. His motives for this might have been pride, self-confidence and distrust of God. He may have wanted to confirm whether he had a sufficiently strong army for further military conquest. The act of taking a census of the Israelites was a breach of God's law which required that Israel should continue a separate people different from other people.

On the other hand, we read that it was God Himself who instigated David to number the Israelites because He was angry with the people of Israel. *Again the anger of the Lord was aroused against Israel, and He moved David against them to say, "Go, number Israel and Judah."* (2 Sam 24:1) For the sin of the Israelites David was prompted to act wrongly for which the Israelites were punished. This incident shows us how God governs the world, and brings out a useful lesson as well. The pride of David's heart was his sin in numbering the people. He was trusting in an arm of flesh more than he should have done in trusting God alone. God looks at sin differently than us. What appears to us harmless, or, a small offence may be a great sin in the eye of God, who discerns the very thoughts and intents of the heart. David's eyes were not opened to the gravity of his sin till God had spoken unto him by His commissioned prophet Gad.

From this incident we can note that admitting our mistakes before God brings deliverance to us. When we humble ourselves and admit to God that we were wrong, we are shifting from pride (that God hates) to humility (that God desires from His children). Let us acknowledge our sins before God and allow God to bring a healing and deliverance in our lives. Let us join with King David as he acknowledged his sins before God: *"**For I acknowledge my transgressions** and my sin is always before me. **Against You, You only, have I sinned, and done this evil in Your sight**— that You may be found just when You speak, and blameless when You judge."* (Psalms 51:3-4)

APRIL 7   *Bible Reading: 1 Kings Chapters 1-3*

EXALTATION COMES FROM GOD ALONE

*Then **Adonijah** the son of Haggith **exalted himself, saying, "I will be king"**; and he prepared for himself chariots and horsemen, and fifty men to run before him.* (1 Kings 1:5). *Then Zadok the priest took a horn of oil from the tabernacle and **anointed Solomon**. And they blew the horn, and all the people said, **"Long live King Solomon!"*** (1 Kings 1:39)

King David had become old and advanced in years (1 Kings 1:1), and the time had come for his successor to take over the throne of Israel. It appears that King David had already decided that Solomon, the second son of Bathsheba should become king after him by the promise that he had made to Bathsheba earlier, which we can see from her words to King David: *Then she said to him, "My lord, **you swore by the Lord your God to your maidservant, saying, 'Assuredly Solomon your son shall reign after me, and he shall sit on my throne.'***
(1 Kings 1:17). King David renewed the pledge that he had given her earlier: *And the king took an oath and said, "As the Lord lives, who has redeemed my life from every distress, **just as I swore to you by the Lord God of Israel, saying, 'Assuredly Solomon your son shall be king after me, and he shall sit on my throne in my place,'** so I certainly will do this day."* (1 Kings 1:29-30)

We need to understand that it was God's will as well that Solomon would succeed the throne of Israel after David, and we can find this from the account of Solomon's birth in 2 Sam 12:24-25: *Then David comforted Bathsheba his wife, and went in to her and lay with* *her. So she bore a son, and he called his name Solomon.* **Now the Lord loved him** *and He sent word by the hand of Nathan the prophet: So he called his name* **Jedidiah**, *because of the Lord.* The word Jedidiah literally means **'Beloved of the Lord'**, since **God loved Solomon from his birth**. Also, it was God's will that Solomon should become king after David that we see from the following verses **that God had spoken to David**:

· *"When your days are fulfilled and you rest with your fathers,* **I will set up your seed after you, who will come from your body**, *and I will establish his kingdom. He shall build a house for My name, and I will establish the throne of his kingdom forever.* (2 Sam 7:12-13).

· **Behold, a son shall be born to you, who shall be a man of rest**; *and I will give him rest from all his enemies all around.* **His name shall be Solomon**, *for I will give peace and quietness to Israel in his days. He shall build a house for My name, and he shall be My son, and I will be his Father; and I will establish the throne of his kingdom over Israel forever.'* (1 Chron 22:9-10).

The Lord had reserved to Himself the right of nominating the king (Deut 17:15), which was acted upon in the appointments both of Saul and David. In the case of David the rule was so far modified that his descendants were guaranteed the perpetual possession of the sovereignty of Israel but only those whom God chooses (2 Sam 7:12).

Let us understand one simple fact: "exaltation comes from God alone". *"For exaltation comes neither from the east nor from the west nor from the south. But God is the Judge: He puts down one, and exalts another"* (Psalms 75:6-7). **Let us humble ourselves under the mighty hand of God so that He alone will exalt us in due time.** *"Therefore humble yourselves under the mighty hand of God, that He may exalt you in due time"* (1 Peter 5:6)

APRIL 8   *Bible Reading: 1 Kings Chapters 4-6*

GOD IS MORE INTERESTED IN US THAN IN WHAT WE DO

Then the word of the Lord came to Solomon, saying: "Concerning this temple which you are building, if you walk in My statutes, execute My *judgments, keep all My commandments, and walk in them, then I will perform My word <u>with you</u>, which I spoke to your father David. And I will dwell among the children of Israel, and will not forsake My people Israel." So Solomon built the temple and finished it.* (1 Kings 6:11-14)

God gave King Solomon everything in abundance – more than anyone could ever imagine. Solomon had wisdom surpassing everyone on the earth during his time, exceedingly great understanding, largeness of heart like the sand on the seashore (1 Kings 4:29-31), the ability to speak 3000 proverbs and write 1005 songs (v. 32), and rest from his enemies as God promised him earlier (compare 1 Kings 5:4-5 with 1 Chron 22:9-10). He also had food and provisions in abundance (1 Kings 4:22-23, 27) along with numerous horses and chariots (1 Kings 4:26, 28) for his personal use. As a token of gratitude for all the blessings that he had received from God, Solomon decided to build a temple for God with the help of his neighbor Hiram, the king of Tyre (1 Kings 5:7-11) and a large labor force to work on his building project (1 Kings 5:13-18).

In 1 Kings 6:11 we read that the word of the Lord came to Solomon — probably through a prophet. God acknowledged Solomon's effort in building His temple thus confirming the promise made to his father David (2Sam 7:12-16). However more than the work of Solomon, God spoke about his personal lifestyle. God wanted Solomon to walk in His statutes, execute His judgments, keep ALL His commandments and walk in them. Then only God would perform His word with him (1 Kings 6:12), dwell among the children of Israel and not forsake them (v.13). The dwelling of God among the children of Israel refers to those symbols of His presence in the temple, which were the visible tokens of His spiritual relation to that people. There was an underlying warning in this message as well - against the pride and presumption of supposing that after building such a magnificent temple, Solomon would always enjoy the presence and favor of God. God plainly let Solomon know that all his efforts for building the temple, God would neither excuse him from obedience to the law of God, nor shelter him from God's judgments, in case of disobedience.

What is the object lesson for us from God's message to Solomon? **God is more interested in us than in what we do for Him!** Every day we should be more concerned regarding our personal relationship with God, try to know His will for us by reading and meditating His word, and walk with Him daily pleasing Him in all that we say and do. When we persevere in our walk with God, we will receive the rich reward that God has promised for us. May our life statement reflect that of the great Apostle Paul: *"**I have** fought the good fight, **I have** finished the race, **I have** kept the faith.** Finally, there is laid up for me the crown of righteousness, which the Lord, the righteous Judge, will give to me on that Day, and not to me only but **also to all who have loved His appearing.***" (2 Tim 4:7-8)

APRIL 9   *Bible Reading: 1 Kings Chapters 7-9*

HUMILITY – A HALLMARK OF AN EFFECTIVE PRAYER

*"Then Solomon **stood** before the altar of the Lord in the presence of all the assembly of Israel, **and spread out his hands toward heaven**; and he said..."* (1 Kings 8:22-23).

Solomon's prayer of dedication of the temple that he had built in Jerusalem is recorded in 1 Kings 8:23-53, a long and descriptive prayer of thirty verses in which he covered any possible future scenarios that may happen in the life of the children of Israel. It is remarkable to note that Solomon started his prayer (v. 22) standing up and lifting his hands to God in surrender, but he ended his prayer kneeling down with his hands still being lifted up to God in humility. *"And so it was, when Solomon had finished praying all this prayer and supplication to the Lord, that **he arose from before the altar of the Lord, from kneeling on his knees with his hands spread up to heaven**"* (1 Kings 8:54). Sometime during his prayer, Solomon realized the greatness of God, and his posture changed from standing to kneeling as an act of humility and acknowledging the awesomeness of God.

At the start of his dedication prayer Solomon stood before the altar — this position was in the court of the people, on a brazen scaffold erected for the occasion (2 Chron 6:13), in front of the altar of burnt offering, and surrounded by a multitude of people. However, during the course of prayer Solomon assumed the attitude of a suppliant, kneeling (1 Kings 8:54; compare 2 Chron 6:24) and with uplifted hands, he performed the solemn act of consecration. This sublime prayer referred to the national blessing and curse contained in the

Law of Moses. Solomon specified *seven cases* in which the merciful intervention of God would be required on the condition of people praying towards that holy place. In this excellent prayer, Solomon did as we should do in every prayer: *he gave glory to God.* He recalled God's promises and praised God as he pleaded for grace and favor from God. Under one word *"forgive"* Solomon expressed all that he could ask in behalf of his people. *Forgiveness of sin prepares the way to receive goodness from God.* A fuller realization of God's greatness, goodness and mercy drove Solomon to his knees as he spread out his hands in prayer.

Let us understand that **humility is a hallmark of an effective prayer. Humility is necessary to the service of God** (Micah 6:8) and **is a characteristic of the saints of God** (Psalms 34:2). **Those who have humility are regarded by God.** *"Though the Lord is on high, yet He regards the lowly"* (Psalms 138:6). *"For all those things My hand has made, and all those things exist" says the Lord. "But on this one will I look: on him who is poor and of a contrite spirit, and who trembles at My word"* (Isaiah 66:2). Those who pray with humility are heard by God as His word assures us: *"He does not forget the cry of the humble"* (Psalms 9:12)

Let us therefore humble before God in prayer like Solomon, and He will lift us up in due time. *"Humble yourselves in the sight of the Lord, and He will lift you up"* (James 4:10).

APRIL 10   *Bible Reading: 1 Kings Chapters 10-12*

COMPROMISE – A PATH TO DESTRUCTION

*"For it was so, when Solomon was old, that his wives turned his heart after other gods; and **his heart was not loyal to the Lord his God,** as was the heart of his father David"* (1 Kings 11:4). *"**Solomon did evil in the sight of the Lord, and did not fully follow the Lord,** as did his father David"* (v. 6). *"So the Lord became angry with Solomon, because **his heart had turned from the Lord God of Israel**, who had appeared to him twice"* (v. 9).

Solomon's extraordinary gift of wisdom was not sufficient to preserve him from falling into grievous and fatal errors. His love for the world and a ceaseless quest for pleasure (Eccl. 2:1-11) had corrupted his heart and had produced in him a state of mental darkness away from God's truth. The grace of God then deserted him and the son of the pious David, the religiously trained child of Bathsheba and pupil of Nathan, instead of showing the stability of sound principle and mature experience became an old and foolish king (Eccl. 4:13).

Solomon's fall from grace can be traced to his "love for many foreign women" (1 Kings 11:1). In fact, we can see that **compromise to godly principles led Solomon on the path to destruction. In fact, Solomon broke every principle of restraint that the king of Israel was commanded by God to follow:**

1.   **The king should NOT multiply horses:** <u>**LAW**</u>: *When you come to the land which the Lord your God is giving you, and possess it and dwell in it, and say, 'I will set a king over me like all the nations that are around me,' you shall surely set a king over you whom the Lord your God chooses; one from among your brethren you shall set as king over you; you may not set a foreigner over you, who is not your brother.* ***But he shall not multiply horses for himself, nor cause the people to return to Egypt to multiply horses,*** *for the Lord has said to you, 'You shall not return that way again.'* (Deut 17:14-16) è <u>**SOLOMON'S DISOBEDIENCE**</u>: ***Solomon had forty thousand stalls of horses for his chariots and twelve thousand horsemen.*** (1 Kings 4:26) *And Solomon gathered chariots and horsemen; he had one thousand four hundred chariots and twelve thousand horsemen, whom he stationed in the chariot cities and with the king in Jerusalem. Also* ***Solomon had horses imported from Egypt*** *and Keveh; the king's merchants bought them in Keveh at the current price.* (1 Kings 10:26, 28)

2.   **The king shall NOT multiply wives:** <u>**LAW**</u>: *"Neither shall he multiply wives for himself, lest his heart turn away"* (Deut 17:17a) è <u>**SOLOMON'S DISOBEDIENCE**</u>: ***But King Solomon loved many foreign women, as well as the daughter of Pharaoh****: women of the Moabites, Ammonites, Edomites, Sidonians, and Hittites— from the nations of whom the Lord had said to the children of Israel, "You shall not intermarry with them, nor they with you. Surely they will turn away your hearts after their gods." Solomon clung to these in love.* ***And he had seven hundred wives, princesses, and three hundred concubines****; and his wives turned away his heart.* (1 Kings 11:1-3). In fact, Solomon's compromise started early

when he made a treaty with Pharaoh, king of Egypt and married his daughter. *"Now Solomon made a treaty with Pharaoh king of Egypt, and **married Pharaoh's daughter**..."* (1 Kings 3:1a). He built a house for her that took 13 years. *"Solomon also made a house like this hall for Pharaoh's daughter, whom he had taken as wife"* (1 Kings 7:8)

3.   **The king shall NOT multiply silver or gold: <u>LAW</u>:** *"...nor shall he (King of Israel) greatly multiply silver and gold for himself"* (Deut 17:17b). è **<u>SOLOMON'S DISOBEDIENCE</u>:** *"The weight of gold that came to Solomon yearly was six hundred and sixty-six talents of gold. All King Solomon's drinking vessels were gold and all the vessels of the House of the Forest of Lebanon were pure gold. Not one was silver, for this was accounted as nothing in the days of Solomon."* (1 Kings 10:14, 21)

Thus, Solomon went on a path of compromise to destruction. To Solomon may be applied the words of Apostle Paul (Gal. 3:3), of Apostle John (Rev. 3:17) and of Prophet Isaiah (Isa 14:21). **Let this be a lesson for us as well.** If our sinful passions are not crucified and mortified by the grace of God, they never will die of themselves. **Let him that thinks he stands, take heed lest he fall.** We see how weak we are of ourselves, without the grace of God; **let us therefore live in constant dependence on that grace. Let us watch and be sober**: ours is a dangerous warfare, and in an enemy's country, while our worst enemies are the sins lurking in our own hearts. Let the following words of Apostle Paul be true in our lives as well: *"I have been crucified with Christ; it is no longer I who live, but Christ lives in me; and the life which I now live in the flesh I live by faith in the Son of God, who loved me and gave Himself for me."* (Gal 2:20)

APRIL 11   *Bible Reading: 1 Kings Chapters 13-15*

DISOBEDIENCE TO GOD BRINGS DEATH

*But the man of God said to the king, "If you were to give me half your house, I would not go in with you; nor would I eat bread nor drink water in this place. **For so it was commanded me by the word of the Lord, saying, 'You shall not eat bread, nor drink water, nor return*** *by the same way you came."* So he went another way and did not return by the way he came to Bethel. (1 Kings 13:8-10)

In 1 Kings 13, we read the story of an unnamed 'man of God' who travelled from Judah to Bethel to pronounce a prophecy to the ungodly King Jeroboam. We cannot get more specific details about this prophet except that He came by divine authority as he accurately predicted an event that took place three hundred sixty years later. His boldness and fortitude to stand and pronounce judgment before the king of Israel was remarkable. The two incidents that happened rapidly in close succession – the withering of King Jeroboam's hand (v. 4) and the altar splitting apart with the ashes pouring out (v. 5) - were truly dramatic. When King Jeroboam requested this 'man of God' to pray for healing and restoration, he did that and the king's hand was restored immediately (v. 6). By all accounts, this young prophet was in the will of God, and he was clearly told what he should not do after completing his ministry – he was <u>not</u> to eat bread or drink water in Bethel, and he was <u>not</u> to return back to Judah using the route that he had travelled.

This young prophet obeyed God by refusing the reward that King Jeroboam offered as a bribe (v. 7-9), and also took a different way to return to his home town. **However, we see some definite steps that led this fiery young prophet to an early death through disobedience:**

1. **DELAY**: This young prophet delayed in his return journey, and we read that the old deceitful prophet found him sitting under an oak (v. 14). This act of delay allowed for the encounter with the old prophet. Our act of obedience to God should have no delays or looking back. Let's remember Lot's wife (Gen 19:26).

2. **DECEPTION**: When the young prophet delayed in his obedience, he allowed himself to be deceived by the old prophet who was actually lying (v. 18).

3. **DISOBEDIENCE**: Instead of recalling the specific command of God and following it completely, the young prophet disobeyed God's word and went back with the old prophet to eat bread and drink water in his house (v. 19)

4. **DAMNATION**: The old prophet showed his true color and intention only after the disobedience was complete. He cried out with passion (as a result of his own guilt and due to the young

prophet's approaching misery) and pronounced the ultimate death sentence as damnation.

5. **DEATH**: Just as the old prophet had cursed, the young prophet was killed by a lion on his return journey (v. 24), and was buried in the old prophet's tomb instead of his fathers' (v. 22b, 30).

This incident teaches us an important lesson that disobedience to God's word will result ultimately in death. Adam and Eve disobeyed God's word (Gen 2:16-17) through Satan's deception (Gen 3:3), which resulted in their eternal death (separation from God's fellowship). *"Do you not know that to whom you present yourselves slaves to obey, you are that one's slaves whom you obey, whether of sin leading to death, or of obedience leading to righteousness?"* (Romans 6:16) *"For the wages of sin is death, but the gift of God is eternal life in Christ Jesus our Lord."* (Romans 6:23).

Let us decide to obey God's word completely and without any delay – no matter what happens in our lives or who tells us otherwise...!!!

APRIL 12   *Bible Reading: 1 Kings Chapters 16-18*

OBEDIENCE TO GOD WILL MANIFEST FOR US DIVINE PROVISIONS

And Elijah the Tishbite, of the inhabitants of Gilead, said to Ahab, "As the Lord God of Israel lives, before whom I stand, there shall not be dew nor rain these years, except at my word." (1 Kings 17:1)

Elijah was the first of the many important prophets that God had sent to warn Israel and Judah as these two kingdoms departed from God's ruling. Elijah who hails from Tisbeh, a place east of Jordan, is abruptly introduced in 1 Kings 17 as a prophet and servant of God. Elijah's warning that both rain and dew will be stopped completely in Israel was a direct message from the God of Israel since drought was the threatened punishment of national idolatry (Deut 11:16, 17; 28:23). Also, the drought and control of the weather was a direct challenge to Baal's credibility as a deity, as this Canaanite storm god supposedly brought life-giving rain to the land.

However, the next set of events reveals a very important truth: **complete obedience to God will manifest divine provisions in our lives.**

- When Elijah proclaimed the word of God to King Ahab boldly in complete obedience to God (1 Kings 17:1), **then God told him to hide by the brook Cherith,** where he could get water for drink and the ravens to feed him bread and meat both morning and evening. *Then the word of the Lord came to him, saying, "Get away from here and turn eastward, and hide by the Brook Cherith, which flows into the Jordan. And it will be that you shall drink from the brook, and I have commanded the ravens to feed you there."* (1 Kings 17:2-4)

- Elijah obeyed God and stayed by the brook Cherith as God had directed him. *"So he went and did according to the word of the Lord, for he went and stayed by the Brook Cherith, which flows into the Jordan."* (1 Kings 17:5) **Only after the brook dried up, did God direct Elijah to Zarephath for a widow to provide food for him.** *Then the word of the Lord came to him, saying, "Arise, go to Zarephath, which belongs to Sidon, and dwell there. See, I have commanded a widow there to provide for you."* (1 Kings 17:8-9)

- **Only after the widow of Zarephath obeyed the word of the prophet Elijah did she receive the heavenly provisions that sustained her during the period of famine in the land of Israel.** *And Elijah said to her, "Do not fear; go and do as you have said, but make me a small cake from it first, and bring it to me; and afterward make some for yourself and your son. For thus says the Lord God of Israel: 'The bin of flour shall not be used up, nor shall the jar of oil run dry, until the day the Lord sends rain on the earth.'" So she went away and did according to the word of Elijah; and she and he and her household ate for many days. The bin of flour was not used up, nor did the jar of oil run dry, according to the word of the Lord which He spoke by Elijah.* (1 Kings 17:13-16)

Let us be assured that when we obey God and seek HIM before anything else, He will provide for us. *"Therefore do not worry, saying, 'What shall we eat?' or 'What shall we drink?' or 'What shall we wear?' For after all these things the Gentiles seek.* **For your heavenly Father knows that you need all these things. But seek first the kingdom of God and His righteousness, and all these things shall be added to you."** (Matt 6:31-33)

We have a God who will provide for us in the midst of famine and among our enemies. **Let us obey God completely as we trust His divine provisions in our lives** as we join King David in his famous psalm: "*You prepare a table before me in the presence of my enemies; You anoint my head with oil; My cup runs over.*" (Psalms 23:5)

APRIL 13   *Bible Reading: 1 Kings Chapters 19-22*

GOD'S WORD PROVIDES STRENGTH FOR OUR LIFE JOURNEY

Then as he (Elijah) lay and slept under a broom tree, suddenly an angel touched him, and said to him, "Arise and eat." Then he looked, and there by his head was a cake baked on coals, and a jar of water. So he ate and drank, and lay down again. And the angel of the Lord came back the second time, and touched him, and said, "Arise and eat, because the journey is too great for you." So he arose, and ate and drank; and he went in the strength of that food forty days and forty nights as far as Horeb, the mountain of God. (1 Kings 19:5-8)

God had displayed his tremendous power for Elijah on Mount Carmel by sending down fire from heaven, as he triumphed over the prophets of Baal. However, soon after the mountain top experience, Elijah became afraid and discouraged as he ran away unable to challenge the death threat from Queen Jezebel. He travelled a day's journey into the wilderness, and sat down under a broom tree giving up and praying that he might die (1 Kings 19:4). It is at this time that God send His angel and fed Elijah twice with food (cake), drink (water) and rest (sleep). The sustaining power of that food from heaven was remarkable – with the strength that he received from God, Elijah travelled for forty days and nights (without any food, drink or sleep) and reached Mount Horeb where he could position himself to hear the "*still small voice*" of God and move forward in his ministry.

God's Word is compared to food in Psalm 119:103: "*How sweet are Your words to my taste, sweeter than honey to my mouth!*" This symbol is repeated in Jeremiah 15:16 and 1 Peter 2:2. Both Prophet Ezekiel and Apostle John are described as "*eating*" a book (Ezek. 3:1-3; Rev. 10:9, 10). This is a powerful symbol of God's servants literally eating and digesting God's Word. Food gives us strength to do our daily activities. If we neglect food, we will become weak and tired. In the same way, when we neglect God's Word we will become spiritually under-developed, and consequently unable to resist temptation and to withstand the Devil's onslaughts.

Only those who regularly meditate on God's Word grow into strong virile Christians (1 John 2:14) who get strength for their onward spiritual journey. We need to read, meditate and hide God's Word in our hearts by memorizing it (Psa.119:11). Job said that he esteemed the words of God's mouth more even than his necessary daily food (Job 23:12) as he truly understood the importance of God's Word that sustained him during his difficult days of trial and pain.

Let us daily take time to intake God's Word in our life. Let our daily prayer be: *"Give us this day our daily bread."* (Matt 6:11). Just like Prophet Elijah, let us not become discouraged due to the onslaught of the enemy and give up on our dream and ministry. Let us trust in God who *"makes me to lie down in green pastures"* of His Word (Psalms 23:2a). Then we can join with Apostle Paul and with his following statement: *"Therefore we do not lose heart. Even though our outward man is perishing, yet the inward man is being renewed day by day."* (2 Cor 4:16)

APRIL 14   *Bible Reading: 2 Kings Chapters 1-3*

FAITHFULLNESS – THE KEY TO AN EFFECTIVE MINISTRY

And so it was, when they had crossed over, that Elijah said to Elisha, "Ask! What may I do for you, before I am taken away from you?" Elisha said, "Please let a double portion of your spirit be upon me." (2 Kings 2:9)

Elisha, the son of Shaphat, was a farmer engaged in plowing his field when the mantle of the prophet Elijah first fell upon him signifying the call from God for a higher ministry (1 Kings 19:19). Elisha demonstrated his commitment to his new calling by destroying the means of his former livelihood, turning his back on his parents and friends and following Elijah as his servant (v. 20-21). In fact, his new assignment was described by others as *'pouring water on the hands of Elijah'* (2 Kings 3:11b).

After following Elijah for so long, it was now time for the transfer of the prophetic mantle to Elisha (2 Kings 2:1-7). The Lord had let Elijah know that his time was at hand. He therefore went to the different schools of the prophets in Gilgal, Bethel and Jericho to give them his last exhortations and blessing. All his efforts, however, to prevail on his attendant Elisha to remain behind, were fruitless. Elisha knew that the time was at hand, and at every place the sons of the prophets spoke to him of the approaching removal of his master. Elisha had long followed Elijah, and he would not leave him now as he hoped to receive the God's anointing through Elijah's parting blessing. Like the rod of Moses, the mantle of Elijah had the divinely operating power of the Spirit and parted the Jordan River which enabled both Elijah and Elisha to cross over on dry ground (v. 8).

The request by Elisha for a *"double portion of Elijah's Spirit"* (v. 9) was applied to the first-born (Deut 21:17), and therefore Elisha's request was, simply, to be heir to the prophetic office and gifts of his master. His request was granted because Elisha was *faithful to his calling* and stuck with Elijah like glue even until the very moment when Elijah was transported to heaven in a chariot of fire (v.10-12). The prophetic mantle of Elijah now fell upon Elisha as he continued his ministry with double fervor.

The removal of Elijah from the world was a type and figure of the ascension of Jesus Christ, and the opening of the kingdom of heaven to all believers. Like Elisha, we are following Christ and His teachings. *It is very important that we should be faithful in our commitment to our calling even unto death.* When God will take up His faithful children to heaven, death is signified by the Jordan River which they must pass through. The death of Christ has already divided those waters so that the ransomed of the Lord may pass over, and boldly say: *"O Death, where is your sting? O Hades, where is your victory?"* (1 Cor 15:55)

Let us *"not become sluggish, but imitate those who through faith and patience inherited the promises"* (Heb 6:12). *"Let us hold fast the confession of our hope without wavering, for He who promised is faithful"* (Heb 10:23). Let us *"be faithful until death, and God will give us the crown of life"* (Rev 2:10).

Bible Reading: 2 Kings Chapters 4-6

TOTAL OBEDIENCE WILL BRING HEALING TO OUR LIVES

"So he (Naaman) went down and dipped seven times in the Jordan, **according to the saying of the man of God; and his flesh was restored like the flesh of a little child, and he was clean.** *And he returned to the man of God, he and all his aides, and came and stood before him; and he said,* **"Indeed, now I know that there is no God in all the earth, except in Israel..."** (2 Kings 5:14-15)

The story of Naaman in 2 Kings 5 gives us **many valuable lessons that we can use in our practical life:**

1. *Even though Naaman was the Syrian General, <u>through him God had given victory to Syria</u>* (v.1a). He was a great and honorable man in the sight of the Syrian King due to his accomplishments. When we are sincere and passionate in our profession, God will surely prosper us.

2. *Even though Naaman was a mighty man of valor to others, he was a leper* (v. 1b). As Rick Warren has once said: *"No matter how good things are in your life, there is always something bad that needs to be worked on...and no matter how bad things are in your life, there is always something good you can thank God for."*

3. *Even though the young girl was a captive in a foreign country, she was a witness of the God of Israel who would heal through His prophet in Samaria* (v. 2-3). We need to be a witness of the saving knowledge of God wherever we are placed – even in hostile territory.

4. *Even though Naaman knew that his healing will originate from the prophet in Samaria, he went with the letter from the King of Syria to the King of Israel – falsely assuming that the king of Israel will heal Naaman* (v. 4-6). Naaman got sidetracked in his desire to get healed – we need to go directly to our Lord Jesus Christ only, by *"whose stripes we are healed"* (Isaiah 53:5).

5. *Even though the king of Israel knew about Prophet Elisha who had done so many miracles and healing, he forget about him and got dismayed at the strange request from the Syrian King* (v. 7). When

troubles confront us, it is so easy to forget that we have a God who still hears our prayers and who still delivers us.

6. *Even though the instruction from Prophet Elisha was simple – to dip in the river Jordan seven times – to get healing (v. 10), Naaman became furious as things did not happen as he had anticipated and he felt that the rivers in Syria were of better quality for cleansing (v. 11-12).* Even though God tells us to do something out of the ordinary and simple, we should not feel offended and get distracted by doing *'what we have always done before'.*

Naaman took the excellent advice from his servants, went down and dipped seven times in the Jordan River. When Naaman completely obeyed the word of God, he received healing and his flesh was restored to the flesh of a little child (v. 14). **When we obey God, the blessings we receive are more than we can normally expect!**

On a final note, **the biggest lesson that we can take from this story is that God uses ordinary people to carry out His extraordinary plan!** God used a lowly servant girl to bring healing in Naaman's life, and brought him to realize that Jehovah was the ONLY God on earth (v. 15). **Let us never dismiss anyone as insignificant – for we never know whom God us using to speak to us today!**

APRIL 16　　　　　　　*Bible Reading: 2 Kings Chapters 7-9*

SHARING THE GOSPEL IS OUR RESPONSIBILITY

Then they (the four lepers) said to one another, **"We are not doing right. This day is a day of good news, and we remain silent."** (2 Kings 7:9a)

The king of Syria sent his army against Samaria, and surrounded the capital city. With the city surrounded, the people could not go out to get food. A terrible famine gripped the city. Food became so scarce that the head of a donkey sold for two pounds of silver. A pint or two of dove dung sold for about two ounces of silver. The people were starving in this desperate situation. They actually resorted to cannibalism. Outside the city wall sat four lepers. They were not allowed into the city because of their leprosy. They were in an even worse situation than the people inside the city walls.

The story of these four lepers is told to us in 2 Kings 7:3-10, and **there are <u>five things</u> we can learn from them:**

1. **They were leprous** (2Kings 7:3a). Leprosy in the Bible is often spoken of as a type of sin. Leprosy speaks of sin as in the blood, becoming overt in loathsome ways and incurable by human means (Scofield Study Bible, note on Leviticus 13:1). Leprosy is a picture of man's totally depraved condition, ruined by sin (Isaiah 1:4-6). This is a terrible description of man's sinful nature *"dead in trespasses and sins"* (Ephesians 2:1), which was our state before salvation.

2. **They were outsiders** (2 Kings 7:3a) at the entrance of the gate. In the parable of the 'Prodigal Son' we read that both of these brothers were outside salvation (Luke 15:13, 25, 28) not understanding the love of their father. Just as these lepers were shut out of the city and the two brothers of the 'Prodigal Son' parable, we were also shut out of salvation without God.

3. **They were dying** (2 Kings 7:4) of starvation. Our state was also the same as *"Death has passed upon all men"* (Romans 5:12), and *"It is appointed unto men once to die"* (Hebrews 9:27).

4. **They used reason** (2 Kings 7:3b) to find a solution to their problem. God has said: *"Come now, and let us reason together, says the Lord: though your sins be as scarlet, they shall be white as snow..."* (Isaiah 1:8). The only solution out of eternal death is to use our reason and turn to God by accepting Jesus Christ as our Lord and Savior.

5. **They rose up and got what they needed** (2 Kings 7:5, 8). There is a great evangelistic truth illustrated from the riches that the lepers got from the abandoned Syrian camp. It speaks of *"the exceeding riches of His grace in His kindness toward us through Christ Jesus"* (Ephesians 2:7) and *"...the riches both of the wisdom and knowledge of God..."* (Romans 11:33) that we have stumbled upon as well like the lepers.

As we relate the story of these four lepers to our lives, we are like the four lepers who have discovered the true riches of the glorious gospel of Jesus Christ. This is truly "good news" that we should not keep to ourselves. *Are we keeping silent or are we telling people we know who are trapped in sin and darkness of the glorious way out?* Think about Andrew in the New Testament who was always bringing someone to

Jesus. *First*, it was his brother Peter (John 1:41), *then* it was a young boy (John 6:8-9); *later*, he, along with Philip, brought a group of Greeks to Jesus (John 12:22). He knew what he had and he wanted to share it with others.

Let us understand that *sharing the gospel* is both our commission and our responsibility! In obedience to Acts 1:8, let us take efforts to be a witness of the saving knowledge of the gospel today!

APRIL 17   *Bible Reading: 2 Kings Chapters 10-12*

NOT ONE WORD OF GOD SHALL EVER FAIL

"Know now that __nothing shall fall to the earth of the word of the Lord__ which the Lord spoke concerning the house of Ahab; for the Lord has done what He spoke by His servant Elijah." (2 Kings 10:10)

Jehu was selected by God through prophetic revelation to be the king of Israel and destroy the entire household of Ahab. This was done in order to avenge the blood of God's servants the prophets of God. *"And he (a young prophet) poured the oil on his (Jehu's) head, and said to him, "Thus says the Lord God of Israel: 'I have anointed you king over the people of the Lord, over Israel. You shall strike down the house of Ahab your master, that I may avenge the blood of My servants the prophets, and the blood of all the servants of the Lord, at the hand of Jezebel. For the whole house of Ahab shall perish; and I will cut off from Ahab all the males in Israel, both bond and free."* (2 Kings 9:6-8)

In accordance to the above prophecy, through the instigation of Jehu, the rulers and elders of Jezreel killed all the seventy sons of Ahab (2 Kings 10:1-9), and Jehu killed all who remained of the house of Ahab in Jezreel (v. 11) and Samaria (v. 17). This was the punishment of God upon Ahab and his wife Jezebel for all the wickedness that they had done in their life.

Let us be clear about three FACTS about the WORD OF GOD:

1. **God's word CANNOT be taken lightly.** *"Knowing this first that no prophecy of Scripture is of any private interpretation, for prophecy never came by the will of man, but holy men of God spoke as they were moved by the Holy Spirit."* (2 Peter 1:20-21)

2. **God's word WILL accomplish its purpose**, and this is what God says: *"For as the rain comes down, and the snow from heaven, and do not return there, but water the earth, and make it bring forth and bud, that it may give seed to the sower and bread to the eater,* ***so shall My word be that goes forth from My mouth; it shall not return to Me void, but it shall accomplish what I please, and it shall prosper in the thing for which I sent it."*** (Isaiah 55:10-11)

3. **God's word shall NEVER FAIL** and this is what God says: *"Heaven and earth will pass away,* ***but My words will by no means pass away."*** (Mark 13:31). *"Search from the book of the Lord, and read:* ***not one of these shall fail; not one shall lack her mate.*** *For My mouth has commanded it, and His Spirit has gathered them."* (Isaiah 34:16)

APRIL 18   *Bible Reading: 2 Kings Chapters 13-15*

GOD ALWAYS LISTENS TO SINCERE PRAYERS

"So Jehoahaz pleaded with the Lord, and the Lord listened to him; for He saw the oppression of Israel, because the king of Syria oppressed them. Then the Lord gave Israel a deliverer, so that they escaped from under the hand of the Syrians; and the children of Israel dwelt in their tents as before." (2 Kings 13:4-5)

Jehoahaz became king over Israel in Samaria and ruled for seventeen years during which time he did evil in the sight of Jehovah, and continued all the wrongful religious institutions of Jeroboam in making Israel to sin before God. Under his government, which pursued the policy of his predecessors regarding the support of the calf-worship, Israel's apostasy from the true God became greater and more confirmed than in the time of his father Jehu. God became angry at the increasing apostasy of King Jehoahaz and people of Israel, and allowed Syria to dominate over them. Under the domination of Syria, Israel was oppressed. It is at that time that Jehoahaz sincerely prayed to God for the first time in seventeen years, and God listened to his prayers and delivered Israel from the Syrian oppression.

God always listens to any person who prays sincerely for mercy after removing the iniquity from the heart. *"If I regard iniquity in* my heart, the Lord will not hear. But certainly God has heard me; He has attended to the voice of my prayer." (Psalms 66:18-19). Further down in 2 Kings chapter 13 we get another insight that God was gracious to Israel because of His ancient covenant with the patriarchs: *"But the Lord was gracious to them, had compassion on them, and regarded them, because of His covenant with Abraham, Isaac, and Jacob, and would not yet destroy them or cast them from His presence."* (2 Kings 13:23)

We see many examples in the Bible about God listening to sincere prayers even from very wicked people like Ahab (1 Kings 21:27-29) and the people of Nineveh during the time of Jonah the prophet (Jonah 3:5-10).

God is now looking across the earth to find those whose hearts are totally committed to Him. As it is written *"The eyes of the Lord move to and fro throughout the whole earth **that He may strongly support those whose heart is completely His.**"* (2 Chronicles 16:9, NASB).

When we approach the throne of God, let us sincerely seek Him in prayer. God will surely reward us for our sincerity. *"It is impossible to please God without faith. Anyone who wants to come to Him must believe that God exists, and that **He rewards those who <u>sincerely</u> seek Him.**"* (Hebrews 11:6, NLT)

APRIL 19   *Bible Reading: 2 Kings Chapters 16-18*

DOING RIGHT
IN THE SIGHT OF GOD

*"Now it came to pass in the third year of Hoshea the son of Elah, king of Israel that **Hezekiah the son of Ahaz**, king of Judah, began to reign. He was twenty-five years old when he became king, and he reigned twenty-nine years in Jerusalem. His mother's name was Abi the daughter of Zechariah. **And he did what was right in the sight of the Lord, according to all that his father David had done.**"* (2 Kings 18:1-3)

Hezekiah became the king of Judah when he was twenty-five years old. It is very important to note that his father Ahaz was one of the most rebellious and ungodly kings who ever ruled Judah who even dedicated his son (probably Hezekiah) to false gods by making him pass through the fire. *"Ahaz was twenty years old when he became king, and he reigned sixteen years in Jerusalem; and he did not do what was right in the sight of the Lord his God, as his father David had done. But he walked in the way of the kings of Israel; indeed he made his son pass through the fire, according to the abominations of the nations whom the Lord had cast out from before the children of Israel. And he sacrificed and burned incense on the high places, on the hills, and under every green tree."* (2 Kings 16:2-4). Taking over the throne from such an ungodly father, Hezekiah would have been inclined to follow his footsteps. Also, the neighboring Israel was in total sin and depravity, due to which the people of Israel were carried away captive to Assyria (2 Kings 17:5-39). Their lifestyle was summarized in the following verses: *"However they did not obey, but they followed their former rituals. So these nations feared the Lord, yet served their carved images; also their children and their children's children have continued doing as their fathers did, even to this day."* (2 Kings 17:40-41)

In the midst of all these ungodliness, Hezekiah did what was right in the sight of God. What exactly did Hezekiah do that pleased God?

1. **He destroyed all false gods and idols.** *"He removed the high places and broke the sacred pillars, cut down the wooden image and broke in pieces the bronze serpent that Moses had made; for until those days the children of Israel burned incense to it, and called it Nehushtan."* (2 Kings 18:4)

2. **He trusted in the Lord God of Israel.** *"He trusted in the Lord God of Israel, so that after him was none like him among all the kings of Judah, nor who were before him."* (2 Kings 18:5)

3. **He held fast to God and followed Him.** *"For he held fast to the Lord; he did not depart from following Him..."* (2 Kings 18:6a)

4. **He obeyed all the commandments of God.** *"(He) kept His commandments, which the Lord had commanded Moses."* (2 Kings 18:6b)

When Hezekiah did what was right in God's sight, *"the Lord was with him; he prospered wherever he went."* (2 Kings 18:7). Hezekiah stands before us as a good example of trusting and following God in the midst of people who are committing evil.

Let the words of Psalm 37 be an inspiration to us: *"Do not fret because of evildoers, nor be envious of the workers of iniquity. For they shall soon be cut down like the grass, and wither as the green herb.*

Trust in the Lord, and do good; dwell in the land, and feed on His faithfulness. Delight yourself also in the Lord, and He shall give you the desires of your heart. Commit your way to the Lord, trust also in Him, and He shall bring it to pass. He shall bring forth your righteousness as the light, and your justice as the noonday." (Psalms 37:1-6)

APRIL 20   *Bible Reading: 2 Kings Chapters 19-21*

TAKING OUR BURDENS DIRECTLY TO GOD

*"And so it was, when **King Hezekiah** heard it, that he tore his clothes, covered himself with sackcloth, and **went into the house of the Lord"*** (2 Kings 19:1) *"And Hezekiah received the letter from the hand of the messengers, and read it; and **Hezekiah went up to the house of the Lord, and spread it before the Lord."*** (2 Kings 19:14)

When King Hezekiah was threatened by an invasion from Sennacherib the king of Assyria, he tore his clothes in anguish, covered himself with sackcloth as an outward expression of grief and **took his burdens directly to God**. He tore his clothes to express horror at the daring blasphemy of Sennacherib and put on sackcloth to show his mental distress. He went into the temple to pray to God for refuge from his affliction (2 Kings 19:1). He then sent his people to Isaiah to obtain the prophet's counsel and comfort, and received an immediate answer from God through Isaiah. *And Isaiah said to them, "Thus you shall say to your master, 'Thus says the Lord: "Do not be afraid of the words which you have heard, with which the servants of the king of Assyria have blasphemed Me. **Surely I will send a spirit upon him, and he shall hear a rumor and return to his own land; and I will cause him to fall by the sword in his own land."*** (2 Kings 19:6-7)

However, when Sennacherib sent a letter to King Hezekiah threatening him again with total destruction by, **he again took his burden directly into God's presence. Hezekiah went into the temple of God, spread the letter before God and prayed to God for deliverance.** *"Now therefore, O Lord our God, I pray, save us from his hand, that all the kingdoms of the earth may know that You are the Lord God, You alone."* (2 Kings 19:19)

God answered King Hezekiah's prayer by giving a verbal assurance of deliverance (v. 20-34), and sent His angel to the Assyrian camp to kill 185,000 during the night time (v. 35). This caused Sennacherib the king of Assyria to return back to Nineveh (v. 36, compare 2 Kings 19:7), where he was murdered by his own two sons in cold blood while he was worshipping his god (v. 37).

When we face any burden in our life - like King Hezekiah - let us take it directly to God who has promised to answer our prayers. Let us join with the Psalmist in seeking God's help for He will never let us down. *"I sought the Lord, and He heard me, and delivered me from all my fears. They looked to Him and were radiant, and their faces were not ashamed. This poor man cried out, and the Lord heard him, and saved him out of all his troubles. The angel of the Lord encamps all around those who fear Him, and delivers them."* (Psalms 34:4-7)

APRIL 21   *Bible Reading: 2 Kings Chapters 22-25*

OUTWARD REFORM BEGINS WITH INWARD RENEWAL

"Josiah was eight years old when he became king...and he did what was right in the sight of the Lord, and walked in all the ways of his father David; he did not turn aside to the right hand or to the left." (2 Kings 22:1-2)

At the tender age of eight, Josiah became the king of Judah. He obeyed God with undivided devotion and initiated sweeping reforms in the land. Throughout his godly leadership of 31 years, Josiah followed the Lord with his whole heart and led his people wisely. His own spiritual passion began to influence Judah and eventually brought about widespread public reforms.

After about ruling for ten years, while Josiah was still a teenager, he sent some people to the high priest to speed up the work of repairing the temple. While clearing the rubble, the high priest found "the Book of the Law" (2 Kings 22:8). Shaphan the scribe thereafter read the word of God to the young king (v. 10). How did the king react? *"...when the king heard the words of the Book of the Law, that he tore his clothes"* (v. 11). His heart was tender (v. 19a), and he had an inner transformation when he heard the word of God. In fact, Josiah humbled himself before God and quickly sent people to Huldah, the prophetess to discern God's plan for them (v. 12-20). He then made a covenant before God to follow the Lord, keep all the commandments

145

and do exactly what God's word required them to do (2 Kings 23:3). This was the beginning of a drastic spiritual reform that spread throughout the land of Judah (v. 4-24) that caused the following statement to be written about King Josiah: *"Now before him there was no king like him, who turned to the Lord with all his heart, with all his soul, and with all his might, according to all the Law of Moses; nor after him did any arise like him."* (2 Kings 23:25)

There is a key principle that we can learn from Josiah's life: **outward reform begins with inward renewal**. Josiah experienced a personal change in his life before he could implement public change. It all began with a personal renewal, which initiated personal transformation in King Josiah's life. This resulted in him implementing public changes and spiritual reforms in his area of influence and realm of power.

For us too, everything begins with a personal inward renewal and a transformation so that we can obey God's perfect will for our lives. May this be God's counsel for us today: *"I beseech you therefore, brethren, by the mercies of God, that you present your bodies a living sacrifice, holy, acceptable to God, which is your reasonable service. And do not be conformed to this world, but **be transformed by the renewing of your mind, that you may prove what is that good and acceptable and perfect will of God.***" (Romans 12:1-2)

APRIL 22   *Bible Reading: 1 Chronicles Chapters 1-3*

CONFIRMING OUR PLACE IN OUR GENERATION

"One generation passes away, and another generation comes; but the earth abides forever." (Eccl 1:4)

The book of Chronicles was written soon after the exile in order to help those returning to Israel how to worship God. It was written after the destruction of Jerusalem in order to answer the question "Why did God choose to punish His people in such a way?" The answer is found in history, and it is beneficial to learn from others mistakes so that we will repeat them again.

As we go through the initial chapters of 1 Chronicles, the following thoughts come to mind:

- **God knows every person who has ever lived in this earth.** He knows each of us by name, and we are not just a faceless number to him. He is intimately concerned with our welfare and we should never feel insignificant. As the Psalmist has exclaimed: *"How precious also are Your thoughts to me, O God! How great is the sum of them! If I should count them, they would be more in number than the sand..."* (Psalms 139:17-18)

- **God records all our activities in His book of remembrance.** *"Then those who feared the LORD spoke to one another, and the LORD listened and heard them; so a book of remembrance was written before Him for those who fear the LORD and who meditate on His name."* (Malachi 3:16). We have to be very careful how we act, and even what we speak every day.

- **God is working on a plan throughout history.** As we see the names of people recorded for each generation in Chronicles, there is a distinct pattern that can be traced from Adam and goes to Abraham through Seth, and thereafter goes to David through Israel. It is obvious that God is creating a family tree for His Son Jesus Christ to be born in due time.

Even today, God is working on a plan of redemption that is already set in place through the death and resurrection of His only begotten Son Jesus Christ (John 3:16). **We should be aware that God has an individual plan for each one of us as well and we need to confirm our place in our generation by fulfilling God's plan in our lives.**

Let us shine the light of the saving knowledge of Jesus Christ into the dark world that we live in and fulfill God's plan in our lives. *"You are the light of the world. A city that is set on a hill cannot be hidden. Nor do they light a lamp and put it under a basket, but on a lampstand, and it gives light to all who are in the house. **Let your light so shine before men, that they may see your good works and glorify your Father in heaven.**"* (Matt 5:14-16)

APRIL 23   *Bible Reading: 1 Chronicles Chapters 4-6*

PRAYING FOR GOD'S SUPERNATURAL BLESSINGS

"Now Jabez was more honorable than his brothers, and his mother called his name Jabez, saying, "Because I bore him in pain." And Jabez

*called on the God of Israel saying, "**Oh, that You would bless me indeed, and enlarge my territory, that Your hand would be with me, and that You would keep me from evil, that I may not cause pain!**" So God granted him what he requested."* (1 Chron 4:9-10)

There is a virtually unknown Bible character hidden in First Chronicles named Jabez. Jewish writers affirm that he was an eminent doctor in the law, whose reputation drew so many scribes around him that a town was called by his name (1Chron. 2:55). The name 'Jabez' literally means, *"He will cause pain"* given by his mother at birth as that was her expectation about him in the future. Yet, Jabez apparently overcame his "painful" background because he alone was singled out as being blessed by God. Why? Because Jabez said a prayer and God granted his request. Obviously, this is a very special prayer that we should note.

The Prayer of Jabez is not about asking God for more material wealth. It is not about placing specific personal demands. It is about asking for God's maximum blessing in our life—whatever, wherever, whenever, and however He wants it to be. It is about using those blessings to become a person of influence for His glory.

As we carefully examine this prayer of Jabez, **we can distill five elements** that we can use in our own personal prayers to God:

1. **Oh, that You would bless me indeed…**sounds selfish, but not when we understand that this blessing can be *'supernatural favors from God'*. Asking for a blessing is seeking the power of God to flow through us. We are asking God to make us a channel of His blessing.

2. **And enlarge my territory…**challenges us to go beyond what is comfortable. Let us begin each day asking God to do something new in our lives. Let us go into new places (that we have never gone before) taking new risks for God that He may use us to expand His kingdom.

3. **That Your hand would be with me…**reminds us that stepping beyond what is comfortable can be dangerous as we are in uncharted territory. We need God's presence with us and His favor upon us at all times to be truly successful.

4. **And that You would keep me from evil…**is a simple recognition that we will be tempted in so many ways as we move forward. As

in the Lord's Prayer (Matt. 6:13a) we need to ask for God's protection everyday from the constant attacks of the enemy (Eph. 6:12; 1 Pet. 5:8).

5. **That I may not cause pain**…gives us the sober realization that our blessings may cause us to inflict pain upon others through our condescending attitude and pride. We need to ask God to give us a clearer perspective about ourselves, and make us humble especially when He blesses us.

Jabez was a good and honorable man who asked God to bless him and God answered his prayer. It's an example of God providing for and caring for His chosen people. The focus of Jabez's prayer is on God and His provision and protection. Jabez asked and God gave him what He requested—not because Jabez said the right thing or manipulated God into granting his request, but because God decided to be glorified through Jabez by answering his prayer.

Let us earnestly ask God to truly bless us with His supernatural favor so that God's name may be glorified through us as we become channels of His blessing to everyone around us!

APRIL 24   *Bible Reading: 1 Chronicles Chapters 7-9*

TEAM BUILDING IN THE HOUSE OF GOD

"For we are God's fellow workers" (1 Corinthians 3:9)

A careful study of 1 Chronicles 9:10-34 reveal that there were specific responsibilities assigned to different people to work in God's Temple in Jerusalem, which was according to God's plan and the abilities of the people to do the work. They belonged to the tribe of Levi – the tribe that God had chosen to serve Him. They all worked as a team so that the temple of God could operate smoothly for the rest of the tribes of Israel. These were the categories of the people of Levi who worked in the temple of God:

1. **Priests** (v. 10-13): They performed the priestly duties within the temple, and *"were very able men for the work of the service of the house of God."* (v. 13b)

2. **Levites** (v. 14-15): They assisted the priests to perform their duties within the temple.

3. **Gatekeepers** (v. 17-27): They provided security service both for the camp of Levi (v. 18) and the temple as they provided security for the treasuries kept securely inside (v. 26). *"And they lodged all around the house of God because they had the responsibility, and they were in charge of opening it every morning."* (1 Chron 9:27)

4. **Those in charge of the serving vessels** (v. 28) – they brought out the vessels and put them back after counting them.

5. **Those in charge of the furnishings and the implements of the sanctuary** (v. 29a)

6. **Those in charge over the fine flour, wine, oil, incense and spices** (v. 29b)

7. **Sons of priests who prepared the ointment of the spices** (v. 30)

8. **Those in charge over the things baked in the pans** (v. 31)

9. **Sons of the Kohathites who were in charge of preparing the showbread for every Sabbath** (v. 32)

10. **Singers – who sang in the temple day and night** (v. 33). They *"lodged in the chambers, and were free from other duties; for they were employed in that work day and night."* (v. 33)

There is a spiritual application for our lives in seeing how work was assigned in the temple of God. We are called to be a **holy priesthood** *"to offer up spiritual sacrifices acceptable to God through Jesus Christ"* (1 Peter 2:5). We are also a **royal priesthood** called to *"proclaim the praises of Him who called us out of darkness into His marvelous light"* (1 Peter 2:9). As the **priests of God**, we are **God's fellow workers** to work in the house of God, the Church (1 Cor. 3:9). We are **stewards** of different talents that God has endowed upon us and must contribute to God's work and to the upkeep of the Church. God has given everyone gifts and abilities that we need to use as a team and work effectively without any dispute or murmuring. We should pursue the same goals that God has instituted for the Church and make effective contribution to benefit the team.

We need to work in team harmony and mutual care, not competing but complimenting each other so that the Church will be built in the fashion that God intends it. *"Now, therefore, you are no longer* *strangers and foreigners, but fellow citizens with the saints and members of the household of God, having been built on the foundation of the apostles and prophets, Jesus Christ Himself being the chief corner stone, in whom the whole building, being joined together, grows into a holy temple in the Lord, in whom you also are being built together for a dwelling place of God in the Spirit."* (Eph 2:19-22)

APRIL 25   *Bible Reading: 1 Chronicles Chapters 10-12*

SEEKING GUIDANCE FROM GOD ALONE

*"So Saul died for his unfaithfulness which he had committed against the Lord, because he did not keep the word of the Lord, and **also because he consulted a medium for guidance. But he did not inquire of the Lord; therefore He killed him, and turned the kingdom over to David the son of Jesse.**"* (1 Chron 10:13-14)

The writer of Chronicles does not repeat the history of Saul's reign, but only of his death, by which a way was made for David to the throne of Israel. Saul died for his transgressions which he committed against the Lord — in having spared the king of the Amalekites and taken the flocks of the people as spoils (1Sam 15:9), as well as in having consulted a woman involved in witchcraft (1Sam 28:7). Both of these acts were great sins - the first was a violation of God's express and positive command (1Sam 15:3), and the second was disobedience to a well-known statute of God's law: *"Give no regard to mediums and familiar spirits; do not seek after them, to be defiled by them: I am the Lord your God."* (Lev. 19:31).

Saul did not inquire of the Lord from his heart – when he tried to get guidance from God (1Sam 28:6-7) he was totally out of touch with God due to his prior sins. Saul appears as a person who had gone so far away from God that he had to resort to witchcraft for his personal guidance.

Let us learn from Saul's tragic end, and follow the principles listed below for our guidance:

· **Ask God to give us guidance.** *"Show me Your ways, O Lord; teach me Your paths. Lead me in Your truth and teach me, for You are the God of my salvation; on You I wait all the day."* (Psalm 25:4-5)

- **God will guide us according to His promise** in Psalm 32:8: *"I will instruct you and teach you in the way you should go; I will guide you with My eye."*
- **The Bible gives us guidance.** Let's join with the Psalmist in asking for daily guidance through His Word: *"Direct my steps by Your word, and let no iniquity have dominion over me."* (Psalm 119:133) *"Your word is a lamp to my feet and a light to my path."* (Psalms 119:105)
- **God directs our path when we trust Him.** *"Trust in the Lord with all your heart, and lean not on your own understanding; in all your ways acknowledge Him, and He shall direct your paths."* (Proverbs 3:5-6)

Let us seek guidance from God alone – for He is the best guide that we can ever find for our daily living!

APRIL 26   *Bible Reading: 1 Chronicles Chapters 13-15*

CONSULTING WITH GOD & HIS WORD IS OUR BEST OPTION

*Then David **consulted** with the captains of thousands and hundreds, and with every leader. And David said to all the assembly of Israel, "If it seems good to you, and if it is of the Lord our God, let us...**bring the ark of our God back to us, for we have not inquired at it since the days of Saul.**" Then all the assembly said that they would do so, for the thing was right in the eyes of all the people.* (1 Chron 13:1-4)

*Then David said, **"No one may carry the ark of God but the Levites, for the Lord has chosen them to carry the ark of God and to minister before Him forever."** (1 Chron 15:2) **"For because you did not do it the first time, the Lord our God broke out against us, because we did not consult Him about the proper order."*** (1 Chron 15:13)

The children of Israel had neglected the Ark of God since the days of Saul, so King David resolved to bring the Ark to its rightful place in Jerusalem from the house of Abinadab in Kirjath Jearim. Like a wise ruler, David consulted with every leader and everyone in Israel and he received a unanimous approval to go ahead with this project. However, David did not consult with the law that was already given through Moses in this matter in Numbers 4:5; 7:9; 10:17 that the Ark of God should only be transported on the shoulders of the Levite priests. Instead, David prepared a new cart, and got two excellent people to guide the oxen. However, a mishap occurred when one of the cart drivers Uzza tried to stabilize and keep the Ark of God from falling down when the oxen stumbled. Inadvertently he broke the law of God and received a swift death punishment from God (1 Chron. 13:7-10). We may question the fairness of this judgment of God, but God had clearly stated in Numbers 4:15 that He would put to death anyone who touched the Ark of God.

After the lapse of three months (1Chron 13:14) the purpose of transporting the ark to Jerusalem was resumed. Time and reflection had led to a discovery of the cause of the painful catastrophe that marred the first attempt. In preparing for the solemn procession that was now to usher the sacred symbol into its resting place, David took special care that the Ark of God should be transported in strict conformity to the law of God. David now realized that earlier he had neither consulted with God nor His Word properly and the results were not good.

Let us understand that consulting with God and His Word is our best option before taking any crucial decision in our lives. God is great in His counsel, as the prophet Jeremiah has expressed to God: *"You are great in counsel and mighty in work, for your eyes are open to all the ways of the sons of men, to give everyone according to his ways and according to the fruit of his doings"* (Jer 32:19). **Our God is "...wonderful in counsel and excellent in guidance"** (Isaiah 28:29). Let us look to Him alone for giving us excellent counsel every step of our way.

APRIL 27   *Bible Reading: 1 Chronicles Chapters 16-18*

REGULAR WORSHIP – A KEY FOR VICTORIOUS LIVING

"So he left Asaph and his brothers there before the ark of the covenant of the Lord **to minister before the ark <u>regularly</u>,** *as every day's work required...and Zadok the priest and his brethren the priests, before the tabernacle of the Lord at the high place that was at Gibeon,* **to offer burnt offerings to the Lord on the altar of burnt offering <u>regularly</u> <u>morning and evening</u>,** *and to do according to all that is written in the*

*Law of the Lord which He commanded Israel; and with them Heman and Jeduthun and the rest who were chosen, who were designated by name, **to give thanks to the Lord, because His mercy endures forever**; and with them Heman and Jeduthun, **to sound aloud with trumpets and cymbals and the musical instruments of God**."* (1 Chron 16:37, 39-42)

King David brought the Ark of God and set it up in the midst of the tabernacle in Jerusalem that he had erected for this purpose and the priests offered burnt offerings and peace offerings before God (1 Chron 16:1). **Then King David went a step further – he appointed some of the Levites to minister before the Ark of God, to commemorate, to thank, and to praise the Lord God of Israel on a regular basis** (v. 4-6). They included worship leaders/singers, instrument players, priests and gatekeepers (1 Chron16:5, 38, 41). **They were to worship and praise God regularly (both morning and evening) – to give thanks to God for His mercy endures forever.**

Due to King David's decision to set regular worship, God was so pleased with David that He made an everlasting covenant with him that would outlast his lifetime (1 Chron 17:3-14). Also, **God preserved David wherever he went** (1 Chron 18:6b, 13b) and **helped him to be victorious over all his enemies** (1 Chron 18:1-13). It is therefore no surprise that David became a man after God's own heart (1 Sam 13:14).

In his book *'The Ultimate Priority'*, John McArthur has argued that **there is nothing self-centered about genuine worship**. Believers need to maintain a lifestyle of continuous worship – both through an individual lifestyle of worship and also get encouragement from other believers as they assemble for group worship. **Individual worship and corporate worship should constantly feed each other. The source of most of the problems Christian believers have relates to two things: either they are not worshipping six days a week with their life, or they are not worshipping one day a week with the assembly of saints.**

Let us maintain a lifestyle of regular worship – that is truly the key of a victorious Christian life!

Fighting our common enemy TOGETHER

When Joab saw that the battle line was against him before and behind, he chose some of Israel's best and put them in battle array against the Syrians. And the rest of the people he put under the command of Abishai his brother, and they set themselves in battle array against the people of Ammon. Then he said, "If the Syrians are too strong for me, then you shall help me; but if the people of Ammon are too strong for you, then I will help you. Be of good courage, and let us be strong for our people and for the cities of our God. And may the Lord do what is good in His sight." (1 Chron 19:10-13)

In 1 Chronicles 19:1-9, the people of Ammon hired Syrian mercenaries to fight against King David and the people of Israel. Joab, the commander of the Israelite army goes out to fight against the dual forces of the Syrians and the Ammonites. It is interesting to note the battle strategy that Joab laid out to his brother Abishai who commanded the other regiment. Joab and his mighty men would fight against the Syrians, while Abishai and his mighty men would fight against the Ammonites. In the event that one regiment faces a stronger enemy, the other regiment will provide them assistance. Moreover, they would put their trust in the God of Israel who would help them to win the battle as they would make themselves strong for the people of Israel and for the land that God had provided for them through His covenant (v. 10-13).

During the battle, the Syrians first fled before Joab and his army, and as a result Ammonites also fled before Abishai and his army (v. 14-15). Finally, King David came with his mighty forces and defeated the Syrians into total submission that they made peace with David and became his servants (v. 16-19). It was a great victory for King David and the people of Israel.

There is a spiritual application through this incident for us today. We are also *"fighting the good fight of faith"* (1 Tim 6:12; 2 Tim 4:7) against a common enemy who is Satan and his forces of darkness (Eph. 6:12). As children of God (John 1:12-12), we all belong to the family of God where God is our heavenly Father (Rom 1:7; 8:15). Together, we are the body of Christ as well (1 Cor 12:27). **So, how do we fight our common enemy since we are so linked together?**

- By staying united with each other (Psalms 133:1; 1 Cor 1:10)
- By being of same mind with each other (Rom 12:16; 15:5; Phil 1:27; 2:2; 3:16; 1 Pet 3:8)
- By keeping peace and harmony with each another (Eph 4:3)
- By bearing the burdens of one another during times of need (Gal 6:1-2)
- By edifying, exhorting and comforting one another through our spiritual gifts (Rom 14:19; 1 Cor 14:3)
- By praying and interceding for one another (Eph 6:18; James 5:16)

Let us help each other sincerely in fighting this battle of faith until our Lord Jesus Christ will one day come and defeat our enemy once and for all. *"Fight the good fight of faith, lay hold on eternal life, to which you were also called and have confessed the good confession in the presence of many witnesses."* (1 Tim 6:12)

APRIL 29   *Bible Reading: 1 Chronicles Chapters 22-24*

SETTING PRIORITIES RIGHT WITH OUR CHILDREN

"Now, my son, may the Lord be with you; and may you prosper, and build the house of the Lord your God, as He has said to you. **Only may the Lord give you wisdom and understanding,** *and give you charge concerning Israel,* **that you may keep the law of the Lord your God. Then you will prosper, if you take care to fulfill the statutes and judgments** *with which the Lord charged Moses concerning Israel. Be strong and of good courage; do not fear nor be dismayed."* (1 Chron 22:11-13)

Before David died and completed his earthly duties, one of the most important things that he did was to call his son Solomon to himself and lay out to him the things that were in his heart. He told Solomon that he had desired to build a temple in Jerusalem as God had now given rest to His people so that they may dwell in Jerusalem forever (1 Chron 22:6-7; 23:25), but God did not allow him to proceed forward in this building venture as he had shed a lot of blood in his lifetime (1 Chron 22:8). However, God had wanted Solomon to undertake this building project after his death (v. 9-10), for which David had prepared all the required building materials for this project (v. 14-16).

David then **set out the priorities** for his son Solomon in this manner – **that God would give Solomon** *'wisdom and understanding'* **to keep the commandments of God completely** so that he would fulfill the statutes and judgments that God had previously charged Moses concerning Israel. In doing so, he would prosper in his life. Solomon must have pondered over this final charge of his father, and decided that getting *'wisdom and understanding'* from God is the primary thing above everything else in his life. That must be reason that when God appeared to Solomon later and asked him what he desired in his life, Solomon asked for *'wisdom and understanding'* above anything else that he could have asked from God (2 Chron 1:7-12). God truly blessed Solomon with abundant *'wisdom and understanding'* that he became the wisest king and the most prosperous ruler of Israel.

This is a wonderful lesson for all parents everywhere about setting priorities for their children. It is good that the children study and achieve greatness on the secular side. **But more important is that they desire for** *'wisdom and understanding'* **from God so that they obey the word of God completely all the days of their lives. Then only are they going to be truly prosperous and successful and can influence many people towards God.**

In order to get started in obtaining wisdom from God, they should **develop a godly fear and reverence for God** (Prov 1:7) and a **love for reading and meditating on God's word** (Joshua 1:8) while they are still young. This is the training that parents are supposed to give to their children as per Proverbs 22:6. **If they lack wisdom, they can also ask in faith to God**: *"If any of you lacks wisdom, let him ask of God, who gives to all liberally and without reproach, and it will be given to him. But let him ask in faith, with no doubting, for he who doubts is like a wave of the sea driven and tossed by the wind."* (James 1:5-6)

APRIL 30   *Bible Reading: 1 Chronicles Chapters 25-27*

SERVING GOD USING OUR MINISTRY GIFTS

*"As each one has received a gift, minister it to one another, as good stewards of the manifold grace of God. If anyone speaks, let him speak as the oracles of God. **If anyone ministers, let him do it as with the***

ability which God supplies, that in all things God may be glorified through Jesus Christ, to whom belong the glory and the dominion forever and ever. Amen." (1 Peter 4:10-11)

King David made elaborate preparations prior to his death to gather the materials and funding to build the temple of God. Along with that, he also planned elaborately and selected people to serve the temple and his kingdom in various capacities according to their inherent gifts and talent for the common good of all the people of Israel. Each person was handpicked and given specific responsibilities according to his/her abilities so that the operations would go smoothly. In fact, 1 Chronicles 25-27 discusses seven areas of service for the children of Israel:

1. **Singers and Musicians (1 Chron 25:1-31):** David appointed singers and musicians in the temple who would *prophesy* with harps, stringed instruments and cymbals according to a specific set order for the service of the temple. *To prophesy* means to praise God with great earnestness and passion under the influence of the Holy Spirit. A total of 288 *skillful and talented singers and musicians* were meticulously selected and commissioned for service (v. 7-8).

2. **Gatekeepers and Porters (1 Chron 26:1-19):** David appointed gatekeepers and porters to guard the sacred treasures of the temple. They would *use their physical strength and valor* to resist those who wrongly would attempt to enter the sanctuary and steal the various items including flour, wine, oil, salt and fuel, along with the lamps, sacred vestments and utensils that were the treasures of the house of God.

3. **Treasurers and Storekeepers (1 Chron 26:20-28):** David appointed treasurers and storekeepers who would oversee the treasuries, and keep an accurate tally of all the treasures dedicated to maintain the temple. They were *people with accounting and math skills* who would make sure that all things are accounted in the house of God.

4. **Judges and Officials (1 Chron 26:29-32):** David appointed judges to determine solutions to questions and controversies which might arise among the Israelites as they interpret God's law in specific situations. The officials were appointed to serve the king in the execution of his decrees by which the several

rights of the king and people were established. These were clearly people of superior intellectual abilities and leadership skills.

5. **Military Captains (1 Chron 27:1-15):** David appointed military Captains to oversee the twelve legions (corresponding to the number of tribes) who were enlisted in the king's service. Each legion comprised a body of twenty-four thousand men, whose term of service was a month in rotation, and who were stationed either at Jerusalem or in any other place where they might be required. Thurs, there was always a force sufficient for the ordinary purposes of state, as well as for resisting sudden attacks or popular uprising.

6. **Tribal Princes (1 Chron 27:16-24):** David appointed princes of the tribes to be tribal rulers who had a superior power to the military Captains, and were probably the king's chief counselors and assistants in the great affairs of his kingdom.

7. **State Officials (1 Chron 27:25-34):** Last but not the least, David appoint state officials who had oversight and charge of the king's property, his vineyards, his herds, and his flocks which formed the wealth of the king.

God requires that we serve His spiritual kingdom faithfully using the ministry gifts that He has endowed upon us. As mentioned in 1 Peter 4:10-11, we need to serve God by ministering to one another as good stewards using the abilities that God has given us so that in all things God may be glorified in and through us!

May

Bible Reading: 1 Chronicles Chapters 28-29

OFFERING OURSELVES WILLINGLY TO GOD

"Moreover, because I have set my affection on the house of my God, I have given to the house of my God, over and above all that I have prepared for the holy house, my own special treasure of gold and silver: **Who then is willing to consecrate himself this day to the Lord?"** *(1 Chron 29:3, 5)*

As King David assembled all the leaders of Israel, he spoke to them all the desires that he had about the temple of God that he was planning to construct and how God did not allow him to do that task. He then spoke about how God had chosen Solomon among all his sons to be the ruler of Israel after him. However, David understood that Solomon was young and inexperienced, and the work in building the temple was great and needed everyone's support (1 Chron 29:1). David then explained about all the treasures that he had kept aside for building the temple, and challenged the leaders and all people to offer willingly to God. What really happened after King David issued the challenge to the leaders and the people of Israel?

· Everyone offered willingly their treasures to the work of God (v. 6-8).
· After giving so willingly, everyone (including King David) rejoiced because they were able to offer so willingly to God from a loyal heart. (v. 9)
· David blessed the God of Israel who gave them riches, honor and strength to do such a task (v. 10-12)

· David thanked God out of a humble heart as God allowed them to give Him out of what God had already given them (v. 13-14)

· David acknowledged that they were pilgrims on the earth and that their life was a shadow that would soon disappear (v. 15)

· Finally, King David spoke these words out of his heart: *"I know also, my God, that You test the heart and have pleasure in uprightness. As for me, in the uprightness of my heart **I have willingly offered all these things; and now with joy I have seen Your people, who are present here to offer willingly to You.***" (1 Chron 29:17)

Let us understand clearly that God gives us blessings and then tests us to see if we are able to offer willingly to God. God is the true owner of everything we possess. All of heaven and earth belongs to God (1 Chron 29:11). Even our bodies belong to God (1 Cor. 6:19-20), and God has given us all things to enjoy in this life (1 Tim 6:17).

Let us offer our bodies as living sacrifices to God so that we become a sweet smelling aroma to God as we obey Apostle Paul's pleading: *"I beseech you therefore, brethren, by the mercies of God, that you present your bodies a living sacrifice, holy, acceptable to God, which is your reasonable service."* (Romans 12:1).

In doing so, we also become a fragrance of Christ to everyone we meet: *"Now thanks be to God who always leads us in triumph in Christ, and through us diffuses the fragrance of His knowledge in every place. For we are to God the fragrance of Christ among those who are being saved and among those who are perishing. To the one we are the aroma of death leading to death, and to the other the aroma of life leading to life."* (2 Cor 2:14-16)

MAY 2   *Bible Reading: 2 Chronicles Chapters 1-3*

PUTTING GOD FIRST IN OUR LIVES

*"Then Solomon, and all the assembly with him, **went to the high place that was at Gibeon; for the tabernacle of meeting with God was there**, which Moses the servant of the Lord had made in the wilderness. And **Solomon went up there to the bronze altar before the Lord**, which was at the tabernacle of meeting, **and offered a thousand burnt offerings on it.**"* (2 Chron 1:3, 6)

After the death of King David, his son Solomon started his rule upon the right priorities that he had learned from his father – he began his reign with a pious, public visit to God's altar. The altar and the tabernacle were enclosed in the ark of God inside a tent in the midst of Jerusalem (2 Chron 1:4-5). Solomon went to the bronze altar before the Lord at the tabernacle of meeting and offered a thousand burnt offerings upon it (v. 6). Actually God did not require Solomon to offer more than one burnt offering as a token of his appreciation to God. However, Solomon wanted to express his appreciation to God profusely and offered a thousand burnt offerings at the very beginning of his reign. He had truly put God first in his life – before anything else. God was so pleased with Solomon that He appeared to Solomon that very night in a dream and offered him back *anything* that he wanted! Solomon then asked for wisdom and understanding, and he received everything else that he needed – including riches, wealth and honor – to rule over the people of Israel superbly (v.7-12).

There is a very important message for us here – **when we put God first in our lives, He will provide to us all the other needed resources for our lives.** Our Lord Jesus Christ has told us a powerful life principle: *"But seek first the kingdom of God and His righteousness, and all these things shall be added to you."* (Matt 6:33). Instead of making the pursuit of success, fame and wealth as our priority as the worldly people do, we need to seek God and His will first and foremost in our daily life routine. Then God will provide us everything that we actually need in our lives, and even more in abundance as in the case of Solomon.

We need to understand that God is waiting for us to seek Him earnestly: *"The Lord looks down from heaven upon the children of men, to see if there are any who understand, who seek God."* (Psalms 14:2). Let this be our desire for today and all the days of our lives: *"One thing I have desired of the Lord, **that will I seek**: that I may **dwell** in the house of the Lord all the days of my life, to **behold** the beauty of the Lord, and to **inquire** in His temple."* (Psalms 27:4)

Bible Reading: 2 Chronicles Chapters 4-6

SEEKING GOD'S GLORY FOR HIS TEMPLE

*Indeed it came to pass, when the trumpeters and singers **were as one, to make one sound** to be heard in **praising and thanking the Lord**, and when they **lifted up their voice** with the trumpets and cymbals and instruments of music, and praised the Lord, saying: "For He is good, for His mercy endures forever," **that the house, the house of the Lord, was filled with a cloud, so that the priests could not continue ministering because of the cloud; for the glory of the Lord filled the house of God.** (2 Chron 5:13-14)*

Once the construction of the temple in Jerusalem was complete, King Solomon took the right steps of bringing the Ark of God into the inner sanctuary (Holy of Holies) of the temple. A careful reading of 2 Chron 5:2-14 provides us the steps that King Solomon took in properly installing the Ark of God (the visible manifestation of God's presence) in the temple in Jerusalem, *and provides to us a symbolism of God's presence filling the living temples of God in Jerusalem on the day of Pentecost in Acts 2:*

King Solomon assembled everyone together in one place (including the elders, the heads of the tribes, the chief fathers and all men of Israel (v. 2-4a). *Similarly, our Lord Jesus Christ also told His disciples to gather together in Jerusalem: "And being assembled together with them, He commanded them not to depart from Jerusalem, but to wait for the Promise of the Father" (Acts 1:4).*

The Levite priests bore the Ark of God on their shoulders (v. 4b-5) exactly as per God's prior instruction. Solomon must have learned a lesson from his father David when he chose an alternate means to transport the Ark of God. *Similarly, it was the disciples of Jesus who assembled in the upper room in Jerusalem – no outsiders or unbelievers participated in that prayer meeting (Acts 1:12-15)*

King Solomon and all the congregation of Israel sacrificed sheep and oxen in abundance (v. 6). *Similarly, during the ten days of waiting, the 120 disciples must have humbled themselves before God and got right with God as required in Psalms 51:17: "The sacrifices of God are a broken spirit, a broken and a contrite heart— these, O God, You will not despise."*

The sanctified Levite priests sounded the trumpets while the Levite singers clothed in white linen made one sound in praising God (v. 11-13). *Similarly, all the disciples gathered in the upper room "continued with one accord in prayer and supplication" (Acts 1:14a).*

When all this happened, the temple of God was filled with the glory of God (v. 13b-14). *Similarly, on the day of Pentecost the Holy Spirit filled all the disciples waiting in the upper room: "When the Day of Pentecost had fully come, they were all with one accord in one place. And suddenly there came a sound from heaven, as of a rushing mighty wind, and it filled the whole house where they were sitting. Then there appeared to them divided tongues, as of fire, and one sat upon each of them. And they were all filled with the Holy Spirit and began to speak with other tongues, as the Spirit gave them utterance." (Acts 2:1-4)*

Let us clearly understand that God has designated our body as the temple of God as mentioned in 1 Cor 6:19: *"Do you not know that your body is the temple of the Holy Spirit who is in you?"* **We need to seek the glory of God to fill our temples everyday of our lives.** In order to do that, we also need to take the very steps that King Solomon and the 120 disciples took for the glory of God to descend in the temple.

When the glory of God fills us, we can be the light of the world - the city on the hill that is visible to everyone *outside* and the lamp that gives light to everyone *inside* the house (Matt 5:14-15). **Let our light so shine before others that they would see our good works and glorify our Father in heaven** (Matt 5:16).

MAY 4   *Bible Reading: 2 Chronicles Chapters 7-9*

GOD IS LOOKING AT US CONTINUALLY

*"For now I have chosen and sanctified this house, that My name may be there forever; and **My eyes and My heart will be there perpetually.**"* (2 Chron 7:16)

After King Solomon had dedicated the temple in Jerusalem, God gave wonderful promises of His commitment towards the temple that has been erected for Him. There are three promises from God regarding the physical temple in Jerusalem:

1. **God had chosen and sanctified the temple in Jerusalem.** This means that God will dwell in the inner sanctuary of the temple going forward, and God will accept the sacrifices and prayers that Solomon or anyone else would be making in the future.

2. **God promised that His name would be in the temple forever.** The great "I AM" would seal His name so that everyone will understand that He is the God of the universe.

3. **God's eyes and His heart will be upon the temple continually forever.** Everything that happens in the temple will be known by God, and He will participate in the worship of the people of Israel.

As mentioned earlier, God has designated our body as the temple of God as mentioned in 1 Cor 6:19: *"Do you not know that your body is the temple of the Holy Spirit who is in you?"* As God's temples, we too have the three promises in our lives as well:

1. **God has chosen us and sanctified us with the precious blood of His Son Jesus Christ.** John 15:16 tells us the following: *"You did not choose Me, but I chose you and appointed you that you should go and bear fruit, and that your fruit should remain, that whatever you ask the Father in My name He may give you."* As per 1 John 1:9, it is the precious blood of Jesus that sanctifies us and cleanses us from all unrighteousness.

2. **God has promised us unlimited access to Him through the name of His Son Jesus Christ.** John 14:13-14 gives us this precious promise: *"And **whatever you ask in My name, that I will do**, that the Father may be glorified in the Son. **If you ask anything in My name, I will do it."***

3. **God's eyes and heart are upon me continually from the beginning to the end of the year.** *"The eyes of the Lord your God are always on it, from the beginning of the year to the very end of the year."* (Deut 11:12).

Seeing that we have such precious promises from God, let us always be sensitive to the fact that **God is always watching us.** In fact, **God is constantly looking at us to come to our aid at all times:** *"For the eyes of the Lord run to and fro throughout the whole earth, to show Himself strong on behalf of those whose heart is loyal to Him."* (2 Chron 16:9)

TAKE WISE COUNSEL TO MAKE THE RIGHT DECISIONS

*Then King Rehoboam **consulted the elders** who stood before his father Solomon while he still lived, saying, "How do you advise me to answer these people?" And they spoke to him, saying, "If you are kind to these people, and please them, and speak good words to them, they will be your servants forever." **But he rejected the advice which the elders had given him, and consulted the young men who had grown up with him, who stood before him.*** (2 Chron 10:6-8)

Rehoboam became the king of Israel after the death of his father Solomon. We know that Solomon had corrupted his wisdom towards the later part of his life. Unlike his father David, Solomon did not make any attempts to teach or train his son in righteousness or the ways of God. So, when King Rehoboam became the king of Israel, he did not have any relationship with the God of Israel nor Shemaiah the man of God (2 Chron 11:2). That is the reason why King Rehoboam turned to both the elders (his father's advisers) and the young men (his peers) in order to make an appropriate decision.

Unfortunately, Rehoboam rejected the good counsel of his father's advisers and consulted his peers, who told him he should not give an inch and in fact should increase the pressure on the people (2 Chron 10:6-11). Foolishly Rehoboam agreed and thus forfeited the Northern Kingdom (2 Chron 10:12-14, 16). We should however note that the young king's stupidity was itself playing into the will of God, who had already decreed that the kingdom would split up after Solomon (2 Chron 10:15; 11:4; 1 Kings 11:29-39). Rehoboam's last-ditch efforts at reconciliation failed, and the united kingdom of Israel was torn into two parts (2 Chron. 10:19). The grandeur and glory of the days of King David and Solomon would never return back to Israel...!!!

This incident teaches us the importance of taking wise counsel to make the right decisions in life. We can't always make right decisions but with God's help and godly counsel we can always make decisions right. The word of God has much to say about heeding to wise counsel:

· *A wise man will hear and increase learning, and a man of understanding will attain wise counsel* (Prov 1:5)

- *Give instruction to a wise man, and he will be still wiser; teach a just man, and he will increase in learning.* (Prov 9:9)
- *Where there is no counsel, the people fall; but in the multitude of counselors there is safety.* (Prov 11:14)
- *The way of a fool is right in his own eyes, but he who heeds counsel is wise.* (Prov 12:15)
- *Without counsel, plans go awry, but in the multitude of counselors they are established.* (Prov 15:22)
- *Listen to counsel and receive instruction, that you may be wise in your latter days.* (Prov 19:20)

Let us be careful to seek God and wise godly counselors when it comes time to take major decisions in life. Let us learn from the story of Rehoboam and be wise in not repeating his mistake in our lives!

MAY 6 *Bible Reading: 2 Chronicles Chapters 13-15*

SEEK GOD WHEN HE WILL BE FOUND

"The Lord is with you while you are with Him. **If you seek Him, He will be found by you***; but if you forsake Him, He will forsake you. For a long time Israel has been without the true God, without a teaching priest, and without law; but when in their trouble* **they turned to the Lord God of Israel, and sought Him, He was found by them.** *Then they* **entered into a covenant to seek the Lord God of their fathers** *with all their heart and with all their soul; and* **whoever would not seek the Lord God of Israel was to be put to death,** *whether small or great, whether man or woman. And all Judah rejoiced at the oath, for they had sworn with all their heart and* **sought Him with all their soul;** *and* **He was found by them,** *and the Lord gave them rest all around."* (2 Chron 15:2-4, 12-13, 15)

The prophet Azariah went to meet King Asa, as he was returning from his victorious pursuit of the Ethiopians, and publicly conveyed a message from the God of Israel in the presence of his army. The message was that God's presence will continue to be with King Asa as long as he earnestly seeks God from all his heart. The past history of Israel is clear that whenever they turned to God and sought Him, He was found by them and God troubled all their adversaries (2 Chron 15:1-7).

King Asa listened to the word from the prophet, took courage destroyed all the idols and restored the altar of the Lord that signified worship (v. 8). He then gathered all the people together (v. 9-10), offered sacrifices for their sins and trespasses (v. 11) and **entered into a covenant with Jehovah that they would seek God with all their heart and soul** (v. 12). Whoever would not seek God would be put to death (v. 13). **The whole assembly took a solemn oath as they swore to seek God from their innermost being** (v. 14-15a). **The result was that God was found by them, and gave them rest all around** (v. 15). There was no war until the thirty-fifth year of the reign of King Asa (v. 19).

The word for us today is that we should earnestly seek God when He will be found by us. We have many precious promises and exhortations in the word of God, a few of which are listed below for our edification:

- *But from there you will seek the Lord your God, and you will find Him if you seek Him with all your heart and with all your soul.* (Deut 4:29)
- *Seek the Lord and His strength; seek His face evermore!* (1 Chron 16:11)
- *Now set your heart and your soul to seek the Lord your God.* (1 Chron 22:19)
- *If you seek Him, He will be found by you; but if you forsake Him, He will cast you off forever.* (1 Chron 28:9)
- *And in every work that he began in the service of the house of God, in the law and in the commandment, to seek his God, he did it with all his heart. So he prospered.* (2 Chron 31:21)
- *And those who know Your name will put their trust in You; for You, Lord, have not forsaken those who seek You.* (Psalms 9:10)
- *The Lord looks down from heaven upon the children of men, to see if there are any who understand, who seek God.* (Psalms 14:2)
- *When You said, "Seek My face," my heart said to You, "Your face, Lord, I will seek."* (Psalms 27:8)
- *I sought the Lord, and He heard me, and delivered me from all my fears.* (Psalms 34:4)

· *The young lions lack and suffer hunger; but those who seek the Lord shall not lack any good thing.* (Psalms 34:10)

MAY 7   *Bible Reading: 2 Chronicles Chapters 16-18*

LOYALTY IS THE TEST OF TRUE LOVE

"For the eyes of the Lord run to and fro throughout the whole earth, to show Himself strong on behalf of those whose heart is loyal to Him." (2 Chron 16:9)

When Baasha the king of Israel came against Judah, King Asa took silver and gold from the treasuries of the house of God and sent them to Ben-Hadad the king of Syria asking for help. In the past, King Asa had trusted in God but now his heart was not loyal to God. He had lost his trust in God being able to deliver him from the army of Israel. In this connection, a reproof was given to King Asa by a prophet of the Lord, for making a league with Syria.

God is displeased when we distrust Him, and when we look to others for help rather than God. It is foolish to lean on a broken reed when we have the Rock of ages to rely upon. To convince Asa of his folly, the prophet shows that he, of all men, had no reason to distrust God, who had found him such a powerful Helper. The many experiences we have had of the goodness of God to us should never lead us to distrust Him. In all conflicts and sufferings we need especially to look to our own hearts that they may be perfect towards God, by faith, patience, and obedience.

Let us remember the words of Jesus and not put our confidence in uncertain riches and money: *"No one can serve two masters; for either he will hate the one and love the other, or else **he will be loyal to the one and despise the other**. You cannot serve God and mammon."* (Matt 6:24).

Let us never love the world or the things of the world over the things of God. *"Do not love the world or the things in the world. If anyone loves the world, the love of the Father is not in him. For all that is in the world—the lust of the flesh, the lust of the eyes, and the pride of life—is not of the Father but is of the world. And the world is passing*

169

away, and the lust of it; but he who does the will of God abides forever." (1 John 2:15-17)

Let us be loyal to God alone, since God will show Himself strong on our behalf during the time of our need. **Let us never forget that loyalty is the test of our true love for God!**

MAY 8   *Bible Reading: 2 Chronicles Chapters 19-21*

A SUPERNATURAL RESPONSE TO TROUBLE

"O our God, will You not judge them? For we have no power against this great multitude that is coming against us; nor do we know what to do, but our eyes are upon You." (2 Chron 20:12)

When trouble comes against us, we can choose to respond either *naturally* or *supernaturally*. When we respond *naturally*, we either confront the trouble head-on with our own strength or we try to run away from the trouble as far as we can. We can also deny that the trouble exists and wish that it would go away. However, we can also respond to trouble *supernaturally* like King Jehoshaphat, who turned to God during the time of his trouble. Let us look into the sequence of events how King Jehoshaphat responded to trouble in his life as recorded in 2 Chron 20:1-30:

- When King Jehoshaphat heard that three great armies were about to attack, fear motivated him to seek the Lord as he proclaimed a fast and gathered everyone together to ask help from the Lord (vv. 1-4).

- His prayer began with praise, which shifted his focus from the magnitude of his problem to the greatness of his God (vv. 5-7).

- After making petitions and receiving an answer through the prophet Jahaziel, King Jehoshaphat and all the people exalted and worshipped the Lord (vv. 18-19).

- As King Jehoshaphat focused on the greatness of his God, he approached the battle, not with soldiers, but with a choir leading the way (vv. 20-21).

- When they began to sing praises to God, the Lord intervened by routing their enemies (vv. 22-25).

· The people reacted with gratitude and worship to the great deliverance that they had received from God (vv. 26-28).

This *supernatural* response from King Jehoshaphat and the people of Judah resulted in peace and rest for them as well as a reverence for God from the surrounding nations (vv. 29-30). Let us also respond *supernaturally* to any trouble that confronts us – God will intervene in our behalf when we praise Him lavishly. Praise affects our outlook and faith, opens the door for God to do great things for us and through that makes us living witness of His acts of deliverance!

"Make a joyful shout to God, all the earth! Sing out the honor of His name; make His praise glorious. Say to God, "How awesome are Your works! Through the greatness of Your power Your enemies shall submit themselves to You. All the earth shall worship You and sing praises to You; they shall sing praises to Your name." (Psalms 66:1-4)

MAY 9   *Bible Reading: 2 Chronicles Chapters 22-24*

THE INFLUENCE OF COUNSELORS IN OUR LIVES

*"**Blessed is the man who walks not in the counsel of the ungodly**, nor stands in the path of sinners, nor sits in the seat of the scornful; but his delight is in the law of the Lord, and in His law he meditates day and night."* (Psalms 1:1-2)

In the readings of 2 Chron 22-24, we come across two kings of Judah whose lives were influenced by counselors – both ungodly and godly.

King Ahaziah: *"Ahaziah was forty-two years old when he became king, and he reigned one year in Jerusalem. His mother's name was Athaliah the granddaughter of Omri. **He also walked in the ways of the house of Ahab, for his mother advised him to do wickedly. Therefore he did evil in the sight of the Lord, like the house of Ahab; for they were his counselors after the death of his father, to his destruction.**"* (2 Chron 22:2-4)

We see that Ahaziah had ungodly and wicked counselors like his own mother and the Ahab family who influenced him to do evil in God's sight. So, God brought about his downfall and eventual death (vv. 7-9). The counsel of the ungodly ruins many young people when they are setting out in the world. Ahaziah gave himself up to be led by evil men and his own evil mother. Those who advise us to do wickedly, counsel us to our destruction; while they pretend to be friends, they are our worst enemies. We need to stay away from these people at all cost.

King Joash: *"Joash was **seven years old** when he became king, and he reigned forty years in Jerusalem. His mother's name was Zibiah of Beersheba. **Joash did what was right in the sight of the Lord all the days of Jehoiada the priest.**"* (2 Chron 24:1-2) *"Now **after the death of Jehoiada** the leaders of Judah came and bowed down to the king. **And the king listened to them.** Therefore they left the house of the Lord God of their fathers, and served wooden images and idols; and wrath came upon Judah and Jerusalem because of their trespass. **Yet He sent prophets to them, to bring them back to the Lord; and they testified against them, but they would not listen.**"* (2 Chron 24:17-19)

In the case of Joash, he ascended the throne of Judah at a tender age of seven. He was greatly influenced by the godly priest Jehoiada and his wife Jehoshabeath, so he started his reign taking the right decision of making a covenant to serve God alone (vv. 3, 16). He destroyed idol worship (v. 17), and *repaired*, *restored* and *reinforced* the house of God to its original condition (vv. 4-14). However, after the death of Jehoiada (vv. 15-16), Joash listened to wicked leaders of Judah and *reinstated* the idol worship that was long forsaken (vv. 17-18). When Zechariah, the son of Jehoiada spoke prophetical words of destruction, Joash had him stoned to death. He did not remember the kindness that the Jehoiada family had done to him nor the fact that it was because of them only that he became the king of Judah (vv. 20-22). Eventually, Joash was killed by the Syrian army who executed God's judgment against Joash, and he was not even buried in the tombs of the kings (vv. 23-25). What a tragedy!

Let us be very careful taking counsel from others – this may decide our decisions, actions and eventual destiny. *"The thoughts of the righteous are right, but the counsels of the wicked are deceitful."* (Prov 12:5). **Let us trust in the Lord who alone can give us good counsel.** *"I will bless the Lord who has given me counsel; my heart also instructs me in the night seasons."* (Psalms 16:7)

Bible Reading: 2 Chronicles Chapters 25-27

KEYS TO SUCCESS AND CAUSE OF FAILURE

*"Uzziah was sixteen years old when he became king, and he reigned fifty-two years in Jerusalem. His mother's name was Jecholiah of Jerusalem. And **he did what was right in the sight of the Lord**, according to all that his father Amaziah had done. **He sought God** in the days of Zechariah, who had understanding in the visions of God; and **as long as he sought the Lord, God made him prosper.**"* (2 Chron 26:3-5) *"**But when he was strong his heart was lifted up**, to his destruction, for **he transgressed against the Lord his God** by entering the temple of the Lord to burn incense on the altar of incense."* (2 Chron 26:16)

Uzziah (also called Azariah in 2 Kings 14:21) was appointed to be the king of Judah by the people through popular demand in place of his father Amaziah (2 Chron 26:1). As we read the early part of his rule in 2 Chron 26:1-15, there are some definite keys to success in Uzziah's life:

· Uzziah's father (Amaziah) had set a good example for him to follow (v. 4)

· A wise and pious counselor called Zechariah, who was skilled in understanding the meaning and lessons of the ancient prophecies, instructed Uzziah (v. 5)

· Uzziah had a good army and able generals to assist him in battle (vv. 11-15)

· Last, but not the least, Uzziah sought the Lord. As long as he sought the Lord, God made him prosper (v. 5). His fame spread far and wide, for he was marvelously helped until he became strong (v. 15b).

However, when Uzziah became strong, he became proud that caused a downward slide in his life. It is written in 2 Chron 26:16 that his heart was lifted up to his destruction. Due to his pride, he thought of himself as invincible and above God's law. He entered the temple of the Lord to burn incense on the altar without approval from God. Uzziah fell from God's favor and God punished him with leprosy. Uzziah was a leper until he died as he lived in isolation being cut off from the house of God (v. 21). We need to understand that pride causes us to set ourselves as gods. Because of pride, we sin without any regard to God's standard. The great Evangelist D. L. Moody has once said: *"When I think I have become strong and I have a good deal of strength – my downfall has already commenced"*.

Let us learn the keys of success and the cause of failure from the life of King Uzziah, and seek the face of God always! Remember the following: *"The fear of the Lord is to hate evil; pride and arrogance and the evil way."* (Prov 8:13)

MAY 11   *Bible Reading: 2 Chronicles Chapters 28-30*

IT'S TIME TO REPAIR OUR BROKEN WORSHIP

"Hezekiah became king when he was twenty-five years old, and he reigned twenty-nine years in Jerusalem. His mother's name was Abijah the daughter of Zechariah. ***And he did what was right in the sight of the Lord, according to all that his father David had done. In the first year of his reign, in the first month, he opened the doors of the house of the Lord and repaired them.""*** (2 Chron 29:1-3)

When Hezekiah had ascended to the throne of Judah, the spiritual condition was very bad. His father Ahaz had *"gathered the articles of the house of God, cut in pieces the articles of the house of God, shut up the doors of the house of the Lord, and made for himself altars in every corner of Jerusalem. And in every single city of Judah he made high places to burn incense to other gods, and provoked to anger the Lord God of his fathers."* (2 Chron 28:24-25) In order to make a new start that was right in the sight of God, Hezekiah had to repair and reinstate the worship back in the temple in Jerusalem, which he did as follows:

1. He opened the closed doors of the house of the Lord and repaired them (2 Chron 29:3)

2. He gathered the priests together, who sanctified themselves for worship as well as sanctified the house of God along with all the articles in the temple (vv. 4-19)

3. He rose early in the morning, gathered the rulers of the city and went into the house of God (v. 20)

4. On their behalf, the priests sacrificed burnt offering and sin offering to God (vv. 21-24)

5. As the burnt offerings were offered, the Levites started worshiping God with songs of praise accompanied by musical instruments (vv. 25-30)

6. Finally, King Hezekiah reinstated the Passover celebrations, even though it was delayed from the time set by God.

To summarize, **the following was the result of King Hezekiah repairing the worship in Jerusalem**:

·   *"So the service of the house of the Lord was set in order. Then Hezekiah and all the people rejoiced that God had prepared the people, since the events took place so suddenly."* (2 Chron 29:35-36)

·   *"And the Lord listened to Hezekiah and healed the people."* (2 Chron 30:20)

·   *"So there was great joy in Jerusalem, for since the time of Solomon the son of David, king of Israel, there had been nothing like this in Jerusalem."* (2 Chron 30:26)

·   *"Then the priests, the Levites, arose and blessed the people, and their voice was heard; and their prayer came up to His holy dwelling place, to heaven."* (2 Chron 30:27)

It is high time that we also repair our broken worship altar in order to experience the blessings of God. *"Come now, and let us reason together,"* says the Lord, *"though your sins are like scarlet, they shall be as white as snow; though they are red like crimson, they shall be as wool. If you are willing and obedient, you shall eat the good of the land"* (Isaiah 1:18-19)

MAY 12   *Bible Reading: 2 Chronicles Chapters 31-33*

GOD IS TRYING TO DRAW OUR ATTENTION TODAY

"And the Lord spoke to Manasseh and his people, but they would not listen. Therefore the Lord brought upon them the captains of the army of the king of Assyria, who took Manasseh with hooks, bound him with bronze fetters, and carried him off to Babylon. Now when he was in affliction, he implored the Lord his God, and humbled himself greatly before the God of his fathers, and prayed to Him; and He received his

entreaty, heard his supplication, and brought him back to Jerusalem into his kingdom. **Then Manasseh knew that the Lord was God.**" (2 Chron 33:10-13)

It is often said that *one's faith is always within one generation of dying out.* This observation finds validation over and over in the Old Testament record. No sooner had Hezekiah died than his son Manasseh began to subvert all the good things his father had done. Most particularly Manasseh reintroduced idolatry to Judah, going so far as to practice human sacrifice and to place images within the holy temple of the Lord (33:1–9). This makes one wonder if the fifteen years extension that Hezekiah had received from God was actually a good thing in the end – for it was during this period that Manasseh was born to him who would resort to all evil activities.

In 2 Chron 33:10, we read that God patiently tried to talk Manasseh out of his evil deeds, but Manasseh *would not listen* (v. 10). To draw his attention, God used the Assyrians to invade Judah and capture Manasseh. Manasseh had now lost his throne, power, and even his freedom. He was separated from his evil counselors and companions, and had no chance of freedom from the wretched prison (v. 11). He must have thought upon what had passed and humbled himself greatly before God as he began to cry for mercy and deliverance (v. 12). God, displaying His loving kindness and tender mercies once again, heard the supplication of Manasseh and restored his kingdom back by bringing him back to Jerusalem into his kingdom. *Then Manasseh* **knew** *that the Lord of Israel was truly God.*

It is possible that like Manasseh, we may drift away from God as we are engaged to fulfill our own agendas and plans. God is always trying to communicate with us through dreams, through His word and even through His prophets but if we do not pay attention, God may bring adversity in our lives to draw our attention. If God knows every thought in our hearts, every cell in our bodies, and every hair on our heads – God knows definitely what we are going through. If we have sinned against God, today let us turn back to God and call upon His name. He will hear our prayer and will deliver us.

God is trying to draw our attention today - let us remember His timeless promises as we turn to Him:

· *"Call to Me, and I will answer you, and show you great and mighty things, which you do not know."* (Jer 33:3)

- *"It shall come to pass that before they call, I will answer; and while they are still speaking, I will hear."* (Isaiah 65:24)
- *"Come to Me, all you who labor and are heavy laden, and I will give you rest."* (Matt 11:28)

MAY 13   *Bible Reading: 2 Chronicles Chapters 34-36*

SEEK GOD WHILE YOU'RE YOUNG

*"Josiah was **eight years old** when he became king, and he reigned thirty-one years in Jerusalem. And **he did what was right in the sight of the Lord**, and walked in the ways of his father David; he did not turn aside to the right hand or to the left. For **in the eighth year of his reign, while he was still young, he began to seek the God of his father David...all his days they did not depart from following the Lord God of their fathers**."* (2 Chron 34:1-3, 33)

Josiah was a very young boy when he ascended the throne of Judah. At the tender age of 8, he was naïve and not having the maturity to make important decisions, he started with doing the right things as he closely followed the steps of his great ancestor David (2 Chron 34:1-2).

However, Josiah made a very important decision when he entered into the eighth year of his reign. At the age of 16 when he was entering into the age of temptation, and had the administration of his kingdom wholly in his own power and nobody to restrain him; even then **he began to seek God earnestly** (v. 3a). He cleaned up Judah and Jerusalem of all idols and images (v. 3b-7) thus obeying the first of the Ten Commandments that God had given to Israelites through Moses. Then, he repaired the house of the Lord his God (v. 8-26). Even God testified through Huldah the prophetess that his heart was tender (v. 27a) and he was sincere in his devotion to God. When he was convicted by God's word, he humbled himself by tearing his clothes and weeping before God (v. 27b). On hearing God's words of judgment on Judah and Jerusalem, he gathered all the elders (v. 29) and went into the house of God for a public reading of the Book of the Covenant (v. 30). Thereafter, he made a renewed covenant with all the inhabitants of Jerusalem *"...to follow the Lord, and to keep His commandments and His testimonies and His statutes with all his heart and all his soul, to perform the words of the covenant that were written* in the book" (v. 31). The chapter concludes with the following words: "...*all his days they did not depart from following the Lord God of their fathers*" (v. 33b). **What a wonderful example Josiah is for all young people everywhere!**

Remember now your Creator in the days of your youth, *before the difficult days come and the years draw near when you say, "I have no pleasure in them"* (Eccl 12:1). As David has written in his psalms - *"For You are my hope, O Lord God; You are my trust from my youth"* (Psalms 71:5) - **let God be your trust when you are young.**

It is a great decision to seek God earnestly when you're young!

MAY 14   *Bible Reading: Ezra Chapters 1-3*

ELEMENTS OF TRUE WORSHIP

When the builders laid the foundation of the temple of the Lord, the priests stood in their apparel with trumpets, and the Levites, the sons of Asaph, with cymbals, to **praise the Lord,** *according to the ordinance of David king of Israel. And they* **sang responsively, praising and giving thanks to the Lord:** *"For He is good, for His mercy endures forever toward Israel."* *Then all the people* **shouted with a great shout,** *when they praised the Lord, because the foundation of the house of the Lord was laid. But many of the priests and Levites and heads of the fathers' houses, old men who had seen the first temple,* **wept with a loud voice** *when the foundation of this temple was laid before their eyes. Yet* **many shouted aloud for joy,** *so that the people could not discern the noise of the shout of joy from the noise of the weeping of the people, for the people shouted with a loud shout, and* **the sound was heard afar off.** (Ezra 3:10-13)

Cyrus, King of Persia, allowed the captive Jews to return to Jerusalem to rebuild the temple as well as subsidized the journey back to their homeland. It was only by the second month of the second year of their coming to Jerusalem that they could get together to begin the work of temple restoration. When the builders laid the foundations of the temple of God, we can note some elements of true worship that we can adopt in our worship as well:

1.   The priests put on their priestly garments and **blew their trumpets loudly.**

2. The Levites **praised God using cymbals** according the ordinance of King David.

3. The priests and Levites **sang responsively praising and giving thanks to God** for His goodness and for His mercy towards Israel.

4. The entire congregation **shouted with a great shout as they praised God** – the sound was heard from a long distance away.

5. The **older people** (including the priests, Levites and heads of families) **wept with a loud voice** as they became emotionally carried away with the significance of the occasion as they remembered the glory of Solomon's Temple that was destroyed.

6. The **younger people shouted aloud with pure joy** as they could not contain the excitement of anticipation about what God was about to accomplish among them.

Our worship to God should include one or more of the above elements listed above – but the more importantly, **our worship must be sincere.** Worship is an encounter with the living and holy God and **we should worship with reverence for God** (Hebrews 12:28). In worship, we ascribe to the Lord the glory due to Him (Psalm 29:1-2), and we can worship boldly because of Christ's sacrifice on our behalf (Hebrews 10:1-10). **Let us be sincere in our worship to God!**

MAY 15   *Bible Reading: Ezra Chapters 4-6*

GOD WILL TURN EVERY BLOCKADE TO OUR BENEFIT

*"So Zerubbabel the son of Shealtiel and Jeshua the son of Jozadak **rose up and began to build the house of God which is in Jerusalem; and the prophets of God were with them, helping them.**" (Ezra 5:2) "Now the temple was finished on the third day of the month of Adar, which was in the sixth year of the reign of King Darius. Then the children of Israel, the priests and the Levites and the rest of the descendants of the captivity, **celebrated the dedication of this house of God with joy.**"* (Ezra 6:15-16)

When the Jews under the leadership Zerubbabel and Jeshua started building the Temple, the Gentiles in the area of Judah and Jerusalem tried to block the efforts. These were the Samaritans who had been planted in the land of Israel (2 Kings 17) who did not mean to unite in the worship of the Lord according to His word. At first they attempted to join forces and requested that they wanted to be a part of the Temple reconstruction (Ezra 4:1-2). However, Zerubbabel and Jeshua did not allow them to participate as they were wise and discerning. Then these adversaries tried to discourage the people of Judah (v. 4a), troubled the people who were building (v. 4b), and hired counselors to frustrate the building efforts (v. 5). When these attempts still did not succeed, they wrote a letter of accusation against the building efforts (v. 6-16), to which the king responded by promptly halting the construction (v. 17-24).

However, God used prophets Haggai and Zechariah to encourage the leaders (Ezra 5:12) as well as the elders of the Jews to secure permission to resume building the Temple (v. 3-17). In response to this request, King Darius issued a decree for rebuilding the Temple immediately (Ezra 6:1-7). Not only that, the entire cost of rebuilding will be borne by King Darius through the money taken from the taxes of the people (v. 8). All the sacrificial animals and other materials would be provided by the king as well (v. 9-10). If anyone resists the building efforts any more, they would be hanged to death (v. 11-12). *"So the elders of the Jews **built**, and they **prospered** through the prophesying of Haggai the prophet and Zechariah the son of Iddo. And **they built and finished it**, according to the commandment of the God of Israel, and according to the command of Cyrus, Darius, and Artaxerxes king of Persia."* (Ezra 6:14)

This teaches us a very important principle – **when we are doing God's work according to God's plan in God's timetable, God will turn every blockade that comes against our efforts to our benefit. If we are steadfast in our work of God, we will definitely succeed when we put our trust in God.** Today, we are involved in the work of God in building the church of God. Our Lord Jesus Christ has issued this wonderful promise to us: *"...I will build My church, and the gates of Hades shall not prevail against it."* (Matt 16:18). Let us not become intimidated or discouraged by the attacks of Satan, who is our enemy. **Through God's help, let us rise up and do our part without fear in building the church of God** as Zerubbabel and Jeshua did in their time (Ezra 5:2).

Bible Reading: Ezra Chapters 7-10

ACCOMPLISH GREAT THINGS THROUGH GOD'S MIGHTY HAND

*"On the first day of the first month he (Ezra) began his journey from Babylon, and on the first day of the fifth month he came to Jerusalem, **according to the good hand of his God upon him. For Ezra had prepared his heart to seek the Law of the Lord, and to do it, and to teach statutes and ordinances in Israel."** (Ezra 7:9-10)*

About sixty years had passed after the Temple in Jerusalem was completed and dedicated under the leadership of Zerubbabel. During this time the priest Ezra, who was a direct descendant of the High Priest Aaron (Ezra 7:1-5), a skilled scribe and an expert in interpreting the laws of God through Moses, had remained in Babylon to compile a historical record of the Israelites. As Ezra prepared his heart to seek God and do His will, he felt inspired to travel to Jerusalem to teach law to the Jews living there and got permission plus all provisions from King Artaxerxes on this venture. God's mighty hand was upon Ezra, as he explains thus: *"So I was encouraged, as the hand of the Lord my God was upon me; and I gathered leading men of Israel to go up with me."* (Ezra 7:28b).

Ezra found strength and courage knowing that God was with him every step of the way (Ezra 7:9, 10, 28). He sought God through fasting and prayer at the river Ahava for both provision and protection to back up the following words he had spoken to the king earlier: *"The hand of our God is upon all those for good who seek Him, but His power and His wrath are against all those who forsake Him."* (Ezra 8:22b). As Ezra writes his travelogue, the same hand of God delivered him from the enemy and every ambush that would take place during the way: *"Then we departed from the river of Ahava on the twelfth day of the first month, to go to Jerusalem. **And the hand of our God was upon us, and He delivered us from the hand of the enemy and from ambush along the road."** (Ezra 8:31)*

Indeed, Ezra could accomplish great things through God's mighty hand – he led the Jews living in Jerusalem to a great spiritual renewal as they put away their foreign wives, confessed their sins to God and made a covenant to serve God alone (Ezra 10:1-44). We too can accomplish great things for God when we trust God for support and rely on His mighty hand for help.

· **"Behold, the Lord's hand is not shortened, that it cannot save; nor His ear heavy, that it cannot hear."** (Isaiah 59:1)

· **"Fear not, for I am with you; be not dismayed, for I am your God. I will strengthen you, yes, I will help you, I will uphold you with My righteous right hand."** (Isaiah 41:10)

· **"Therefore humble yourselves under the mighty hand of God, that He may exalt you in due time."** (1 Peter 5:6)

MAY 17   *Bible Reading: Nehemiah Chapters 1-3*

WEEPING OVER THE BROKEN WALLS

It came to pass in the month of Chislev, in the twentieth year, as I (Nehemiah) was in Shushan the citadel, that Hanani one of my brethren came with men from Judah; and I asked them concerning the Jews who had escaped, who had survived the captivity, and concerning Jerusalem. And they said to me, "The survivors who are left from the captivity in the province are there in great distress and reproach. The wall of Jerusalem is also broken down, and its gates are burned with fire." **So it was, when I heard these words that I sat down and wept, and mourned for many days; I was fasting and praying before the God of heaven**. (Neh 1:1-4)

Nehemiah served as the official cupbearer of King Artaxerxes of Babylon even though he was a Jew displaced by the Babylonian captivity. As a high official of the king's court, Nehemiah had immediate access to the king as the king trusted him to serve wine that was not poisoned. Nehemiah had everything that he could ask for – position, worldly success, power, wealth, etc. However, he was concerned about his own people who had survived the Babylonian captivity and lived in Jerusalem. Upon inquiry Nehemiah came to know that the Jews were *greatly distressed* due to the broken wall of Jerusalem and the absence of any gates upon the walls that were burned with fire (Neh 1:1-3).

Upon hearing this terrible news, Nehemiah sat down, wept, mourned, fasted and prayed for many days to God (Neh 1:4-11). This reflects the tender heart of Nehemiah, and the passion that he had for the city of Jerusalem where the temple of God was built. In the absence of a strong wall to surround the city and proper gates to regulate the entry and exit of people, the security of God's temple was compromised. What else could Nehemiah do being away in a foreign country under the authority of a foreign king who had absolute power over him but to weep, fast and pray over this matter? *It is possible that Nehemiah wept and prayed over this matter for over three months at least* – from the time he heard the bad news in the month of Kislev ~ Nov/Dec (Neh 1:1) to the time he presented his burden to the king in the month of Nissan ~ Mar/Apr (Neh 2:1). While Nehemiah *prayed*, God enlightened him with a *plan* and he could thoroughly *prepare* himself before he showed himself sorrowful to the king. That was the reason why Nehemiah had a plan of action ready when the king asked him what he needed to alleviate his distress (Neh 2:5-8).

Like Nehemiah, we should also feel the burden and weep concerning the broken walls of God's kingdom and work towards improving the current situation. Our Lord Jesus Christ had promised us: *"...I will build My church, and the gates of Hades shall not prevail against it."* (Matt 16:18). However, lately we are seeing much causality in the body of Christ. Immorality, politics and compromise are rampant within the church leadership and laity. How true is the following statement? - *"Whoever has no rule over his own spirit is like a city broken down, without walls."* (Prov 25:28). **It is high time for us to weep over the broken walls and work towards rebuilding them like Nehemiah did in his time!**

MAY 18   *Bible Reading: Nehemiah Chapters 4-6*

WATCH OUT FOR YOUR ENEMY'S ATTACK

*"And it happened, when our enemies heard that it was known to us, and that God had brought their plot to nothing, that **all of us returned to the wall, everyone to his work**. So it was, from that time on, that half of my servants worked at construction, while the **other half held the spears, the shields, the bows, and wore armor; and the leaders were behind all the house of Judah**. Those who built on the wall, and those who carried burdens, **loaded themselves so that with one hand***

they worked at construction, and with the other held a weapon. Every one of the builders had his sword girded at his side as he built. And the one who sounded the trumpet was beside me." (Neh 4:15-18)

From the time Nehemiah started rebuilding the wall of Jerusalem, he started experiencing a constant attack of some enemies including Sanballat the Horonite, Tobiah the Ammonite official and Geshem the Arab (Neh 2:19). Here's the chronology of the events showing the way they reacted and schemed together to thwart the work of God from the very beginning:

1. When they heard that the walls of Jerusalem were being rebuilt, *they were deeply disturbed* (Neh 2:10).

2. They *laughed* at Nehemiah and the Jews who were engaged in the construction efforts and *despised them with taunting words* that they were rebelling against the king (Neh 2:19)

3. When they got the report that the walls were still being rebuilt, *they were furious and very indignant,* and they *mocked* the Jews who were engaged in this task (Neh 4:1).

4. They became so *angry* that they *conspired together to come and attack Jerusalem and create confusion* (Neh 4:7). Their objective was to kill the Jews and cause the rebuilding work to stop (Neh 4:11).

5. They *called for a 'peace' meeting* with Nehemiah with the *intention of harming him bodily* (Neh 6:1-2).

6. When Nehemiah refused to meet with them, they *hired a secret informer* called Shemaiah to *prophesy falsely* against Nehemiah in order to make him afraid and sin against God. Then they would flash this news around and discredit Nehemiah among all the Jews (Neh 6:10-13).

7. Finally, *they were so disheartened by their failed attempts* to dissuade Nehemiah from his tasks (Neh 6:16) that *they sent letters* to Nehemiah *to scare him into giving up* (Neh 6:19b).

In spite of all these attempts, Nehemiah stood firm and escaped the clutches of his enemies with God's help.

We must watch out always against the attack of Satan, our spiritual enemy. Do not expect that our warfare will be over until our earthly work is ended. The word of God is the sword of the Spirit, which we should always have at hand in our conflicts as Christians. Every true

Christian is both a laborer and a soldier, working with one hand, and fighting with the other. Satan fears to attack the watchful Christian, and if he attacks we can be assured that our Lord will fight for us. Thus must we wait until our life's journey ends when we shall be welcomed to the rest and joy of our Lord!

- *"Put on the whole armor of God that you may be able to stand against the wiles of the devil."* (Eph 6:11)
- *"Be sober; be vigilant; because your adversary the devil walks about like a roaring lion, seeking whom he may devour. Resist him, steadfast in the faith, knowing that the same sufferings are experienced by your brotherhood in the world."* (1 Peter 5:8-9)

MAY 19   *Bible Reading: Nehemiah Chapters 7-9*

GUARDING THE DOORS OF OUR LIVES

And I (Nehemiah) said to them, **"Do not let the gates of Jerusalem be opened until the sun is hot; and while they stand guard, let them shut and bar the doors; and appoint guards from among the inhabitants of Jerusalem, one at his watch station and another in front of his own house."** (Neh 7:3)

Bruce Wilkinson says this about Ezra and Nehemiah..."*While Ezra deals primarily with the religious restoration of God's people, Nehemiah is concerned with the political, geographical, and economic restoration. The first seven chapters (of the book of Nehemiah) are devoted to the rebuilding of Jerusalem's walls because Jerusalem was the political and spiritual center of God's people. Without walls, Jerusalem could hardly be considered a city at all. Ezra and Nehemiah worked together to rebuild the people spiritually and morally so that the restoration would be complete.*"

The focus of rebuilding activities in Nehemiah is on the walls of Jerusalem. The walls of the city had lain in ruins since 586 B.C. Then Nebuchadnezzar, king of Babylon, had breached them, entered Jerusalem, burned the temple, carried most of the remaining Jews off to Babylon, and knocked the walls down. Consequently the few Jews who remained could not defend themselves (2 Kings 25:1-11). The returned exiles had attempted to rebuild the walls in or shortly after

458 B.C., but that project had failed because of local opposition (Ezra 4:12, 23). However, despite much opposition from Sanballat, Tobiah and Geshem, Nehemiah and the Jews had now finally rebuilt the walls of Jerusalem and hung the doors securing the city.

Nehemiah, having finished the wall, returned to the Persian court, and came to Jerusalem again with a new commission. He knew that the safety of a city, under God, depends more upon the inhabitants than upon its walls. That is the reason that he instructed his brother Hanani and Hananiah (the leader of the citadel) that they should take utmost care to shut the gates of Jerusalem and stand guard both at the watch station and in front of every house. Only the doors should be opened during clear and broad daylight when the people are ready in case of an assault from the enemy. (Neh 7:2-3). As Isaiah 62:6 tell us: *"I have set watchmen on your walls, O Jerusalem; they shall never hold their peace day or night. You who make mention of the Lord, do not keep silent."*

We need to understand that our safety depends on how well we guard ourselves and our family against sin. We should always guard the doors of our lives, and not allow Satan to make any inroads as we set our minds on things above and not on things on the earth (Col 3:2). Let's pay attention to the following words as we guard the doors of our lives: *"Therefore put to death your members which are on the earth: fornication, uncleanness, passion, evil desire, and covetousness, which is idolatry. Because of these things the wrath of God is coming upon the sons of disobedience, in which you yourselves once walked when you lived in them. But now you yourselves are to put off all these: anger, wrath, malice, blasphemy, filthy language out of your mouth. Do not lie to one another, since you have put off the old man with his deeds, and have put on the new man who is renewed in knowledge according to the image of Him who created him."* (Col 3:5-10)

MAY 20   *Bible Reading: Nehemiah Chapters 10-13*

RENEWING OUR COVENANT & COMMITMENT WITH GOD

"We make a sure covenant, and write it; our leaders, our Levites, and our priests seal it" (Neh 9:38). *"Now the rest of the people—the priests, the Levites, the gatekeepers, the singers, the Nethinim, and all*

*those who had separated themselves from the peoples of the lands to the Law of God, their wives, their sons, and their daughters, everyone who had knowledge and understanding— **these joined with their brethren, their nobles, and entered into a curse and an oath to walk in God's Law, which was given by Moses the servant of God, and to observe and do all the commandments of the Lord our Lord, and His ordinances and His statutes.***" (Neh 10:28-29)

The privilege of leading the nation of Israel in covenant renewal fell to the Levites who are listed in Neh 9:5 *with a notable omission of Nehemiah.* After exhorting the crowd to stand and praise the Lord, they addressed Him in prayer, recognizing His incomparability and glory. The prayer itself follows, at least in a general way, the pattern of covenant texts found elsewhere in the Old Testament and in the ancient Near East as well. After this lengthy prayer devoted primarily to the dismal history of Israel's past failures contrasted with the unlimited patience and grace of God, the secular and religious leaders led by Nehemiah whose names appear in Neh 10:1–27 affixed their signatures to the covenant text, the provisions of which follow in Neh 10:28–39.

In what appears to be a univocal response, all segments of the community pledged themselves to keep all the terms of the Law that God had revealed to Moses long before (Neh 10:28–29). Addressing an issue that Ezra had already dealt with, they promised never again to intermarry with the heathen (Neh 10:30; Ezra 9:1–10:44). Besides this, they vowed to honor the Sabbath, to pay the required temple taxes, to offer the first fruits of their labor, and to care for the needs of the Levites (Neh. 10:31–39).

During our spiritual life journey, there are times when we veer away from the race that is set for us (Heb 12:1). **At these times, more importantly, we need to renew our covenant with God.** Just like a married couple renews their marriage vows and reaffirms their commitment to each other, we also need to pause at times and renew our commitment to follow God and be faithful to our heavenly calling. God remembers His covenant with us all the time, as it says in Psalms 105:8-11: *He remembers His covenant forever, the word which He commanded, for a thousand generations, the covenant which He made with Abraham, and His oath to Isaac, and confirmed it to Jacob for a statute, to Israel as an everlasting covenant, saying, "To you I will give the land of Canaan as the allotment of your inheritance".*

187

God is ever mindful of His covenant with us: *"He has given food to those who fear Him; He will ever be mindful of His covenant"* (Psalms 111:5). **From our end, let us renew our commitment and covenant with Him today!**

MAY 21   *Bible Reading: Esther Chapters 1-3*

GOD HAS CHOSEN US TO FULFILL HIS GREATER PLANS

*"**And Esther obtained favor in the sight of all who saw her.** So Esther was taken to King Ahasuerus, into his royal palace, in the tenth month, which is the month of Tebeth, in the seventh year of his reign. **The king loved Esther more than all the other women, and she obtained grace and favor in his sight more than all the virgins**; so he set the royal crown upon her head and made her queen instead of Vashti."* (Esther 2:15-17)

The Jews had been in exile for many years in the land of Babylon. When power changed to the hands of the Persians, they were still there. At the beginning of the story of Esther, the King of Persia is displeased with his queen, and removes her from her royal position. Advisors suggest that all the fairest young maidens in the land be brought to the King over a period of time that he might choose a new queen from among them.

A young Jewess Hadassah, whose Persian name is Esther, is among the young maidens brought to the palace. At the insistence of her guardian, Uncle Mordecai, she conceals her national identity. After winning the favor of the King, she becomes Queen. The mystery of why Esther was chosen as the queen among all the other beautiful young women is only revealed at the end of this narrative where God is not mentioned – not even once! However, God was working behind the scenes all the time to thwart the schemes of the enemy to annihilate His children. Esther, who was barely out of girlhood, was thrust into a setting where she ultimately had influence with one of the most powerful men in the world, King Xerxes of Persia.

God has sometimes used armies and sometimes performed spectacular miracles in order to rescue His children. But He is not limited to those strategies. He can just as easily use one obscure person

– like Joseph or Esther - and manipulate the circumstances around them to allow them to be the agent of His salvation. God can use young women, like Esther, just as easily as young warriors, like David, to accomplish His plans for His people.

We can serve God and fulfill the role that He called us even in an environment where everyone around us is ungodly. It is more important for us to understand that God chooses us to fulfill His greater plans that we cannot even comprehend. This is what our Lord Jesus has told us: *"You did not choose Me, but I chose you and appointed you that you should go and bear fruit, and that your fruit should remain, that whatever you ask the Father in My name He may give you."* (John 15:16)

Like Esther, if we are sensitive to God's greater purposes in our lives, we can be a blessing to others and effective in the kingdom of God. Let us be content where God has placed us and serve Him faithfully with the best of our abilities!

"Let each one remain in the same calling in which he was called. Were you called while a slave? Do not be concerned about it; but if you can be made free, rather use it. For he who is called in the Lord while a slave is the Lord's freedman. Likewise he who is called while free is Christ's slave. You were bought at a price; do not become slaves of men. Brethren, let each one remain with God in that state in which he was called." (1 Cor 7:20-24)

MAY 22 *Bible Reading: Esther Chapters 4-6*

CHOOSING TO SERVE GOD FAITHFULLY

Mordecai told them to answer Esther: "Do not think in your heart that you will escape in the king's palace any more than all the other Jews. ***For if you remain completely silent at this time, relief and deliverance will arise for the Jews from another place, but you and your father's house will perish. Yet who knows whether you have come to the kingdom for such a time as this?"*** *Then Esther told them to reply to Mordecai: "Go, gather all the Jews who are present in Shushan, and fast for me; neither eat nor drink for three days, night or day. My maids and I will fast likewise.* ***And so I will go to the king, which is against the law; and if I perish, I perish!"*** *(Esther 4:13-16)*

189

Chapter 4 tells us about the agony of Mordecai and Esther after they came to know that the king had ordered upon the persuasion of the wicked Haman to kill all the Jews. Mordecai urged Esther to intercede on behalf of the Jews (v. 13). Esther realized that God had placed her as queen for this reason, and she finally resolves that she will come out of her own "closet," and try to use her influence with the King to stop the slaughter of the Jews. There's only one small problem. By law, even Queen Esther was expected never to initiate contact with the King sitting in his court, unless summoned (v. 10-11). His advisors and sycophants had seen to that – that no one could approach the King unless summoned, on pain of death! But Esther resolves to risk her life for her people!

Why would a beautiful young queen decide to do so, to take such an enormous risk in "lobbying" the King to stop the slaughter of her people—the people she had conveniently declined to identify with once she had been chosen as Queen? Esther fasted for three days and nights before she approached the king (v. 15-16) and we see that God granted her favor before the king when she approached him publicly in court (Esther 5:2).

This episode teaches us an important lesson: **there are times we must take a stand for the good against the evil, even if it is at great cost or great risk.** Every day we are being urged to take the moral high ground, live what is right, not wrong, and when necessary speak the truth to people of power even if we personally must suffer for it. When we do that, God may work a miracle on our behalf - like the case of Esther who found favor from the king or, the three young men who escaped the fiery furnace in the book of Daniel. However, God may also keep silent at times – like in the case of His only begotten Son Jesus Christ who stood before Pilate but was crucified on the cross or, the Lutheran theologian Dietrich Bonhoeffer who stood up to Adolf Hitler and was executed for his faith.

We must realize that we may have been placed where we are for such a times as this! Whether we are great or small, or think ourselves too insignificant or too important, we should ask ourselves, *"Has God placed me where I am to do the right thing, to take the risk, to stand up or stand out so that the day might be saved?"* The answer is a resounding "YES". **Whatever happens to us personally, like Esther, let's choose to serve God faithfully…!!!**

Bible Reading: Esther Chapters 7-10

WE WILL REAP WHAT WE SOW

"You have plowed wickedness; you have reaped iniquity. You have eaten the fruit of lies, because you trusted in your own way, in the multitude of your mighty men." (Hosea 10:13)

The above verse from the book of Hosea aptly describes Haman, the enemy of the Jews. Out of the wickedness in his heart, he had devised and attempted to annihilate all the Jews in the province by taking advantage of the king's naivety. However, God used Queen Esther to destroy the schemes of the enemy Haman.

At the banquet that Esther had prepared for King Ahasuerus and Haman, she revealed her true identity and begged the king for her life and the lives of her people (Esther 7:3-4). When the king asked her to reveal who was responsible for this dastardly act, Esther pointed to Haman as the cause of her grief. As Haman began to beg Esther for forgiveness he fell on her couch in sheer desperation causing the King to accuse him of attacking the Queen. Haman was immediately taken to be hung to death - on the very gallows that he had built for Mordecai. Also, his ten sons were also hanged on the gallows later (Esther 9:13-14). Haman had indeed reaped what he sowed!

Mordecai received Haman's official position and all his property. A proclamation was issued allowing all the Jews to defend themselves and because of Mordecai's new position, they even received help from non-Jews. So on the day that Haman had planned for the annihilation of the Jewish nation, all the enemies of the Jews were destroyed. *"On the day that the enemies of the Jews had hoped to overpower them, the opposite occurred, in that the Jews themselves overpowered those who hated them."* (Esther 9:1) This victorious day is still celebrated as Purim every year on the 14th and 15th days of Adar on the Jewish calendar. An annual feast and celebration is held to honor God for delivering the Jews from their enemies. *Clearly, God had perfect timing in arranging the events of Esther's life, showing His faithful care of His chosen people!*

One thing that we can learn from these series of events is that we will reap what we sow – this is the law of God. *"Those who sow in tears shall reap in joy. He, who continually goes forth weeping, bearing seed for sowing, shall doubtless come again with rejoicing, bringing his sheaves with him"* (Psalms 126:5-6).

Let us turn back to the book of Hosea to understand what God truly wants from our lives: *"Sow for yourselves righteousness; reap in mercy; break up your fallow ground, for it is time to seek the Lord, till He comes and rains righteousness on you."* (Hosea 10:12)

MAY 24   *Bible Reading: Job Chapters 1-3*

"HAVE A DIFFERENT PERSPECTIVE OF LIFE"

Job was an extremely wealthy and influential man who lived in the land of Uz that was located in northern Arabia. At a time when one's wealth is assessed by livestock, Job's enormous wealth and position is described in Job 1:3: *"Also, his possessions were seven thousand sheep, three thousand camels, five hundred yoke of oxen, five hundred female donkeys, and a very large household, so that **this man was the greatest of all the people of the East**"* (Job 1:3). Job's patriarchal family-clan and the offering of sacrifice by Job as the head of the family (rather than a priest) indicate that Job lived during a time period before the Exodus of the Israelites. It is probable that Job was a contemporary of Abraham.

However, more significantly Job is described as *"blameless and upright"* and as *"one who feared God and shunned evil"* (Job 1:1). He was a good father of his ten children, and loved them enough to pray and intercede daily for them (Job 1:5). **It was when calamity struck Job head-on due to no fault of his life that we are able to understand that Job had an entirely different perspective of life.**

When Job lost all his ten children and his entire livestock all within a matter of hours, we can see how Job reacted to this tragedy: ***Then Job arose, tore his robe, and shaved his head; and he fell to the ground and worshiped. And he said: "Naked I came from my mother's womb, and naked shall I return there. The Lord gave, and the Lord has taken away; blessed be the name of the Lord." In all this Job did not sin nor charge God with wrong.*** (Job 1:20-22) Job was aware of three important aspects of his life:

1. He came into this world carrying nothing and he will leave this world carrying nothing.

2. Everything that he had was a gift of God from His bounty. "Blessed be the name of God".

3. The God who has gifted him can also take it back as well. "Blessed be the name of God".

After this, the intensity of Job's problems increased when God allowed Satan to inflict Job with painful boils (Job 2:7). This was when Job's wife instead of being a *'helper'* to him (Gen 2:20) suggested that he should *'curse God and die'*: **Then his wife said to him,** *"Do you still hold fast to your* **integrity?** *Curse God and die!"* *But he said to her, "You speak as one of the foolish women speaks.* **Shall we indeed accept good from God, and shall we not accept adversity?"** **In all this Job did not sin with his lips.** (Job 2:9-10). Here again Job's perspective towards life is reflected – **he was willing to accept both good and bad from God with complaining or rebelling**.

Job was willing to accept adversity that came to his life along with the good things that he had enjoyed earlier from God (compare Job 1: 10 with Job 2:10). The Apostle Paul also learned to rejoice both in plenty and in want (Phil 4:10-13). Let us have a different perspective in life – like that of Job and Apostle Paul. Let us know that God is working everything good in our lives – whether good or bad. *"And we know that all things work together for good to those who love God, to those who are the called according to His purpose."* (Romans 8:28)

MAY 25 *Bible Reading: Job Chapters 4-6*

DO TROUBLES ORIGINATE FROM OUR PAST SINS ONLY?

"Behold, happy is the man whom God corrects; therefore do not despise the chastening of the Almighty. For He bruises, but He binds up; He wounds, but His hands make whole. He shall deliver you in six troubles, yes; in seven no evil shall touch you." (Words of Eliphaz to Job in 5:17-19)

After sitting silent for seven days and nights, Job opened his mouth and started out by publicly cursing the day of his birth (Job 3:1). This reaction to his suffering is the same that Jeremiah also would emulate later (Jer. 20:14–18). Job intensified his anguish by wishing that he would be born dead in his mother's womb (Job 3:11). To have been stillborn at birth would have been better (Job 3:11–19). Since that option was impossible, Job finally longed for death (Job 3:20–26).

Job's first respondent, Eliphaz, was from Teman in the Arabian Desert (see Job 2:11; 6:19). He first rebuked Job for his lack of composure in difficulty, especially since Job himself had comforted others in similar circumstances (4:1–4). But he then drove straight to the heart of the issue: **No one ever suffered or died prematurely without sin having brought it on.** Job therefore must have sinned (Job 4:5–11). Sinners suffer because they sin; to say otherwise is to assert that God is not just (Job 4:12–21).

Continuing his charge against Job, Eliphaz became more personal in his accusations. He had seen people who started out well but their world came crashing down later because of their sin. They suffered calamities similar to those of Job, which could not be attributed to *"bad luck"* or external causes. This is definitely God's judgment for sin in Job's life (Job 5:1–7). The only solution for Job, Eliphaz said, was for him to turn back to God (Job 5:8–16). What God did in Job's case, Eliphaz implied, was to bring suffering into his life as an alarm to help him come to grips with the reality of his sin. If Job would make things right with God, he would once more enjoy the blessing of many children and abundant riches (Job 5:17–27).

The question before us is this - do our troubles originate from past sins only? **The answer is a resounding "NO".** We know that Job was a righteous man as asserted in Job 1:1 and Ezekiel 14:14, 20. **His troubles were NOT as a result of his past sins.**

Our Lord Jesus Christ also answers this question very clearly as seen in the passage below: *"There were present at that season some who told Him about the Galileans whose blood Pilate had mingled with their sacrifices. And Jesus answered and said to them, "Do you suppose that these Galileans were worse sinners than all other Galileans, because they suffered such things?* **I tell you, no; but unless you repent you will all likewise perish.** *Or those eighteen on whom the tower in Siloam fell and killed them, do you think that they were worse sinners than all other men who dwelt in Jerusalem?* **I tell you, no; but unless you repent you will all likewise perish."** (Luke 13:1–5).

Let us always remember that our troubles DO NOT originate from our past sins ONLY...!!!

Bible Reading: Job Chapters 7-9

SEIZE OPPORTUNITIES DURING OUR LIFETIME!

*"As the cloud disappears and vanishes away, so he who goes down to the grave **does not come up**. He shall **never return** to his house, **nor shall his place know him anymore**."* (Job 7:9-10)

In his response to Eliphaz, Job compares life to a term of service whose end is something to be desired (Job 7:1–2). In his case, life was so burdensome that it seems to lack any meaning or purpose (vv. 3–4). Yet Job was acutely aware that life was fragile, slipping away from him towards certain and gloomy destination (vv. 5–8). He would soon move into another realm, one from which he would never return (vv. 9–10).

Such plain truth as the brevity of our life and the certainty of our death will enlighten us when we use this in our daily life application. Glorified saints shall no more return to the cares and sorrows of their homes; nor condemned sinners to their worldly pleasures. We should secure a better place for us before we die. To do that, we should seize every opportunity that is presented to us. Recently I heard a wonderful statement that is worth repeating here: *"An opportunity of a lifetime should be seized during the lifetime of that opportunity"*. At times, God opens certain doors and windows of opportunity in our lives. We need to seize those chances and attempt to do great things for God and His kingdom!

The great Apologist **C.S. Lewis** has once said like this: *"We are like eggs at present. We cannot go indefinitely being just an ordinary 'decent' egg. We must be hatched or go bad"*. With God's help, let us boldly seize today – 'Carpe diem' - and make our lives extraordinary! Let us boldly declare with Apostle Paul: *"I can do all things through Christ who strengthens me."* (Phil 4:13)

TRUST IN THE WISDOM AND SOVEREINTY OF GOD

"But now ask the beasts, and they will teach you; and the birds of the air, and they will tell you; or speak to the earth, and it will teach you; and the fish of the sea will explain to you. Who among all these does not know that the hand of the Lord has done this, in whose hand is the life of every living thing, and the breath of all mankind? Does not the ear test words and the mouth taste its food? Wisdom is with aged men, and with length of days, understanding. **With Him are wisdom and strength, He has counsel and understanding.***"* (Job 12:7-13)

In Job chapter 11, Zophar launched a personal attack on Job himself by calling him a hypocrite for protesting his innocence in the face of contrary evidence (vv. 1–6). Without any sympathy, Zophar tried to convince Job that his troubles stemmed from hidden sin, and God was punishing Job as a result of his sin. He also contended that Job lacked a healthy respect for the wisdom of God, the omniscient One who knows all about human wickedness despite efforts to conceal it (vv. 7–12).

As a rejoinder, Job wishes his miserable friends could understand that disaster often comes on those least prepared and least deserving of it (Job 12:4–6). Then Job reflected on the sovereign ways of God that are manifest in **nature** (vv. 7–9) and in **man's very existence** (v. 10). In the light of this lofty concept, the arguments of Job's friends appeared to be shallow (vv. 11–12). The only way Job could explain his condition was that God's omniscience and omnipotence were incomprehensible with respect to **nature** (vv. 13–15), **individuals** (vv. 16–21), the **mysteries of the unseen** (v. 22), and the **affairs of whole nations** (vv. 23–25).

God Himself tells us this unchanging reality: *"For My thoughts are not your thoughts, nor are your ways My ways," says the Lord. "For as the heavens are higher than the earth, so are My ways higher than your ways, and My thoughts than your thoughts."* (Isaiah 55:8-9)

Let us trust in the wisdom and sovereignty of God – in the fact that He is working behind the scenes on our behalf and preparing us to be effective tools in His kingdom!

IT IS BETTER TO TRUST IN GOD – NO MATTER WHAT HAPPENS

*"Though He slay me, **yet will I trust Him**. Even so, I will defend my own ways before Him. **He also shall be my salvation**..."* (Job 13:15-16)

As Job processed his current pitiful situation, **he made a very important decision** that would go a long way in providing him fortitude for his arduous journey ahead. **He purposed to put himself in God's hands despite his ignorance of God's purposes for him.** He could not save himself after all (Job 13:13–14), so no matter what God did to him—even to the point of taking his life—he would trust God completely (vv. 15–16). By thus submitting himself to God, Job was not conceding that his friends' accusations about him were justified. Indeed, he maintained that his defense before them was indisputable (vv. 17–19).

Job then turned to the Lord with **two requests** and **five questions**. He begged for God (a) to take away His hand of wrath and (b) to deliver him from fear (vv. 20–21). He asked God (1) to reveal the gravity of his sins, (2) why God was hiding from him, (3) why God was treating him as an enemy, (4) why God was scaring him who was like a leaf tossed in the wind, and (5) why God was going after him whose life had turned to dry wood (vv. 22–25). To Job it seemed that God had put him in the impossible situation of holding him accountable for misdeeds that He refused to disclose to him (vv. 26–28). Job then concluded that human beings by nature and birth were hopelessly fragile and impaired. Their existence is temporal (Job 14:1–2), and their days were predetermined by God (vv. 3–5). **It was therefore better to trust in God – no matter what happens!**

Job is a good example to emulate – he resolved to trust God even though life had turned sour for him. Even though darkness was on every side, Job decided to look up to the 'light of the world' for guidance and comfort. **During times of intense trouble, let us also resolve to trust in God and wait on Him to act on our behalf.** *"Trust in the Lord with all your heart, and lean not on your own understanding; in all your ways acknowledge Him, and He shall direct your paths. Do not be wise in your own eyes; fear the Lord and depart from evil.* (Prov 3:5-7)

ARE WE 'MISERABLE COMFORTERS' TO OTHERS IN THEIR DISTRESS?

Then Job answered and said: "I have heard many such things; **miserable comforters** *are you all!"* (Job 16:1-2)

Job's three friends had travelled from their home town, from a long distance, to be with Job when they had heard of his adversities. In fact, they had made appointments together to come and mourn with him, and to comfort him (Job 2:11). When they met Job, they could not recognize him due to the physical infirmity that had afflicted him. They wept aloud in sorrow, tore their clothes and sprinkled dust upon themselves as an outward expression of grief (v. 12). They sat down on the ground with Job for seven days and seven nights without speaking a word, seeing that Job's grief was too intensive to be expressed aloud (v. 13).

However, when each of Job's friends started speaking – Eliphaz (Job 4:1-5:27; 15:1-35), Bildad (Job 8:1-22), and Zophar (Job 11:1-20) – the words that came out of their mouths were words of condemnation and not of comfort. Instead of providing relief to Job, they were like inflicting pain to his wounds. To all the previous allegations from his three 'friends' Job simply responded, in essence, *"I've heard it all before - you are all miserable comforters"* (Job 16:2).

In his book *'How to Get Along with Almost Anyone'*, H. Norman Wright has categorized **four** different kinds of people who express various forms of destructive criticism:

1. First, there are the **'blamers'**. They avoid accepting responsibility for their actions by criticizing other people or blaming past experiences which cannot be changed or undone.

2. Next, there are the **'hurtful jokers'**. Humor is a positive method of relating with others, but hurtful jokers make others the butt of their humor. They specialize in laughing at people instead of laughing with them.

3. Then, there are the **'fault-finders'**. These people have the insatiable need to point out others' defects, but usually do that with a smile and the words, "I'm just trying to be helpful…"

4. Finally, there are the **'cannibals'**. These people do not criticize in a joking manner or settle for mere nitpicking. They go for the jugular…they attack through the most severe forms of personal criticism and put others down with complete disregard of their feelings. These destructive critics are intent in tearing down and manipulating the hurting person.

As children of God, we should never engage in destructive criticism or turn out to be 'miserable comforters' like Job's friends. In fact, Satan engages in these activities, and he is referred to as a **thief** by our Lord Jesus Christ. *"The thief does not come except to steal, and to kill, and to destroy."* (John 10:10). Satan is the **"accuser of God's children"** who accuses them before God day and night (Rev 12:10).

If we are engaged in destructive criticism, let us detest from this activity once and for all. This is what God's word counsels us to do: *"Brethren, if a man is overtaken in any trespass, you who are spiritual restore such a one in a spirit of gentleness, considering yourself lest you also be tempted. Bear one another's burdens, and so fulfill the law of Christ."* (Gal 6:1-2)

Let us never be 'miserable comforters' to others in their distress!

MAY 30   *Bible Reading: Job Chapters 19-21*

TACKLING OUR PROBLEMS WITH A DIFFERENT PERSPECTIVE

"For I know that my Redeemer lives, and He shall stand at last on the earth; and after my skin is destroyed, this I know, that in my flesh I shall see God, whom I shall see for myself, and my eyes shall behold, and not another." (Job 19:25-27)

In the earlier discourses of Job, he had mentioned death (Job 16:18), God (Job 12:13, 16, 18; 13:15-18) and hope in immortality (Job 14:13-17) as possible avenues of redemption from the present tragic reality. While responding to the harsh criticism of Bildad who listed the horrible fate of sinners, it seemed that Job would again respond with despair and self-pity. Job wished first that there could be a present but permanent record testifying to his innocence before God (Job 19:23–24).

However, Job then had a wonderful revelation that boosted his confidence as a ray of hope once more penetrated his gloom. Job became convinced that God was his Redeemer (v. 25) whom he would see some day in the future. In one of the grandest resurrection texts of the Old Testament, Job affirmed that he would survive death and not just in some disembodied form. From within his body he would see God and with literal, physical eyes (vv. 26–27). This passage may be a prophetical reference to the doctrine of bodily resurrection seen in 1 Corinthians 15.

What we can understand here is that Job feels that he will be vindicated after death through a bodily resurrection. We know that this truth was made possible into reality when our Lord Jesus Christ rose from the dead. Resurrection, then, is necessary not only to ensure unending life but also to certify the fact that our God is just. If there is no resolution of moral inequities in this life, there must be one in the life to come. Otherwise, God is not fair, which is an unthinkable conclusion.

Like Job, let us tackle our problems with a different perspective. Let us pay close attention to what Apostle Paul speaks about this matter:

- *"For I consider that the sufferings of this present time are not worthy to be compared with the glory which shall be revealed in us. For the earnest expectation of the creation eagerly waits for the revealing of the sons of God. For the creation was subjected to futility, not willingly, but because of Him who subjected it in hope; because the creation itself also will be delivered from the bondage of corruption into the glorious liberty of the children of God."* (Romans 8:18-21)

- *"Therefore we do not lose heart. Even though our outward man is perishing, yet the inward man is being renewed day by day. **For our light affliction, which is but for a moment, is working for us a far more exceeding and eternal weight of glory,** while we do not look at the things which are seen, but at the things which are not seen. For the things which are seen are temporary, but the things which are not seen are eternal."* (2 Cor 4:16-18)

- *But we speak the wisdom of God in a mystery, the hidden wisdom which God ordained before the ages for our glory, which none of the rulers of this age knew; for had they known, they would not* *have crucified the Lord of glory. But as it is written: **"Eye has not seen, nor ear heard, nor have entered into the heart of man the things which God has prepared for those who love Him."** But God has revealed them to us through His Spirit. For the Spirit searches all things, yes, the deep things of God.* (1 Cor 2:7-10)

MAY 31   *Bible Reading: Job Chapters 22-24*

TRACE THE HEART OF GOD WHEN YOU CANNOT SEE HIM

*"Look, I go forward, but He is not there, and backward, but I cannot perceive Him; when He works on the left hand, I cannot behold Him; when He turns to the right hand, I cannot see Him. **But He knows the way that I take; when He has tested me, I shall come forth as gold.**"* (Job 23:8-10)

Eliphaz exhorted Job to admit that his sufferings resulted from sin (Job 22:1-11) to which Job disagreed. However, when Eliphaz reminded that God is in heaven (v. 12) - this statement may have triggered Job's lament about God's inaccessibility. First of all, Job wanted to make it clear that his suffering was even worse than it appeared or than he could describe (Job 23:1–2). This made it all the more urgent that he be able to confront God in a legal setting and arrive at a fair resolution of his case. Job believed that if only he could meet God face to face, he could persuade Him of his innocence (vv. 3–7). Of course, that was not possible, as Job could not see God anywhere he turned – whether it was forward or backward or at his left hand or at his right hand (vv. 8–9).

When Job could not see God around him, he then traced the heart of God. In the very next statement Job declared that God *knows* the way that he is taking at this time. Job then hit the core of his problems so far – **God was testing him as gold is tested through all his afflictions**. However, he will surely come out his distress one day – more valuable and more precious - free from all his impurities.

Here are three precious lessons that we can learn from Job's life:

1. At the most difficult times, we should trace the heart of God even when we cannot visualize His presence anywhere around us.

2. God will provide us the strength and comfort to see us through our troubles.

3. God will also intervene in our lives and with His peace fill up the place that is emptied of the comforts of this life.

*"Be anxious for nothing, but in everything by prayer and supplication, with thanksgiving, let your requests be made known to God; **and the peace of God, which surpasses all understanding, will guard your hearts and minds through Christ Jesus.**"* (Phil 4:6-7)

*"Cast your burden on the Lord, and **He shall sustain you; He shall <u>never</u> permit the righteous to be moved.**"* (Psalms 55:22)

June

Bible Reading: Job Chapters 25-27

MAINTAINING OUR INTEGRITY ALWAYS

*Moreover Job continued his discourse, and said: "As God lives, who has taken away my justice, and the Almighty, who has made my soul bitter, as long as my breath is in me, and the breath of God in my nostrils, **my lips will not speak wickedness, nor my tongue utter deceit**."* (Job 27:1-4)

Job had lost everything that was important in his life – his wealth, his children and even his health. Even his wife had turned her back on him, and had suggested that he *"curse God and die"* (Job 2:9). His friends added salt to his wounds through their accusations and vain philosophy. Everything was dark around Job's life as he realized that God had allowed all these afflictions to happen in his life. However, Job still maintained his integrity as he vowed to himself that he will not speak any wickedness or deceitful words to God in any form of accusation.

When things go wrong in our life, our first tendency is to accuse God for allowing bad things to happen to us. However, Job stands out as a good example who would not speak any wickedness in times of trouble. We can see other examples in the scriptures as well – Joseph and Daniel in the Old Testament and our Lord Jesus Christ in the New Testament who maintained their integrity as they faced great evil in their lives.

Let us maintain our integrity always – no matter what happens in our lives!

"...But with the humble is wisdom. The integrity of the upright will guide them..." (Prov 11:2-3)

"Blessed is the man who walks not in the counsel of the ungodly, nor stands in the path of sinners, nor sits in the seat of the scornful; but his delight is in the law of the Lord, and in His law he meditates day and night. He shall be like a tree planted by the rivers of water that brings forth its fruit in its season, whose leaf also shall not wither; and whatever he does shall prosper." (Psalms 1:1-3)

JUNE 2   *Bible Reading: Job Chapters 28-30*

SEEKING GODLY WISDOM IN OUR LIVES

"But where can wisdom be found? And where is the place of understanding? *Man does not know its value, nor is it found in the land of the living. The deep says, 'It is not in me'; and the sea says, 'It is not with me.' It cannot be purchased for gold, nor can silver be weighed for its price. It cannot be valued in the gold of Ophir, in precious onyx or sapphire. Neither gold nor crystal can equal it, nor can it be exchanged for jewelry of fine gold. No mention shall be made of coral or quartz, for the price of wisdom is above rubies. The topaz of Ethiopia cannot equal it, nor can it be valued in pure gold. God understands its way, and He knows its place. And to man He said,* **'Behold, the fear of the Lord, that is wisdom, and to depart from evil is understanding.'"** (Job 28:12-19, 23, 28)

Job continued his long reply to Bildad, and the centerpiece of Job's soliloquy is an exquisite poem on wisdom (chapter 28:12-28). Job claimed that God's wisdom supersedes all human wisdom.

In discussing the source of wisdom, Job used the imagery of mining. Gold, silver, and precious stones lie beneath the earth's surface all the time, but they can be extracted only by lot of human effort. They are hidden from our sight, and therefore are of no practical value until they are found and brought to light (vv. 1–11). The same is true of wisdom. It too lies hidden but even more so than mere stones and metals (vv. 12–14). It is actually far more valuable than these metals (vv. 15–19) precisely because it is so difficult to recover (vv. 20–22).

True wisdom, in fact, cannot be mined from the earth but must come from God, who alone knows where it is to be found (v. 23). We cannot separate godliness from godly wisdom (vv. 23–28; Psalms 111:10; Prov. 1:7). It is only when we fear God, revere and worship Him that we can know anything of godly wisdom. **Let us always seek godly wisdom in our lives!**

Give instruction to a wise man, and he will be still wiser; teach a just man, and he will increase in learning. "The fear of the Lord is the beginning of wisdom, and the knowledge of the Holy One is understanding." (Prov 9:9-10)

JUNE 3   *Bible Reading: Job Chapters 31-33*

THE IMPORTANCE OF SELF-DISCIPLINE

"I have made a covenant with my eyes; why then should I look upon a young woman? Does He (God) not see my ways, and count all my steps? (Job 31:1, 4)

After defending his position before his friend, Job speaks about the self-discipline that he had always maintained so far. Job did not speak anything by way of boasting, but in answer to the charge of hypocrisy. Job understood that the spiritual nature of God's commandments reaches to the thoughts and intents of his heart so Job made certain decisions in his life that evolved out of self-discipline.

In his final defense, Job recounted his life of strict moral integrity (Job 31:1–4). He had been scrupulously honest in all his business dealings (vv. 5–8), had never committed the sin of adultery (vv. 9–12), had treated his servants gently and with respect (vv. 13–15), had met the needs of the poor and needy (vv. 16–23), had resisted the attractions of material wealth (vv. 24–25), had not fallen into idolatry (vv. 26–28), had not engaged in any form of personal revenge (vv. 29–30), was careful to entertain strangers (vv. 31–32), did not conceal his sins from God (vv. 33–34), and did not abuse his stewardship of fields and properties (vv. 35–40).

Job's only regret was that God seemed not to have noticed his life of integrity and self-discipline (vv. 35–37). However, we know that God had noticed that Job *"was blameless and upright, and one who feared God and shunned evil"* (Job 1:1), and the end of the story of Job was much better than the beginning.

As a child of God, it is very important for us to maintain self-discipline in our lives. It is very easy to get tempted by Satan and the pleasures that the world has to offer us. However, the path of sin is very slippery (Psalms 73:18) and we have to set some guards in our lives early on so that we are not drawn away by our desires and enticed to sin (James 1:13-15).

Early on in his ministry in 1948, the famous evangelist Billy Graham and his core leadership team took certain decisions for maintaining self-discipline in four areas listed below:

1. *Financial Accountability*: Billy's team committed themselves to integrity and openness in all their financial dealings.

2. *Sexual Indiscretions*: Due to the possibility as well as the appearance of sexual indiscretions, Billy and his team committed together to guard themselves against sexual sin. Billy committed to never be alone with a woman other than his wife, and made other commitments safe-guarding this purity.

3. *Model of evangelists working in concert with the local churches*: Billy's team committed to work with the local churches wherever possible in the proclamation of the Gospel.

4. Finally, Billy's team noted that many evangelists inflate their numbers to validate their ministry. They *committed to doing their best in accurately reporting crowd size and decisions*. To do otherwise was rooted in pride and had no place in the proclamation of the Gospel.

Due to their adherence to these four major areas of self-discipline, Billy Graham has been used by God to draw millions into God's kingdom. **Let us also realize the importance of self discipline and make the following decision with Apostle Paul**: *"But I discipline my body and bring it into subjection, lest, when I have preached to others, I myself should become disqualified."* (1 Cor 9:27)

JUNE 4   *Bible Reading: Job Chapters 34-36*

DON'T JUMP INTO CONCLUSIONS

*"Therefore listen to me, you men of understanding: Far be it from God to do wickedness, and from the Almighty to commit iniquity. **For He***

repays man according to his work, and makes man to find a reward according to his way." (Job 34:10-11)

Elihu started his long and final discourse with the assertion that the three friends of Job did not have any understanding even though they were many years older than him (Job 32:4). *"Great men are not always wise, nor do the aged always understand justice. Therefore I say, 'Listen to me, I also will declare my opinion.'"* (Job 32:9-10). **However, Elihu also jumped into a conclusion that God repays people according to his work and rewards people on this earth according to their deeds.**

Elihu continued his speech with a scathing criticism of Job's hypocrisy and cynicism. He said he could discern the flavor of Job's speech and could expose it as a feeble attempt at self-justification (Job 34:1–6; 13:18). In reality, however, Job was no better than the sinner who loves to say that it never pays to serve the Lord (Job 34:7–9). Elihu then concluded on a theological ground that since God was holy and just, **the reason for Job's suffering lies with Job himself** (vv. 10–12). God is sovereign over all His creation (vv. 13–15), and so He cannot be coerced or persuaded by earthly rulers to do what is unjust (vv. 16–19). Such beings, powerful as they are, will die, but God lives on, dealing with human beings only as they deserve (v. 20).

The premise of Job's accusation was that Job was suffering because of his past misdeeds. This was wrong because Job was indeed a righteous man and God wanted to prove to Satan that Job would hold fast to his integrity even though he undergoes suffering in his life. At the end of the story, we see that Job was reinstated back to his original position and he got back double of what he had earlier.

Let us be careful that we never jump into any conclusions as to why someone is suffering in this earth. The wisdom and ways of God are beyond our comprehension. *"For My thoughts are not your thoughts, nor are your ways My ways," says the Lord. "For as the heavens are higher than the earth, so are My ways higher than your ways, and My thoughts than your thoughts."* (Isaiah 55:8-9)

Let us know that everything that happens in our lives happens only with the knowledge and plan of God and everything will work out for good at the end. *"And we know that all things work together for good to those who love God, to those who are the called according to His purpose."* (Romans 8:28)

UNDERSTAND AND ACKNOWLEDGE THE GREATNESS OF GOD

Then the Lord answered Job out of the whirlwind, and said: "Who is this who darkens counsel by words without knowledge? Now prepare yourself like a man; I will question you, and you shall answer Me." (Job 38:1-3)

When Job and his friends had said everything they knew with their flawed collective wisdom, God at last had the final word. Job and his *"comforters"* had repeatedly spoken out of a misguided theology that was based on deduction, intuition, observation, and mere feeling. Although there were some correct conclusions and great declarations about God in the earlier discourses of Job and his friends, they had argued based out of flawed premises. God had to speak, in order to allow revelation to correct and clarify the faulty theological arguments of Job and his friends.

God appeared unexpectedly into the scene in a whirlwind - a symbol of *"judgment"* (Psalms 50:3-4) - the same phenomenon associated with the taking of Elijah up into heaven (Job 38:1; 2 Kings 2:1, 11). Then, God engaged Job as though he were on trial in a courtroom, asking challenging questions and demanding appropriate responses (Job 38:2–3). Can Job explain the phenomena of God's *natural* government? If not, how can Job then hope to understand the principles of God's *moral* government?

The dominant theme of God's discourse is that of *divine sovereignty* - the idea that because He is God, everything that He does is just and right - even though we cannot comprehend them with our limited understanding. This *begins* historically with *creation* itself. Turning to Job specifically, God asked where Job was on that momentous occasion (vv. 4–7). Since Job himself did not then exist at that time, Job had nothing to comment. Similarly, Job had nothing to say about the limitation of the seas (vv. 8–11; see Gen. 1:6–10), the ordering of time and seasons (vv. 12–15; see Gen. 1:14–19), and the details of the structure of the cosmos with its perceived layers of compartments (vv. 16–38).

God's questions were not intended to be answered, but only to be acknowledged that God was great, His works were marvelous, and everything under the heavens that He had created belonged to Him alone. God does not owe us anything, which makes the fact that He gave us everything that He had created even more astounding!

When troubles come in our lives, we need to reflect on the greatness of God instead of questioning the justice of God. When Job questioned God's justice as it related to his troubles, God answered Job by telling him to notice the power and might with which He created the world, and to observe God's ability to control every element in this world. **God's power is beyond our understanding. All we need to do is to submit to His divine will and trust God in the midst of the darkness in our lives.**

Let us join with Moses and the Israelites in acknowledging the greatness of God: *"Who is like You, O Lord, among the gods? Who is like You, glorious in holiness, fearful in praises, doing wonders?"* (Exodus 15:11)

JUNE 6   *Bible Reading: Job Chapters 40-42*

SEEING GOD IN THE MIDST OF OUR TRIALS

Then Job answered the Lord and said: "I know that You can do everything, and that no purpose of Yours can be withheld from You...I ***have heard of You by the hearing of the ear, but now my eye sees You.*** *Therefore I abhor myself, and repent in dust and ashes."* (Job 42:1-2, 5-6)

As God Almighty questioned Job within the context of His creation and the wonders of nature that could not be fathomed by a finite human being, Job could truly learn the greatness of God. All his life Job lived as a righteous man and believed in God as well as prayed to God daily. This was based out of a knowledge that he had about God. However, it was in the midst of the storms in his life that Job could actually SEE God...and that was enough for him. All the questions that he had were answered by God through the profound revelation.

When Job saw the greatness of God, he did not have any more words of complaint or self-pity. As Job was brought to his senses by this recounting of God's unfathomable, inexpressible sovereignty, all Job could do is confess that he had spoken out of turn. When he was questioning the activities of God earlier, he should have been praising. What Job thought he knew about God through prior theological knowledge, he now had come to know by experience of revelation. The answer now was obvious—repentance and full trust in his God (Job 42:1–6).

We need to understand that **sometimes the best answers to life's most baffling and troubling questions lie not in what God says, but in who He is.** When we recognize that truth, we will begin to see that God does not just know the answers but, in fact, is the answer. To know Him is to know all one needs to know. We can know God better when we pass through trials and sufferings like Job. We will get more clarity in our life's vision as God will speak to us in the midst of our trials and sufferings. **We can truly see God in the midst of our trials if we look hard for Him and try to listen intently to His still small voice!**

But as it is written: "Eye has not seen, nor ear heard, nor have entered into the heart of man the things which God has prepared for those who love Him." But God has revealed them to us through His Spirit. (1 Cor 2:9-10)

JUNE 7   *Bible Reading: Psalms Chapters 1-9*

MAINTAINING GODLY ROUTINES ON A DAILY BASIS

"Give ear to my words, O Lord, consider my meditation. Give heed to the voice of my cry, my King and my God, for to You I will pray. **My voice You shall hear in the morning, O Lord; in the morning I will direct it to You, and I will look up.***"* (Psalms 5:1-3)

King David was a busy man – he had to take care of the affairs of his kingdom, watch out for people who were looking to unseat him from his throne (incl. his son Absalom who was successful for a short time), take care of his many wives and his multiple children as well as prepare materials for the building of the temple in Jerusalem. However in the midst of his busy daily agenda, he still had time for God and prayer. Early on in his life, he took a very important decision – every day in the morning he will call upon God in prayer. For David, mornings were the appropriate time to praise God and ask for directions (Psalms 5:3). In another Psalms, David has this to say: *"Cause me to hear Your lovingkindness in the morning, for in You do I trust; cause me to know the way in which I should walk, for I lift up my soul to You."* (Psalms 143:8)

Even when King David was in the wilderness, he sought God's help early in the morning: *"O God, You are my God; early will I seek You; my soul thirsts for You; my flesh longs for You in a dry and thirsty land where there is no water. So I have looked for You in the sanctuary, to see Your power and Your glory."* (Psalms 63:1-2)

Godly routines will go a long way in keeping us in the right perspective and help us to achieve great things for the glory of God. Daniel maintained a godly routine of praying three times a day, and he was so faithful that not even a death threat could change his daily routine (Daniel 6:10). God honored Daniel among all his companions because he disciplined himself and gave priority to godly matters.

Let us also spend quality time God daily and give God the first place in our daily routines – He will surely bless us greatly!

JUNE 8   *Bible Reading: Psalms Chapters 10-17*

EXPERIENCING THE 'FULLNESS OF JOY' IN GOD'S PRESENCE

"You will show me the path of life; in Your presence is fullness of joy; at Your right hand are pleasures forevermore." (Psalms 16:11)

King David's prayer reveals his trust and reliance upon God. There are four components in this verse: a guide (God), a traveler (me), a way (path) and an end (life). The guide is but one, the traveler, one; the way one; and the life, the only one. If God is to be our guide, there are **three things that we should do**, which are recorded in this Psalm:

1. Put our trust in God alone (Psalms 16:1)
2. Bless the Lord at all times (Psalms 16:7; 34:1)
3. Set the Lord always before us (Psalms 16:8)

This psalm is about a person who obeys God by putting total confidence in God alone (Psalms 16:1). There is nothing good in our lives except what God has given us (v. 2; James 1:17). When we speak about the virtue of goodness, there are two aspects: *being good* and *doing good*. Goodness is the fruit of walking with God, and the goodness of God is associated with His patience. Further, we should prefer the company of the saints of God (v. 3) and avoid people who do not serve Christ (v. 4). God will then bless us and lead us through the right way (v. 7). He will not leave us in the place of the dead, but will resurrect us into the land of the living (v. 10) – into the very presence of God (v. 11). We will then enjoy the blessings of God in this life and beyond all that we can have confidence in a life to come, one filled with joy and eternal pleasures. Our Lord Jesus Christ being raised from the dead has already ascended into glory, to dwell in constant nearness to God, where joy is at its full for ever – that is the place where we will go one day in the future.

In the meantime, let us experience the fullness of joy in God's presence. When we live close to God, we will truly experience joy in our lives and this will spill over to others as joy is a fruit of the Spirit (Gal. 5:22). *"But let all those rejoice who put their trust in You; let them ever shout for joy, because You defend them; let those also who love Your name be joyful in You."* (Psalms 5:11)

JUNE 9   *Bible Reading: Psalms Chapters 18-22*

APPRECIATE THE GLORY & GOODNESS OF GOD IN NATURE

"The heavens declare the glory of God; and the firmament shows His handiwork. Day unto day utters speech and night unto night reveals knowledge. There is no speech nor language where their voice is not heard." (Psalms 19:1-3)

Psalms 19 is one of the most beautiful hymns penned by King David that praises God for the excellence of all His creative works. This *"general revelation"* by which His power and glory may be seen in the *'works of God'* (vv. 1-6) is complemented by the *"special revelation"* of the *'Word of God'* (vv. 7–9) that enables people to understand Him as One who gives wisdom and who provides a means by which sin can be forgiven for every human being (vv. 10–14).

When we look at nature, we can see that it is a grand symphony conducted by the creator God. The beauty and grandeur of nature can never be surpassed by anything that humans have created so far – just think how God created all that we see around us in just six days by the power of His spoken Word (Gen. 1: 3-31). We should get both visual and hearing stimulus as we see, observe and hear from nature.

However, we should not stop at just appreciating the grandeur of nature but comprehend the **glory of God** – for nature *"declares the glory of God"* (Psalms 19:1). The word *"glory"* in scripture refers to the essential worth, beauty and value, so when we behold nature, we visualize the intrinsic worth, brilliance and the radiant beauty of the Creator God Himself. Not only do we see the glory of God in creation, but we also see the **goodness of God** in creation. *"The Lord is good to all, and His tender mercies are over all His works."* (Psalms 145:9) God is the architect and engineer of all creation. God spoke and His glorious beauty poured out through His creation.

Let us pause a moment from our busy schedules today and tune our hearts to God's creation so that the beauty we see around us in nature may catapult us to praising and glorifying God for His glory and goodness!

· *"The Lord is high above all nations, His glory above the heavens."* (Psalms 113:4)

· *"O Lord, our Lord, how excellent is Your name in all the earth, who have set Your glory above the heavens!"* (Psalms 8:1)

JUNE 10   *Bible Reading: Psalms Chapters 23-31*

HIDING IN THE SECRET PLACE OF GOD FOR REFUGE

*"One thing I have desired of the Lord, that will I seek: that I may dwell in the house of the Lord all the days of my life, to behold the beauty of the Lord, and to inquire in His temple. **For in the time of trouble He shall hide me in His pavilion; in the secret place of His tabernacle He shall hide me**; He shall set me high upon a rock."* (Psalms 27:4-5)

Psalms 27 is a timeless poem written by King David, where he first of all expresses his confidence in God (vv. 1-3) and his love of communion with God in His temple (vv. 4-6). David then concludes with an acknowledgment of the sustaining power of faith in his own case (vv. 7-11), and an exhortation to others to follow his example (vv. 12-14).

There is a place of refuge from the storms of this life, which is called the *'secret place'* (v. 5). This is the place where God hides His beloved – this is the sanctuary of His presence. We can read about this in one of the other prayers of David: *"You shall hide them in the **secret place** of Your presence from the plots of man; You shall keep them secretly in a pavilion from the strife of tongues"* (Psalms 31:20). This was the sanctuary that David looked to see God's power and glory when he was in the wilderness (Psalms 63:1-2). This secret place is like the eye of the storm – an inner sanctuary of peace and tranquility.

In order to dwell in the *'secret place'* of God, there are **six important** principles that we need to remember (based on Psalms 27:1-5):

1. Remember to *have confidence* in God (v. 1)
2. Remember to *commit ourselves* to God (v. 4)
3. Remember to *live near* to God always (v. 4)
4. Remember to *love* God from the heart (v. 4)
5. Remember to *lean on* God during trouble (v. 5)
6. Remember to *take comfort* in God always (v. 5)

When we hide in the secret place of God during trouble, He will secure and protect us from any calamity that might happen in our lives. Let us take assurance from the words of the psalmist: *He who dwells in the secret place of the Most High shall abide under the shadow of the Almighty. I will say of the Lord, "He is my refuge and my fortress; My God, in Him I will trust." Surely He shall deliver you from the snare of the fowler and from the perilous pestilence. He shall cover you with His feathers, and under His wings you shall take refuge; His truth shall be your shield and buckler.* (Psalms 91:1-4)

JUNE 11   *Bible Reading: Psalms Chapters 32-37*

RESTING AND WAITING ON GOD ALONE

*"**Rest in the Lord, and wait patiently for Him**; do not fret because of him who prospers in his way, because of the man who brings wicked schemes to pass. Cease from anger, and forsake wrath; **do not fret**—it*

only causes harm. For evildoers shall be cut off; but those who wait on the Lord, they shall inherit the earth. **Wait on the Lord, and keep His way**, *and He shall exalt you to inherit the land; when the wicked are cut off, you shall see it. Mark the* **blameless man**, *and observe the upright;* **for the future of that man is peace.**" (Psalms 37:7-9, 34, 37)

Despite the unfairness of life, King David prays that he will not retaliate against the evil people but rest in the Lord and wait patiently for God – for God will bring justice in the earth in due time (vv. 7, 9). As we wait patiently on God, we should also stop being angry at our current situation for our anger tends to be vindictive and punitive. On the other hand, God's anger is untainted by self-interest and tempered with mercy. God's wrath can even be His love that brings us to repentance and faith in Him (Romans 12:19, 21).

How do we rest in the Lord? *Listed below are six areas where we can rest upon:*

1. Rest in the *will of God*, for whatever he wills for us is for our highest good (Rom. 12:1-2)

2. Rest in the *love of God*, and meditate on the ultimate sacrifice of our Lord Jesus Christ on the cross (John 3:16).

3. Rest in the *mercy of God*, for it is by His mercies that we are not consumed (Lam 3:22; Psalms 37:26)

4. Rest in the *word of God*, for His word will nourish us and guide us in the path of life (Psalms 23:2; Psalms 119:105)

5. Rest in our *relationship with God*, for He is our heavenly Father after we receive Him into our lives (John 1:14; Romans 8:14-17)

6. Rest in the *Lord Himself* as he guides us continually through the Holy Spirit who indwells us (John 14:26; 15:26; 16:8, 13)

How do we wait upon the Lord? *Consider the three ways listed below:*

· *By pouring our heart to God in prayer* like Hannah (see Psalms 62:1-2, 5-6, 8)

· *By saturating ourselves in the Holy Scriptures* (Psalms 130:5) *and waiting for His direction* like Simeon (Luke 2:25-32)

· *By keeping serving God faithfully* like Anna the prophetess (Luke 2:36-38)

Every day we have a choice how to live every moment. We can live God's way and enjoy His approval or we can live in the worldly way and end up in destroying ourselves. **When we live God's way – by resting and waiting for God alone – we can have peace with God and be in harmony with our surroundings** (Psalms 37:37). We will then enjoy God's favor and we live to please Him alone on this earth!

JUNE 12   *Bible Reading: Psalms Chapters 38-44*

THE ONLY DRINK THAT WILL REALLY SATISFY

*"As the deer pants for the water brooks, so pants my soul for You, O God. **My soul thirsts for God, for the living God**. When shall I come and appear before God?"* (Psalms 42:1-2)

Psalm 42 is a contemplation of the sons of Korah along with several other psalms (44–49). Korah was the great-grandson of Levi who had rebelled against the leadership of the High Priest Aaron (Num. 16:1–2). However, his own sons did not participate in the evil deeds long with their father and others, and ended up as leaders in Israel's worship (1 Chron. 6:32–38).

This psalm is the cry of a person detached from the worship of God in Jerusalem and is now sighing for the house of God. This portrays an intense longing for God and his desire to worship God with others in the temple (Ps. 42:4). This is also the voice of a spiritual believer under depression who is longing for the renewal of the divine presence while struggling with doubts and fears but yet holding on to the faith in the living God.

The psalmist's *"thirst"* for God must be seen not only in the comparison he made *("as the deer pants after streams of water")*, but also against the background of the desert where he was currently. To him, fresh water to drink was not just a refreshing luxury–it was tantamount to staying alive itself! For the psalmist, his thirst for God's presence was comparable to the thirst of a deer dehydrated and craving for a drink of water.

Do we have a similar thirst for God as well? Or, are we satisfied with what the world is offering us so far as substitute 'artificial' drinks?

When Jesus spoke to the Samaritan women by the well in Sychar, this is what he told her: *"Whoever drinks of this water will thirst again, but whoever drinks of the water that I shall give him will never thirst. But the water that I shall give him will become in him a fountain of water springing up into everlasting life."* (John 4:13-14) **The water that Jesus was referring to was the Holy Spirit that He poured on the believers on the Day of Pentecost.** The evidence for that is found in John 7:37-39: *On the last day, that great day of the feast, Jesus stood and cried out, saying, "If anyone thirsts, let him come to Me and drink. He who believes in Me, as the Scripture has said, out of his heart will flow rivers of living water."* **But this He spoke concerning the Spirit, whom those believing in Him would receive; for the Holy Spirit was not yet given, because Jesus was not yet glorified.**

Let us understand that God alone can only satisfy our real thirst. Let us respond to God's invitation: *"Ho! Everyone who thirsts, come to the waters..."* (Isaiah 55:1). For God alone can satisfy our inward longing: *"For He satisfies the longing soul, and fills the hungry soul with goodness."* (Psalms 107:9)

JUNE 13   *Bible Reading: Psalms Chapters 45-51*

REST AND REFOCUS UNDER GOD'S CARE

"Be still, and know that I am God; I will be exalted among the nations, I will be exalted in the earth! The Lord of hosts is with us; the God of Jacob is our refuge." (Psalms 46:10-11)

Psalms 46 is a wonderful poem penned by the sons of Korah that speaks about God, in particular, about His presence (vv. 1-3), His protection (vv. 4-7) and His promise (vv. 8-11). This psalm is a *'Song of Zion'* and is thematically linked to Psalms 47 and 48. This psalm begins with the confession that God is a refuge (v. 1) and this point summarizes the next two main sections as well (vv. 7, 11). So long as God is with His people, they need have no fear (v. 2). Zion itself is secure from all the threats of the nations because of God's role as a defensive fortification (v. 7). This is not a temporary measure for God will usher in a day when all the nations will acknowledge His lordship (v. 10).

Verse 10 exhorts us that we should be still and know that He is God and He will be exalted in the earth. We cannot *try* (requires effort and exertion) to **relax** (requires absence of effort and exertion). We can *'be still'* and rest confidently in God's care as He knows our future – we are safe in His Hands. Elijah heard the *'still small voice'* after great demonstrations of wind, earthquake and fire (1 Kings 19:12). To tune into hearing the *'still small voice'* of God, we must *'be still'* and tune out noises from the world. **We need to quiet our hearts to listen to God as we meditate on His Word.**

Psalms 23:1-3 gives us the following assurance: *"The Lord is my shepherd; I shall not want. He makes me to lie down in green pastures; He leads me beside the still waters. He restores my soul; He leads me in the paths of righteousness for His name's sake."* We need to **know** God as our Good Shepherd who **makes us** lie down in the green pastures of His Word and **leads us** beside the still waters of His Spirit and in the paths of righteousness.

Let us understand one important fact: **God promises rest and refocus for us when we are still and rest confidently in His providential care!**

JUNE 14   *Bible Reading: Psalms Chapters 52-59*

TAKING OUR BURDENS TO GOD IN PRAYER

*"As for me, **I will call upon God**, and the Lord shall save me. Evening and morning and at noon **I will pray, and cry aloud**, and He shall hear my voice."* (Psalms 55:16-17)

Bible scholars have suggested that King David was in a foreign city (away from Jerusalem) when he penned Psalm 55. David complained to God because of "the voice of the enemy" and the "oppression of the wicked" (v. 3). He was burdened and terrified of death (vv. 4-5) and he wanted to flee away from his problems or fly away from the storms in his life (vv. 6-8).

King David's problems happened because he was betrayed, not by anybody but by his trusted friend (vv. 12-14). We can assume that David was referring to the disloyalty of his counselor Ahithophel, whose duplicity contributed to David's having been forced into exile (2 Sam. 15:12; 16:15–23; 17:14). He perhaps was the "friend" referred to in Psalm 55:13. In a strong imprecation David urged God to deal with these traitors as they deserved (v. 15). Their hypocritical professions of friendship were treacherous (vv. 20–21), but God would have the last word, vindicating the righteous and condemning the wicked (vv. 22–23).

At the moment of crisis in his life, King David took his burdens to God in prayer (v. 16). He called for help from God as he prayed and cried aloud at least three times of the day (v. 17). We know that God heard those prayers of David and restored back his kingdom by defeating the counsel of Ahithophel to his son Absalom.

At times when our lives get fragmented as different problems arise in our lives, we should also take our burden to God in prayer. *"Cast your burden on the Lord, and He shall sustain you; He shall **never** permit the righteous to be moved."* (Psalms 55:22) Our prayers can help to defragment our lives, and God will show us what to God and what only He can do for us. God is always available to hear our prayers as He truly cares for us.

Let us remember what our Lord Jesus Christ has promised us: *"Come to Me, all you who labor and are heavy laden, and I will give you rest. Take My yoke upon you and learn from Me, for I am gentle and lowly in heart, and you will find rest for your souls. For My yoke is easy and My burden is light."* (Matt 11:28-30) Let us boldly sing the words of the famous hymn penned by Joseph Scriven:

"What a friend we have in Jesus, All our sins and griefs to bear!

What a privilege to carry, everything to God in prayer!"

JUNE 15　　　　　　　　　*Bible Reading: Psalms Chapters 60-67*

HOW CAN WE BE RICHLY FULFILLED IN OUR LIVES?

*"For You, O God, have tested us; You have refined us as silver is refined. You brought us into the net; You laid affliction on our backs. You have caused men to ride over our heads; we went through fire and through water; **but You brought us out to rich fulfillment.**"* (Psalms 66:10-12)

Psalms 66 is one of the hymns whose author is not specified, but the Bible scholars ascribe this psalm to King David judging by the style and the fact that house of God is mentioned (v. 13). The initial verses (vv. 1-4) calls upon all nations to praise God, while the next set of

219

verses (vv. 5-7) invites us to *"come and see"* the works of the Lord, pointing attention to the Israelites crossing the Red Sea or even crossing the Jordan river. Towards the later part of the psalms (vv. 13-15) the psalmist becomes personal and confesses his own obligations to God. Finally, the psalmist bursts out with a repeated *"come and hear"* as he declares with thanksgiving the special favor of the Lord to himself (vv. 16-20).

Between the passage of *telling others* to worship God (v. 1-9) and *telling himself* what he needs to do (vv. 13-20), we read in verses 10-12 what the psalmist is *telling God*. Like someone describing his past looking at the rearview mirror, the psalmist is telling God how He has tested him to refine him as silver is refined with the objective to remove all the impurities. Malachi 3:3 describes God as someone who *"shall sit as a refiner and purifier of silver."* *"Behold, I have refined you, but not as silver; I have tested you in the furnace of affliction."* (Isaiah 48:10)

The psalmist then describes to God how He has allowed him to be entrapped in the net that the enemy has laid (v. 11a), brought stressful burdens into his life (v. 11b), and caused others to ride over his head (v. 12a). This is an allusion to beasts of burden, particularly to camels, whose heads the rider almost sits over, and so domineers over them as he pleases. Finally the psalmist says that he went through fire and water (v. 12b). Fire is the extremity of heat and dryness; water is the extremity of moistness and coldness. This means that God allowed the psalmist to go through extreme situations. However, **God was with him during his affliction** as His word describes in Isaiah 43:2-3: *"When you pass through the waters, I will be with you; and through the rivers, they shall not overflow you. When you walk through the fire, you shall not be burned, nor shall the flame scorch you. For I am the Lord your God, the Holy One of Israel, your Savior..."*

The end result was that the psalmist found 'rich fulfillment' in the process. Let us also remember that when God allows us to go through trials the end result is that God wants us to be richly fulfilled in our lives.

"In this you greatly rejoice, though now for a little while, if need be, you have been grieved by various trials, that the genuineness of your faith, being much more precious than gold that perishes, though it is tested by fire, **may be found to praise, honor, and glory at the revelation of Jesus Christ,** *whom having not seen you love."* (1 Peter 1:6-8)

Bible Reading: Psalms Chapters 68-71

DECLARING GOD'S POWER TO THE PRESENT GENERATION

"O God, You have taught me from my youth; and to this day I declare Your wondrous works. **Now also when I am old and grayheaded, O God, do not forsake me, until I declare Your strength to this generation, Your power to everyone who is to come."** (Psalms 71:17-18)

Psalm 71 is the testimony of an old man who is reflecting on God's goodness to him over the years but who also had ongoing needs in his old age (v. 9). As he is being threatened by those who would harm him (v. 13), he prays that God will continue to preserve him (v. 18), and promises to proclaim God's name to all who will hear him (v. 16). He then hopes that beyond this life God will vindicate the sufferings of this world with renewed life in the world to come (v. 20). This psalm can be divided into four parts: reflection on the past (vv. 1–6), request for the present (vv. 7–12), resolution for the future (vv. 13–18), and restoration at the end (vv. 19–24).

As the psalmist reflects on his past life, he is aware of one thing – God has taught him many things from his youth. He has gone through different life experiences from his young age until now, and these experiences have taught him lessons that are always useful and important. One of the lessons was that *"God is our refuge and strength, a very present help in trouble"* (Psalm 46:1). Another lesson would be *"The Lord is my shepherd; I shall not want"* (Psalms 23:1). As an old man, the psalmist reflects on the countless ways how God had intervened during his life journey and had taught him invaluable lessons that are so precious to him. He had leaned on God many times and could speak about His all sufficiency to the new generation. So, the psalmist prays to God that he may be able to transmit his testimony to the youth so that they may be trained in the fear of God, and get intimately acquainted with the power of God so that they would be inspired to walk by faith as well.

The best gift that we can give to our present generation is to declare to them the strength and power of God that has worked in our lives. Just like the psalmist requests God to keep him alive until he has declared God's strength to his generation and God's power to the youth, let our prayer be that we too can pass on the lessons that we have learned during our life's journey to our next generation so that they also will follow God intimately. *Truly, that will be our life's greatest achievement!*

Bible Reading: Psalms Chapters 72-77

GET A HEAVENLY PERSPECTIVE FROM GOD'S PRESENCE

"Behold, these are the ungodly, who are always at ease; They increase in riches. Surely I have cleansed my heart in vain, and washed my hands in innocence. For all day long I have been plagued, and chastened every morning. If I had said, I will speak thus, behold, I would have been untrue to the generation of Your children. When I thought how to understand this, it was too painful for me—until I went into the sanctuary of God; then I understood their end. But it is good for me to draw near to God; I have put my trust in the Lord God, that I may declare all Your works." (Psalms 73:12-17, 28)

Psalms 71 is the second psalm ascribed to Asaph and the first of eleven consecutive psalms bearing his name. It is a *wisdom psalm* whose sentiments are similar to Psalm 1 and follows Psalms 37 in content. In this psalm, Asaph explains how he became envious of the prosperous boastful wicked (Psalm 73:3), and admits that in the midst of life's difficulties and dangers he perceived that evil people seem exempt from such things (v. 5). They arrogantly refuse to consider God (v. 11), and they seem to be blessed in spite of such arrogance (v. 12).

However, Asaph decides to go into the sanctuary of God and spend time in His presence and that put everything in the proper perspective. Having come to his senses, Asaph described his change of heart as almost a conversion as he understood what is finally going to happen to the ungodly people (v. 17). He understood that the prosperity of sinners is only a mirage and that they are headed for certain disaster (v. 18). *In reality, the righteous are the ones who are blessed with divine insight and guidance (v. 23–24) as they have hope in both heaven and earth* (v. 25). The righteous must therefore celebrate this hope and share it with others who need it (v. 28).

We need to spend time in God's presence and see everything that is happening around us from God's point of view. *We will get a heavenly perspective of earthly happenings by getting closer to God.* When we visualize everything from God's viewpoint, we will not be jealous at the prosperity of the wicked (like Asaph). Instead, we will praise God for this blessed life and for His promise of the eternal life that He has granted us! *Our God is everything we need – even when life seems unfair!* Like the psalmist, let us take a decision today: *"One thing I have desired of the Lord, that will I seek: that I may dwell in the house of the Lord all the days of my life, to behold the beauty of the Lord, and to inquire in His temple."* (Psalms 27:4)

"Blessed is the man You choose, and cause to approach You, that he may dwell in Your courts. We shall be satisfied with the goodness of Your house, of Your holy temple." (Psalms 65:4)

JUNE 18   *Bible Reading: Psalms Chapters 78-81*

OPEN YOUR MOUTH WIDE AND GOD WILL FILL IT

"I am the Lord your God, who brought you out of the land of Egypt; ***open your mouth wide, and I will fill it.****"* (Psalms 81:10)

In Psalm 81, the psalmist Asaph requests the Israelites to observe the festival because of God's faithfulness in the past in delivering Israel from Egypt (v. 6) and providing for her in the wilderness (v. 7). Israel had rebelled against God in the past and was still continuing in rebellion (v. 13). If only the people would repent, God would forgive them and enable them to prevail over their enemies (v. 14).

In the middle of this discourse, Asaph points out in verse 10 that because God had brought them out of the clutches of slavery in Egypt, He could do great things for them. God had proved his power over the mighty Egyptian empire and it required that the Israelites believe in God and ask great things from Him. *Just like the little birds in the nest open their mouths wide for food and the parent birds fills them, God will fill the deepest need of His children when they open their mouths wide to Him!*

What is meant by opening our mouths wide? This may mean being fervent in our prayers, being unashamed with our petitions to God, and having enlarged hope and expectations from God. One example of a prayer that God challenges us to pray with enlarged hope and expectation is found in Psalms 2:8: *"Ask of Me, and I will give you the nations for Your inheritance, and the ends of the earth for Your possession."* By praying in this expansive manner, we increase our ability to pray, and receive greater things from God. God will then fill our mouths with abundant thanksgivings when we see the answers of our prayers right before our eyes. We shall also be filled with those blessings that we pray for: *"And my God shall supply all your need according to His riches in glory by Christ Jesus."* (Phil 4:19) Let us open our mouths wide and see how God fills them in the coming days!

"Ask, and it will be given to you; seek, and you will find; knock, and it will be opened to you. For everyone who asks receives, and he who seeks finds, and to him who knocks it will be opened. Or what man is there among you who, if his son asks for bread, will give him a stone? Or if he asks for a fish, will he give him a serpent? If you then, being evil, know how to give good gifts to your children, how much more will your Father who is in heaven give good things to those who ask Him!" (Matt 7:7-11)

JUNE 19   *Bible Reading: Psalms Chapters 82-89*

LET'S HAVE OUR HEARTS SET ON A PILGRIMAGE

"Blessed is the man whose strength is in You, whose heart is set on pilgrimage. *As they pass through the Valley of Baca, they make it a spring; the rain also covers it with pools. They go from strength to strength; each one appears before God in Zion."* (Psalms 84:5-7)

Psalm 84 is a song of pilgrimage penned by the sons of Korah whose duties included being gatekeepers of the temple (1 Chron. 26:1, 12–19). This psalm reveals an intense longing for God's house – the temple in Jerusalem (Psalm 84:1-4), and this impulse for worship was so strong as to overcome any obstacle that might stand in the way of the pilgrim (v. 7). God was there, and to worship Him there ultimately was the height of all joy and blessing (v. 10).

There are **five lessons** that we can learn from the above verses 5-7 that are listed below:

1. *God considers those people blessed who have learned the secret of putting their focus/trust in God*: We are blessed *(divine favored)* when our strength to believe, obey and suffer lies in God alone. This happens when the doctrines, precepts, and promises of God are deeply engraved upon our hearts, and we are passionate in following God's ways during our life's journey.

2. *God is not only their power source, but their hearts are set on a pilgrimage*: Pilgrimages to the tabernacle were a grand feature of Jewish life and these blessed people had an earnest desire to take this journey, even though they lived far off from the tabernacle. We need to realize that this earth is not our own – we are just passing through. We need to closely follow the footsteps of the fathers in faith who confessed that they were strangers and pilgrims on this earth (Heb 11:13).

3. *As these pilgrims pass through the Valley of Baca, they make it a spring (or, well)*: The Valley of Baca represents the valley of weeping – the testing/trial experiences in the life of a believer. These tragic experiences should create wells of testimony regarding the faithfulness of God, and these experiences may be used to bless others as we go through similar experiences. Let's always remember that "the steps of a good man are ordered by the Lord" (Psalms 37:23).

4. *When we use our life experiences to bless others, God will fill our wells of experience with His rain*: God will pour His showers of blessings upon our efforts to glorify Him through our life tragedies. God will help us to overcome our tragic situations and help us to be "more than conquerors" (Romans 8:37).

5. *We will go from strength to strength until we appear before God*: At the end of all our valley experiences, we will appear before God in Mount Zion, the holy mountain of God. Even though weary from the demands of the journey, we will gather strength as we trudge along in God's ways, and *finally* reach the wonderful presence of God.

Let's set on our heart on a pilgrimage today knowing that our ultimate destination is the presence of God! Let's follow the example of the Old Testament saints who did exactly that: *"(They)…died in faith, not having received the promises, but having seen them afar off were assured of them, embraced them and confessed that they were* strangers and pilgrims on the earth. 14 For those who say such things declare plainly that they seek a homeland. And truly if they had called to mind that country from which they had come out, they would have had opportunity to return. But now they desire a better, that is, a heavenly country. Therefore God is not ashamed to be called their God, for He has prepared a city for them." (Heb 11:13-16)

JUNE 20 *Bible Reading: Psalms Chapters 90-97*

LORD, TEACH US TO NUMBER OUR DAYS!

"So teach us to number our days that we may gain a heart of wisdom." (Psalms 90:12)

Psalms 90 is the <u>only</u> psalm attributed to Moses, the man of God. Moses prays to His Redeemer in the context of the frailty of man and the shortness of life, contrasting this with the eternity of God. It is a contrast between *the everlasting God* and *the temporal man*, between *what is eternal* and *what is temporary*, between *what is permanent* and *what is perishing* and between *the divine view point* and *the human viewpoint*. This prayer is a powerfully honest look at the brevity and significance of life in which Moses compares our entire lifetime to grass that grows up in the morning and withers in the evening (v. 5-6). This is a prayer contemplating the snapshots of our life with the final image in view.

Moses had realized the significance of his life early at the age of 40, when he chose *"to suffer affliction with the people of God than to enjoy the passing pleasures of sin"* (Heb 11:24-26) as he was well aware that he was fast moving to his eternal destiny. This is exactly what Job knew as well when he said the following words: *"My days are swifter than a weaver's shuttle, and are spent without hope. Oh, remember that my life is a breath! My eye will never again see good. The eye of him who sees me will see me no more; while your eyes are upon me, I shall no longer be. As the cloud disappears and vanishes away, so he who goes down to the grave does not come up. He shall never return to his house, nor shall his place know him anymore."* (Job 7:6-10)

So, Moses prayed that we may gain a heart of wisdom (v. 12), so God would teach us to number our days! There are four reflections we can distill from this short prayer:

1. *This prayer came from the heart of an **objective man** who knew that his death was certain.* During the 40 years that he had led the children of Israel through the wilderness, he had seen over 1.2 million deaths. As the popular saying goes - if there are two things certain in this life, they are death and taxes. *"And as it is appointed for men to die once, but after this the judgment"* (Heb 9:27)

2. *This prayer came from the heart of an **old man** who knew how short his life is.* Moses has categorized the life span of a 'normal' human being to 70 years only, which will soon be carried away like a *flood* or gone away like *sleep in the night* (v. 5).

3. *This prayer came from the heart of a **godly man** who knew that there is something abiding and meaningful in life.* Time is only significant when we visualize it in the light of eternity. God had placed us here on earth with a purpose, and we should ensure that our lives are significant. We should invest our time in people and projects that will live on after we die!

4. *This prayer came from the heart of a **wise man** who knew the importance of setting deadlines.* We need to maintain discipline in our lives – this is the secret of spiritual living. We need to consider making the right choices and how we should spend our time every day.

Lord, help us to do Your will and be effective as we travel quickly from our home here on earth to our heavenly home that You are preparing for us. Lord, help us to redeem our time that You have given us each day, to avail every opportunity that we get and follow in your footsteps in total obedience!

JUNE 21 *Bible Reading: Psalms Chapters 98-104*

COUNTING THE BLESSINGS IN OUR LIVES

"Bless the Lord, O my soul; and all that is within me, bless His holy name! Bless the Lord, O my soul, and forget not all His benefits: who forgives all your iniquities, who heals all your diseases, who redeems your life from destruction, who crowns you with lovingkindness and tender mercies, who satisfies your mouth with good things, so that your youth is renewed like the eagle's." (Psalms 103:1-5)

Psalms 103 is one of the beautiful hymns penned by King David, in which he blesses God for who He is and for all the blessings He has bestowed on his life. At the outset, David sings of the personal mercies which he had himself received (vv. 1-5), and having been forgiven and redeemed, he felt like a renewed person (v. 5). Then David magnifies the attributes of Jehovah as displayed in his dealings with his people (vv. 6-19); and he closes by calling upon all the creatures in the universe to adore the Lord and join with himself in blessing the ever gracious Jehovah God.

Psalms 103:2 reminds us that we should not forget "all the benefits" that God has poured in our lives. In verses 3-5, David lists out **five core blessings** that God has granted to us:

1. God has forgiven ALL our iniquities.
2. God has healed ALL our diseases.
3. God has redeemed our life from total destruction.
4. God has crowned us with His lovingkindness and tender mercies.
5. God has satisfied us with good things in our lives so that we are renewed in strength and purpose.

Let us remember that God *daily loads us with benefits* (Psalms 68:19). We need to acknowledge God's abundance in our lives, and counting these blessings will multiply the joys in our lives. In the midst of trouble, acknowledging God's role in our lives can redirect our thinking from the hurts of our hearts and forces us instead to dwell upon the greatness of our God who cares about us so deeply. There is a healing power in praise, so praising God's greatness will put hope and instill joy in our troubled hearts!

Read carefully the following words of the famous hymn penned by Johnson Oatman, Jr.:

When upon life's billows you are tempest-tossed,

When you are discouraged, thinking all is lost,

Count your many blessings, name them one by one,

And it will surprise you what the Lord hath done.

Count your blessings, name them one by one,

Count your blessings, see what God hath done!

Count your blessings, name them one by one,

*Count your many blessings, see what God hath done.

[*And it will surprise you what the Lord hath done.]

"In everything give thanks; for this is the will of God in Christ Jesus for you." (1 Thess 5:18)

JUNE 22   *Bible Reading: Psalms Chapters 105-110*

BE THANKFUL
TO GOD EVERY DAY

"Oh, give thanks to the Lord! Call upon His name; make known His deeds among the peoples!" (Psalms 105:1)

Psalm 105 was evidently composed by King David, for the first fifteen verses of it were used as a hymn at the carrying up of the ark from the house of Obed-edom, and we read in 1 Chronicles 16:7, *"Then on that day David delivered first this psalm to thank the Lord, into the hand of Asaph and his brethren."* The first verses are full of joyful praise, and call upon the people to extol Jehovah (vv. 1-7); then the earliest days of the infant nation are described (vv. 8-15); the going into Egypt (16-23), the coming forth from it with the Lord's outstretched arm (vv. 24-38), the journeying through the wilderness and the entrance into Canaan (vv. 39-45). Psalms 105 is one of four psalms that begin with a note of thanksgiving (see also Psalms 107, 118, 136).

It is so important that we are thankful to God every day of our lives, as it is the will of God that we are sincerely thankful to Him (1 Thess. 5:18). Just as David recounted the blessings of God by leafing through the pages of history in the lives of the children of Israel, we need to look back in our lives and recall the many good things that God has done for us. He has been our Ebenezer – our God has thus far helped us in our spiritual journey (1 Sam 7:12). Through our thankfulness, we can also worship God (Heb. 12:28). We also need to understand that if we are not thankful to God, we are slipping on a slippery slope of sin, uncleanness and debauchery (Rom. 1:21-32).

Let us make thankfulness a priority in our worship to God today – when we call upon the name of God. After that, let us turn around and make known His workings to the other people around us. (Psalms 105:1).

*"Serve the Lord with gladness; come before His presence with singing. Know that the Lord, He is God; it is He who has made us, and not we ourselves; we are His people and the sheep of His pasture. **Enter into His gates with thanksgiving, and into His courts with praise. Be thankful to Him, and bless His name.**"* (Psalms 100:2-4)

JUNE 23   *Bible Reading: Psalms Chapters 111-118*

DELIGHT IN READING & MEDITATING GOD'S WORD

*"Praise the Lord! **Blessed is the man** who fears the Lord, who delights greatly in His commandments."* (Psalms 112:1)

Psalms 111 and 112 begin each phrase with a successive letter of the Hebrew alphabet and is referred to as an *acrostic*. Psalm 112 is a *'wisdom'* psalm and generally regarded as an exposition of Psalms 111:10, presenting the happiness of those who fear and obey God, and contrasting the fate of the ungodly. The psalmist connects blessing to covenant obedience through reading and meditating on God's word (v. 1), which involved not only worship of the Lord but also attention to the needs of those around him who were suffering deprivation and persecution (vv. 8–9).

Psalms 112 starts with declaring a person blessed (divine favored) who does two things: (a) *Fears God (has a holy reverence of God)*; and (b) *Delights in reading and meditating God's word*. We need to understand that *belief determines behavior*, and that is why it is so important to *have a true view of God* which is obtained only from His word. When we have a *true view of God*, our lives will *prioritize in doing the things that please God*. **When we please God, He will reward us with *seven great blessings* that are listed in Psalm 112:**

1. Our children will be blessed (v. 2)
2. We will enjoy abundance of wealth and prosperity (v. 3)
3. We will bless others with what we have (v. 5)
4. We will not be distressed when calamities happen in our lives (vv. 7-8)
5. We will help the poor and the downtrodden (v. 9a)
6. We will be honored among people, and this honor will last beyond our lifetime (v. 9)

7. Our enemies will envy us but will not be able to bring us down (v. 10)

A good example in the Bible who experienced all these blessings is **Job**, whose life reflected all the above blessings even though he went through tragic situations in his life. **Let us delight in reading and meditating on God's word every day.** If we do that, we can also be assured of **stability** and **strength** (*"like a tree planted by the rivers of water"*), **fruitfulness** (*"that brings forth its fruit in its season"*) and **endurance** (*"whose leaf also shall not wither"*). To summarize, **there will be prosperity in our lives** (*"whatever he does shall prosper"*).

*"**Blessed is the man** ... (whose) delight is in the law of the Lord, and in His law he meditates day and night. He shall be like a tree planted by the rivers of water that brings forth its fruit in its season, whose leaf also shall not wither; and whatever he does shall prosper."* (Psalms 1:1-3)

JUNE 24 *Bible Reading: Psalms Chapter 119*

BE DIRECTED DAILY THROUGH GOD'S WORD

"Your word is a lamp to my feet and a light to my path." (Psalms 119:105)

Psalms 119 is the longest psalm in the Bible and contains meditations on the excellencies of the Word of God. This psalm is divided into twenty-two parts or stanzas, denoted by the twenty-two letters of the Hebrew alphabet. Each stanza contains eight verses, and the first letter of each verse is that which gives name to the stanza. The Word of God is alluded to in almost every one of the 176 verses by the words "law," "statutes," "ways," "precepts," "decrees," "commands," "word," and "promise." The lesson to be learned above all others is that knowledge and practical application of the Word will keep one from sin and thus enable him to know and serve God appropriately (119:9, 11, 92, 98, 105, 130, 133, 176). God has revealed Himself in Scripture, and only in that revelation can one find forgiveness, life, and meaning. Above all, God's word is wholly sufficient for godly living.

R.C. Sproul, in his famous book *'Pleasing God'*, tells us that for real sanctification to occur in our lives, three absolute changes are necessary. There must be a change in our *consciousness, convictions* and *conscience. Consciousness* involves knowledge. Before we can willfully do what God commands and what pleases Him, we must first understand what God requires. *Conviction* is the knowledge that is settled, and that which penetrates our conscience. Our *conscience* is the inner voice that either accuses or excuses us, but we can train it in the direction of self-approval and is not totally reliant. For our *conscience* to function in godly ways, it must be influenced by *godly convictions*, which is sharpened only through reading and meditating on God's word daily.

Through His Word, God wants to direct us daily. His Word is a lamp unto our feet and a light to our path. When we look forward by using the light provided by God's Word, we will not stumble in the dark. All we need is the light ahead to take the next step forward, and God's Word is able to do that if we read, meditate, memorize and delight ourselves in His Word every day. Daily focus on God's Word and constant meditation are the keys to our godly success. Then, we will not slip into the pit holes of bitterness and despair as we look at Jesus while running our race everyday with the light shed through God's Word.

*"And so we have the prophetic word confirmed, **which you do well to heed as a light that shines in a dark place**, until the day dawns and the morning star rises in your hearts; knowing this first, that no prophecy of Scripture is of any private interpretation, for prophecy never came by the will of man, but holy men of God spoke as they were moved by the Holy Spirit."* (2 Peter 1:19-21)

JUNE 25   *Bible Reading: Psalms Chapters 120-127*

GOD'S PRINCIPLE OF SOWING AND REAPING

*"Those who **sow in tears shall reap in joy**. He, who **continually goes forth weeping, bearing seed for sowing, shall doubtless come again with rejoicing, bringing his sheaves with him**."* (Psalms 126:5-6)

Psalms 126 is the seventh step of the 'Song of Ascents' that the pilgrims recited as they journeyed to the temple in Jerusalem. This psalm divides itself into a *narrative* (vv.1-2), a *song* (v.3), a *prayer* (v.4), and a *promise* (vv.5-6). Psalm 126 has also been *divided into three parts* by Bible scholars as *this psalm describes the joy that should arise in us as a result of our position in Christ*:

1. **Joy is freedom (vv.1-3)…in Christ**: As we yield ourselves to Christ in total obedience, He reproduces Himself in us and enables us to be totally free to do His will.
2. **Joy is fullness (v.4)…in Christ**: God can fill our empty lives the way that the rains fill the dry riverbeds in the desert.
3. **Joy is fruitfulness (vv.5-6)…in Christ**: A fruitful Christian experiences God's power and fulfills complete potential which can only come through understanding and adhering God's principle of sowing and reaping.

What is God's principle of sowing and reaping?

Psalms 126:5-6 describes a process that goes against our natural tendencies when we are taken into a difficult period in our lives. Whenever we are hurled into a crisis that brings tears, our natural tendency is to recoil in fear and hurt, and subsequently retreat into a corner. However, there is a better way that God tells us to handle such times of travail and pain. God is telling us that *if we do something unnatural, we will reap extraordinary joy* in our lives. When faced with difficult circumstances, rather than sitting back and allowing self-pity and discouragement to consume us, we should plant seeds during this time. We need to reach out and see where we can be a blessing to others as we give ourselves in this task.

The psalmist acknowledges that we are sowing seeds while we are in our pain. The seeds will return to us in another form – in the form of sheaves, which represents multiplied blessings. We will receive joy and fruit from the seeds that we plant during this time. Sheaves represent the fruit of a harvest – we will gain abundant harvest from the seeds that we plant in other people's lives.

If we find ourselves in a difficult place today, let us attempt to go against our natural tendencies to sow seeds of blessings in other people's lives – undoubtedly we shall soon reap great harvest of joy. These seeds can also be the word of God that we plant in other's hearts – no doubt these seeds will germinate through the power of the Holy Spirit and we will see the fruit of a great harvest right before our eyes!

*"Do not be deceived, God is not mocked; for **whatever a man sows, that he will also reap**. For he who sows to his flesh will of the flesh reap*

*corruption, but **he who sows to the Spirit will of the Spirit reap everlasting life. And let us not grow weary while doing good, for in due season we shall reap if we do not lose heart. Therefore, as we have opportunity, let us do good to all**, especially to those who are of the household of faith." (Gal 6:7-10)*

JUNE 26   *Bible Reading: Psalms Chapters 128-136*

PRAISE GOD FOR HIS GREATNESS AND GOODNESS

*"**Praise the Lord, for the Lord is <u>good</u>**; sing praises to His name, for it is pleasant. For the Lord has chosen Jacob for Himself, Israel for His special treasure. **For I know that the Lord is <u>great</u>, and our Lord is above all gods**" (Psalms 135:3-5)*

Psalm 135 is one of the *"Hallelujah"* psalms (similar to Psalms 146–150) that exhorts us praise lifted up to the Lord because of His worth and works (vv. 1-3). This psalm appears to be directed to Israel, particularly to the tribe of Levi and the house of the High Priest Aaron (vv. 19-21). God chose Israel as His own people and for this He alone is deserving of praise (v. 4). His works as Creator also speak of His glory, as does His miraculous deliverance of Israel from bondage and subsequent conquest of their enemies in Canaan (vv. 8–9, 12). In comparison to Him the gods of the nations are impotent and useless (vv.15–18). No wonder all should praise the Lord—people and priests alike (vv. 19–21).

However, we are exhorted to praise God due to His two wonderful attributes: He is GREAT (v. 5) & He is GOOD (v. 3).

How can we say that our God is GREAT?

When we look around in nature, we will soon realize that our God is GREAT in maintaining order (vv. 6-7). Our God has created everything. He displayed His greatness in the lives of the Israelites as He delivered them from the bondage in Egypt and brought them to the Promised Land that He had promised to their father Abraham (vv. 8-12). His greatness is *beyond* our human understanding – all we can do is to praise Him for His greatness.

How can we say that our God is GOOD?

Our God is essentially good, and He let Moses see His goodness, and this is what God told Moses: *"I will make all My goodness pass before you, and I will proclaim the name of the Lord before you. I will be gracious to whom I will be gracious, and I will have compassion on whom I will have compassion."* (Ex 33:19) Later on, Jesus clarified that no one is good, except God alone (Matt. 19:17). God's goodness extended to Israel in that He chose Israel for Himself (Psalms 135:4) just like He chose us as well (John 15:16). His goodness is *beyond* our human understanding – all we can do is to praise Him for His goodness.

- **Understanding the _greatness of God_ should send us to our knees in humility as we thank Him for saving us from destruction.**

- **Understanding the _goodness of God_ should lift us back to our feet to offer Him our grateful praise as He used His goodness to reach out to us and save us.**

"The Lord is slow to anger and _great_ in power, *and will not at all acquit the wicked. The Lord has His way in the whirlwind and in the storm, and the clouds are the dust of His feet.* **The Lord is _good_, a stronghold in the day of trouble; and He knows those who trust in Him.**" (Nahum 1:3, 7)

JUNE 27   *Bible Reading: Psalms Chapters 137-142*

"TRUSTING IN THE SAFETY OF GOD'S HANDS"

Though I walk in the midst of trouble, You will revive me; **You will stretch out _Your hand_ against the wrath of my enemies, and _Your right hand_ will save me.** *The Lord will perfect that which concerns me; Your mercy, O Lord, endures forever; do not forsake the* **works of _Your hands_.** *(Psalms 138:7-8). You have hedged me behind and before, and laid* **_Your hand_** *upon me. Such knowledge is too wonderful for me; it is high, I cannot attain it. Where can I go from Your Spirit? Or where can I flee from Your presence? If I ascend into heaven, You are there; if I make my bed in hell, behold, You are there. If I take the wings of the morning, and dwell in the uttermost parts of the sea, even there* **_Your hand_** *shall lead me, and* **_Your right hand_** *shall hold me.* (Psalms 139:5-10)

Both Psalms 138 and 139 are hymns penned by King David. While Psalm 138 speaks about God's goodness to the faithful, Psalm 139 talks about God's perfect knowledge about us – He knows everything about us – our thoughts, fears, hopes – and yet He loves us in spite of them.

From Psalms 138:7-8, we can understand that our God has the safest pair of hands, and His right hand will save us when we fall into trouble. Like King David, we can look to the safety of God's hand and trust Him to keep us from spiritual danger and possible defeat. Jude reminds us that *'God will keep us from stumbling and present us before the presence of His glory with great joy'* (Jude 1:24-25). Even though we may stumble and even fall down, we shall not be utterly cast down *for the Lord will uphold us with His hand* (Psalms 37:23-24). When we are at the point of falling down or sinking during our faith-walk like Peter walking on the water (Matt. 14:29-31), all we need to do is to call upon His name "Lord, save me!" and God will stretch out His hands and save us.

During the fierce storms that come in our lives when our stable world is shaken, we tend to grip tightly to the provisions that have helped us in the past using our own power, reason, feeling and endurance. It is at these times that **we need to loosen our grips on everything around us and trust in the safety of God's all powerful hands**! We can come close to Him through confession, repentance and trusting in His grace to lead us through.

"Behold, __the Lord's hand__ is not shortened, that it cannot save; nor His ear heavy, that it cannot hear. But your iniquities have separated you from your God; and your sins have hidden His face from you, so that He will not hear." (Isaiah 59:1-2)

JUNE 28   *Bible Reading: Psalms Chapters 143-150*

TRUE SATISFACTION IN LIFE COMES FROM GOD ALONE

*"The **eyes of __all__ look expectantly to You**, and You give them their food in due season. You open Your hand and **satisfy the desire of __every living thing__**."* (Psalms 145:15-16)

Psalm 145 is another hymn penned by King David who directs his praises to God for *God's greatness in the past* (vv. 1–7), *God's glory in* the future (vv. 8–13) and *God's grace in the present* (vv. 14–21). To expand this further, David praises God *for His glory* (vv. 1-7), *for His goodness* (vv. 8-10), *for His kingdom* (vv. 11-13), *for His providence* (vv. 14-16), and *for His saving mercy* (vv. 17-21).

In the midst of rendering his praises to God, David looks around him to all the animals on the earth, all the fishes in the water and all the birds in the air and realizes a profound truth. God has created all the animals, fishes and birds (Gen 1:20-25), and God is sustaining all the living creatures on this earth by giving them food in due season as they all look expectantly to God for their daily survival. David realizes that every living being on this earth look expectantly to God for nourishment and survival. God knows the need of every animal, fish and birds and He satisfies their desires every day.

When Jesus started His public ministry, He pointed this out as part of His lengthy discourse called The Sermon on the Mount: *"Look at the birds of the air, for they neither sow nor reap nor gather into barns; yet your heavenly Father feeds them. Are you not of more value than they?"* (Matt 6:26) As we understand that God our heavenly Father feeds all the animals on this earth, all the fishes in the rivers, seas and oceans and all the birds that fly in the air, God definitely knows our needs and He is well able not only to sustain and nourish us, but also to satisfy our every need and longing. On a personal level, our God is also our Good Shepherd and we shall not want anything as He will satisfy our every need (Psalms 23:1-2).

Let us realize that true satisfaction comes from God alone, he will satisfy every thirst and longing that we have in our lives (John 4:13-14). Today, let us join Joni Eareckson Tada in praying this simple but profound prayer: *'Lord, there are many things I desire, but I really don't need. Subtract my desires and keep me from adding my own wants. Help me to find satisfaction in You, for only then will I find real and lasting contentment.'*

JUNE 29   *Bible Reading: Proverbs Chapters 1-3*

SEEK GODLY WISDOM FOR OUR DAILY LIVING

"The proverbs of Solomon the son of David, king of Israel: **to know wisdom and instruction, to perceive the words of understanding, to**

receive the instruction of wisdom, justice, judgment, and equity; to give prudence to the simple, to the young man knowledge and discretion— a wise man will hear and increase learning, and a man of understanding will attain wise counsel. Wisdom calls aloud outside - whoever listens to me will dwell safely, and will be secure, without fear of evil." (Prov 1:1-5, 20, 33)

The book of Proverbs is attributed to King Solomon (Prov. 1:1) who obtained his wisdom as a gift from God (1 Kings 3:11–12). Using this wonderful extraordinary ability to understand profound matters, he penned wonderful proverbial sayings that attest to his wisdom.

"And God gave Solomon wisdom and exceedingly great understanding and largeness of heart like the sand on the seashore. Thus Solomon's wisdom excelled the wisdom of all the men of the East and all the wisdom of Egypt...for he was wiser than all men...and his fame was in all the surrounding nations. He spoke three thousand proverbs and his songs were one thousand and five. Also he spoke of trees, from the cedar tree of Lebanon even to the hyssop that springs out of the wall; he spoke also of animals, of birds, of creeping things, and of fish. And men of all nations, from all the kings of the earth who had heard of his wisdom, came to hear the wisdom of Solomon." (1 Kings 4:29-34)

The book of Proverbs provides wisdom and guidance for living an obedient life. Here, the wise king Solomon instructs his *"son,"* and thus ultimately every young person, in the importance of knowing the Lord, for it is God who imparts wisdom sufficient for all the complexities and challenges of life. This book also imparts to all young people (and to all who are wise enough to listen) the principles by which life must be lived if it is to be successful (Prov. 1:2–5).

Let us understand that wisdom is the God-given ability to see life with objectivity and handle life with stability imparted from God's word. Wisdom is the ability to apply knowledge in the proper way that benefits man and honors God. To be able to attain wisdom, we need to seek God with godly fear and reverence that is the foundational step for all wisdom (Prov. 1:7) and take time to listen to God in the midst of all the noises that tries to capture our attention.

Let us seek godly wisdom for our daily living – we will then *'dwell safely and be secure without any fear of evil'* (Prov. 1:33).

"The fear of the Lord is the beginning of wisdom; a good understanding have all those who do His commandments. His praise endures forever." (Psalms 111:10) *"**See then that you walk circumspectly**, not as fools but **as wise**, redeeming the time, because the days are evil. Therefore do not be unwise, but **understand what the will of the Lord is**."* (Eph 5:15-17)

JUNE 30   *Bible Reading: Proverbs Chapters 4-6*

SEVEN THINGS THAT GOD HATES

*"These six things the Lord hates, yes, **seven** are an abomination to Him: **a proud look, a lying tongue, hands that shed innocent blood, a heart that devises wicked plans, feet that are swift in running to evil, a false witness who speaks lies, and one who sows discord among brethren**."* (Prov 6:16-19)

Solomon lists **seven things that God hates** – these sins are detested by God and are also hurtful in our dealings with other people. These things which God hates, we must hate them ourselves. The seven sins mentioned are committed by five of our body organs: <u>one</u> **sin is committed by our eyes** *(a proud look)*, <u>three</u> **sins are committed by our tongue** *(a lying tongue, a false witness who speaks lies, one who sows discord among brethren)*, <u>one</u> **sin is committed by our hands** *(hands that shed innocent blood)*, <u>one</u> **sin is committed by our heart** *(a heart that devises wicked plans)*, and <u>one</u> **sin is committed by our feet** *(feet that are swift in running to evil)*.

In reality, all sins evolve from our heart. Our heart represents our will and evil is plotted in our hearts first before it goes into action by other body organs. God has declared that the human heart is capable of all evil (Genesis 6:5), so we must guard our heart very carefully. *"Keep your heart with all diligence, for out of it spring the issues of life."* (Prov 4:23).

Our *proud eyes* refer to willful rebellion against all authority (Daniel 11:2) and goes before our destruction (Numbers 14:40-45). *Our hands should not shed innocent blood* because people are made in the image of God and murder is breaking God's commandment (Genesis 9:6). Our *feet that are quick to rush to do evil* refer to our involvement in unlawful activities. We should never rejoice about evil (1 Cor 13:6). A *lying tongue* is harmful (Prov 26:28) and we can never enter God's kingdom if we lie (Rev 21:8). We should never lie and *give false witness* (Deut 19:16-19) nor *gossip about others.*

Among the seven things that God hates, pride tops the list! Pride happens when we overvalue ourselves and undervalue others, and that is revealed through our looks. This may even lead to devising evil and sowing discord. **Let's be careful to be humble always and guard our heart and tongue from doing wrongful things and displeasing God!**

*"Likewise you younger people, **submit yourselves** to your elders. Yes, all of you **be submissive to one another, and be clothed with humility**, for 'God resists the proud, but gives grace to the humble.' Therefore **humble yourselves under the mighty hand of God**, that He may exalt you in due time, **casting all your care upon Him**, for He cares for you."* (1 Peter 5:5-7)

July

Bible Reading: Proverbs Chapters 7-9

SEEKING GODLY WISDOM DAILY IN OUR LIVES

*"For wisdom is better than rubies and **all the things one may desire cannot be compared with her.** I (wisdom) love those who love me, and those who seek me diligently will find me. Blessed is the man who listens to me, watching daily at my gates, waiting at the posts of my doors. For whoever finds me finds life, and obtains favor from the Lord. But he who sins against me wrongs his own soul; all those who hate me love death"* (Prov 8:11, 17, 34-36)

Proverbs 8 introduces wisdom as a lady who takes her stand at the top of a high hill and cries out to all the people passing by the entrance of the city gates (v. 1-3). In fact, eminent scholars have categorized Proverbs 8 as containing the *longest sustained personification* in the Bible, introducing *'lady wisdom'* who does most of the speaking in this chapter. She takes a highly visible position in order to attract the attention of as many people as possible (v. 1–3; see 1:20–21). She describes her audience as fools who need hearts to understand prudence and wisdom (v. 5). She speaks nothing but truth and righteousness (vv. 7–8), virtues that are more rare and valuable than gold and rubies (vv. 10–11).

This is a poetic way of teaching us that God Himself is the very essence of wisdom. The very foundation of wisdom is the holy reverence (fear) and knowledge of God. *"The fear of the Lord is the beginning of wisdom, and the knowledge of the Holy One is understanding."* (Prov 9:10) What is meant by the fear of the Lord? Prov. 8:13 answers it this way: *"The fear of the Lord is to hate evil; pride and arrogance and the evil way and the perverse mouth I hate."*

The key passage chosen for today's devotion speaks to us that nothing can be compared in this world to finding godly wisdom. We need to earnestly search for godly wisdom in our daily activities. When we find godly wisdom, we will find both life and obtain godly favor in our lives. When we understand godly wisdom, then we will know God more clearly (v. 35; see John 14:6), but if we despise godly wisdom, we will surely die (v. 36; see John 3:36). **Let us seek after godly wisdom today and every day for the rest of our lives!**

*"However, **we speak wisdom among those who are mature**, yet not the wisdom of this age, nor of the rulers of this age, who are coming to nothing. But **we speak the wisdom of God** in a mystery, **the hidden wisdom which God ordained before the ages for our glory**, which none of the rulers of this age knew; for had they known, they would not have crucified the Lord of glory. But as it is written: "Eye has not seen, nor ear heard, nor have entered into the heart of man the things which God has prepared for those who love Him.' **But God has revealed them to us through His Spirit. For the Spirit searches all things, yes, the deep things of God.**" (1 Cor 2:6-10)*

JULY 2   *Bible Reading: Proverbs Chapters 10-12*

WATCHING OUR WORDS CAREFULLY

*"In the multitude of words sin is not lacking, but **he who restrains his lips is wise. The tongue of the righteous is choice silver**; the heart of the wicked is worth little. **The lips of the righteous feed many**, but fools die for lack of wisdom. The **truthful lip shall be established forever**, but a lying tongue is but for a moment. Lying lips are an abomination to the Lord, but **those who deal truthfully are His delight**."* (Prov 10:19-21; 12:19, 22)

The message from God's Word for us is very clear – we who call ourselves as God's children cannot afford the luxury of speaking idle words. We have an added responsibility to guard our tongues at all times. A word that we speak improperly and without thinking can have great repercussions. A word that is spoken at a moment of passion or anger can never be taken back. No matter how much we apologize, the wounds caused by our hurtful words takes a very long time to heal. People may forgive us, but some will never forget the hurt and pain that the words had caused. James counsels us that our tongue is a fire, a world of iniquity (James 3:6), it is evil and full of deadly poison (v. 8b). That may be the reason why our tongues are not exposed, but is caged in our mouth and sealed with our lips. If we do not stumble with our words, we can be 'perfect' and will be able to control our whole body as well (v. 2).

We should honor God through our words by doing the following:

- *We should show discernment and carefully filter the words that we speak* (Prov 10:19; 21:23)
- *We should use positive words always – even to address things that we are passionate about* (Prov 15:1-2)
- *We should avoid words that reflect poorly on us, since we are God's children.* Eph 4:29 tells us that no corrupt words should come out from our mouth, but only words that would edify others and impart grace upon the people who hear us.
- *We should restrain ourselves and allow all gossip about others to end with us* – nothing should go beyond us. We can never know when any words that we speak without thinking can come back to haunt us later on.

Let us follow the example of our Lord Jesus Christ, whose words were gracious (Luke 4:22) and life giving (John 6:63). He restrained His words before the Roman Governor Pilate in such a way that Pilate was amazed (Matt 27:11-14). **Let us also watch our words wisely – for they have the power of life and death!**

"A man has joy by the answer of his mouth, and a word spoken in due season, how good it is!" (Prov 15:23) *"A word fitly spoken is like apples of gold in settings of silver."* (Prov 25:11) *"The Lord God has given Me the tongue of the learned that I should know how to speak a word in season to him who is weary."* (Isaiah 50:4)

JULY 3   *Bible Reading: Proverbs Chapters 13-15*

GOD'S STANDARDS OF BLESSING A NATION

"Righteousness exalts a nation, but sin is a reproach to any people." (Prov 14:34)

About 3,000 years ago, King Solomon penned these profound words that holds true even today. This is God's law stated as clearly as possible: *"Righteousness exalts a nation."* **What is righteousness?** God has answered this through His Word: *"All Your commandments are righteousness"* (Psalm 119:172). When we keep aside the commandments of God – the divine standard that God has laid for us - we have no basis to even know what is right and what is wrong. *"Sin is a reproach to any people."* **What is sin?** Again, the Bible defines it: *"Sin is the transgression of the law"* (1 John 3:4). In other words, sin is lawlessness, or the breaking of God's law.

The United States of America is celebrating **Independence Day** tomorrow to commemorate the adoption of the Declaration of Independence on July 4, 1776, that declared its independence from Great Britain. This is a good time to ponder and pray for our nation. Let us understand that God has established the government authorities and laws to insure that society could function in order. *"Everyone must submit himself to the governing authorities, for there is no authority except that which God has established. The authorities that exist have been established by God"* (Romans 13:1). Our country is in grave danger after having removed the ancient landmarks (Prov 22:29) and having veered away from the godly foundations like prayer, word of God, sanctity of marriage between a man and woman, right of life for the unborn, etc, etc.

*What should **we do** as God's children who are seeing the crumbling of God's standards?* **We need to <u>stay true</u> to God's standard of Righteousness—the Word of God - we need to <u>rely upon</u> the source of righteousness: the Lord Jesus Christ - we need to <u>elect leaders</u> who uphold these godly standards.**

All those who believe in God and in His eternal principles are to stand out like lighthouses on a darkened coast. This is the time when Christian example is a most precious commodity. May we *let our lights shine* in such a way that others may see the beauty and appeal of true Christian living! May *we live like Christians* and make known in every legitimate way God's message for our faltering world! May we also *spend much time in prayer* for those whose lives are troubled - whose hearts have never been touched by the gospel!

*"If My people who are called by My name will humble themselves, and pray and seek My face, and turn from their wicked ways, then **I will***

hear from heaven, and will forgive their sin and heal their land." (2 Chron 7:14)

JULY 4   *Bible Reading: Proverbs Chapters 16-18*

OUR REAL SECURITY IS IN THE NAME OF GOD

"The name of the Lord is a strong tower; the righteous run to it and are safe." (Prov 18:10)

One of the richest kings in days, Solomon, looked at his immense wealth, position, power, wives, children and friends but did not feel that they provided him with the security that he needed in his life. However, he received a revelation as he pondered about where he could obtain the 'real' security that he was longing for - **it was only in the name (character) of God that he could get 'real' security in his life!**

The need for security/safety is an inherent need that every human being has – as per Maslow's hierarchy of needs. This includes the need for security of body, of employment, of resources, of morality, of the family, of health and of property (see diagram below).

However, of late it is very clear that everything that people have held as security has crumbled and has proven to be of no security at all. Many people have tried to find safety/security in their wealth. However, the Bible is clear that wealth and riches will not last forever (Prov. 23:5; 27:24; Eccl. 5:14; I Tim. 6:17). False safety and security in wealth and riches has lead to laziness, pride and destruction. There is no 'real' security in position and power – for people rise and fall in power as the waves of the sea. This is evident from the stories of many world leaders who have fell down from places of influence and power. There is no 'real' security these days in anyone – family or friends – as many have realized in pain after going through divorces and separation.

Let us be rest assured that our 'real' security is in God and upon His word – by faith we trust Him to be who He is and what He says. *"The wicked in his proud countenance does not seek God; God is in none of his thoughts."* (Psalms 10:4) However, let us place our trust on God, His Name that is above every other name, and in His character – for He alone is our 'real' security!

*"**God is our refuge and strength, a very present help in trouble. Therefore we will not fear,** even though the earth be removed, and though the mountains be carried into the midst of the sea; Though its waters roar and be troubled, though the mountains shake with its swelling."* (Psalms 46:1-3)

JULY 5   *Bible Reading: Proverbs Chapters 19-21*

DO YOUR PART *THEN* GOD WILL DO HIS PART

"The horse is prepared for the day of battle, but deliverance is of the Lord." (Prov 21:31)

King Solomon with his profound wisdom uses the example of a battle that Israel might encounter and how to win the battle. Does he just trust in God only and do nothing from his part hoping that God will grant him deliverance? The answer is 'NO' - he and his people *should* prepare the horse for battle, but deliverance is only from the Lord!

"There are many plans in a man's heart, nevertheless the Lord's counsel— that will stand." (Prov 19:21) Men's best devices and self-reliance are vain compared with God's, without His aid. Means are to be used, but, after all, our safety and salvation are only of the Lord. Only His counsel will stand and only His plans for us will survive!

The wise man or woman is blessed with God's grace and power to accomplish the otherwise impossible. Such resources enable one to overcome whole cities (Prov. 21:22) and to achieve victory in the day of conflict (21:31). To be wise, then, is to be mighty, for wisdom recognizes and is able to tap into the awesome power of Almighty God.

Even though we do our part in preparing the horses for battle, **we should *not* put our trust in them**. *"Some trust in chariots, and some in horses; but we will remember the name of the Lord our God."* (Psalms 20:7) Our trust should be in power and strength of God, for without Him we can do nothing. (John 15:5b). **Let us do our part and *then* God will do His part!**

*"**A horse is a vain hope for safety; neither shall it deliver any by its great strength.** Behold, the eye of the Lord is on those who fear Him,*

on those who hope in His mercy, to deliver their soul from death, and to keep them alive in famine. **Our soul waits for the Lord; He is our help and our shield.** *For our heart shall rejoice in Him,* **because we have trusted in His holy name.**" (Psalms 33:17-21)

JULY 6   *Bible Reading: Proverbs Chapters 22-24*

WORDS OF PRACTICAL WISDOM FOR DAILY LIVING

"By wisdom a house is built, and through understanding it is established; through knowledge its rooms are filled with rare and beautiful treasures." (Prov 24:3-4)

Today's readings from Proverbs 22-24 provides us practical words of wisdom not only from King Solomon, but also words of other wise men other than Solomon (22:17-24:22) and more words of the wise (24:23-34).

We need to understand that *knowledge* is nothing more than an accumulation of raw facts, but *wisdom* is the ability to see people, events, and situations as God sees them. In the Book of Proverbs, it is *wisdom* that *takes center stage*—a grand, divine wisdom that transcends the whole of history, peoples, and cultures. Solomon and other wise men reveal the mind of God in matters high and lofty and in common, ordinary, everyday situations, too.

The recurring promise of the Book of Proverbs is that those who choose wisdom and follow God will be blessed in numerous ways: with *long life* (9:11); *prosperity* (2:20-22); *joy* (3:13-18); and the *goodness of God* (12:21). Here are a few practical words of wisdom for daily living that we can glean from Proverbs 22-24:

1. **We need to choose a good name and loving favor (from God) over accumulating wealth** (22:1). In our modern, pleasure-seeking culture, character and reputation have a way of being ignored by everyone. True value must be seen, however, not in what one has but in what he or she truly is. A good name is an asset whose currency is unaffected by the boom or bust of the material world. In fact, as per Eccl 7:1, a *"good name is better than precious ointment"*.

2. **If we excel in our work, we will stand before leaders** (22:29). We need to be hardworking and diligent in our work, and the natural

consequence is that *"the hand of the diligent makes rich"* (10:4) and *"the plans of the diligent lead surely to plenty"* (21:5). This will definitely increase our standing in life and we will keep company with leaders.

3. **We should not withhold in giving timely correction to our children** (23:13-14). We need to maintain strong discipline in the home, and 'train' up our children in godly ways (22:6). While there is little danger that the use of the *"divine ordinance of the rod"* will produce bodily harm, there is great hope of spiritual good.

4. **We should not associate with those who are given to change** (24:21). We need to avoid the company of restless people who are unstable in their convictions and are fickle-minded.

5. **We should not be lazy but always work hard** (24:30-34). Verses 30 & 31 give us a striking picture of the effects of laziness. We need to learn wisdom from the folly of the lazy person. *"How long will you slumber, O sluggard? When will you rise from your sleep? A little sleep, a little slumber, a little folding of the hands to sleep — so shall your poverty come on you like a prowler, and your need like an armed man."* (Prov 6:9-11)

Let us incorporate these words of practical wisdom in our life and daily living for God's blessings and favor upon our lives!

JULY 7   *Bible Reading: Proverbs Chapters 25-27*

THE IMPORTANCE OF SELF-CONTROL IN OUR LIVES

"Whoever <u>has no rule over his own spirit</u> is like a city broken down, without walls." (Prov 25:28)

God uses the clear illustration of an undefended city to show us how important self-control is for our spiritual protection. *Self-control is the ability to rule over our own spirit; to judge all things by the word of God; to say yes to what pleases God, and to reject what God hates.* It is important to give attention to this because destructive things can barge into our lives once they find an entrance or foothold in our weakness. *Broken down walls can be compared to a weak and undefended spirit that leaves us vulnerable to the attacks of the enemy.* These include the incursions of evil thoughts and successful temptations. Lacking self-control means that we will lack our most important line of defense and it is inevitable that we will soon lie in spiritual ruin.

Self-control is thus very important in our spiritual life. It is mentioned as being the fruit of the Spirit in Galatians 5:23, and one of the Christian virtues that must be added to our faith in 2 Peter 1:6. One who lacks self-control is one who has already allowed himself to be drawn away by his own desires (James 2:14). He has given up the very thing that will prevent sin from entering in, and death will be the end result (v. 15). King David failed to exercise self-control when he lingered in looking at Bathsheba bathing (2 Samuel 11:2). If his *"wall of defense"* had been in place, he would have turned away and thought nothing else of it, but his lack of self-control led to temptation entering in and, subsequently, sin!

We can improve self-control in our lives by *building defense against the attack of our one and only enemy - Satan.* We can do that by putting on the whole armor of God (Eph 6:11) and by quenching the fiery darts of Satan through our faith in God (v. 16). Instead of filling up our minds with the worldly *"junk"*, we should think only those things that are true, noble, just, pure, lovely and of a good report (Phil 4:8). *Secondly,* we should always determine that we are *training to win.* To do that we need to read/meditate/memorize the word of God regularly so that we can know the truth (John 8:31-32) and have a ready answer for every temptation (e.g. Jesus - see Matt 4:1-11). The devil will always flee if we resist him (1 Peter 5:8, 9), but we must first resist! We need to set aside our sins and patiently run the race before us (Hebrews 12:1, 2). *Finally,* we must *stay alert at all times.* It is vital that we are ready at all times for our enemy is always looking to attack us in a weak moment (1 Peter 5:8). We must be always ready to give an answer (1 Peter 3:15) and we must always stand ready to fight the enemy (Eph 6:13). **It is therefore essential for us to have self-control to be able to fulfill God's plan in our lives!**

"He who is slow to anger is better than the mighty, and <u>he who rules his spirit</u> than he who takes a city." (Prov 16:32)

SEVEN QUALITIES OF A VIRTUOUS WIFE

"Who can find a virtuous wife? For her worth is far above rubies."
(Prov 31:10)

In Christian marriages, by biblical mandate, the husband is the head of the wife and family. But many husbands, unfortunately, are unskilled at managing the affairs of family life. The *"virtuous wife"* described in Proverbs 31:10-31 provides a good role model for every wife who (through godly submission) exercises her gifts and talents in such a way as to bless her husband and children. It is interesting to note that each of the verses (10 through 31) begin with the letters of the Hebrew alphabet in alphabetical order as in Psalms 119.

This exquisite picture of a virtuous wife is conceived and drawn in accordance with the customs of Eastern nations but its moral teachings are timeless and relevant for today as well. Here are **seven qualities of a virtuous wife** that every woman should aspire for in her own life:

1. **She is TRUSTWORTHY** (vv. 11-12). She can be safely trusted by her husband (v. 11a) and he will allow her to manage everything for him as she makes attempts always to do him good only (v. 12).

2. **She is INDUSTRIOUS** (vv. 13-15). She takes both pain and pleasure in her hard work. She manages time well as she rises early in the morning to provide food for her home (v. 15).

3. **She is a VISIONARY** (vv. 16-19). She understands the generation of future wealth as she "considers" and "perceives" buying both land (v. 16) and property (v. 18) by prudent management.

4. **She is BENEVOLENT** (vv. 20-23). She is willing to cheerfully share her wealth with the less fortunate who need a helping hand (v. 20), and due to her benevolence her household is well cared of (v. 21) and her husband has a place of honor in his community (v. 23).

5. **She is RESOLUTE** (vv. 24-25). She is firm in her affairs as she creates goods with her own hands and generates money for her home (v. 24). This can be compared to a wife who works outside her home in order to supplement her family income.

6. **She is WISE** (vv. 26-29). Her wisdom is revealed in her talks with others (v. 26). She not only takes prudent measures herself, but gives prudent advice to others. She conducts the affairs of her home with discretion (v. 27) due to which both her children and husband can only lavish praises upon her (v. 28).

7. **She is GOD-FEARING** (vv. 30-31). Above all, she fears God as she conducts herself. The fear of God reigning in her heart is the true beauty of her soul. While outward beauty is only skin-deep and charm is pretentious – a woman who fears God shall be praised by everyone (v. 30). *The result of her labor is her best eulogy for everyone to see* (v. 31).

"Charm is deceitful and beauty is passing, but a woman who fears the Lord, she shall be praised. Give her of the fruit of her hands, and let her own works praise her in the gates." (Prov 31:30-31)

JULY 9   *Bible Reading: Ecclesiastes Chapters 1-3*

THE VANITY OF PLEASURE AND WORLDLY HAPPINESS

"Whatever my eyes desired I did not keep from them. I did not withhold my heart from any pleasure, for my heart rejoiced in all my labor; and this was my reward from all my labor. Then I looked on all the works that my hands had done and on the labor in which I had toiled; and indeed all was vanity and grasping for the wind. There was no profit under the sun." (Eccl 2:10-11)

King Solomon had everything that any man or woman could dream of having in this world. Not only did he have godly wisdom but God also granted to him both riches and honor (1 Kings 3:12-13; 2 Chron 1:11-12). In fact, he had everything that this world could offer him, incl. pleasure, laughter, wine, wisdom, houses, gardens, money, possessions, music, and servants. He also had about 700 wives and 300 concubines. However, he soon realized that they were all in vain (Eccl. 2:11). He understood that lasting satisfaction does not come from possessing tangible things like money, material goods, projects, entertainment and work.

Solomon also understood that pleasure is vain (2:1–3), as are human accomplishments (2:4–11). Houses, gardens, reservoirs, a house full

251

of servants, herds and flocks, silver and gold, professional musicians for entertainment—all fail to yield satisfaction. Solomon's kingly office afforded him anything he wanted, but he always wanted more and did not get the satisfaction that he wanted.

Let us understand that happiness in our lives do not arise not from the situation in which we are placed or from the worldly pleasures that we have. **It is only through Jesus Christ that lasting joy can be attained!**

*"As the Father loved Me, I also have loved you; abide in My love. If you keep My commandments, you will abide in My love, just as I have kept My Father's commandments and abide in His love. **These things I have spoken to you, that My joy may remain in you, and that your joy may be full.**"* (John 15:9-11)

JULY 10   *Bible Reading: Ecclesiastes Chapters 4-6*

THE ADVANTAGES OF MUTUAL ASSISTANCE

*"**Two are better than one**, because they have a good reward for their labor. For if they fall, one will lift up his companion. But woe to him who is alone when he falls, for he has no one to help him up. Again, if two lie down together, they will keep warm; but how can one be warm alone? Though one may be overpowered by another, two can withstand him. **And a threefold cord is not quickly broken.**"* (Eccl 4:9-12)

When God made man and placed him in the Garden of Eden, God himself noticed that it was not good for man to be alone. *And the Lord God said, "It is not good that man should be alone; I will make him a helper comparable to him."* (Gen 2:18) We need to understand and realize that the ties of union, marriage, friendship and religious communion are better than a person to be alone. There are advantages that accrue from efforts that being conjoined. The Talmud says, *"A man without a companion is like a left hand without the right."*

Verses 9-11 speaks to us that two are far better than one. It is good to have someone with us to share our life's burdens. Then in verse 12b, it mentions that a threefold cord is not quickly broken. The clear meaning is that there is strength in numbers, and if two are better than one, then three are even better. Perhaps this is an echo of the

Trinity - the ultimate strength – or even the union of man and a woman in marriage where God is right at the center of the marriage.

In all things union tends to success and safety. Above all, the union of Christians assists each other by encouragement or friendly reproof. They warm each other's hearts while they converse together of the love of Christ, or join in singing his praises. Then let us improve our opportunities of Christian fellowship. Where two are closely joined in holy love and fellowship, Christ will by his Spirit come to them; then there is a threefold cord!

"Now I plead with you, brethren, by the name of our Lord Jesus Christ, that you all speak the same thing, and that there be no divisions among you, but that you be perfectly joined together in the same mind and in the same judgment." (1 Cor 1:10)

JULY 11   *Bible Reading: Ecclesiastes Chapters 7-9*

NEED FOR PRAYER/ DISCERNMENT IN CHOOSING A LIFE PARTNER

*"I applied my heart to know, to search and seek out wisdom and the reason of things, to know the wickedness of folly, even of foolishness and madness. **And I find more bitter than death the woman whose heart is snares and nets, whose hands are fetters. He who pleases God shall escape from her, but the sinner shall be trapped by her.**"* (Eccl 7:25-26)

Ecclesiastes 7:1–8:15 is targeted towards frustrations that can creep up in our lives and how to overcome them. Keeping this in context, we can note that King Solomon extols the value of wisdom (7:11–29) pointing out that it preserves our life (7:12), provides us strength to overcome (7:19), and makes it clear that *wickedness is utter foolishness* (7:25). An *example* of such foolishness is *in succumbing to the seduction of an evil woman* (7:26), a theme found frequently in the wisdom literature (for example, Prov. 2:16–19; 5:1–6; 6:20–25; 7:1–27).

In Eccl 7:26, Solomon writes from his personal experience with marriage. As someone whose multiple wives (700) and concubines (300) led him astray from serving God (1 Kings 11:4), Solomon had ample first-hand experience about the influence of a wife upon her husband in spiritual matters. Of course, he was not a hater of women, but had realized that an unwise marriage could be a trap and bring downfall to the husband. Like the other wisdom literature in the Bible, the book of Ecclesiastes was written from a male perspective – as a source of counsel to young men in Israel. Had this book been written from the perspective of a woman, it would have targeted on the misery of a woman married to a cruel and brutal man.

It should be noted that much of Ecclesiastes is taken up with reflections on Genesis chapter 3 – the account of the first sin – which may be one reason why this book is so much concerned with death and the brevity of life (Gen 3:19). After Eve was deceived, Adam stood with her and participated in the sin (Gen 3:6), which brought sin upon humankind in general (Eccl. 7:20-29). So, in effect Solomon was urging readers not to repeat Adam's mistake.

The need for every young man and young woman today is prayer and discernment in choosing a life partner! There are *evil* men and women in this world and a child of God should not be hasty in committing his/her life with anyone unless he/she is totally convinced of the godly character of the person. Solomon has pointed out that a good lifelong marriage is one of the greatest joys in life (Eccl 9:9). If the marriage relationship has to last a lifetime, the marriage partners will have to count the cost of this union well in advance and enter into this relationship that will last a lifetime.

Our Lord Jesus describes a couple of scenarios of the dire need to count the cost: before we start a building project and before we initiate war against another country (Luke 14:28-32). *How can we count the cost of our future marriage unless we clearly weigh our relationship and ensure that we are fully aware about our future marriage partner?* It is a known fact that *much prayer and discernment through premarital counseling* will help the couple greatly in making the right decision concerning their future marriage and lifelong commitment.

"Where there is no counsel, the people fall; but in the multitude of counselors there is safety" (Proverbs 11:14).

HOW TO FIND REAL JOY AND MEANING IN LIFE?

*"Rejoice, O young man, in your youth, and let your heart cheer you in the days of your youth; walk in the ways of your heart, and in the sight of your eyes; but know that for all these God will bring you into judgment. **Remember now your Creator in the days of your youth**, before the difficult days come and the years draw near when you say, "I have no pleasure in them."* (Eccl 11:9; 12:1)

As King Solomon brings the book of Ecclesiastes to a conclusion, he turns his attention to the young people in his kingdom and gives them some **timeless advice** of how they can find real joy and meaning in life. Let us understand the philosophy of many young people these days – *"Eat, drink and be merry, for tomorrow we die"* is actually a conflation of two biblical sayings: *"...a man has nothing better under the sun than to eat, drink, and be merry..."* (Eccl 8:15) and *"Let us eat and drink, for tomorrow we die!"* (Isaiah 22:13). This is a wrong approach to life, and will surely end in utter failure.

In order to find real joy and meaning in life, *there are three things that we should do* even when we are young:

1. **We must recognize that we are ultimately accountable to God alone** (11:9). We can go in our own ways and do whatever we want with our life, but we should be aware that we will one stand before God who will judge us for what we have done in our life. *"For we must all appear before the judgment seat of Christ, that each one may receive the things done in the body, according to what he has done, whether good or bad."* (2 Cor 5:10)

2. **Early on in life we should recognize the existence and claims of our Creator God** (12:1). In a brilliant metaphor describing the aging process (12:2–7), Solomon suggests that we should not wait until our old age before turning to the Lord and serving Him. We should do so when we are young so that we can live our entire life with significance.

3. **We should revere God and obey His commandments** (12:13). All the teachings in the book of Ecclesiastes lead to this conclusion (12:9–10). The bottom line is to *fear God by revering Him and*

displaying that by keeping His commandments, for a day is coming when He will judge everyone and call them to account for all their works (12:14).

"Let us hear the conclusion of the whole matter: Fear God and keep His commandments, for this is man's all. For God will bring every work into judgment, including every secret thing, whether good or evil." (Eccl 12: 13-14)

JULY 13   *Bible Reading: Song of Solomon Chapters 1-3*

GOD'S LOVE IS BETTER THAN ALL EARTHLY PLEASURES

"Let Him kiss me with the kisses of His mouth - **For Your love is better than wine.** *"* (Song 1:2)

King Solomon is the author of this eight chapter love song in approximately 900 BC. It was probably written before his spiritual decline (1 Kings 11:3-4). Solomon was a prolific songwriter, who wrote about 1005 songs in his lifetime (1 Kings 4:32).

The Song of Solomon is the greatest song in redemptive history and the longest song in the Bible. This song reveals *God's pattern in how we grow in passion for Jesus*. It touches the significant principles and practical realities needed to develop mature love for God.

The *symbolic interpretation* of this song is to see the spiritual truths in our relationship with Jesus behind the natural love story. Solomon shows forth *the joy of life that can be attained without regard to how our circumstances are going*. Here, *the Holy Spirit is calling us to make intimacy with God the goal of our life.* The song highlights how full our life is when our consuming passion is to love and know Jesus. Even with hard circumstances, our spirit can be alive in God.

The *theme of the song* is the *Bride's cry for the kiss of God's Word to touch the deepest place in her heart.* This refers to *encountering the Word in the deepest and most intimate way.* In other words, the Word as it reveals the King's emotions for His Bride and awakens our heart in the three-fold love of God (love from God - then for God - which overflows to others).

The greatest "pleasures" that we can experience are spiritual ones. These are *best experienced by encountering Jesus as the Bridegroom God.* This intoxicates our heart and makes us lovesick. **It is when we encounter Jesus that we realize that God's love is better than ALL the earthly pleasures that we can ever hope to experience. God has called us to holiness so that we can experience complete joy and undiluted pleasure that is perfect and eternal.**

"In Your presence is fullness of joy...Your right hand are pleasures forevermore." (Psalms 16:11)

JULY 14   *Bible Reading: Song of Solomon Chapters 4-6*

THE CHRISTIAN PARADIGM OF GOD

"You have ravished My heart, My sister, My spouse (bride); You have ravished My heart with one look of your eyes, with one link of your necklace. How fair is your love, My sister, My spouse! **How much better than wine is your love***..."* (Song 4:9-10c)

In his studies in the Song of Solomon entitled *"Progression of Holy Passion"* Mike Bickle has categorized the Christian paradigm of God using the above passage. According to him, **the Christian paradigm of God is founded on the revelation of God's deep emotions of love.** The revelation of God as a **tender Father** and a **passionate Bridegroom** was a new idea in religious history during the first century.

In **Jewish tradition**, what was most emphasized about God was that *He is holy* in the sense of *being totally separate from sin.* They did not think of a holy God as sharing human experience. They thought of God as incapable of sharing it simply because He is God. In other words, they saw God as being "above" sharing the human dilemma by the very definition of being God.

The **Greek philosophers** saw God as *emotionally distant from humans.* The most prominent Greek thinkers were the **Stoics.** They saw the main attribute of God as being *apatheia,* by which they meant *God's inability to feel anything.* They reasoned that if God felt something then He might be influenced or even controlled by what He felt. They argued that those who felt sorrow or joy were vulnerable to being hurt and thus controlled by those they had feelings for. They believed that anyone who affected God's emotions would be greater than God for that moment.

The **Epicureans** (a school of Greek philosophy) believed that *the gods lived detached in eternal bliss.* They lived in the intermediate world and thus, were not aware of events occurring on earth. They were therefore, *totally detached from human affairs as they lived in great happiness.*

Thus, the Jews understood God as a *holy God* separated from humans; the Stoics a god *without any feelings*; the Epicureans a *detached god.* **In to this context of religious thought came the totally new idea of the Christian God who deliberately subjected Himself to human emotion, pain and weakness.** Jesus Christ came as the One who embraced human experience and was therefore, sympathetic. *"For we do not have a High Priest who cannot sympathize with our weaknesses, but was in all points tempted as we are, yet without sin."* (Heb. 4:15)

It was inconceivable to the religious mindset of the first century that a holy God would have capacity for tenderness, sympathy and affection – one who even wrapped Himself in the garments of humanity and then experienced God's wrath on a cross. **The capacity to deeply love is unique to the human spirit. This capacity for** *agape love* **brings us to unimaginable heights in God's glory – we need to love God and others with that kind of sacrificial love that God has already loved us!**

"For when we were still without strength, in due time Christ died for the ungodly. For scarcely for a righteous man will one die; yet perhaps for a good man someone would even dare to die. ***But God demonstrates His own love toward us, in that while we were still sinners, Christ died for us.*** *Much more then, having now been justified by His blood, we shall be saved from wrath through Him."* (Romans 5:6-9)

JULY 15   *Bible Reading: Song of Solomon Chapters 7-8*

OUR TWO-FOLD SPIRITUAL IDENTITY IN GOD'S LOVE

"I am my Beloved's, and His desire is toward me." (Song 7:10)

King Solomon is unfolding this beautiful love poem between the Beloved and the Shulamite, which is symbolic of the relationship between Jesus and the individual believer, and gives us spiritual principles to aid us in our progression of holy passion for Him. We need to understand that our obedience is rooted in our two-fold spiritual identity in God's love. Our first spiritual identity is that *we should see ourselves as ones that Jesus desire.* Our second spiritual identity is that *we should see ourselves as totally belonging to Jesus.* **We are our Beloved's because His desire is towards us.** We need to first understand that Jesus loves us with an eternal love and His desire is for us at all times. *"We love Him because He first loved us."* (1 John 4:19)

Spiritual Identity #1: We see ourselves as ones that Jesus desire. *The prominent theme in the Song is the revelation of God's desire for us.* We should have a deep insight into Jesus' affection and enjoyment of us as His spiritual bride. This revelation will powerfully change us, and this should be our primary motivation for obedience and diligence in the ways of God (Song 4:9; 6:4-5; 7:6-10). Insight into God's desire gives us the strength to refuse to live by the opinions of others as this gives us emotional security. We speak the Word to the enemy, saying, *"It is written: His desire is towards me, regardless if others reject me".*

Spiritual Identity #2: We see ourselves as lovers of God in saying, *"I am my Beloved's"* or *"I belong to Jesus, I'm under His leadership, I want to please Him, His desires are what I care most about."* We should have the revelation of Jesus' total ownership of us (1 Cor 6:20). We exist for Him without any other considerations (Rev. 14:4). We should serve God without any concern for what will happen to us. Our focus should now be entirely on Jesus, the author and finisher of our faith (Heb 12:1-2). The question of what Jesus desires in us should be the most relevant issue in our lives. This is what we should value more than anything else in this world.

We should thus be defined by the fact that we are desired by God and that we desire (love) Him. We confess our identity, *"I'm a lover of God. That is who I am. That is what I do."* **We should live a life of sacrificial obedience because He already desires and loves us.**

God loves us in the same measure that He loves His only begotten Son Jesus Christ (John 15:9; 17:23). **Let us understand the depth of**

God's love as well as our two-fold spiritual identity in that love as we live to please Him alone in this world. *"Now may the Lord direct your hearts into the love of God..."* (2 Thess. 3:5)

"For this reason I bow my knees to the Father of our Lord Jesus Christ, from whom the whole family in heaven and earth is named, that He would grant you, according to the riches of His glory, to be strengthened with might through His Spirit in the inner man, **that Christ may dwell in your hearts through faith; that you, being rooted and grounded in love, may be able to comprehend with all the saints what is the width and length and depth and height— to know the love of Christ which passes knowledge; that you may be filled with all the fullness of God."** (Eph 3:14-19)

JULY 16   *Bible Reading: Isaiah Chapters 1-3*

THE IMPORTANCE OF 'GETTING RIGHT' WITH GOD

"Wash yourselves, make yourselves clean; put away the evil of your doings from before My eyes. Cease to do evil, learn to do good; seek justice, rebuke the oppressor; defend the fatherless, plead for the widow. **"Come now, and let us reason together," says the Lord, "Though your sins are like scarlet, they shall be as white as snow; though they are red like crimson, they shall be as wool.** *If you are willing and obedient, you shall eat the good of the land; but if you refuse and rebel, you shall be devoured by the sword"; for the mouth of the Lord has spoken.* (Isaiah 1:16-20)

God called Isaiah as a prophet to denounce the sins of Judah and Jerusalem, and the book of Isaiah is regarded as the first of the series of prophecies by the 'major' prophets, the others being Jeremiah, Ezekiel and Daniel. In chapters 1–5, Isaiah highlights the sin of Judah and Jerusalem while weaving together the themes of sin, judgment, and deliverance in the subsequent chapters.

The first chapter of Isaiah describes **three charges of God's indictment against His children:**

·   The **first charge** was that *they had "rebelled" against God* (1:2–9) and had *'turned their backs'* on the Holy One of Israel. Their rebellion brought judgment from God that was tempered only by God's mercy in graciously leaving a remnant.

· The **second charge** was that *their worship was not sincere* (1:10–20) and the people displayed their rebellion through insincere worship. Rather than following God's command to "love the Lord your God with all your heart and with all your soul and with all your strength" (Deut. 6:5), the people sought to buy off God with their many sacrifices. God saw through their hypocritical worship.

· The **third charge** was that *they did not keep justice* (1:21–31). A city once faithful to God had now prostituted itself for material gain. Murder, thievery, bribery, and injustice characterized the rulers and people in the similar manner. God vowed to avenge and purge the people as He promised one day to judge the rebels and restore His city to a place of righteousness.

In the midst of these charges, God extends a unilateral offer to His children to reconsider their ways. As God's children, this offer also extends to us and we need to understand that our heart attitude (whether obedience or rebellion) will display itself in how we relate to God and others.

What does God require from us to get right with Him?

1. **Cleanse ourselves from our sins through the blood of Jesus.** (Isa 1:16a, 18). *"If we confess our sins, He is faithful and just to **forgive us our sins and to cleanse us from all unrighteousness.**"* (1 John 1:9)

2. **Forsake everything that stands between our relationship with worshipping and serving God** (Isa 1:16b). *"He who covers his sins will not prosper, but whoever **confesses and forsakes them** will have mercy."* (Prov 28:13)

3. **Do good to others and stand for righteousness and justice** (Isa 1:17). *"He has shown you, O man, what is good; and what does the Lord require of you but **to do justly, to love mercy, and to walk humbly with your God?**"* (Micah 6:8)

JULY 17   *Bible Reading: Isaiah Chapters 4-6*

SEEING THE VISION OF GOD'S MAJESTY

*In the year that King Uzziah died, **I saw the Lord sitting on a throne, high and lifted up, and the train of His robe filled the temple.** Above* *it stood seraphim; each one had six wings: with two he covered his face, with two he covered his feet, and with two he flew. And one cried to another and said: "Holy, holy, holy is the Lord of hosts; the whole earth is full of His glory!" And the posts of the door were shaken by the voice of him who cried out, and the house was filled with smoke."* (Isaiah 6:1-4)

Isaiah chapter six is a record of God's divine call to the prophet Isaiah through a marvelous vision of God's majesty and splendor. Bible scholars believe that this was most likely Isaiah's original call to prophetic ministry. The reason why this heavenly vision was placed in chapter six instead of chapter one is because it served as a climax to the preceding five chapters and as a bridge to chapters 7–12. God called Isaiah to serve as His messenger because the nation stood on the brink of national calamity. His message was one of judgment—and hope. God would judge the nation for sin, and the judgment would continue until the coming of the Messiah.

Isaiah's call to prophetic ministry began with a vision of the awesome majesty and holiness of God (6:1–8). We should note that Isaiah saw this vision "in the year King Uzziah died" (6:1a). King Uzziah represents the pride of a king as he attempted to take over the role of a priest in worshipping God (2 Chron 26:19-21). However, this vision shows the humility of the angels (seraphims) who covered their face and feet and proclaimed only the holiness and glory of God (6:2). As the angels proclaimed God's absolute holiness, Isaiah realized his own sin as well as the sin of the nation (6:5). God forgave Isaiah (6:6-7) and then asked for a willing messenger (6:8a). In gratitude Isaiah stepped forward and responded, "Here I am. Send me!" (6:8b).

What is the need for seeing the vision of God's majesty in our lives?
The answer to this question lies in the fact that when we truly see and know the greatness, majesty and holiness of God, then we can truly see a clearer vision about our *real* state – about who we truly are! We cannot hide behind the façade that we put every day before other people before the holiness of God. When we see the majesty of God, we understand the great need for God's grace in our lives. We will then make a greater commitment to live and speak for God among the people in our sphere of influence.

Isaiah's vision of God led to a true vision of himself and others as unholy and unclean before God. This recognition of sin led Isaiah to a need for God's cleansing grace (6:7), and this vision commissioned him to spread God's message (6:9) about a holy God to unholy people! We too need to see the vision of God's majesty in our lives so that we can see ourselves as we truly are, get right with God and cleansed through the blood of Jesus Christ (1 John 1:9) and take God's message of salvation to everyone we know.

And Jesus came and spoke to them, saying, **"All authority has been given to Me in heaven and on earth. Go therefore and make disciples of all the nations, baptizing them in the name of the Father and of the Son and of the Holy Spirit, teaching them to observe all things that I have commanded you; and lo, I am with you always, even to the end of the age."** *Amen.* (Matt 28:18-20)

JULY 18   *Bible Reading: Isaiah Chapters 7-9*

JESUS CHRIST ("GOD-WITH-US"): GOD'S PLAN FOR OUR SALVATION

"Therefore the Lord Himself will give you a sign: **Behold, the virgin shall conceive and bear a Son, and shall call His name Immanuel.** *Curds and honey He shall eat, that He may know to refuse the evil and choose the good."* (Isaiah 7:14-15)

Isaiah, whose name means *"the Lord is salvation,"* ministered in the Southern Kingdom of Judah after the Northern Kingdom of Israel had fallen to Assyria. God had raised Isaiah as a prophet not only to minister to Judah and Jerusalem, but as God's spokesman to let the world know about His plans for salvation for humankind about 700 years before his birth. The purpose of this book is to display God's glory and holiness through His judgment of sin and His deliverance and blessing of a righteous remnant.

Many Bible scholars have debated whether the birth of the child predicted in Isaiah 7:14 is a prophecy of a child in Isaiah's day or a prophecy of the virgin birth of Christ (or both). However, this prophecy specifically points out to the virgin birth of Jesus Christ (Luke 1:31–35) who was the long-awaited Messiah of the Jews and the Savior of the world.

Let us examine some **specific prophecies** that Isaiah made relating to Jesus Christ:

- **Isaiah 7:14**: A young woman/virgin is to give birth to a son named **Immanuel**, meaning *"God with us."*
- **Isaiah 9:6–7**: The child to be born is named **"Wonderful Counselor, Mighty God, Everlasting Father, Prince of Peace,"** and will reign on David's throne forever.
- **Isaiah 11:1–9**: The child, called **"a shoot … from the stump of Jesse"** and a **"Branch,"** will reign with righteousness and justice and bring universal peace.
- **Isaiah 11:10–12**: The "Root of Jesse" will rule over the nations and re-gather the people of Israel and Judah.

The birth of Jesus Christ into this world is no accident, but was part of God's plan that He conceived before the foundation of the world. Jesus Christ is a historical fact who made such a tremendous impact in this world that even our timeline (B.C. /A.D.) is determined by His birth. God planned His only begotten Son Jesus Christ to be the Savior of all humankind. Have you accepted Him as your Lord and Savior yet? If not, today is the best day to accept Him in your heart and turn away from sin and the worldly life!

*"**Now the birth of Jesus Christ was as follows**: After His mother Mary was betrothed to Joseph, before they came together, she was found with child of the Holy Spirit…**So all this was done that it might be fulfilled which was spoken by the Lord through the prophet, saying: "Behold, the virgin shall be with child, and bear a Son, and they shall call His name Immanuel," which is translated, "God with us."** (Matt 1:18, 22-23)*

JULY 19 *Bible Reading: Isaiah Chapters 10-12*

IT'S TIME TO CHANGE OUR ATTITUDE FROM PRIDE TO PRAISE

*"Shall the **ax** boast itself against him who chops with it? Or shall the **saw** exalt itself against him who saws with it? As if a **rod** could wield itself against those who lift it up or as if a **staff** could lift up, as if it were not wood!"* (Isaiah 10:15)

In chapter 10:5–11, prophet Isaiah is pronouncing God's strong displeasure with Assyria, the heathen country He had chosen as a tool of judgment against His own people Israel for her multiplied sins. Having announced the coming of an enemy who would ravage Israel, God then identified that nation and said He would judge her for her sin as well. Though Assyria was *"the rod of (God's) anger"* (v. 5), she was still held accountable by God for her actions. Though God sent Assyria to loot Judah, the Assyrians went beyond what God had permitted. Their king Sennacherib stepped over the line when he raised his hand even against the God of Judah.

The role of Assyria was only that of an instrument of punishment in God's Hand – an instrument like an axe, saw, rod and staff (v. 15). However, due to Assyria's pride God's pronounced judgment on her: *"I will punish the fruit of the arrogant heart of the king of Assyria, and the glory of his haughty looks"* (v. 12). God said He would punish Assyria for her pride by sending *"a wasting disease"* on her soldiers (v. 18). This occurred in 701 B.C. when Sennacherib was attacking Judah and "the angel of the Lord" put to death 185,000 Assyrian soldiers overnight (see Isaiah 37:36–37).

It is time to change our attitude from pride to humility, which will happen only when we realize who we truly are – just instruments in the Hands of the Almighty God. When we are humble before God then ***our vision will be clarified as we realize how much we depend on God daily in our lives!*** This was what was prophesied by Isaiah concerning the returning remnant of Israel: *"And it shall come to pass in that day that the remnant of Israel, and such as have escaped of the house of Jacob, will never again depend on him who defeated them, but* ***will depend on the Lord, the Holy One of Israel, in truth"*** (Isaiah 10:20). ***Our dependence on God will ultimately lead to our praising God for becoming our salvation, our strength and our song.*** This is what God ultimately wants from us every day!

And in that day you will say: ***"O Lord, I will praise You****...behold,* ***God is my salvation****, I will trust and not be afraid;* ***for YAH, the Lord, is my strength and song; He also has become my salvation."*** *Therefore with joy you will draw water from the wells of salvation. And in that day you will say:* ***"Praise the Lord, call upon His name****; declare His deeds among the peoples, make mention that His name is exalted.* ***Sing to the Lord, for He has done excellent things****; this is known in all the earth."* (Isaiah 12:1-5)

PRIDE LEADS TO DESTRUCTION BUT EXALTATION COMES FROM GOD

"How you are fallen from heaven, O Lucifer, son of the morning? How you are cut down to the ground, you who weakened the nations? For you have said in your heart: 'I will ascend into heaven, I will exalt my throne above the stars of God; I will also sit on the mount of the congregation on the farthest sides of the north; I will ascend above the heights of the clouds, I will be like the Most High.' Yet you shall be brought down to Sheol, to the lowest depths of the Pit." (Isaiah 14:12-15)

Satan's fall from heaven is symbolically described in Isaiah 14:12-14 and Ezekiel 28:12-18. While these two passages are referring specifically to the kings of Babylon and Tyre, they reference to the spiritual power behind those kings, namely, Satan who is referred here as Lucifer (in Latin) or, Morning Star (in English). We know that Jesus Christ is *"the bright and morning star"* (Rev. 22:16), so Lucifer (Satan) is only a *counterfeit* version of Jesus.

Bible scholars are of the opinion that Lucifer's fall from heaven in all probability happened during the first earth age. Lucifer wanted to sit *"on the mount of the congregation"*, which according to Psalms 82:1 was where God stands. He also wants to sit *"on the farthest sides of the north"* where God's throne is situated (Psalms 75:6-7). He wanted to be like the *"Most High"*, which is one of the divine names of God as being the possessor of heaven and earth. However, Isaiah 14:15 says that Lucifer would be *"brought down to Sheol, to the lowest depth of the Pit"*. This will happen in the millennium when Satan is cast into the bottomless pit for a thousand years (Revelation 20:2-3).

Why did Satan fall from heaven? 1 Timothy 3:6 indicates that pride caused Satan's downfall. Satan fell because of pride. He desired to be God, not to be a servant of God. Notice the many "I will..." statements in Isaiah 14:12-15. Ezekiel 28:12-15 describes Satan as an exceedingly beautiful angel. Satan was likely the highest of all angels, the most beautiful of all of God's creations, but he was not content in his position. Instead, Satan desired to be God, to essentially 'kick God off His throne' and take over the rule of the universe.

How did Satan fall from heaven? Actually, a fall is not an accurate description. It would be far more accurate to say God cast Satan out of heaven (Isaiah 14:15; Ezekiel 28:16-17). Let us be careful not to follow the footsteps of Lucifer, who became Satan because of his pride. Let us clearly understand that *"pride goes before destruction and a haughty spirit before a fall."* (Prov 16:18)

"I said to the boastful, 'Do not deal boastfully,' and to the wicked, 'Do not lift up the horn. Do not lift up your horn on high; do not speak with a stiff neck.' **For exaltation comes neither from the east nor from the west nor from the south. But God is the Judge: He puts down one, and exalts another."** (Psalms 75:4-7)

JULY 21   *Bible Reading: Isaiah Chapters 16-18*

IT'S TIME TO TURN TO GOD & LIVE TO PLEASE HIM

"In that day a man will look to his Maker, and his eyes will have respect for the Holy One of Israel. He will not look to the altars, the work of his hands; He will not respect what his fingers have made, nor the wooden images nor the incense altars." (Isaiah 17:7-8)

The northern kingdom of Israel had allied with Syria (Damascus), and both would fall to the Assyrians (Isaiah 17). *If the people we trust do not trust the Lord, we will partake in the judgment that God has prepared for them.* God's judgment on Israel is pictured by a sunset and a heavy person losing weight (v. 4), as well as a field that has no grain for the harvester and no fruit for the gleaners (vv. 5–6). Israel had decayed, and all her efforts at recovery were wasted (vv. 10–11). If only they had turned to God before the sun set or the disease wasted away the body or the blight destroyed the harvest! But they trusted their own idols and not the true God (vv. 7–8). *How easy it is to put confidence in the work of our own hands and not in the God who made those hands!*

However, there is still hope for Northern Israel as they will turn to the true and living God, their Maker, the Holy One of Israel, and will renounce everything that has to do with idolatry that they had followed all this time. *"Their land is also full of idols; they worship the work of their own hands, that which their own fingers have made."*

267

(Isaiah 2:8) These idols included the Canaanite goddess Asherah who was a fertility goddess symbolized by sacred groves and poles (27:9; Ex. 34:13; Deut. 16:21; Judg. 2:13). Since their idols could not deliver them, the people of Northern Israel will be prompted to turn back to God one day. *Often it is only after some disaster that we realize how far we have drifted from God!*

We have a choice to make today – either we follow after our self-manufactured idols (which may be anything that takes the place of God in our lives and may include our jobs, hobbies, leisure, friends, social networking, television, internet, music, etc.) or, we seek and follow after God and His kingdom (Matt. 6:33). The Bible is clear that we cannot serve two masters – we will hate one and love the other or else we will be loyal to one and despise the other (Matt. 6:24). Whether we like it or not – if we do not bow to Jesus Christ today, we <u>will</u> bow to Him one day. *Turn to Jesus today – look to Him and live to please Him in our lives* – otherwise a day is coming when we will bow before Him and acknowledge that He is Lord over all…!!!

"Therefore God also has highly exalted Him (Jesus Christ) and given Him the name which is above every name, that at the name of Jesus every knee should bow, of those in heaven, and of those on earth, and of those under the earth, and that every tongue should confess that Jesus Christ is Lord, to the glory of God the Father." (Phil 2:9-11)

JULY 22   *Bible Reading: Isaiah Chapters 19-21*

WILL ISRAEL, EGYPT AND ASSYRIA BE UNITED IN THE FUTURE?

"In that day Israel will be one of three with Egypt and Assyria—a blessing in the midst of the land, whom the Lord of hosts shall bless, saying, "Blessed is Egypt My people, and Assyria the work of My hands, and Israel My inheritance." (Isaiah 19:24-25)

Egypt, Israel's oppressor at the time of the Exodus, centuries later became her ally against Assyria. Isaiah prophesied that God would come in judgment against Egypt, bringing division and defeat. Egypt, with the life-giving Nile River, was a haven for others in times of drought. But *"the waters of the river will dry up"* (19:5) —a picture of great calamity. However, Isaiah prophesies future blessing for Egypt.

He described a time (called *"that day"* in 19:16, 18, 19, 21, 23–24) when Egypt will acknowledge the Lord and will join with Israel in worshiping Him.

We can observe the conversion of Egypt described in sequence:

1. They shall speak the language of Canaan (v. 18a)
2. They shall swear allegiance to the Lord of hosts as their King (v. 18b)
3. They shall set up the public worship of God (altar & pillar) in their land (v. 19)
4. When they are in distress, they shall seek the God of Israel (v. 20)
5. The knowledge of God shall prevail among them (v. 21)
6. They shall come into the communion of saints (v. 23)

When Egypt and Assyria become partners in serving God Israel shall make a third with them (v. 24); they shall become a three-fold cord, not easily broken. *Israel will be one of three with Egypt and Assyria, that is, they will form a triple alliance, enjoying the blessings of Christ's kingdom.* The Savior and a Mighty One (v.20) who brings universal blessing refers to Jesus Christ Himself ruling over Egypt during the millennial kingdom. The highway running from Egypt to Assyria through Israel pictures a time of international peace when Egypt and Assyria will become God's people.

Thus, prophet Isaiah sees a time when Israel will be a partner and ally of her former foes, and together they will become a blessing to all the inhabitants of the earth. Isaiah promises that one day the God of Israel will be the God not only of the Arab and Jewish nations, but also of the whole world. *This was what God had promised many years ago, when He had called Abraham, the father of the nations, to serve Him:*

Now the Lord had said to Abram: "Get out of your country, from your family and from your father's house, to a land that I will show you. I will make you a great nation; I will bless you and make your name great; and you shall be a blessing. **I will bless those who bless you, and I will curse him who curses you; and in you all the families of the earth shall be blessed.***"* (Gen 12:1-3)

PRAISING GOD IN THE MIDST OF JUDGMENT

*"When it shall be thus in the midst of the land among the people, it shall be like the shaking of an olive tree, like the gleaning of grapes when the vintage is done. **They shall lift up their voice, they shall sing**; for the majesty of the Lord they shall cry aloud from the sea. Therefore glorify the Lord in the dawning light, the name of the Lord God of Israel in the coastlands of the sea. From the ends of the earth we have heard songs: "Glory to the righteous!"* (Isaiah 24:13-16)

The four chapters from Isaiah 24 to 27 form one continuous poetical prophecy. In particular, Isaiah 24 is descriptive of the dispersion and successive calamities of the Jews (vv. 1-12); the preaching of the Gospel by the first Hebrew converts throughout the world (vv. 13-16); the judgments on the adversaries of the Church, and the final triumph of the Church (vv. 16-23).

What we can understand from Isaiah 24:13-16 is that God's intervention and judgment will not be dreaded by everyone. The prophecy of gloom and doom is interrupted by the sound of a distant song of praise by a redeemed remnant as they sing the praises of Jehovah for His saving grace. From the east to the west (and everywhere in between) *a believing remnant will glorify God for His righteous actions. Those who had been persecuted and oppressed by the world will rejoice to see God's punishment of the wicked.*

This passage in Isaiah is thus a prophetical reference to the fact there will be a righteous remnant that will remain in this earth who will suffer through the Great Tribulation. This remnant that remains shall lift up their voice and shall sing in recognition of God's divine deliverance of them from the Great Tribulation. The new song that they sing is in response to God's act of salvation (see Isaiah 12; 35:6; 42:10–13; 44:23; 49:13; 52:8, 9; 65:14). The reference to the *"ends of the earth"* (v. 16) emphasizes the universal nature of the prophecy in this passage. The phrase *"glory to the righteous"* (v. 16) refers to the righteous people of God who have lived to please God.

The lesson for us from this passage is that we should love God and be willing to suffer for the sake of righteousness to escape the coming judgment of God against the wicked!

We have this wonderful assurance given by our Lord Jesus himself: *"Blessed are those who are persecuted for righteousness' sake, for theirs is the kingdom of heaven."* (Matt 5:10) Here's another prophecy by Jesus concerning the upcoming tribulation: *"For then there will be great tribulation, such as has not been since the beginning of the world until this time, no, nor ever shall be. And unless those days were shortened, no flesh would be saved; but for the elect's sake those days will be shortened."* (Matt 24:21-22)

JULY 24   *Bible Reading: Isaiah Chapters 25-27*

HAVING THE 'PERFECT' PEACE FROM GOD

"You will keep him in perfect peace, whose mind is stayed on You, because he trusts in You. Trust in the Lord forever, for in Yah, the Lord, is everlasting strength." (Isaiah 26:3-4)

In Isaiah 26:1-6, Isaiah predicted a day when the people of Judah will sing about Jerusalem as a *"strong city"* that will open its gates to the righteous. God will be known as the One who humbles the proud (*"those who dwell on high"*) and levels their cities, allowing the oppressed to triumph over them. Here, the city of God is in contrast to man's city (Isaiah 24:10). The righteous nation (redeemed Israel) experiences the *"perfect peace"* that comes from leaning hard on Jehovah.

The famous evangelist D.L. Moody tied verses 3 and 4 in the following manner: *"The tree of peace strikes its roots into the crevices of the Rock of Ages."* The people of God realize that *"in YAH the Lord is everlasting strength"* or, *"the Rock of Ages"* (In Hebrew, YAH is the shortened form of YHWH, the revered name of Jehovah God). It was from this expression that Augustus Toplady got the idea for one of the greatest hymns in all times called *"Rock of Ages."* Seeking shelter in a cleft of a rocky crag during a violent thunderstorm, he started writing this hymn using the following words: *"Rock of Ages, cleft for me, let me hide myself in Thee."*

The expression *'perfect peace'* indicates a peace that goes beyond our human comprehension. To have one's mind stayed on God means to lean on God in total confidence and security. Trust is the ultimate expression of that confidence, and this *"perfect peace"* is only found in Immanuel (Isaiah 9:6; 11:6–9; 14:7). This peace of God is only that which the righteous receive from God (v. 12; 32:17, 18; 55:12; 66:12) and will extend to the wicked (48:22; 59:8).

Let us remember that in the midst of turmoil and disarray in our lives where we tend to be anxious and troubled in our hearts. It is at these times that we can turn to God in prayer to provide us both strength in our hearts and peace in our minds.

"Be anxious for nothing, but in everything by prayer and supplication, with thanksgiving, let your requests be made known to God; and **the peace of God, which surpasses all understanding, will guard your hearts and minds through Christ Jesus.***"* (Phil 4:6-7)

JULY 25 *Bible Reading: Isaiah Chapters 28-30*

JESUS CHRIST IS OUR SURE FOUNDATION

Therefore thus says the Lord God: **"Behold, I lay in Zion a stone for a foundation, a tried stone, a precious cornerstone, a sure foundation; whoever believes will not act hastily."** (Isaiah 28:16)

The prophecy in Isaiah 28:16 is God's plan and promise concerning Jesus Christ as the only foundation of hope for escaping the wrath to come. This foundation was laid in Zion, in the eternal counsel of God. This foundation is a stone, firm and able to support His church. It is a tried stone, a chosen stone, and approved of God.

God promises to lay in Zion ... a precious cornerstone. The Messiah is the tried and true cornerstone of God's kingdom. The apostles and the New Testament writers have clearly identified this cornerstone as Jesus Christ. Here are a few verses that will verify Jesus Christ to be the foundation and the cornerstone of the Church that He has established on the earth:

- *The stone which the builders rejected* (speaking prophetically about Jesus Christ) *has become the chief cornerstone. This was the Lord's doing; it is marvelous in our eyes.* (Psalms 118:22-23)
- *For they* (the Israelites who rejected Jesus) *stumbled at that stumbling stone. As it is written: "Behold, I lay in Zion a stumbling stone and rock of offense, and whoever believes on Him will not be put to shame."* (Romans 9:32-33)

272

- *If you confess with your mouth the Lord Jesus and believe in your heart that God has raised Him from the dead, you will be saved. For with the heart one believes unto righteousness, and with the mouth confession is made unto salvation. For the Scripture says, "Whoever believes on Him will not be put to shame." (Romans 10:9-11)*
- *For no other foundation can anyone lay than that which is laid, which is Jesus Christ. (1 Cor 3:11)*
- *Now, therefore, you are no longer strangers and foreigners, but fellow citizens with the saints and members of the household of God, having been built on the foundation of the apostles and prophets, **Jesus Christ Himself being the chief corner stone**, in whom the whole building, being joined together, grows into a holy temple in the Lord, in whom you also are being built together for a dwelling place of God in the Spirit. (Eph 2:19-22)*
- *Therefore it is also contained in the Scripture, "Behold, I lay in Zion a chief cornerstone, elect, precious, and he who believes on Him will by no means be put to shame." Therefore, to you who believe, He is precious; but to those who are disobedient, the stone which the builders rejected has become the chief cornerstone," and "a stone of stumbling and a rock of offense." They stumble, being disobedient to the word, to which they also were appointed. (1 Peter 2:6-8)*

Thus, we can understand clearly that God has established Jesus Christ, the Messiah, as the only worthy object of trust, a sure foundation. Those who rely on Him never need to be scared regarding the future. Those who believe in Jesus Christ as their Lord and Savior will find Him as a sure foundation. To those who reject Jesus, He will become a stumbling stone who will seal their fate to eternal death and judgment. Under His reign, everything will have to meet the test of justice and righteousness, and His judgment will sweep away every false objects of trust.

JULY 26   *Bible Reading: Isaiah Chapters 31-33*

SIX GODLY QUALITIES OF A RIGHTEOUS PERSON:

"He who walks righteously and speaks uprightly, he who despises the gain of oppressions, who gestures with his hands, refusing bribes, who

stops his ears from hearing of bloodshed, and shuts his eyes from seeing evil: He will dwell on high; his place of defense will be the fortress of rocks; bread will be given him, his water will be sure." (Isaiah 33:15-16)

As Isaiah is prophesying about the impending judgment that is destined for everyone (Isaiah 33:10-14), there is hope for the righteous. As in some of the Psalms, which contain questions and answers regarding the conditions for admittance to worship (Psalms 15 and 24), Isaiah describes the qualities of those who will escape punishment and dwell with the Lord in safety forever (vv. 15-16). The **six** qualities of a righteous person (Isaiah 33:15) are listed below:

1. Lives a life displaying righteous behavior - walks righteously

2. Speaks only what is right and true - speaks uprightly

3. Does not oppress weak people in order to make money – hates money from dishonesty

4. Makes it plain that his/her integrity cannot be bought with bribes – refuses to take bribes

5. Does not listen to suggestions for eliminating opponents by resorting to violence (Job 31:31; Prov. 1:14, 16)

6. Cannot tolerate evil at any time – even the very appearance of evil

The conduct of the godly are also described in the following scripture passages: Psalms 1:1, 2; 15:2–5; 24:4; Galatians 5:22–25; Ephesians 5:1 and James 3:13–18. The person who pursues a godly character will enjoy **two** major benefits (Isaiah 33:16):

1. **He shall be safe**; he shall escape the devouring fire and the everlasting burning in hell.

2. **He shall be supplied**; he shall want nothing that is necessary for him.

"On high" (v. 16) refers to God's dwelling (v. 5)—the place the righteous will go to live with God forever. God will make their lives secure when He comes to reside in and rule over Jerusalem.

Let us sincerely attempt to live godly lives every day – this will surely pay off in the end!

Bible Reading: Isaiah Chapters 34-36

NOT ONE OF THE BIBLE PROPHECIES SHALL EVER FAIL

*"Search from the book of the Lord, and read: **not one of these shall fail; not one shall lack her mate**. For My mouth has commanded it, and His Spirit has gathered them."* (Isaiah 34:16)

Isaiah chapter 34 ends with a reference to the book of the Lord, which is apparently the book of inspired prophecies and probably refers to Isaiah's own writing found in vv. 1–15. This may be the volume in which the various prophecies and other parts of Scripture began henceforward to be collected together. *"Now go, write it before them on a tablet, and note it on a scroll, that it may be for time to come, forever and ever"* (Isaiah 30:8).

The book of the Lord also refers to God's inspired prophecies predicting the future judgment, and the Holy Spirit will see to it that what the Word announces is fulfilled. So severe will this coming eschatological judgment be that we need to be reminded that it is part of the divinely inspired prophetic Scripture; and therefore, it will certainly come to pass as God has predicted it.

While referring to specific prophecies, Isaiah brings out the image from pairing of animals mentioned in the previous verse 15 ("mate"). What it means is that no prediction shall want a fulfillment as its companion…every single Bible prophecy will be fulfilled. There is a change of person ("My" to "His") and Bible scholars have pointed out that such changes of person are frequent in Hebrew poetry.

Taking this verse for a spiritual application in our lives - the book of the Lord is the Bible we have in our hands. We ought to read it with the understanding that it has divine origin and authority. *"Knowing this first that no prophecy of Scripture is of any private interpretation, for prophecy never came by the will of man, but holy men of God spoke as they were moved by the Holy Spirit"* (2 Peter 1:20-21). We must not only read the scriptures, but see out of it, search into it, turn first to one text and then to another and compare them together. We can thus extract abundant wisdom through diligent search of the scriptures, which we cannot get through a casual superficial reading.

When we read the various predictions in the scriptures, we will understand not one of these shall fail. What God has spoken through

His written word will surely come to pass, and the Holy Spirit will ensure that each and every word will be fulfilled. This is what our Lord Jesus Christ has spoken concerning the word of God: *"Truly I say to you, till heaven and earth come to an end, not the smallest letter or part of a letter will in any way be taken from the law, till all things are done."* - Matt 5:18 (Bible in Basic English)

JULY 28   *Bible Reading: Isaiah Chapters 37-39*

HOW TO BE VICTORIOUS WHEN ATTACKED BY OUR ENEMIES?

And Hezekiah received the letter from the hand of the messengers, and read it; and Hezekiah went up to the house of the Lord, and spread it before the Lord. Then Hezekiah prayed to the Lord, saying: "O Lord of hosts, God of Israel, the One who dwells between the cherubim, You are God, You alone, of all the kingdoms of the earth. You have made heaven and earth. Incline Your ear, O Lord, and hear; open Your eyes, O Lord, and see…that all the kingdoms of the earth may know that You are the Lord, You alone." (Isaiah 37:14-20)

When King Hezekiah was confronted with a threatening letter from King Sennacherib of Assyria, he did not respond directly. Instead, he took this letter and *"spread it out before the Lord"* in a magnificent display of humble trust and utter dependence upon God as he turned to the Lord in prayer. The idea was not that God must read the message, but rather that He might consider the matter. Hezekiah used this means to indicate that he was committing the entire matter to the Lord for His judgment. His first concern was not for his own safety but for God's glory and he attributes deity exclusively to Jehovah (Isaiah 44:8; 45:5, 6, 14, 22; 46:9).

The eminent Bible Scholar, Warren Wiersbe has expounded Isaiah 37 beautifully and listed **five simple steps** *(through King Hezekiah's experience)* **that we should take when we are attacked by our enemies**:

1. *Take our burdens to God.* It is good to talk things over with others, but only God can work in our hearts and turn fear into faith. God knows everything our enemies are saying and writing,

and God has a perfect plan for us. By faith, we should take everything to God in prayer.

2. ***Listen for God's message.*** The words of the enemy will discourage us, but God's Word will encourage us. In every battle, His word to us is, *"Do not be afraid"* (v. 6). After all, God has everything under control.

3. ***Seek to glorify God alone.*** More than anything else, Hezekiah was concerned for the glory of God (vv. 4, 16–20). *"Hallowed be Your name"* must be our primary prayer (see Matt. 6:8).

4. ***Trust God to work.*** Sennacherib defied the God of Israel, and yet he died in the house of his god who could not protect him (v. 38). God can handle our enemies far better than we can.

5. ***Trust God after the victory.*** The Assyrians had devastated the land, but God promised to feed His people and give them a harvest (vv. 30-31). Let us always remember that our future is in God's Hands.

Let us always understand that God is willing and waiting for us to go to Him when we are in trouble. Just like He unilaterally destroyed King Hezekiah's enemy, He will destroy all our enemies as well as He will show Himself strong on our behalf. *"For the eyes of the Lord run to and fro throughout the whole earth, to show Himself strong on behalf of those whose heart is loyal to Him."* (2 Chron 16:9)

JULY 29   *Bible Reading: Isaiah Chapters 40-42*

IT'S TIME TO RENEW OUR STRENGTH LIKE EAGLES

"Have you not known? Have you not heard? The everlasting God, the Lord, the Creator of the ends of the earth, neither faints nor is weary. His understanding is unsearchable. **He gives power to the weak, and to those who have no might He increases strength.** *Even the youths shall faint and be weary, and the young men shall utterly fall, but* **those who wait on the Lord shall renew their strength; they shall mount up with wings like eagles, they shall run and not be weary, they shall walk and not faint.***"* (Isaiah 40:28-31)

In Isaiah 40:28, God repeats these rhetorical questions for emphasis (see verse 21). God is not only everlasting *(transcendent over time)* but also the Creator of the ends of the earth *(transcendent over space)*. He is omnipotent (all powerful) and meets all the needs of His people. God will never let His people down (Psalms 121:3, 4) as He gives both power and strength to the weak, and to those who do not rely in their own strength (Jer. 9:23).

To *"wait on the Lord"* refers to **confident expectation** and **hope in God for deliverance** (Psalms 40:1). *'Mount up'… 'Run'… 'Walk'* shows the **spiritual transformation** that faith brings to a person. The Lord gives both **power** and **strength** to those who trust in Him. The illustration of *"mounting up with wings like eagle"* depicts the strength that comes from the Lord. The Lord describes His deliverance of the Israelites in Exodus 19:4 as similar to being lifted up on the strong wings of an eagle. Also, in Psalms 103:5, the strength of people who are nourished by God is compared to the strength of the eagle, which is a common metaphor for strength (Deut. 32:11). **God's strength is available for all who prayerfully wait in patience for God's purposes to be carried out!**

In our personal lives, we may be weak like *grass* (Isaiah 40:6–8), *sheep* (v. 11), *dust* (v. 15), *grasshoppers* (v. 22), and *even worms* (41:14); but when we trust the power of God and wait on Him in prayer, we can be like *an eagle, a runner*, and *a patient pilgrim* (vv. 28–31). In the emergencies of life, God will help us to soar like eagles; in the race set before us He will help us to run with endurance (Heb. 12:1), and in the daily routine of life He will help us to patiently walk one step at a time (Psalms 1:1).

"Now to Him who is able to do exceedingly abundantly above all that we ask or think, according to the power that works in us, to Him be glory in the church by Christ Jesus to all generations, forever and ever. Amen." (Eph 3:20-21)

JULY 30   *Bible Reading: Isaiah Chapters 43-45*

GOD'S AMAZING PROMISE OF PROTECTION

But now, thus says the Lord, who created you, O Jacob, and He who formed you, O Israel: "Fear not, for I have redeemed you; I have called you by your name; you are Mine. When you pass through the waters, I will be with you; and through the rivers, they shall not overflow you. When you walk through the fire, you shall not be burned, nor shall the flame scorch you. For I am the Lord your God, the Holy One of Israel, your Savior..." (Isaiah 43:1-3)

This above passage is a declaration of God to protect His people Israel on the basis that He has created them from the dust of the earth (Gen. 2:7) for good works (Eph. 2:10); redeemed them from Egypt; set them apart for Himself and has entered into an everlasting covenant with them. God claims Israel as His own on the basis of four factors: (1) creation, (2) formation, (3) redemption, and (4) naming, which according to the oriental custom signified ownership.

In spite of Israel's deliberate rejection of God to rule as her rightful king, God reassures them, *"Fear not, for I have redeemed you"*. The theme of *redemption* appears twenty-two times in the Servant passages of the Book of Isaiah, and indicates redemption from physical and spiritual bondage as well as the eschatological redemption that is yet to come (Isaiah 43:5-7; 44:22; 49:16, 17). In tones of tender love, Jehovah assures His people that they need not fear, because He who created, formed, redeemed, and called them *will be with them when they pass through the waters and walk through the fire. Passing through the waters* is an allusion to the crossing of the Red Sea (Ex. 14:21, 22) and the Jordan River (Josh. 3:14–17). *Walking through the fire* is a metaphor for protection in danger (Ps. 66:12) as we consider God's protection of Shadrach, Meshach, and Abednego in the fiery furnace (Dan. 3:25–27).

In our case, there is no reason to be afraid when we understand God's amazing promise of protection and realize what God has done for us. He has formed us (Isaiah 43:1) making us for Himself (v. 21) and for His glory (v. 7). When we have trusted Jesus Christ, God has redeemed us (v. 1) and blotted out all our sins (v. 25). He loves us (v. 4) and knows our names (v. 1). Even more, God promises to be with us (v. 5) and take us through the waters and the fire (v. 2). The waters can make us wet or bring us discomfort, but they will not overwhelm us or overflow over us. God's presence and protection will be there when we walk through the furnace of affliction. We will not be burned nor shall the fire scorch us as we have God's protection over us. Since we are called to holiness (set apart for God), we need to be separated from anything that is unclean or impure. *So, when we walk through* fire, we will realize that God's purpose for us is to purify us and not to destroy us!

"And we know that all things work together for good to those who love God, to those who are the called according to His purpose. For whom He foreknew, He also predestined to be conformed to the image of His Son, that He might be the firstborn among many brethren. Moreover whom He predestined, these He also called; whom He called, these He also justified; and whom He justified, these He also glorified. What then shall we say to these things? If God is for us, who can be against us?" (Romans 8:28-31)

JULY 31   *Bible Reading: Isaiah Chapters 46-48*

GOD CARRIES US FROM CRADLE TO GRAVE!

"Listen to Me, O house of Jacob, and all the remnant of the house of Israel, who have been upheld by Me from birth, who have been carried from the womb: Even to your old age, I am He, and even to gray hairs I will carry you! I have made, and I will bear; even I will carry, and will deliver you. To whom will you liken Me, and make Me equal and compare Me, that we should be alike?" (Isaiah 46:3-5)

In Isaiah 46, there is a vivid picture of the siege of Babylon and the evacuation of its idols. The carriages are creaking under the weight of the idols and the animals are groaning under the load (v. 1). In contrast, God carries His children from birth (v. 3) to the old age (v. 4). Thus, Isaiah 46 has two major contrasts: idols, which must be supported as opposed to Yahweh, who supports Israel (vv. 1-7)

The idols of Babylon, Bel and Nebo, are being carted away by the Persians. As the weary beasts plod on, the idols topple. The gods they represent cannot save the load; instead they are carried off into captivity. In contrast to the idols which are carried by the people, the true God will carry His people even to their old age. We are here told that the false gods will certainly fail their worshippers when they have most need of them (v. 1, 2) and that the true God will never fail his worshippers (v. 3, 4).

There are two kinds of gods in this world: *the idols we carry and the One God who carries us!* Let us understand that an idol is a substitute

280

for God, something that we value and serve other than God. We trust it and sacrifice for it; but in the end, it can do us no good. Isaiah mocked the idols of the nations and affirmed repeatedly that Jehovah was the only true and living God (40:18–20; 41:5–7; 44:9–20; 45:15–21; 46:1–7). Martin Luther said that *"all such as rely and depend upon their art, wisdom, strength, sanctity, riches, honor, power, or anything else are guilty of worshiping idols."*

The idea in this passage is that all the idols that we trust and serve passionately will one day fall before the Lord. The rhetorical question is that to whom can we liken God? The obvious answer—no one! There is no one like the God we serve. Yahweh is the unique and incomprehensible God. It is this great God who has promised to carry us from cradle to grave! Let us put our faith and trust in Him alone for He alone will carry us from our cradle to our grave!

"The eternal God is your refuge, and underneath are the everlasting arms" (Deut 33:27)

"But You are He who took Me out of the womb; You made Me trust while on My mother's breasts. I was cast upon You from birth. From My mother's womb You have been My God." (Psalms 22:9-10)

"For You are my hope, O Lord God; You are my trust from my youth. By You I have been upheld from birth; You are He who took me out of my mother's womb. My praise shall be continually of You." (Psalms 71:5-6)

August

TRUSTING IN GOD WHILE WALKING IN THE DARK

"Who among you fears the Lord? Who obeys the voice of His Servant? Who walks in darkness and has no light? **Let him trust in the name of the Lord and rely upon his God.** *Look, all you who kindle a fire, who encircle yourselves with sparks: walk in the light of your fire and in the sparks you have kindled— this you shall have from My hand: you shall lie down in torment."* (Isaiah 50:10-11)

The prophet Isaiah calls upon those who *"fears the Lord"* and *"obeys the voice of God's Servant"*. The fear of the Lord—that is, the reverence of God—is the beginning of true wisdom (see Prov. 1:7). God's Servant mentioned here prophetically speaks about Jesus Christ, who came into this earth as a lowly servant. So, the exhortation is for those who revere God and obey Christ that they continue to trust God even during times of distress (pictured as walking "in the dark").

On the other hand, the prophet Isaiah issues a warning to those who try to solve their problems by using their own effort (pictured as walking "in the light of" their own "fires"). Those who refuse to trust God and rely instead on their own abilities will ultimately face torment. Those *"who kindle a fire"* means those who are self-reliant, instead of walking in the light of the Lord and His Servant (Isaiah 2:5; 42:6). When the 'Light of Life' comes into the world, some will choose darkness (John 3:17, 18). Torment indicates God's punishment for unbelief.

The above verses describe *two groups of people*. The *first* group of people walks in dependence on the Lord. They confess their own need for guidance. For them God's advice is to trust in the name of the Lord and rely upon their God. Then they will be flooded with illumination. The *second* group of people tries to manufacture their own guidance, feeling no need of divine direction. They can walk in the light of their own sparks but the Lord will see to it that they will lie down in torment.

Let us clearly understand that people who fear and obey God can still end up in the darkness of perplexity. Then they are tempted to light their own fires and try to find their way out by themselves. Instead, these verses exhort them to trust the Lord and wait on Him for help, and He will give us the light that we need when we need it.

Our Christian life is comparable to a walk from the 'outer court' to the 'Holies of Holies' through the 'Holy Place' of the Tabernacle. There is sunlight in the outer court, candlelight in the inner court, but no light in the innermost court. It is when we progress to the near presence of God that we rely and trust completely on God alone as we *'walk by faith and not by sight'* (2 Cor. 5:7). That is what God is expecting from each one of us!

*"**Unto the upright there arises light in the darkness**; He (God) is gracious, and full of compassion, and righteous."* (Psalms 112:4)

*"You who love the Lord, hate evil! He (God) preserves the souls of His saints; He delivers them out of the hand of the wicked. **Light is sown for the righteous**, and gladness for the upright in heart."* (Psalms 97:10-11)

*"The steps of a good man are ordered by the Lord, and He (God) delights in his way. **Though he fall, he shall not be utterly cast down; for the Lord upholds him with His hand.**"* (Psalms 37:23-24)

AUGUST 2   *Bible Reading: Isaiah Chapters 52-54*

JESUS CHRIST – THE SIN-BEARING SUFFERING SERVANT WHO TOOK OUR PLACE

"Surely He has borne our griefs and carried our sorrows; yet we esteemed Him stricken, smitten by God, and afflicted. But He was wounded for

our transgressions, He was bruised for our iniquities; the chastisement for our peace was upon Him, and by His stripes we are healed." (Isaiah 53:4-5)

Isaiah 53 is a prophecy about Jesus Christ – the suffering Servant - God's perfect sacrifice for the sins of the world (Acts 8:26–40). This prophecy actually begins in Isaiah 52:13 telling us that the Servant suffered for doing God's will and yet was highly exalted by the Lord. Jesus was humiliated in His birth and life (vv. 1–3) as well as during His trial, His sufferings and His death (vv. 4–9). He was depicted as a beaten servant (52:13–14), a root (53:2), an innocent lamb (53:7), an offering for sin (53:10), a woman in travail giving birth to spiritual "seed" (53:10–11), and a victorious general (53:12).

Our Lord Jesus suffered *all five kinds of wounds* known to medical science: *contusions* (through blows by a rod), *lacerations* (through scourging on His back), *penetrating wounds* (through crown of thorns on His head), *perforating wounds* (through nails on His hands and feet) and *incised wounds* (through spear on His side). It was for our transgressions, for our iniquities, and in order that we might have peace, in order that we might be healed. The truth is that we were the ones who went astray and who walked in self-will and Jehovah placed our iniquity on Him, the sinless substitute.

Our Lord Jesus literally fulfilled **all** the prophecies made by Isaiah with regards to the Suffering Servant:

· He will be exalted (compare Isaiah 52:13 with Philippians 2:9)
· He will be disfigured by suffering (compare Isaiah 52:14; 53:2 with Mark 15:17, 19)
· He will be widely rejected (compare Isaiah 53:1, 3 with John 12:37, 38)
· He will bear our sins and sorrows (compare Isaiah 53:4 with Romans 4:25; 1 Peter 2:24, 25)
· He will make a blood atonement (compare Isaiah 53:5 with Romans 3:25)
· He will be our substitute (compare Isaiah 53:6, 8 with 2 Corinthians 5:21)
· He will voluntarily accept our guilt and punishment (compare Isaiah 53:7 with John 10:11)
· He will be buried in a rich man's tomb (compare Isaiah 53:9 with John 19:38-42)

- He will justify many from their sin (compare Isaiah 53:10, 11 with Romans 5:15-19)
- He will die with transgressors (compare Isaiah 53:12 with Mark 15:27, 28; Luke 22:37)

Let us consider the glory of the salvation that Jesus has purchased for us on the cross. God, the Father was pleased, not that His Son suffered, but that His sacrifice accomplished eternal salvation. God's justice was satisfied, and believing sinners can be justified (v. 11; Rom. 3:21–31). Griefs (or pain) and sorrows (or sickness) refer to the consequences of sin. Our Lord Jesus came to this earth to suffer and die for our sins and sickness (Isaiah 53:6, 11, 12; Matt. 8:17; Heb. 9:28), so that we can enjoy redemption, health, joy, peace and eternal life. *Have you taken advantage of His sufferings and death by accepting Him as your Lord and Savior?*

"For to this you were called, because Christ also suffered for us, leaving us an example, that you should follow His steps: 'who committed no sin, nor was deceit found in His mouth'; who, when He was reviled, did not revile in return; when He suffered, He did not threaten, but committed Himself to Him who judges righteously; who Himself bore our sins in His own body on the tree, that we, having died to sins, might live for righteousness—by whose stripes you were healed." (1 Peter 2:21-24)

AUGUST 3 Bible Reading: Isaiah Chapters 55-57

GOD'S INVITATION TO ENJOY ABUNDANT LIFE

"Ho! Everyone who thirsts, come to the waters; and you who have no money, come, buy and eat. Yes, come, buy wine and milk without money and without price. Why do you spend money for what is not bread, and your wages for what does not satisfy? Listen carefully to Me, and eat what is good, and let your soul delight itself in abundance. Incline your ear, and come to Me. Hear, and your soul shall live; and I will make an everlasting covenant with you— the sure mercies of David." (Isaiah 55:1-3)

In Isaiah 55, God extends a *general invitation* to everyone to find their satisfaction and their security in Him alone. This is a *call to revival* for all who have wandered far from God or His grace that is the basis for our relationship with Him. This is also a *call to salvation* for those who do not know Him personally, promising a free but abundant and eternal life that is better than money can buy.

God's invitation is issued to the *thirsty* and the *penniless*—all who will recognize their need for spiritual blessing and their inability to meet the need themselves. *"Waters"* and *"wine and milk"* are symbols of abundant spiritual blessings. These blessings are the *waters of the Holy Spirit*, the *wine of joy*, and the *milk of God's Word*. They are the *free gifts of grace*, without money and price. True satisfaction and lasting pleasure are found only in God! As Jesus spoke to the Samaritan woman: *"Whoever drinks of this water will thirst again, but whoever drinks of the water that I shall give him will never thirst. But the water that I shall give him will become in him a fountain of water springing up into everlasting life."* (John 4:13-14)

When we return to God, we will also receive all the *"sure mercies"* promised to David (2 Sam. 7) in the everlasting covenant (Isaiah 55:3b; Psalm 89:3, 4, 28, 29). This covenant promises that a descendant of David will rule eternally over a kingdom that will bless all the nations (Luke 1:32, 33; 2:30–32). This will be fulfilled one day in the Lord Jesus Christ and in His glorious reign. We will share in the benefits of God's kingdom. However, the pathway of blessing lies in seeking the Lord and in forsaking sin. When we thus return to the Lord, we will find Him full of mercy and pardon (Isaiah 55:6-7).

Thus, to those who *"spend money for what is not bread"* and *"wages for what does not satisfy"* (Isaiah 55:2), God offers a compelling invitation: *"Come to Me … and your soul shall live"* (v. 3). This marvelous call of God is extended to everyone in this world. Anyone who is thirsty can drink of His waters of grace (55:1, 5).

This same invitation is still in effect for everyone today. In the Book of Revelation, the Lord says, *"I will give of the fountain of the water of life freely to him who thirsts…and let him who thirsts come. Whoever desires let him take the water of life freely"* (Rev. 21:6; 22:17).

Have you personally responded to God's gift of life, through faith in Jesus Christ? Are you unsatisfied with what the world offers you? Are you still dying of thirst? **God invites you to come, drink and enjoy the abundant life that He has made available for everyone!**

Bible Reading: Isaiah Chapters 58-60

GOD'S DESIRED OUTCOMES FROM OUR FASTING AND PRAYER

"Is this not the fast that I have chosen: to loose the bonds of wickedness, to undo the heavy burdens, to let the oppressed go free, and that you break every yoke? Is it not to share your bread with the hungry, and that you bring to your house the poor who are cast out; when you see the naked, that you cover him, and not hide yourself from your own flesh? Then your light shall break forth like the morning, your healing shall spring forth speedily, and your righteousness shall go before you; the glory of the Lord shall be your rear guard. Then you shall call, and the Lord will answer; you shall cry, and He will say, 'Here I am.'" (Isaiah 58:6-9)

The closing chapters of Isaiah (chapters 58–66) introduce us to the Messiah's program of peace for the world. One crucial element of introducing peace is through our fasting and prayer. In this passage, true fasting is contrasted with the false external show of piety.

Fasting is the discipline of abstaining from food for biblical reasons. It is called "afflicting one's soul" (v. 3), and is often practiced to demonstrate the sincerity of our prayers. There are several biblical reasons for fasting. We should fast when facing a national crisis (2 Chr. 20:3; Ezra 8:21; Esth. 4:16), for individual needs (Matt. 17:21), during periods of distress (2 Sam. 3:35; Ps. 35:13), when facing spiritual decisions (Matt. 4:2; Acts 13:2), and in anticipation of Christ's return (Luke 5:35).

God wants fasting that is accompanied by the loosing of the shackles of wickedness, lifting the yoke of oppression, feeding the hungry, providing shelter for the poor, clothing the naked, and helping the needy neighbor. God is more concerned about how we treat and care for our fellowman than about any vain ritualism. Those who thus practice social justice are assured of guidance, healing, and a protective escort. Fasting and other spiritual disciplines are not ends in themselves, but are intended to result in greater godliness in all our relationships. If they do not have that result, it is obvious that God has no interest in them.

When we strive to be a spiritual, we will fight the constant battle of *"ritual versus reality"*. It is much easier to go through the external activities of religion than it is to love God from our hearts and let that love touch the lives of others. What a difference it makes when we repent and return to the Lord (vv. 8–12). We will have light instead of darkness, healing instead of disease, righteousness instead of defilement, and glory instead of disgrace.

As we fast and pray to God, His love grows in us and flows out to others in acts of piety. This is what God requires as an outcome to our fasting!

"If you extend your soul to the hungry and satisfy the afflicted soul, then your light shall dawn in the darkness, and your darkness shall be as the noonday. The Lord will guide you continually, and satisfy your soul in drought, and strengthen your bones; you shall be like a watered garden, and like a spring of water, whose waters do not fail." (Isaiah 58:10-11)

AUGUST 5   *Bible Reading: Isaiah Chapters 61-63*

LIVING ON MISSION WITH GOD SO THAT HE GETS THE GLORY

"The Spirit of the Lord God is upon Me, because the Lord has anointed Me to preach good tidings to the poor; He has sent Me to heal the brokenhearted, to proclaim liberty to the captives, and the opening of the prison to those who are bound; to proclaim the acceptable year of the Lord, and the day of vengeance of our God; to comfort all who mourn, to console those who mourn in Zion, to give them beauty for ashes, the oil of joy for mourning, the garment of praise for the spirit of heaviness; that they may be called trees of righteousness, the planting of the Lord, that He may be glorified."* (Isaiah 61:1-3)

Although these are words of prophecy spoken by God's servant Isaiah, the words take on greater meaning when Jesus reads from this section (vs.1-2a) during His visit to the synagogue in Nazareth and closes His reading with the statement, *"Today this Scripture is fulfilled in your hearing"* (Luke 4:21). Thus, He applies these verses to Himself. This prophecy was literally fulfilled in the ministry of Christ. Isaiah is included (62:1) as a shadow or forerunner of Jesus.

Jesus Christ was anointed with the Holy Spirit at His baptism and His earthly ministry was concerned with bringing the good tidings of salvation to the poor, binding up the brokenhearted, proclaiming liberty to sin's captives, and opening the prison of those who were bound. The reference to *"liberty"* and *"opening of the prison"* allude to the Year of Jubilee, during which all debts and obligations were erased (Lev. 25:8-10).

These words of prophecy also describe the character and office of the Messiah. We should note that Jesus ended the quotation with the words *"to proclaim the acceptable year of the Lord"* because what follows, *"the day of vengeance of our God"* will not be fulfilled until His Second Coming. At His glorious appearing He will proclaim the day of God's judgment. Then He will comfort those who mourn in Zion, granting to them a garland in place of ashes on their heads, the oil of joy instead of mourning, praise instead of a spirit of heaviness. His chosen people will then be called trees of righteousness, planted by the Lord, and bringing glory to Him. They will rebuild the cities of the Promised Land that have lain in ruins.

What were God's purposes for anointing Jesus with His Spirit? We can see that there are **six purposes** from Isaiah 61:1-3:

1. *To preach good tidings*: This refers to the proclamation of the gospel and to the priority of evangelism.

2. *To bind up the brokenhearted*: This refers to placing the *'balm of Gilead'* (Jeremiah 8:22) to heal the hearts that have been broken by sin and guilt.

3. *To proclaim liberty*: This refers to freeing slaves in captivity of sin, addictions and sickness.

4. *To proclaim the acceptable year of the Lord*: This refers to announcing the *"year of the Lord's favor"*. Through His death and resurrection, Jesus inaugurated the *"day of salvation"* (2 Cor. 6:2) in which the gospel is preached all over the world, and those who are bound in sin and sickness can be liberated through Him (Eph. 2:12, 13; 3:5; 2 Tim. 1:10).

5. *Christ would comfort all that mourn after His great and awesome judgments*: (To be fulfilled in the future.)

6. *Christ would exchange the evidences of mourning with the evidences of rejoicing*: (Also to be fulfilled in the future.)

Through this anointing, *the end result would be that God gets the glory* (61:3c). Like Jesus, the purpose of anointing of God's Spirit in our lives is that through His power we can also be a witness of the gospel, heal people from sickness, deliver them from bondage, comfort the people who are broken hearted and plant God's Word in their hearts. **Let us live on mission with God being anointed by His Spirit so that He gets the glory!**

"But you shall receive power when the Holy Spirit has come upon you; and you shall be witnesses to Me in Jerusalem, and in all Judea and Samaria, and to the end of the earth." (Acts 1:8)

AUGUST 6　　　　　*Bible Reading: Isaiah Chapters 64-66*

DO WE EVER TREMBLE AT THE WORD OF GOD?

*Thus says the Lord: "Heaven is My throne, and earth is My footstool. Where is the house that you will build Me? And where is the place of My rest? For all those things My hand has made, and all those things exist," says the Lord. "**But on this one will I look: on him who is poor and of a contrite spirit, and who trembles at My word.**"*(Isaiah 66:1-2)

The opening words of the last chapter of Isaiah were written to the unrepentant people of Israel. They should not think that, in that condition, they can please God by building a temple for Him. This passage points to the magnitude and immensity of God, who is greater than the heavens. *Heaven is His throne and earth is His footstool.* He is not limited to any house (temple) made by man. The apostle John tells us that in eternity there is no need for a temple, *"for the Lord God Almighty and the Lamb are the temple of it"* (Rev. 21:22). The Lord has no need for a man-made temple because heaven and earth— the whole cosmos—is His sanctuary (Isaiah 40:22). The resting place for the *"feet"* of the Lord extends beyond the Ark of the Covenant (Isaiah 60:13) to the whole earth.

In this passage, God underlines the kind of worship He wants. Any religious act without a truly contrite spirit is an abomination to Him. God hates empty religious expressions as much as paganism (Jer. 7:21–23). Every religious ritual that we participate not accompanied with reverence, justice, and sincerity is despised by God. God is seeking 'true worshipers' who will worship Him in *"spirit and truth"* (John 4:24).

To *"tremble at God's word"* (Isa. 66:2, 5) means *to respect what God says and fear to disobey it* (Ps. 119:120). The Jews experienced this trembling when Ezra exposed their sins (Ezra 9:4; 10:3), and the prophet Habakkuk experienced it when he saw the vision of God's judgment (Hab. 3:16). Saul of Tarsus trembled when he met the Lord near Damascus (Acts 9:6). However, King Jehoiakim did not tremble at the Word; he tried to destroy it (Jer. 36), and that led to his destruction (Prov. 13:13). Paul has urged us to, *"work out our own salvation [Christian life] with fear and trembling"* (Phil. 2:12).

God desires to dwell in us who are of a poor and contrite spirit. Prophet Isaiah foresees the New Testament doctrine of the indwelling of the Holy Spirit in the temple of our bodies: *"Do you not know that your body is the temple of the Holy Spirit who is in you, whom you have from God, and you are not your own?"* (1 Cor 6:19)

Let us be humble and contrite as we tremble at His Word and serve Him with reverence and godly fear! *"...Let us have grace by which we may serve God acceptably with reverence and godly fear. For our God is a consuming fire."* (Heb 12:28-29)

AUGUST 7   *Bible Reading: Jeremiah Chapters 1-3*

DO NOT FORSAKE THE FOUNTAIN OF LIVING WATERS

"For My people have committed two evils: they have forsaken Me, the fountain of living waters, and hewn themselves cisterns—broken cisterns that can hold no water." (Jer 2:13)

Ancient landowners would dig cisterns to collect the rainwater. To insure that the cistern would hold water, the landowner plastered it inside with lime. Often cracks would develop and the water would leak out. In like manner Judah had abandoned Yahweh, the *"fountain of living waters"* (Ps. 36:9; Prov. 13:14; 16:22; Is. 55:1) for man-made powerless gods. The figure of the fountain of living waters emphasizes that God alone can bring the life and refreshment necessary to the thirsty soul (Rev. 21:6). Judah had left the purity of the living waters for the pollution of contaminated broken cisterns that offered no water at all.

The people had committed two evils. *First*, they had forsaken the Lord, the fountain of living waters. Isaiah had already used this imagery of God's blessing (Isa 44:3), and Jesus later alluded to it (John 4:10–15; 7:37–39). The *second sin* was that of idolatry, referring to broken cisterns. To people living in an arid land where the search for fountains of fresh water and good cisterns to hold it was a daily priority, this imagery was a powerful object lesson. God's people had forsaken (1:16) Him and served worthless deities. *God, the fountain of living waters, offered a limitless supply of fresh, life-giving sustenance. Instead the people chose broken cisterns, which were useless for storing water and useless for sustaining life.*

Why was judgment coming to the nation of Judah? The reason was because the people were unfaithful to God and had mixed the worship of Jehovah with the worship of heathen idols. Religion was very popular in Judah, but it was not very spiritual. The people, priests, rulers, and prophets have forgotten all God did for them. Unlike such heathen lands as Cyprus and Kedar, who are loyal to their gods, Judah has forsaken the Lord her God for worthless idols.

Let us not repeat the same mistakes that Judah did – by putting our trust in things or people in this world. Let us never forsake the Lord, who is the fountain of living waters! Instead, let us put our total trust and confidence in Him alone, and join with Jeremiah by praying the following prayer:

*O Lord, the hope of Israel, all who forsake You shall be ashamed. "Those who depart from Me shall be written in the earth, **because they have forsaken the Lord, the fountain of living waters.**" Heal me, O Lord, and I shall be healed; save me, and I shall be saved, for You are my praise.* (Jer 17:13-14)

AUGUST 8   *Bible Reading: Jeremiah Chapters 4-6*

KEEPING OUR END IN MIND IN ALL OUR ACTIVITIES

"An astonishing and horrible thing has been committed in the land: the prophets prophesy falsely, and the priests rule by their own power; and My people love to have it so. But what will you do in the end?" (Jer 5:30-31)

In this terse message, the prophet Jeremiah describes the moral depravity of Judah's leaders as *"an astonishing and horrible thing"*. The deterioration of the leadership of the land had reached to the prophets and priests, the very people who were to be the mainstays of righteousness among the people. Both offices had succumbed to the temptation of abusing their power, rejecting their responsible roles as messengers and servants of God.

Judah's sin was so exceedingly evil that it was described as being appallingly horrible as the people 'loved' being under the ministry of false prophets and wicked priests and desired to continue this farce (Jer. 6:13-15). The worst phase of this national evil was not that only some people were guilty, but even the priests and the prophets have become corrupt and self-serving. It is appalling and horrifying that the priests and prophets would pervert the message of God and that the people would *"love to have it so."* Even Jeremiah's chilling words, *"What will you do in the end?"* referring to the coming judgment, could not shake the people from their false complacency.

What we can understand is that the people of Judah were satisfied with a totally corrupt government. The prophets were telling the people what they wanted to hear. But prophet Jeremiah took his orders from God Almighty who knew what the people needed. If their healing required bitter medicine, that is what they would get.

In our own lives and activities, we need to be aware that God is watching us closely seeing all the activities we are doing and hearing all the words we are speaking. One day we will have to give an account before God regarding everything that we do in this world. *"For we must all appear before the judgment seat of Christ, that each one may receive the things done in the body, according to what he has done, whether good or bad."* (2 Cor 5:10)

Let's keep our end in mind in all our activities as we will reap one day what we sow today! This is what God's word speaks to us about this matter: *"Do not be deceived, God is not mocked; for whatever a man sows, that he will also reap. For he who sows to his flesh will of the flesh reap corruption, but he who sows to the Spirit will of the Spirit reap everlasting life. And let us not grow weary while doing good, for in due season we shall reap if we do not lose heart."* (Gal 6:7-9)

AUGUST 9   *Bible Reading: Jeremiah Chapters 7-9*

KNOWING GOD & HIS ATTRIBUTES – THE ONLY REASON TO GLORY

Thus says the Lord: "Let not the wise man glory in his wisdom, let not the mighty man glory in his might, nor let the rich man glory in his riches; **but let him who glories glory in this, that he understands and knows Me,** *that I am the Lord, exercising lovingkindness, judgment, and righteousness in the earth. For in these I delight," says the Lord.* (Jer 9:23-24)

Jeremiah prophesies from the Temple gates and challenges the people of Judah. After lamenting their foolishness of following vain idols, Jeremiah turns their attention to the true source of wisdom—the Lord Himself (9:23–10:25). True wisdom was to be found in the consistent following of the *three central qualities of spiritual life*: **lovingkindness** (the exercise of true covenant loyalty showing God's faithfulness to His covenant with Israel), **judgment** (the consistent application of true justice for all), and **righteousness** (the maintenance of what was right in the sight of the Lord in all of life). These three characteristic qualities of the Lord are revealed and exercised in His covenant with Israel as well.

All subjects of man's boasting prove untrustworthy. Man glories in wisdom, power, and riches. The wise Solomon, one of the most wealthy and powerful men who ever lived, testifies that all these are vanities (Eccl. 1:2–4). Judah's trust in these brought her destruction. The only way of escape is to seek to know and understand God (Eccl. 12:13). Salvation is for all who know God and trust His attributes (vs. 23–24), while judgment is for all who are unbelievers in heart (vs. 25–26).

This is what Herbert Livingston remarked about our scripture portion (Jer 9:23-24): *"These verses are worthy to be memorized. Humans strive for wisdom, might, and riches, while God delights in lovingkindness, justice, and righteousness. Blessed is the one who understands the Lord so as to delight in what He delights."* The only true reality for us is to understand and know God intimately. All else is transitory, including human wisdom, might, and riches. We should find our real meaning and true worth in the fact that we know God and celebrate His attributes. True knowledge of God resulting from an intimate relationship with God will be demonstrated in our character as well. Knowing God and His attributes – this is the only reason for us to glory!

But God has chosen the foolish things of the world to put to shame the wise, and God has chosen the weak things of the world to put to shame the things which are mighty; and the base things of the world and the things which are despised God has chosen, and the things which are not, to bring to nothing the things that are, that no flesh should glory in His presence. But of Him you are in Christ Jesus, who became for us wisdom from God—and righteousness and sanctification and redemption—that, as it is written, **"He who glories, let him glory in the Lord."** (1 Cor 1:27-31)

AUGUST 10   *Bible Reading: Jeremiah Chapters 10-12*

LOOKING AT OUR LIFE FROM GOD'S PERSPECTIVE

"If you have run with the footmen, and they have wearied you, then how can you contend with horses? And if in the land of peace, in which you trusted, they wearied you, then how will you do in the floodplain of the Jordan?" (Jer 12:5)

Along with many of the Old Testament saints, the prophet Jeremiah too faces the problem of the prosperity of the wicked. In Jeremiah 12:1-4, he asks why the Lord, who is Himself righteous, allows the wicked to prosper — such as the men of Anathoth — and permits the righteous, like himself, to suffer. However, instead of promising Jeremiah better days ahead, God describes the prophet's present unbearable conditions as only a foretaste of worse experiences to come. A metaphor of athletic strength is used to show the prophet that his struggle has just begun.

God's response to Jeremiah's question (v. 4) comes in the form of *two metaphorical questions.* The *first* metaphor, *of foot racing*, was designed to teach Jeremiah that the obstacles he faced in his hometown were meager compared to those he would encounter before the kings of Judah and Babylon (the horses). The *second* metaphor, *of peace*, was designed to remind the prophet of the impending turmoil he would have to endure in proclaiming the message of judgment to an unrepentant leadership. The relatively peaceful setting of Anathoth, with its minor opposition from treacherous family members, served to prepare Jeremiah to struggle against greater antagonists. Thus, God was saying to Jeremiah, *"The worst is yet to come. Do not give up now."*

God's answer helped to prepare Jeremiah for the trials ahead. Serving God is a blessed privilege, but it is also a difficult task; and it gets more and more difficult. Jeremiah would go from racing with men to racing with horses, from a land of peace to the thickets of the Jordan. This is the only way we can mature in life and service.

It is helpful for us to look at our life from a bigger picture and from God's perspective. We need to remember that living for God in this life will not always be easy. We must be prepared for obstacles and trials. Our Lord Jesus Himself has warned us ahead of time that living for God in the midst of a wicked generation is not easy. However, He has already gone through such trials and even more, and have come out triumphant (Hebrews 4:15). This is what He has promised us: *"In the world you will have tribulation; but be of good cheer, I have overcome the world."* (John 16:33b)

Let us trust in God and put our faith in Him alone. This will only get us the victory in the end. *"For whatever is born of God overcomes the world. And this is the victory that has overcome the world—our faith. Who is he who overcomes the world, but he who believes that Jesus is the Son of God?"* (1 John 5:4-5)

AUGUST 11   Bible Reading: Jeremiah Chapters 13-15

GOING "BACK-TO-THE-BASICS" WITH GENUINE REPENTANCE

Therefore thus says the Lord: "If you return, then I will bring you back; you shall stand before Me; if you take out the precious from the vile, you shall be as My mouth. Let them return to you, but you must not return to them. And I will make you to this people a fortified bronze wall; and they will fight against you, but they shall not prevail against you; for I am with you to save you and deliver you," says the Lord. "I will deliver you from the hand of the wicked, and I will redeem you from the grip of the terrible." (Jer. 15:19-21)

Even the great prophet Jeremiah could miss God's way. Self-pity is forbidden because it accomplishes no good. Jeremiah was spiritually facing the wrong direction through self-pity (vv. 15–18) and it was necessary that he must voluntarily *"repent"* (Jer. 3:1, 7, 12), after which God would restore him to his prophetic position as God's spokesman. *"Stand before"* means *"to serve"*, so we can infer that genuine repentance is necessary to serve God faithfully.

The Hebrew term translated *"return"* can be rendered *"to repent."* Therefore, the challenge implies more than a mere return to a former position; it indicates instead *a new moral and spiritual direction of life.* Jeremiah was faced with the options of either repentance for his doubting God's love and wisdom, or dismissal from his prophetic office. The Lord teaches Jeremiah *two important lessons about repentance*: (1) it is necessary and volitional; and (2) God must work this repentance (*"I will bring you back"*). If Jeremiah will return to his work, his words will continue to have divine authority. Only then will Jeremiah be restored to his prophetic task.

Let us always remember that when we fail, God will confront us (v. 19), but He will also encourage us. Rebuking Jeremiah for his doubt and self-pity, God told him to remain steadfast. God then restated the promises He made when He commissioned Jeremiah as a prophet (v. 20). Though opposition would come, God promised to keep Jeremiah safe from his enemies (v. 21).

Sometimes God will take us *"back-to-the-basics"* to remind us what He has promised us during His initial call into His ministry in order that we may *"repent"* and return back to Him. For prophet Jeremiah too, God was taking him *"back-to-the-basics"* to remind him what He had promised when He had initially called him into the ministry (compare vv. 20-21 to 1:18-19) so that Jeremiah will genuinely *"repent"* and return back to his place in ministry.

"For behold, I have made you this day a fortified city and an iron pillar, and bronze walls against the whole land—against the kings of Judah, against its princes, against its priests, and against the people of the land. They will fight against you, but they shall not prevail against you. For I am with you," says the Lord, "to deliver you." (Jer. 1:18-19)

WE ARE CLAY IN THE HAND OF GOD (THE MASTER POTTER)

The word which came to Jeremiah from the Lord, saying: "Arise and go down to the potter's house, and there I will cause you to hear My words." Then I went down to the potter's house, and there he was, making something at the wheel. And the vessel that he made of clay was marred in the hand of the potter; so he made it again into another vessel, as it seemed good to the potter to make. Then the word of the Lord came to me, saying: "O house of Israel, can I not do with you as this potter?" says the Lord. "Look, as the clay is in the potter's hand, so are you in My hand, O house of Israel!" (Jer 18:1-6)

In chapter 18, prophet Jeremiah was commanded by God to go to the potter's house in order to learn a lesson. What he saw there was that the potter was sitting at the wheel and spinning the lower stone with his feet which caused the upper disc to rotate. This enabled both hands of the potter to be free in order to work the clay into shape. Should the vessel become spoiled due to any impurity, the potter would not just discard the clay, but simply remold it into another vessel according to his modified plan.

The lesson for Jeremiah was that God was the potter and Israel was the vessel being formed into shape (Isaiah 45:9; 64:8). The spoiling of the vessel was not God's fault but Israel's. The potter's vessel was marred, and thus not suitable for its intended purpose. The potter's remolding of the clay into an acceptable and unblemished work symbolized God's action in reforming Israel. The people had become marred (defiled) and had to be reformed into a vessel fit to be identified with God.

Thus, God taught Jeremiah a profound lesson about His sovereignty and His right to discipline Israel until she conformed to His plan. Perhaps a hard lump in the clay ruined the vessel as it spun on the potter's wheel. The potter must remove the hard lump to achieve his purpose in reshaping the vessel. Israel was the chosen vessel to bring God's blessing to the world, and Romans 9:1–5 describes what God had put into that vessel. Many times in her history, when Israel would not yield to God, He made her again. She was marred but still in His hands, and He made her again. God will do the same for anyone who yields to His will.

Let us understand that we too are clay in the hand of the Master Potter (God) as we are being shaped everyday by God into vessels fit for His use (Acts 9:15; 2 Cor. 4:7). We should take away all impurities from our lives, and yield to His perfect plan in our lives! This is what God is telling us today: *"You will say to me then, 'Why does He still find fault? For who has resisted His will?' But indeed, O man, who are you to reply against God? Will the thing formed say to him who formed it, 'Why have you made me like this?' Does not the potter have power over the clay, from the same lump to make one vessel for honor and another for dishonor?"* (Romans 9:19-21)

AUGUST 13   *Bible Reading: Jeremiah Chapters 19-21*

CHOOSING THE WAY OF LIFE OVER DEATH

"Now you shall say to this people, Thus says the Lord: "Behold, I set before you the way of life and the way of death. He who remains in this city shall die by the sword, by famine, and by pestilence; but he who goes out and defects to the Chaldeans who besiege you, he shall live, and his life shall be as a prize to him. For I have set My face against this city for adversity and not for good," says the Lord. "It shall be given into the hand of the king of Babylon, and he shall burn it with fire." (Jer 21:8-10)

The prophet Jeremiah delivered *three messages from God* - the *first message* was to the king Zedekiah (vv. 1-7), the *second message* was to the people (vv. 8-10) and the *third message* was to the members of the house of David (vv. 11-14). The passage above was God's message to the people giving them the choice between life and death. Those who would surrender to the Babylonians when they come to capture Jerusalem would live, but those who would resist and fight would perish. Thus, the people had two clear choices: *"the way of life and the way of death"* (v. 8). Those who chose to remain in the city would die, but those who would surrender to the enemy besieging Jerusalem would live (v. 9).

Thus, Jeremiah advised the people to surrender to the Babylonians to save their lives. This counsel was not received well by many people who were flattered by false prophets to fight the enemy and hold on to the end by trusting in their own strength. Even though Jeremiah was not a popular preacher, but his message was truly from God. Those who listened to him and made the right choice would live, but those who resisted the word of God would perish.

This choice of life and death given to the Israelites reminds us of a similar choice given by Moses, the man of God to the Israelites before he died. This is what Moses had said then: *"I call heaven and earth as witnesses today against you, that I have set before you life and death, blessing and cursing; therefore choose life, that both you and your descendants may live; that you may love the Lord your God, that you may obey His voice, and that you may cling to Him, for He is your life and the length of your days; and that you may dwell in the land which the Lord swore to your fathers, to Abraham, Isaac, and Jacob, to give them."* (Deut 30:19-20)

In our present age, we too have a choice to make in our lives: *choosing to travel in the way of life or death.* The way of life is narrow, unpopular and not accepted by the worldly people, but this way will lead us to God. On the other hand, the way of death is popular and many travel this way, but they will finally end up in destruction. Let's obey what Jesus has commanded us: *"Enter by the narrow gate; for wide is the gate and broad is the way that leads to destruction, and there are many who go in by it. Because narrow is the gate and difficult is the way which leads to life, and there are few who find it."* (Matt 7:13-14)

Let us examine our hearts today and ask Him to lead us in the way of life: *"Search me, O God, and know my heart; try me, and know my anxieties; and see if there is any wicked way in me, and lead me in the way everlasting."* (Psalms 139:23-24)

AUGUST 14 *Bible Reading: Jeremiah Chapters 22-24*

PROMISE THAT GOD WILL BE OUR FUTURE RIGHTEOUS KING

"Behold, the days are coming," says the Lord, "that I will raise to David a Branch of righteousness; a King shall reign and prosper, and execute judgment and righteousness in the earth. In His days Judah will be saved, and Israel will dwell safely; now this is His name by which He will be called: THE LORD OUR RIGHTEOUSNESS." (Jer 23:5-6)

With the words *"Behold, the days are coming"*, prophet Jeremiah speaks a message of hope from God for the future. This is one of the great messianic prophecies of Jeremiah in the Old Testament. Judah's many unrighteous kings were like shepherds who had destroyed and scattered God's flock (Jer. 23:1-2). However, God promises to raise up in David's line another King who would be *"a righteous Branch,"* that is, another descendant of the Davidic line (see Isa. 11:1). In Zechariah 3:8, He is *"My servant the BRANCH."* In Zechariah 6:12, He is presented as *"The Man ... the Branch."* And in Isaiah 4:2, He is *"The Branch of the Lord."* These correspond to the four ways Christ is presented in the Gospels—as King, Servant, Son of Man, and Son of God.

Jesus Christ is the fulfillment of this messianic prophecy. As King, He will reign "wisely" and justly; and His name will be *"The Lord Our Righteousness"* or *"Jehovah-Tsidkenu"* (v. 6) is one of seven compound names of Jehovah. His reign will bring about a new exodus when God will summon the Israelites out of all the countries where they have been scattered and restore them to their own land (see Jer. 16:14–15). These verses also speak to us that one day Jesus Christ will return in glory to execute justice and judgment and His reign over all (Luke 1:31–33).

Jesus Christ is the root and offspring of David (Rev. 22:16), the horn of David (Psalms 132:17, 18) and our future righteous King who will judge the world justly as *"The Lord Our Righteousness"*. Today, let us bow before Him and worship Him in holiness!

"Oh, worship the Lord in the beauty of holiness! Tremble before Him, all the earth. Say among the nations, "The Lord reigns; the world also is firmly established, it shall not be moved; He shall judge the peoples righteously.' Let the heavens rejoice, and let the earth be glad; let the sea roar, and all its fullness; Let the field be joyful, and all that is in it. Then all the trees of the woods will rejoice before the Lord. For He is coming, for He is coming to judge the earth. He shall judge the world with righteousness and the peoples with His truth." (Psalms 96:9-13)

AUGUST 15   *Bible Reading: Jeremiah Chapters 25-27*

LISTENING TO AND OBEYING THE WORD OF GOD

Jeremiah the prophet spoke to all the people of Judah and to all the inhabitants of Jerusalem, saying: "From the thirteenth year of Josiah *the son of Amon, king of Judah, even to this day, this is the twenty-third year in which the word of the Lord has come to me; and **I have spoken to you, rising early and speaking, but you have not listened. And the Lord has sent to you all His servants the prophets, rising early and sending them, but you have not listened nor inclined your ear to hear.** They said, 'Repent now everyone of his evil way and his evil doings, and dwell in the land that the Lord has given to you and your fathers forever and ever. Do not go after other gods to serve them and worship them, and do not provoke Me to anger with the works of your hands; and I will not harm you.' **Yet you have not listened to Me,"** says the Lord, "that you might provoke Me to anger with the works of your hands to your own hurt."* (Jer 25:2-7)

Imagine preaching for 23 years and seeing no visible results! Jeremiah was faithful to his calling even though the people opposed him and would not hear God's Word. Jeremiah's final message in chapter 25 concerned *"all the people of Judah"*. Even though he had spoken to the people repeatedly through these many years, they had not listened to his warnings.

God also has been consistent in reaching out to Judah by sending other prophets to speak to His people. These prophets include Habakkuk, Zephaniah, Urijah (26:20), and those of previous centuries who had persistently proclaimed the message of repentance so that the people might remain in the land. Their repeated message to Judah was to *"repent"* (v. 5) or *"return"* since their security and stability in the land was directly related to their covenant faithfulness to God (see Deut. 28; 29). Yet the people would not obey. Instead, they resorted to the pagan worship of idols. This was a breach of the covenant that God had with Israel (see Ex. 20:3–5), which provoked God to anger and judgment.

The Babylonian captivity was God's way of punishing the rebels and purifying the godly remnant of the nation. The nation was deaf to God's Word (vv. 4, 7, 8), but that Word would be fulfilled in due course of time. The people of Judah were eventually taken captive by Nebuchadnezzar, the king of Babylon and remain in exile for 70 years (v. 11). According to 2 Chronicles 36:20–21, the Lord punished Judah for 70 years because that was the number of sabbatical years they had not observed (Lev. 25:1–7). The people did not rest on the weekly Sabbath (Jer. 17:19–27), and they did not give the land its rest every 7 years (Lev. 26:27–35). When we keep to ourselves what belongs to God, we eventually lose it and suffer in the process!

We need to really listen and obey every word that God speaks to us directly through His Word and through His servants. Let us obey what God is speaking to us today: *"If My people who are called by My name will humble themselves, and pray and seek My face, and turn from their wicked ways, then I will hear from heaven, and will forgive their sin and heal their land."* (2 Chron 7:14)

AUGUST 16 *Bible Reading: Jeremiah Chapters 28-30*

GOD'S PLAN TO GIVE US HOPE AND A BETTER FUTURE

"For I know the thoughts that I think toward you, says the Lord, thoughts of peace and not of evil, to give you a future and a hope." (Jer 29:11)

In 597 B.C., the Babylonians began to deport the Jews to Babylon. To those who were deported, Jeremiah sent a letter in which he told them to prepare for a long stay in Babylon. Instead of hoping for Babylon's quick destruction, they were to seek its peace and prosperity. The Lord would restore the exiles only when the seventy years of judgment that He had announced were completed (Jer 25:11–12).

In the above key verse, we can understand that God places considerable emphasis on His unchangeable plan to bring peace and not evil in our lives. He wishes to give us hope and provide us with a better future. Even though Judah was in captivity, God has not terminated His relationship with His people. God remembers His covenant promises of restoration that He had promised in Deut. 30:1–10.

In his exposition of Jer 29:10–14 in *'Preaching'*, Yates makes the following observation: *"God's Word to His people in the day of Jeremiah is still His sure word for men who have sinned and lost touch with the Infinite. He is always available. His longing is that all men may look to Him and live. His arms are always open in loving invitation to any who will turn to Him. Cleansing, peace, joy, victory will be his at the hand of a loving God who delights to welcome His children home."*

According to the Bible scholar Warren Wiersbe, Jeremiah's letter to the exiles helps us understand how we can make the best of a difficult situation:

- *Accept it.* We should live as normal a life as we can and put up with inconveniences without complaining. We should try to be a blessing to others, and be a peacemaker, not a troublemaker.

- *Be patient.* God has the timing all worked out, and His plans never fail. He knows how long and how much.

- *Trust God.* Verse 11 is a powerful promise to claim when we are *"in exile"*. God thinks about us personally and is planning for us. His plans are *for peace*, so we need not fear the future. His plans are *purposeful*, so we should let Him work out His will. No matter how difficult our situation may be, we should not waste our suffering by resisting God.

- *Avoid false hopes.* It is human to indulge in false hopes and grasp at every straw, but this approach leads to despair. We should avoid the subtle voices of the false teachers with their false hopes. The Word of God will tell us what to do.

Today, we are somewhat like the Jewish exiles in Babylon, for we are away from our heavenly home and living among those who do not accept our way of life. We live with a future hope in the return of Christ and spending eternity with Him. In the meantime, we are just visitors and pilgrims on earth. This is what Apostle Peter tells us to do within our context: *"Beloved, I beg you as sojourners and pilgrims abstain from fleshly lusts which war against the soul, having your conduct honorable among the Gentiles, that when they speak against you as evildoers, they may, by your good works which they observe, glorify God in the day of visitation."* (1 Peter 2:11-12)

AUGUST 17   *Bible Reading: Jeremiah Chapters 31-33*

OUR SPIRITUAL TRANSPARENCY THROUGH THE 'NEW COVENANT'

*"Behold, the days are coming, says the Lord, when I will make a new covenant with the house of Israel and with the house of Judah — this is the covenant that I will make with the house of Israel after those days, says the Lord: **I will put My law in their minds, and write it on their hearts; and I will be their God, and they shall be My people.** No more shall every man teach his neighbor, and every man his brother, saying, 'Know the Lord,' for they all shall know Me, from the least of them to*

the greatest of them, says the Lord. **For I will forgive their iniquity, and their sin I will remember no more."** (Jer 31:31-34)

The 'New Covenant' is the fifth and last of the theocratic covenants (pertaining to the rule of God). God made the 'New Covenant' primarily with Israel and Judah (v. 31). This is a covenant of grace through which humans will be given a new moral nature, and knowledge of the Lord will be universal (see Heb. 10:15–17). Unlike the Mosaic Law, it is unconditional. It emphasized what God will do, not what man must do (vv. 33-34).

The 'New Covenant' is the culmination of God's covenant-making with Israel. There are some marked differences between the 'Old' and 'New Covenant' (v. 32; Gen. 9:13):

- The 'Old Covenant' (given at Mount Sinai) demanded obedience, while the 'New Covenant' offers forgiveness of sin.
- The 'Old Covenant' was written on stone tablets, while the 'New Covenant' is carved on the hearts of God's people (see Ezekiel 36:26, 27).
- The 'Old Covenant' was between God and the nation Israel, whereas the 'New Covenant' is between God and all believers.

At the foundation of the 'New Covenant' is the fact that God is everything; He will make His people what they ought to be. The new covenant came into force with the atoning death of Christ. All believers in the present church age are the recipients of its benefits. Eventually those benefits will also be extended to include a repentant and regenerate Israel (Rom. 11:25–29).

Four provisions are made in this 'New Covenant':

1. *Regeneration*—God will put His law in their inward parts and write it in their hearts (v. 33)

2. *A national restoration*—Yahweh will be their God and the nation will be His people (v. 33)

3. *Personal ministry of the Holy Spirit*—they will all be taught individually by God (v. 34)

4. *Full justification*—their sins will be forgiven and completely removed (v. 34)

The 'New Covenant' is made sure by the blood that Jesus shed on Calvary's cross. Jesus' payment for sins is more than adequate to pay for the sins of all who will believe in Him. The 'New Covenant' is called *"new"* in contrast to the covenant with Moses which is called *"old"* (Jer. 31:32; Heb. 8:6–13) because it actually accomplishes what the Mosaic covenant could only point to, that is, *the child of God living in a manner that is consistent with the character of God.*

The New Testament reveals that the words that God has promised to write on the hearts of His people *are written by the Holy Spirit* (2 Cor. 3:1–3), *who empowers them to live in a manner that reflects the very character of God.* This profound truth of God's 'New Covenant' is so significant that *this passage is quoted three times in the New Testament* (John 6:45; Heb. 8:10; 10:16–17).

We are the *'living epistles'* of Christ in these end times, and we must reflect Christ with love and goodness through a steady pattern of living excellence. We have to be spiritually transparent living under the 'New Covenant'. This is what Apostle Paul tells about our status: *"You are our epistle written in our hearts, known and read by all men; clearly you are an epistle of Christ, ministered by us, written not with ink but by the Spirit of the living God, not on tablets of stone but on tablets of flesh, that is, of the heart."* (2 Cor 3:2-3)

AUGUST 18   *Bible Reading: Jeremiah Chapters 34-36*

OBEDIENCE TO GODLY INSTRUCTIONS HAS GREAT REWARDS

And Jeremiah said to the house of the Rechabites, "Thus says the Lord of hosts, the God of Israel: 'Because you have obeyed the commandment of Jonadab your father, and kept all his precepts and done according to all that he commanded you, therefore thus says the Lord of hosts, the God of Israel: "Jonadab the son of Rechab shall not lack a man to stand before Me forever." (Jer 35:18-19)

The Rechabites were named after Rechab whose son Jonadab was active in aiding Jehu in the expulsion of Baal worship in the Northern Kingdom of Israel in 841 B.C., and they descended from the Kenites (Judges 1:16; 1 Chr. 2:55).

Jeremiah obeyed the Lord by inviting the Rechabites into the house of the Lord and by offering them wine to drink (v. 1-5). The Rechabites courteously refused to drink it because of instructions their father had given them (v. 6) in line with the Nazarite vows (Judges 13:5; 2 Kings 10:15). The vow taken by Jonadab the son of Rechab had committed his descendants to a nomadic life and abstinence from wine, which was a voluntary commitment that was not required by the Mosaic Law (Deut. 6:10, 11; 7:13). Further, they refused to build houses, sow seeds, plant or own vineyards due to which they were forced to live in Jerusalem by the advance of the Chaldeans (v. 7-11). They maintained a true pilgrim character. What an example!

In marked contrast were the people of Judah. While the Rechabites obeyed and followed the teachings of Jonadab their father, Judah had neither obeyed the Lord nor followed His instructions. The Rechabites were more loyal to their earthly father and his human judgments than the people of Judah were to their Creator God. Because the Rechabites were faithful to the command of their forefather, the Lord assured them they would always have descendants who would worship the Lord! (vv. 18-19)

People sometimes excuse or justify their immoral behavior with the attitude that *"everybody's doing it."* But that notion is false. Not everyone is doing it. Not everyone is giving way to popular opinion. The Rechabites showed that it is possible to remain obedient and faithful to God, no matter what other people may be doing. God is always looking for individuals whose lives are characterized by obedience and faithfulness. Such individuals will experience God's blessing even in the midst of trials! *"Moreover it is required in stewards that one be found faithful."* (1 Cor 4:2) *"A faithful man will abound with blessings, but he who hastens to be rich will not go unpunished."* (Prov 28:20)

Let us also commit to be faithful to God alone and fully obey His instructions by walking in His will: *"Do not fear any of those things which you are about to suffer. Indeed, the devil is about to throw some of you into prison, that you may be tested, and you will have tribulation ten days. Be faithful until death, and I will give you the crown of life."* (Rev 2:10)

GOD WILL REWARD US ACCORDING TO OUR ACTIONS

"In the ninth year of Zedekiah king of Judah, in the tenth month, Nebuchadnezzar king of Babylon and all his army came against Jerusalem, and besieged it. In the eleventh year of Zedekiah, in the fourth month, on the ninth day of the month, the city was penetrated." (Jeremiah 39:1-2)

Jerusalem was so strong, that the inhabitants believed the enemy could never enter it. But sin provoked God to withdraw his protection, and then it was as weak as other cities. After King Zedekiah had ruled Judah for eleven years, the Babylonians captured Jerusalem in 586 B.C. *What we read in chapter 39 is how God rewarded three different people living in Jerusalem according to their actions:*

1. *God rewarded Zedekiah for his wickedness* (vv. 1–10). King Zedekiah did not pay any attention to the word of God that He spoke through His prophet Jeremiah. *"But neither he (Zedekiah) nor his servants nor the people of the land gave heed to the words of the Lord which He spoke by the prophet Jeremiah."* (Jer 37:2) He was specifically requested by Jeremiah to obey the voice of God and surrender to the Babylonian king as follows: *"...please obey the voice of the Lord which I speak to you. So it shall be well with you, and your soul shall live."* (Jer 38:20) But Zedekiah, his sons, and his men of war tried to flee but were captured. The last thing Zedekiah saw was the execution of his own sons; then he was blinded. He walked by sight and ended up in darkness. He lived to serve himself and lost everything. He learned the truth of these words: *"Be sure your sin will find you out"* (Num. 32:23).

2. *God rewarded Jeremiah for his faithfulness* (vv. 11–14). For forty difficult years, he courageously proclaimed God's Word, even though the people refused to obey it. If we measure ministry by *"results,"* Jeremiah was a failure. Given his freedom, he chose to remain with his people and minister to them. We see that the Babylonian king gave instructions through the captain of his guard that Jeremiah should be well-treated, and eventually the prophet was released from the court of the prison. How true are

these words - *"For the Lord God is a sun and shield; the Lord will give grace and glory; no good thing will He withhold from those who walk uprightly."* (Psalms 84:11)

3. *God rewarded Ebed-Melech for his kindness (vv. 15–18).* This is what God spoke to this Ethiopian eunuch through Jeremiah: *"I will deliver you...and you shall not be given into the hand of the men of whom you are afraid. For I will surely deliver you, and you shall not fall by the sword; but your life shall be as a prize to you, because you have put your trust in Me,"* says the Lord. (Jer 39:17-18) God did not forget the act of kindness done to Jeremiah. God rewarded this Ethiopian for persuading King Zedekiah to release Jeremiah from the slimy pit dungeon for his kindness (38:7–13). Now we know why this foreigner had rescued Jeremiah: he had put his faith in the God of Israel (v. 18). It must have been Jeremiah's witness that won him. An outsider trusted the God of Israel, but the Jews would not trust Him!

Let us clearly understand that God will one day reward us for all that we do in this world. Knowing this fact let our actions be pleasing in God's sight and worthy of His rewards that he will give us one day in the future. This is what our Lord Jesus Christ had promised while He was in this world: *"He who receives you receives Me, and he who receives Me receives Him who sent Me. He who receives a prophet in the name of a prophet shall receive a prophet's reward. And he who receives a righteous man in the name of a righteous man shall receive a righteous man's reward. And whoever gives one of these little ones only a cup of cold water in the name of a disciple, assuredly, I say to you, he shall by no means lose his reward."* (Matt 10:40-42)

AUGUST 20   *Bible Reading: Jeremiah Chapters 40-42*

SEEK DIRECTION FROM GOD ONLY TO FOLLOW THEM

"For you were hypocrites in your hearts when you sent me to the Lord your God, saying, 'Pray for us to the Lord our God, and according to all that the Lord your God says, so declare to us and we will do it.' And I have this day declared it to you, but you have not obeyed the voice of the Lord your God, or anything which He has sent you by me. Now

309

therefore, know certainly that you shall die by the sword, by famine, and by pestilence in the place where you desire to go to dwell." (Jer 42:20-22)

Terrified of the Babylonians after the fall of Jerusalem, and fearful of the Ammonites after the assassination of the appointed governor Gedaliah, the survivors of Jerusalem made preparations to flee to Egypt (41:16–18). These survivors included *"soldiers, women, children, and court officials."* Before departing, however, they made a pretense of seeking God's guidance by asking prophet Jeremiah for a word from the Lord (42:1-3). When the prophet consented, they promised to obey, no matter what the guidance was.

God's answers do not always come immediately but in His own good time. Ten days later the answer came: Don't flee to Egypt but stay in the land. If they stay, God will prosper them. If they flee, all the perils they feared in Judah will overtake them in Egypt. *But it seems that the people were already determined to flee to Egypt, so Jeremiah told them flatly that they would meet disaster there.*

What we can see here is that although the Jewish refugees promised to obey God's will, the Lord's message (vv. 7–22) conflicted with their plans (42:19–43:3). The Lord's will was against seeking refuge in Egypt (Deut. 17:16). The underlying issue here was *false trust* and the *delusion of safety in human power and calculation* (22:20, 22; 30:14).

Many times we seek direction from God, but only want to hear what is *'convenient'* for us (2 Tim. 4:3, 4). We pray falsely and expect God to just validate our desires. We ask God for guidance, but our minds are already made up to do what we want. Unfortunately, such pretense of *"seeking counsel"* from God is just window dressing, and this action does not please God. Let us seek direction from God *only* to follow them!

"Where do wars and fights come from among you? Do they not come from your desires for pleasure that war in your members? You lust and do not have. You murder and covet and cannot obtain. You fight and war. Yet you do not have because you do not ask. You ask and do not receive, because you ask amiss, that you may spend it on your pleasures." (James 4:1-3)

AUGUST 21   *Bible Reading: Jeremiah Chapters 43-45*

DO NOT SEEK AFTER GREAT THINGS, BUT TRUST IN THE LORD

*"Thus says the Lord: "Behold, what I have built I will break down, and what I have planted I will pluck up, that is, this whole land. **And do you seek great things for yourself? Do not seek them**; for behold, I will bring adversity on all flesh," says the Lord. "**But I will give your life to you as a prize in all places, wherever you go.**"* (Jer 45:4-5)

The above passage is a message of comfort to Baruch, the son of Neriah and the brother of Seraiah who served as an official under King Zedekiah (Jer 51:59). Baruch, whose name means *"blessed"*, was a scribe by occupation and served as Jeremiah's secretary and his lifelong friend. It appears that Baruch had been told at the beginning of his ministry of the difficulties ahead (see Jer. 1:10; 36:1–4), but had eventually become discouraged with the sad turn of events like Jeremiah (see Jer. 15:10).

Bible scholars have given different reasons as to why Baruch may have become discouraged:

· Due to his fears regarding the threatened judgments on Judah

· Due to his personal rejection from others because of his association with Jeremiah (Jer 36:15–19; 43:3)

· Due to his disappointment with events after King Jehoiakim burned the original copy of the prophecy and he had to write a second copy all over again (see Jer. 36).

However, God encouraged Baruch with the promise of sparing his life. Baruch's lofty calling was simply to be a faithful minister (see Mark 10:45) and he had be content with God's appointment (see Phil. 4:11). Warren Wiersbe has suggested from this passage that when it seems like our work and witness are useless, we should remember *for whom we are doing them*, and note the *three facts* listed below:

1. *God knows our trials.* Baruch could have had an easier life, but he chose to identify himself with the most unpopular man in the land. God knows what we are going through and will bring us through (Isa. 43:1-2)

2. *God hears our words.* Like any servant of God, Baruch had his difficult days when he felt everything was falling apart. However, God heard his cries of frustration just like He hears our words all the time (Psalms 28:6-7)

3. *God meets our needs.* Baruch was alive and cared for because he was associated with Jeremiah. God will meet all needs if we trust Him. If we are going to seek great things, we should seek them for God and not for ourselves (Matt. 6:33).

Kelly commented on Jeremiah chapter 45 as follows: *"The great lesson for Baruch was that in a day of judgment the proper feeling for a saint and servant of God is an absence of self-seeking. Lowliness of mind always becomes the saint, but in an evil day, it is the only safety. Humility is always morally right, but it is also the only thing that preserves from judgment."*

Unlike Baruch who became bitter with God for withholding what he wanted, we can choose to be thankful because God has already supplied what we need. Let us not seek great things after ourselves but trust in God and remember God's word that instructs us: *"Let your conduct be without covetousness; be content with such things as you have. For He Himself has said, "I will never leave you nor forsake you." So we may boldly say: "The Lord is my helper; I will not fear. What can man do to me?"* (Heb 13:5-6)

AUGUST 22   Bible Reading: Jeremiah Chapters 46-48

GOD WILL ULTIMATELY PRESERVE HIS PEOPLE

"But do not fear, O My servant Jacob, and do not be dismayed, O Israel! For behold, I will save you from afar, and your offspring from the land of their captivity; Jacob shall return, have rest and be at ease; no one shall make him afraid. Do not fear, O Jacob My servant" says the Lord, "for I am with you; for I will make a complete end of all the nations to which I have driven you, but I will not make a complete end of you. I will rightly correct you, for I will not leave you wholly unpunished." (Jer 46:27-28)

The book of Jeremiah has not been arranged chronologically otherwise this section (chapters 46-49) should have historically followed the events of chapter 25 where Jeremiah anticipated the Babylonian conquest (Jer 25:9).

The passage above is a repeat from Jeremiah 30:10, 11, with only a slight variation. These are the words of comfort to Israel, for God will not forget His covenant with its promises of protection, peace, and prosperity (see Gen. 9:13). The purpose of God's chastisement is to refine His people. The word *"correct"* (v. 28b) denotes *discipline*, which will be done *justly*. This prophecy has a double fulfillment— one in the return from exile and the other still in the future (Rom. 11:1–5, 26–32).

God is still Israel's covenant God who will deal with a righteous remnant by restoring it to the land in accordance with his unconditional promises of old. In contrast with Egypt, who would be taken into exile, Israel was not to fear or be dismayed. In the midst of international chaos, Israel had a sure promise of the presence of the Lord and of survival. The destroyers will themselves be destroyed, but God will have compassion on His own. Israel could look forward to a time when she would enjoy "peace and security." A remnant would survive to receive again God's blessings. As the *'new Israel'* the Church of God can also relate to these promises of God.

When the Church (and literal Israel) might seem utterly consumed, there still remains hope because God will even raise His people from the dead (Romans 11:15) and ultimately preserve His people. Through this passage, God gave a message of peace to His people in captivity: they would return to their land and be established again. They had to be corrected in love, but they would not be destroyed: *"I will save you . . . I am with you"* - What words of encouragement!

AUGUST 23   *Bible Reading: Jeremiah Chapters 49-52*

LET'S RETURN TO GOD & RENEW OUR COVENANT WITH HIM:

"In those days and in that time," says the Lord, "the children of Israel shall come, they and the children of Judah together; with continual weeping they shall come, and seek the Lord their God. They shall ask the way to Zion, with their faces toward it, saying, 'Come and let us join ourselves to the Lord in a perpetual covenant that will not be forgotten.'" (Jer 50:4-5)

This is a message of hope for the return and restoration of Israel and Judah interposed in the prophecies against Babylon in Jeremiah chapters 50 & 51. Six times, after Jeremiah speaks of judgment on Babylon, he predicts blessing for Israel and Judah and the above referenced verses (4–5) form the first. Jews in exile are told to lead the return of captives to their own lands because Babylon will be plundered.

Jeremiah announced to the nations the public humiliation of Babylon. She would be captured and her gods would be put to shame. Jeremiah's prophecy looked beyond the fall of Babylon to Cyrus in 539 B.C., to describe an end-time destruction that will reverse the fortunes of Israel and Judah. The destruction of Babylon will be the climax of God's judgment on the gentile powers that have oppressed His people, and will open the way for the fulfillment of His promises to Israel (Isa. 13–14; Zech. 5:5–11; Rev. 17–18).

How would the Israelites return to God & be restored in fellowship with Him?

1. They shall weep and cry in repentance (as the Israelites did in Samuel's time, 1 Samuel 7:2).
2. They shall inquire after the Lord and seek His face for help.
3. They shall renew their covenant and walk with God more closely.

What we see here is that Israel and Judah would be restored one day as they seek the Lord in mournful repentance, looking for help to return home. They would enter into a perpetual covenant with the Lord that they would not forget or reject (see Ezekiel 16:60). Throughout this prophecy, God gives words of hope to His people still in captivity. Both Israel and Judah will be reunited and restored to their land (50:4–5). The scattered flock will be gathered (50:6–7, 17) and the sinful nation forgiven (50:19–20). They are guilty of sin, but God the Judge will plead their case (50:33–34). The forsaken wife will be reunited to her Husband (51:5), and the nation will be vindicated (51:10).

Let's also return to God and renew our covenant with Him!

"Seek the Lord while He may be found, call upon Him while He is near. Let the wicked forsake his way, and the unrighteous man his thoughts; let him return to the Lord, and He will have mercy on him; and to our God, for He will abundantly pardon." (Isaiah 55:6-7)

HOPING IN GOD'S MERCIES, COMPASSION & FAITHFULNESS

*Through the Lord's **mercies** we are not consumed, because His **compassions** fail not. They are new every morning; great is Your **faithfulness**. "The Lord is my portion," says my soul, "therefore I hope in Him!" The Lord is good to those who wait for Him, to the soul who seeks Him. It is good that one should hope and wait quietly for the salvation of the Lord.* (Lam 3:22-26)

The above verses embody the central thesis of the book of Lamentations. In the midst of the lingering depression over his misery, prophet Jeremiah gets his eyes off himself and onto the Lord. Hope is revived when he remembers that the Lord's mercies and compassions are new every morning and that His faithfulness is great (vv. 21–24). The lesson that he had learned in the school of affliction: it is good to wait quietly for the Lord's deliverance (vv. 25–26).

This is one of the poignant expressions of the grace of God found anywhere in the Bible. All would be consumed were it not for God's mercies. The word *"mercies"* is a translation of the Hebrew word *"hesed"* meaning *"lovingkindness"* (Jer. 2:2). This word captures the spirit of the term *"grace"* in the New Testament (Eph. 2:8). Each morning His mercies are fresh, verifying God's great faithfulness to us (v. 23). Every day presents us with a new opportunity to discover and experience more of God's love. God remains *"full of grace and truth"* in every situation (see Ex. 34:6, 7; John 1:14).

These verses mark the turning point in Jeremiah's experience of grief and prayer. As he *looked at himself* (vv. 1–18), he saw an aged man on a winding path in the dark, being pursued by lions. The more he considered his feelings, the more hopeless he felt. Then he *looked away from himself* and *by faith looked to the Lord*. He has hope now (v. 21) because of God's mercies, compassions, and faithfulness. Focusing on our problems can make us discouraged, but focusing on God's never-ending faithfulness gives us hope!

God will not forsake His children today. His mercy and grace have been extended to those who are in Christ Jesus (Rom. 8:1), and nothing can separate us from His love (8:31–39). As a result, we can have hope (5:1–5; 1 Pet. 1:3–5), even in the midst of the gloomiest circumstances (2 Cor. 1:8–11).

"Your mercy, O Lord, is in the heavens; Your faithfulness reaches to the clouds. Your righteousness is like the great mountains; Your judgments are a great deep; O Lord, You preserve man and beast. How precious is Your lovingkindness, O God! Therefore the children of men put their trust under the shadow of Your wings." (Psalms 36:5-7)

AUGUST 25   *Bible Reading: Lamentations Chapters 4-5*

PRAY TO GOD FOR RESTORATION AND RENEWAL

*"You, O Lord, remain forever; Your throne from generation to generation. Why do You forget us forever, and forsake us for so long a time? Turn us back to You, O Lord, and we will be **restored**; **renew** our days as of old, unless You have utterly rejected us, and are very angry with us!"* (Lam 5:19-22)

The Book of Lamentations ends on a note of hope and a powerful bit of wisdom by affirming that God remains forever (v. 19). Jeremiah's sadness concerning the state of Judah and the fall of Jerusalem is ameliorated *only* by his awareness that God alone remains unchangeable. Situations and circumstances may undergo rapid change, but God is eternally on His throne. Therefore, there is cause for hope. In spite of severe suffering because of her sin, Judah had not been abandoned as a nation. In a final burst of faith, this prayer lays hold of restoration and renewal in the Lord.

God's eternal rule and reign are a hope and support during the bleakest moments of suffering and despair (see Psalms 80:1, 2; 89:3, 4; 103:19). In the light of God's unchanging faithfulness and righteousness (Psalms 52:1; Malachi 3:6; James 1:17), Jeremiah pleads with God to act so that the hearts of His people will be turned back to Him in godly sorrow and full repentance. Without genuine repentance and conversion there can be no restoration to the former relationship between God and His people!

From the book of Lamentations, we can note that the *road to renewal* in our lives will also take the following steps:

1. Step 1: *From sin to suffering* (Lam. 1:8)

2. Step 2: *From sorrow to repentance* (Lam. 1:20)
3. Step 3: *From prayer to hope* (Lam. 3:19–24)
4. Step 4: *From faith to restoration* (Lam. 5:21)

Let us always remember that God's chastening is proof that He loves us and has not forsaken us (Heb. 12:5–11). One day, He will take us out of the furnace and give us a new start. We will be restored and renewed if we let Him have His way.

"Restore us, O God; cause Your face to shine, and we shall be saved!" (Psalms 80:3)

AUGUST 26   *Bible Reading: Ezekiel Chapters 1-3*

UNDERSTANDING OUR ROLE AS "SPIRITUAL WATCHMEN"

*"Now it came to pass at the end of seven days that the word of the Lord came to me, saying, "Son of man, **I have made you a watchman for the house of Israel**; therefore hear a word from My mouth, and give them warning from Me: when I say to the wicked, 'You shall surely die,' and you give him no warning, nor speak to warn the wicked from his wicked way, to save his life, that same wicked man shall die in his iniquity; but his blood I will require at your hand. Yet, if you warn the wicked, and he does not turn from his wickedness, nor from his wicked way, he shall die in his iniquity; but you have delivered your soul."* (Ezek 3:16-19)

In ancient Israel, watchmen were stationed on the walls to watch out for approaching enemies and warn people of danger by sounding an alarm (see 2 Sam. 18:24-27; 2 Kin. 9:17-20). Prophets were also called *watchmen* because of the similar role they played *spiritually* (see Jer. 6:17; Hos. 9:8; Hab. 2:1).

In this passage we see that God made Ezekiel a *"spiritual watchman"* over His people, and was asked by God to warn both the *"wicked"* (vv. 18, 19) and the *"righteous"* (vv. 20, 21). As a watchman, Ezekiel was responsible to speak God's Word and warn both the nation of Israel and wayward individuals. If Ezekiel did not warn the people, he would be held as responsible for their murder as if he had killed them himself. However, if he fulfilled his assignment, then he would have delivered himself from any responsibility for the coming calamity. People who refused to heed his warning had only themselves to blame eventually.

We, as the ministers of God, are the *"spiritual watchmen"* on the church's walls, and we must be on the alert always (Isa. 21:8; Gen. 31:40). Of course, all our efforts are in vain if God does not guard the city as well (Psalms 127:1- 2). *What are our duties as watchmen?* We have *"to take notice and give notice"*. We have to *take notice* of what God is saying concerning His people and *"hear the word from His mouth"* (v. 17). Then, we must *give notice* of what we have heard to other people.

It is a serious thing to be watchmen, for the destiny of precious souls is at stake (Ezekiel 3:16–21; 33:1–9). The watchmen must be alert to every opportunity and must not be afraid to sound the alarm. False watchmen are not faithful (Isa. 56:10–12), and will be held accountable on the day of God's final judgment. Apostle Paul was a faithful watchman who was able to say, *"I am innocent of the blood of all men. For I have not shunned to declare to you the whole counsel of God"* (Acts 20:26–27).

One last word…despite his great responsibility Ezekiel was shut up by God and had to wait for God-given opportunities. We also need to be sensitive to God's leading in witnessing. Sometimes we need to be silent. However, most of us are silent when we ought to be witnessing. *Let us understand our role as "spiritual watchmen" of the church and the world, and fulfill our responsibilities faithfully, even today!*

"I have set watchmen on your walls, O Jerusalem; they shall never hold their peace day or night. **You who make mention of the Lord, do not keep silent***"* (Isaiah 62:6)

AUGUST 27   *Bible Reading: Ezekiel Chapters 4-6*

UNDERSTANDING OUR PRIVILEGE & POSITION IN THIS WORLD

"Thus says the Lord God: **'This is Jerusalem; I have set her in the midst of the nations and the countries all around her.** *She has rebelled against My judgments by doing wickedness more than the nations, and*

against My statutes more than the countries that are all around her; for they have refused My judgments, and they have not walked in My statutes.' Therefore thus says the Lord God: 'Because you have multiplied disobedience more than the nations that are all around you, have not walked in My statutes nor kept My judgments, nor even done according to the judgments of the nations that are all around you'— therefore thus says the Lord God: 'Indeed I, even I, am against you and will execute judgments in your midst in the sight of the nations." (Ezek 5:5-8)

The above words were being said *in anguish* by God to prophet Ezekiel. Jehovah God had gifted to the Israelites this magnificent city called Jerusalem as an inheritance. God had loved this city and had established it as the center of the world, because His holy temple was there. Jerusalem was regarded in God's point of view as center of the whole earth, designed to radiate the true light over the nations in all directions. *"Beautiful in elevation, the joy of the whole earth, is Mount Zion on the sides of the north, the city of the great King."* (Psalms 48:2)

God had also planned Jerusalem to be the meeting place of all the nations in the future: *"At that time Jerusalem shall be called The Throne of the Lord, and all the nations shall be gathered to it, to the name of the Lord, to Jerusalem."* (Jer 3:17) This great city lay midway between the oldest and most civilized states, Egypt and Ethiopia on one side, and Babylon, Nineveh, and India on the other, and afterwards Persia, Greece, and Rome. *Israel was thus placed to be the spiritual benefactor of the whole world!* (See Psalms 67:1-7)

However, Jerusalem had rebelled against God and His laws. The people of this favored city had not only stubbornly refused to keep the laws of God, but had sinned even more than all the heathen nations around them—they had even failed to follow the moral laws that were common among the pagans. They started worshipping idols and had literally gone beyond the heathen in provoking God to anger. So, God promised to judge the Israelites more severely in the sight of the nations (v. 8).

God had placed Israel and the city of Jerusalem in a strategic position, and so their punishment would be more severe on account of their disobedience. We, as Christians, have even higher privileges than the Jews. Like Jerusalem set in the midst of the nations, we have also been set in the midst of the unbelievers to be a source of light to them. Let us understand our privilege and position in this world, and live only for eternal rewards that God will give us one day!

"You are the light of the world. A city that is set on a hill cannot be hidden...let your light so shine before men, that they may see your good works and glorify your Father in heaven." (Matt 5:14-16)

AUGUST 28   *Bible Reading: Ezekiel Chapters 7-9*

IT'S TIME TO WEEP OVER THE UNGODLINESS AMONG GOD'S PEOPLE

"Now the glory of the God of Israel had gone up from the cherub, where it had been, to the threshold of the temple. And He called to the man clothed with linen, who had the writer's inkhorn at his side; and the Lord said to him, **"Go through the midst of the city, through the midst of Jerusalem, and put a mark on the foreheads of the men who sigh and cry over all the abominations that are done within it."** *To the others He said in my hearing, "Go after him through the city and kill; do not let your eye spare, nor have any pity. Utterly slay old and young men, maidens and little children and women; but do not come near anyone on whom is the mark; and begin at My sanctuary.* **So they began with the elders who were before the temple.** *"* (Ezek 9:3-6)

In this vision God took Ezekiel back to Jerusalem to show him the wickedness of God's people. The glory of God moved away from the Holy of Holies and began to depart from the temple fulfilling the saying: *"Ichabod—the glory has departed"* (1 Sam. 4:19–22; Jer. 7:1–15). Without the glory of God, the temple was just another building; and without the presence of God in our lives, we are just like other people (Exod. 33:12–16).

In Ezekiel chapter 9, six executioners are seen coming from the north (the direction from which the Babylonians were to come) to destroy the idolaters among God's people. The man clothed with linen *may* symbolize grace. The glory cloud (symbol of God's presence) leaves the holy of holies in the temple, grieved away by the idolatry of the people. Those faithful Jews who sighed and cried being opposed the idolatry were sealed by a mark on their foreheads so that they would not be killed.

According to Bible scholars, the sign (or, mark) on the forehead was the last letter of the Hebrew alphabet (tau), which the rabbis said suggested completeness. It is also the first letter of torâ (law). Feinberg notes a fascinating parallel of this incident with that mentioned in Revelation 7:1–3: *"Christian interpreters have seen a somewhat prophetic allusion to the sign of the cross. In the earlier script the last letter of the Hebrew alphabet (taw) had the form of a cross. Ezekiel, of course, could not have thought of Christian symbolism nor is the passage a direct prediction of Christ's cross. It is a remarkable coincidence, however."*

Then the executioners began to slay the idolaters, starting with the elders of Israel, but God's command has one restriction: *"Do not come near anyone on whom is the mark,"* says God. The literal fulfillment of this judgment is recorded in 2 Chronicles 36:17–19. God's judgment proceeds without exemptions, as it did when the death angel struck all the homes which did not have blood on the doorpost (Exodus 12:13). Those who demonstrated a righteous attitude through true repentance and remorse were marked out from the hardened rebels and spared from the punishment.

Let us note that God's judgment <u>will</u> begin with His people (v. 6b). Those who obey God's commands and weep over the ungodliness among God's people will be spared (see Rev. 7:2–4; 9:4; 14:1). *"For the time has come for judgment to begin at the house of God; and if it begins with us first, what will be the end of those who do not obey the gospel of God?"* (1 Peter 4:17)

AUGUST 29   *Bible Reading: Ezekiel Chapters 10-12*

THE COMFORT OF GOD'S PRESENCE IN OUR LIVES

Therefore say, 'thus says the Lord God: "Although I have cast them far off among the Gentiles, and although I have scattered them among the countries, yet I shall be a little sanctuary for them in the countries where they have gone."' (Ezek 11:16)

God here announced through prophet Ezekiel that He would do just the opposite of what leaders in Jerusalem expected; He would protect the exiles as their sanctuary, and they would become the remnant.

Verses 16–21 include the most comforting words spoken by God so far in the prophecy. They will be taken captive, but also preserved, regathered, given the land, and converted upon their return. God explained to Ezekiel that the Jews taken captive and spread among foreign lands were actually the remnant whom God was protecting. God himself would continue as their sanctuary—a word in Hebrew that literally means a *"holy place"* or a *"set-apart place."*

Wherever God's people go, God goes with them. That was the comforting message that Ezekiel delivered to the Babylonian exiles (v. 16). They were far from home and had no temple such as the one at Jerusalem, where God's presence was said to dwell. That same sense of isolation was going to be felt by the people of Judah when God scattered them throughout the ancient world (see Jer. 9:16; 52:28–30). But the Lord assured His refugees that He would be their *"little sanctuary"* wherever they went. Furthermore, He promised to eventually bring them back to the land of Israel (v. 17).

Since the exiles were far from the temple in Jerusalem, God Himself would substitute as their sanctuary. Jesus later would take the place of the temple (Matt. 26:61; 27:40; John 2:19), and through the Spirit His followers would become His temple (1 Cor. 3:16, 17; 2 Cor. 6:16; 1 Pet. 2:5).

The promise of God's presence among His people can be a great comfort to believers today who find themselves alone among those who do not know or honor God. The Lord is with us wherever we go. We can call on Him no matter what the circumstances around us. Just like God promised to be a *"little sanctuary"* for the Old Testament believers of Ezekiel's day, in the New Testament, we will serve as *"little temples"* for God.

"If you love Me, keep My commandments. And I will pray the Father, and He will give you another Helper, that He may abide with you forever— the Spirit of truth, whom the world cannot receive, because it neither sees Him nor knows Him; but you know Him, for He dwells with you and will be in you. I will not leave you orphans; I will come to you." – Jesus Christ (John 14:15-18)

"Do you not know that your body is the temple of the Holy Spirit who is in you, whom you have from God, and you are not your own? For you were bought at a price; therefore glorify God in your body and in your spirit, which are God's." (1 Cor 6:19-20)

THE PARABLE OF THE FRUITLESS GRAPEVINE

"Therefore thus says the Lord God: 'Like the wood of the vine among the trees of the forest, which I have given to the fire for fuel, so I will give up the inhabitants of Jerusalem; and I will set My face against them. They will go out from one fire, but another fire shall devour them. Then you shall know that I am the Lord, when I set My face against them. Thus I will make the land desolate, because they have persisted in unfaithfulness,' says the Lord God." (Ezek 15:6-8)

Ezekiel chapter 15 is an allegory picturing Israel as God's grapevine that is no longer bearing fruit. The essential use of grapevine is to bear fruit (Psalms 80:8–16; Ezek. 19:10–14; Hosea 10:1). Since a grapevine is not good for wood or building (vv. 2, 3), once it has ceased to bear fruit, it can only be cast into the fire (v. 4). The point was clear: *the nation of Israel had ceased to bear the fruit of righteousness and was therefore destined for judgment.* Both Isaiah (Isa. 5:1-7) and Jeremiah (Jer. 2:21) spoke of Israel's failure to produce proper fruit; however Ezekiel spoke of the total uselessness of Israel (v. 5).

Israel was thus like a charred and fruitless vine. It was not serving the Lord or bringing glory to Him. As the vine with charred ends, it had suffered burning (chastisement and judgment) on previous occasions. The northern end of the branch was charred by the Assyrians. The southern end was charred by the Egyptians. And now the middle – Jerusalem - would be charred by the Babylonians (see 2 Kings 25:9). The second fire of verse 7 pictures the captivity of those who escaped. They would now be given up to complete destruction because of their continued fruitlessness (v. 8).

As believers we have high privileges, but also the responsibility to produce fruit for God's glory. *If we don't glorify Him with our life, our existence is vain and useless.* It is like the vine without fruit, and our testimony will be destroyed. As branches in Christ, the True Vine, our chief function is to bear fruit for God. This would include the development of Christian character in our lives as seen in the fruit of the Spirit. However if we do not bear fruit, our existence is useless, and that was the condition of God's people in Ezekiel's day. Instead, if we share the life of God through faith in Jesus Christ, our lives will reveal itself in the fruit that we bear for His glory.

Let us remember the words of Jesus today and bear much fruit in our lives for His glory: *"I am the vine, you are the branches. He who abides in Me, and I in him, bears much fruit; for without Me you can do nothing. If anyone does not abide in Me, he is cast out as a branch and is withered; and they gather them and throw them into the fire, and they are burned. If you abide in Me, and My words abide in you, you will ask what you desire, and it shall be done for you. By this My Father is glorified, that you bear much fruit; so you will be My disciples."* (John 15:5-8)

AUGUST 31   *Bible Reading: Ezekiel Chapters 16-18*

GOD IS NOT PLEASED WITH THE DEATH OF THE WICKED

"Therefore I will judge you, O house of Israel, every one according to his ways," says the Lord God. "Repent, and turn from all your transgressions, so that iniquity will not be your ruin. Cast away from you all the transgressions which you have committed, and get yourselves a new heart and a new spirit. For why should you die O house of Israel? For I have no pleasure in the death of one who dies," says the Lord God. "Therefore turn and live!" (Ezek 18:30-32)

In this passage, God clarifies His views on individual responsibility to prophet Ezekiel. Everyone is judged equitably and individually. God never enjoys condemning a person, but is just and righteous in dispensing His judgments. Sin can never be taken lightly in one's relationship with God, and repentance is the way to life. The people continued to accuse God of injustice, but He shows that there is no injustice because even a wicked man can be saved by turning from his sins, and that is what the Lord wants them to do.

The problem is not God's unwillingness to save man, but rather man's refusal to be saved. This is God's passionate call to repentance, and displays God's mercy and man's choice. God's burden for His people is that they have life, not death. But life will not be forced upon anyone who wishes to remain in his sin. The individual must personally respond and repent to have life. Each individual is judged separately, so the only way for each person to *live* is to *'repent and turn'*.

God is not pleased in the death of the wicked or in judging them (vv. 23, 32). God will gladly forgive sinners if they would only repent.

The supreme need is for a *"new heart and a new spirit"* (v. 31), which can come only through faith in Christ as the gift of God (36:26) and is not the product of human effort (Eph. 2:8, 9). Ezekiel exhorts his audience to seek these not through their own merit but by repentance (v. 32).

God does not punish the innocent for the guilty except in the case of His Son. On the cross, Jesus took the punishment for our sins. God has no pleasure in the death of the wicked, *"yet it pleased the Lord to bruise Him"* (Isa. 53:10), *"for Christ also suffered once for sins, the just for the unjust, that He might bring us to God"* (1 Pet. 3:18).

September

SEPTEMBER 1   *Bible Reading: Ezekiel Chapters 19-21*

GOD DEALS WITH US FOR HIS NAME'S SAKE

"Then you shall know that I am the Lord, when I bring you into the land of Israel, into the country for which I raised My hand in an oath to give to your fathers. And there you shall remember your ways and all your doings with which you were defiled; and you shall loathe yourselves in your own sight because of all the evils that you have committed. ***Then you shall know that I am the Lord, when I have dealt with you for My name's sake,*** *not according to your wicked ways nor according to your corrupt doings, O house of Israel," says the Lord God.* (Ezek 20:42-44)

In chapter 20, prophet Ezekiel gives us a panoramic view of the history of Israel. It is in two parts: *her rebellious past* (vv. 1–31) and *her glorious future* (vv. 32–44). The *first part* surveys all that God had done for the nation, and the nation's sorely inadequate response. The mood changes dramatically at verse 33 where, in a series of the words *"I will"*, the Lord promises what He will accomplish on behalf of His people. The *second part* describes the coming judgment of those Jews who will be living at the conclusion of the Tribulation period when Christ returns to earth. He will bring the faithful into the blessings of the new covenant in the kingdom.

When the nation is restored to the land of Israel, they will no longer worship idols, but they will worship the Lord in holiness. The summary verse (44) indicates that it is for God's name's sake that

Israel will be restored in spite of their wicked ways and corrupt doings. When God is finished they will know that He is the LORD!

God chastens us that He might restore us and there is always hope. The repeated *"I will"* statements in verses 33-44 assures us that God is working for us and not against us. Remember that God does all this for His name's sake only. For His name's sake, God forgives our sins (1 John 2:12), guides us (Psalms 23:3; 31:3), deals with us (Ps. 109:21), and revives us (Ps. 143:11).

For God's name's sake, we should serve Him faithfully (3 John 7; Rev. 2:3), sacrifice for Him (Matt. 19:29), and be willing to suffer reproach for Him (Matt. 10:22; 24:9). All that we do should be for the honor and glory of God's name alone: *"Therefore, whether you eat or drink, or whatever you do, do all to the glory of God."* (1 Cor 10:31)

SEPTEMBER 2   *Bible Reading: Ezekiel Chapters 22-24*

STANDING IN THE GAP ON BEHALF OF OTHERS

"So I sought for a man among them who would make a wall, and stand in the gap before Me on behalf of the land, that I should not destroy it; but I found no one. Therefore I have poured out My indignation on them; I have consumed them with the fire of My wrath; and I have recompensed their deeds on their own heads," says the Lord God. (Ezek 22:30-31)

In one of the saddest verses in the book of Ezekiel, God Himself confesses that He found no one who could stand in the gap in order to stem the tide that would inevitably bring destruction (v. 30). God could not find a qualified spiritual leader to stand before God in intercession and lead the people to repentance.

·   *"Making a wall"* gives an image of leading the people to repentance. This is what God had to say about the false prophets earlier: *"You have not gone up into the gaps to build a wall for the house of Israel to stand in battle on the day of the Lord."* (Ezek 13:5)

·   *"Standing in the gap"* gives an image of interceding to God for His people (Genesis 20:7; Exodus 32:11; Numbers 16:48). In the history of Israel, God had raised up *"gap people"* to stand in the breach and stay off the judgment. Moses and Phinehas were such men (Psalms 106:23, 30), as were Joseph (Psalms 105:17) and Samuel (1 Samuel 3).

The imagery here is also that of a wall with a section broken down by a siege. If no soldier stands in the gap to repulse the enemy, the city surely will be taken. God represented Himself as against His people, and He was unable to find anyone who could turn away the coming judgment (see Ezek. 14:13–20). All classes of society were guilty before the Lord — rulers (v. 25); priests (v. 26); magistrates (v. 27); prophets (v. 28); and people (v. 29). Thus, not a righteous person, a reformer or an intercessor could be found in Israel to stand before God.

God is not looking for new methods or programs, but is looking for *"gap people"* with the courage to stand for what is right, even if they must stand alone. They will not only build strong walls but become walls by standing in the gap in the hour of danger. As the *"gap people"* we can act as go-betweens in the troubles around us by *"standing in the gap"* to bridge chasms of indifference and oppression. We can do what we can to stem the tide of evil and tell others of the opportunity to know God through His Son Jesus Christ. Above all, we can earnestly intercede to God on behalf of others in prayer.

Remember, *one person can make all the difference*! Will that person be YOU?

SEPTEMBER 3   *Bible Reading: Ezekiel Chapters 25-27*

GOD WILL JUDGE ALL UNBELIEVERS ONE DAY

The word of the Lord came to me, saying, "Son of man, set your face against..., and prophesy against them." (Ezek 25:1-2)

In Ezekiel chapters 25–32 we read of God's judgment on *seven heathen nations,* who included all of Judah's neighbors: *on the east,* Ammon, Moab, and Edom; *on the west,* Philistia; *on the north,* Tyre and Sidon; and *to the southwest,* Egypt. Most of these prophecies were never heard by the nations themselves, but were delivered to Israel to emphasize the sovereignty of God, which includes His guidance of His own people and His rule over and judgment of the nations with whom Israel had come into contact.

Though God's judgment began with His own people, it would extend to all the neighboring nations. These nations are judged for various forms of rebellion against God. They had contact with God's people, knew about Him, but were unwilling to turn to Him. What we can understand from these passages is that God's ways always reveal His thoughts, whether in judgment or in grace.

The *first nation* upon which judgment is pronounced was **Ammon** (25:1–7) because they rejoiced at the fall of God's sanctuary, Israel and Judah, and the Babylonian captivity. The *second nation* was **Moab** (25:8–11), which was hostile toward Judah, and they would know that God was the Lord. The *third nation* was **Edom** (25:12–14) because they took vengeance against the house of Judah, the Lord GOD said, they would know His vengeance. **Philistia** (25:15–17) was the fourth nation for God's judgment. Their never-ending hatred of Judah would bring upon them the vengeance of the Lord. The *fifth nation* that God judged was the seacoast city of **Tyre** (26:1–28:19). Tyre rejoiced when they heard that their business rival city Jerusalem had fallen, thinking that they would now get all the business!

Just as these nations would learn that if they touch God's people, they touch God, even so those who engage in *"Christian-bashing"* today will one day learn that Christian believers are the apple of God's eye. This is even true when God's people fall into sin and are judged for it.

When other believers are experiencing God's chastening or are suffering the consequences of their sins, what is our attitude toward them? Do we pray for them and encourage them to seek the Lord and yield to His will, or do we add to their trials? We should beware of all malicious joy, gloating, or revengeful thoughts against God's children. Instead, like Ezekiel, we should mourn, intercede, and confess the sins of other believers as our own.

"Therefore strengthen the hands which hang down, and the feeble knees, and make straight paths for your feet, so that what is lame may not be dislocated, but rather be healed. Pursue peace with all people, and holiness, without which no one will see the Lord" (Heb 12:12-14)

SELF-PRIDE IS
THE ROOT OF ALL SIN

*"You were the anointed cherub who covers; I established you; you were on the holy mountain of God; you walked back and forth in the midst of fiery stones. You were perfect in your ways from the day you were created, till iniquity was found in you...**your heart was lifted up because of your beauty**; you corrupted your wisdom for the sake of your splendor"* (Ezek 28:14-15, 17)

The prophecies of Ezekiel in verses 11-19 was addressed to the King of Tyre instead of the prince of Tyre. The description of the king of Tyre - as the seal of perfection, full of wisdom and perfect in beauty, as having been in Eden the garden of God, as having every precious stone as a covering, as being the anointed cherub, and as having been on the holy mountain of God - taken together seem too impressive for any earthly ruler. For this reason many Bible students see in these verses a description of Lucifer (Satan) and of his fall from heaven.

As a descriptive passage on Lucifer (Satan), the content reveals more about his fall than any other passage in the Bible. He served near the presence of God (v. 14), was perfect (v. 15), became guilty of the sin of pride (v. 17), and was therefore destined for judgment (vv. 16-19). The statement *"You were perfect... till iniquity was found in you"* (v. 15) is the closest that the Bible ever comes to explaining the *origin of sin*. It began when one of God's previously perfect creatures rebelled against Him. Lucifer was the most beautiful cherub, but because of his self-pride he was destroyed. *If self-pride was deadly enough to destroy a most powerful and wise angel, how much more should we humans make sure not to be proud of ourselves!*

Lucifer was thus expelled from heaven because of his pride and desire to be equal with God. (Isaiah 14:12–15). The origin of Lucifer's sin was pride in his beauty. He allowed his splendor to corrupt his wisdom. *Ultimately, all sin is rooted in this self-pride!*

The essence of self-pride is *self-centeredness* and *selfishness*. It claims that whatever we have achieved is by our own virtue, and leaves God and other circumstances out of our successes. It wants to be center stage always and takes all the credit for oneself. *Self-pride is the opposite of thankfulness and gratitude, and should be avoided at all costs as it is the root of all evil.* Let us give credit and thanks to God for all that we have accomplished so far in our lives!

Likewise you younger people, submit yourselves to your elders. Yes, all of you be submissive to one another, and be clothed with humility, for "God resists the proud, but gives grace to the humble." Therefore humble yourselves under the mighty hand of God, that He may exalt you in due time. (1 Peter 5:5-6)

SEPTEMBER 5   *Bible Reading: Ezekiel Chapters 31-33*

UNDERSTAND THE FAIRNESS OF GOD'S JUDGMENT

Therefore you, O son of man; say to the house of Israel: thus you say, "If our transgressions and our sins lie upon us, and we pine away in them, **how can we then live?"** *Say to them: 'As I live, says the Lord God, I have no pleasure in the death of the wicked, but that the wicked turn from his way and live.* **Turn, turn from your evil ways!** *For why should you die O house of Israel?' Therefore you, O son of man, say to the children of your people:* **'The righteousness of the righteous man shall not deliver him in the day of his transgression; as for the wickedness of the wicked, he shall not fall because of it in the day that he turns from his wickedness; nor shall the righteous be able to live because of his righteousness in the day that he sins.'** (Ezek 33:10-12)

Even though God's message through prophet Ezekiel is to the whole house of Israel, but its application was to be made on an individual basis. This is called *"the doctrine of individual moral responsibility"*. God was not dismissing a person's previous life in the sense of having no interest in it. Rather God emphasizes here that in the entire course of his/her life a person is free to change, through repentance and become accepted by God.

Due to their individual sins and transgressions before God many Israelites ask in despair: *"How can we then live?"* How many people even today have lost all hope and are in depression and despair. The Lord's answer is: *"REPENT"* or, *"TURN AWAY from your wickedness"*. There is hope for the worst sinner, but the *only hope* is in turning from sin. When the people complained that God's dealings with them were not just, God denies this and reminds them that *He will pardon a wicked man who confesses and forsakes his sin*; also, *He will punish a righteous man who turns to wickedness.*

In punishing Israel God was actually being faithful to His covenant stipulations with Israel. This covenant had been approved by the Israelites by agreeing to its commands and accepting the consequences of breaking them, both corporately and individually (see Exodus 19:1–9; Deut. 27). God presents His rationale in these verses for deciding who would be rewarded with life and who would suffer death: He would save those who repent and turn to Him, but would condemn those who trust in themselves and do evil. After presenting His rationale, God declares that His judgment is just and fair.

Each day we have many opportunities to choose to live righteously. As individuals, we are responsible for our actions, and our destiny is determined by our choices. What God wants from us today is *true repentance – turning away from our sins and turning to God!*

"The sacrifices of God are a broken spirit, a broken and a contrite heart—these, O God, You will not despise." (Psalms 51:17)

SEPTEMBER 6   *Bible Reading: Ezekiel Chapters 34-36*

GOD – OUR ONLY TRUE SHEPHERD – IS ALL WE NEED

"I will feed My flock, and I will make them lie down," says the Lord God. *"I will seek what was lost and bring back what was driven away, bind up the broken and strengthen what was sick; but I will destroy the fat and the strong, and feed them in judgment. You are My flock, the flock of My pasture; you are men, and I am your God."* (Ezek 34:15-16, 31)

In Ezekiel 34, the leaders of Israel depicted as *"shepherds"* received a performance review from God that was <u>not</u> good. The leaders were spending most of their energies feeding themselves instead of the flock (vv. 2–8), and they were giving them nothing but leftovers (vv. 18–19). Not only were they neglecting the most vulnerable among the people, the weak, the sick, the broken, and the refugees, but they were actually taking advantage of them (vv. 4–6, 21). There was only one remedy for this situation—to remove the leaders from leadership (vv. 9–10).

Instead, God Himself would heal the hurting, restore the scattered, and feed His flock (vv. 11–16). He will be their Shepherd and will gather them to the land and rule over them (during the Millennium). Evangelist D. L. Moody nicely outlines God's ministry to His sheep:

Notice the "I will's" of the Lord God on behalf of his sheep: *I will* search *them and seek them out* (v. 11). *I will* deliver *them* (v. 12). *I will* bring *them out - I will* gather *them together - I will* bring *them in* (v. 13). *I will* feed *them* (v. 14). *I will* cause *them to lie down* (v. 15). *I will* bind *up the broken - I will* strengthen *the sick* (v. 16).

John Taylor also beautifully ties together the revelations of God as Shepherd in both Testaments for us:

The picture of the shepherd searching out the wanderer (in verse 12) is a remarkable foreshadowing of the parable of the lost sheep (Luke 15:4), which our Lord doubtless based on this passage in Ezekiel. It illustrates as clearly as anything can do, the tender, loving qualities of the God of the Old Testament, and strikes a death-blow at those who try to drive a wedge between Yahweh, God of Israel, and the God and Father of our Lord Jesus Christ. Nor is this the only passage that speaks of God, the tender shepherd (Psalms 78:52; 79:13; 80:1; Isaiah 40:11; 49:9; Jer. 31:10).

Thus, this passage in Ezekiel 34 is a prefiguring of Christ as the Good Shepherd (John 10:1–16), who would bring His sheep back *"to their own land"* (vv. 12, 13). It also speaks of the future day of deliverance when God will seek out His sheep (see 36:16–36). Israel, though guilty and misguided, would eventually be rescued by the divine Good Shepherd and restored to the Promised Land.

Today, Jesus Christ is the Great Shepherd of the sheep (Heb. 13:20–21), and He cares for His own. He sends *"showers of blessing"* on the dry land and makes it into a garden (vv. 26, 29). What a difference it makes when our God is in control! He is ALL we need!

"The Lord is my shepherd; I shall not want." (Psalms 23:1)

SEPTEMBER 7   *Bible Reading: Ezekiel Chapters 37-39*

STAND UP LIKE A MIGHTY ARMY OF GOD

The hand of the Lord came upon me and brought me out in the Spirit of the Lord, and set me down in the midst of the valley; and it was full of bones. Then He caused me to pass by them all around, and behold, there were very many in the open valley; and indeed they were very dry. And He said to me, "Son of man, can these bones live?" So I answered, "O Lord God, You know."…So I prophesied as He commanded me, and breath came into them, and they lived, and stood upon their feet, an exceedingly great army. (Ezek 37:1-3, 10)

In Ezekiel's vision, God's Spirit deposited him in the midst of a valley in which he saw very dry bones of Israel (vv. 1-2). He was ordered to prophesy to those bones so that they would come to life (vv. 4-6). The first time he prophesied, sinews, flesh and skin came upon the bones (vv. 7-8). The next time he prophesied to the wind and the breath came into the bodies (vv. 9-10). This pictured the national restoration of Israel (vv. 11–14), first the restoration of a people spiritually dead, and then their regeneration.

The dry bones symbolized the whole house of Israel, who were identified as *dry* or *spiritually dead* (vv. 2–5); *as dejected*, with no apparent hope of being *"resurrected"* as the people of the living God; and *as dispersed* before being rejoined and rebuilt (vv. 6–10). The major thrust of this passage is the coming spiritual rebirth of God's chosen people through the Spirit of God (vv. 15–28; 36:22–32). This spiritual rebirth would miraculously revive and restore human beings to what God had intended them to be in the beginning.

Through this vision, we can notice a parallel in our own regeneration as well where the Word of God should first revive us and then the Holy Spirit regenerates us. The Bible scholar Yates makes an application for our own need of the Holy Spirit today:

"With weirdness, realism and dramatic force the prophet (Ezekiel) presents the heartening news that Israel may hope to live. A revival is possible! Even dry bones, without sinew and flesh and blood, can live. The coming of God's Spirit brings life. The same thrilling truth is still needed in a world that has dry bones everywhere. What we need is to have the Holy Spirit come with His quickening power that a genuine revival may sweep the earth."

We should note that the breath of God was breathed into man at creation (Gen. 2:7), into the Word when it was written (2 Tim. 3:16), and upon the disciples to empower them for ministry (John 20:22). It will one day sweep over God's chosen people and make them a new nation. Meanwhile, God longs to send the *"wind of revival"* to

His church; and He will, *if we honor His Word, pray, and depend on the Spirit of God.*

Let us desire to stand up like a mighty army of God, even today!

SEPTEMBER 8   *Bible Reading: Ezekiel Chapters 40-42*

THE IMPORTANCE OF TRUE GOD-CENTERED WORSHIP

And the man said to me, "Son of man, look with your eyes and hear with your ears, and fix your mind on everything I show you; for you were brought here so that I might show them to you. Declare to the house of Israel everything you see." (Ezek 40:4)

About 573 B.C., prophet Ezekiel was given a vision of the city of Jerusalem and the millennial temple. In the fourteenth year after Jerusalem was captured, Ezekiel was taken up and set on a very high mountain. He was shown a vision of the city of Jerusalem and the millennial temple by a man whose appearance was like bronze. The prophet was commanded to fix his mind on everything he saw and to declare it to the house of Israel (v. 4).

According to some Bible scholars, Ezekiel's temple will be the final temple to be constructed. The new temple will include the traditional outer court (40:5–27), the inner court (40:28–47), the main building (40:48–41:26), adjacent buildings (42:1–14), outer walls (42:15–20), and the altar (43:13–27). The fact that Ezekiel would spend so much space describing the temple indicates its importance. Some interpret this prophecy as an exact blueprint of a physical temple to be constructed in or near Jerusalem during a future millennial (thousand-year) period. Others see this prophecy not as a blueprint, but *as a vision that stresses the purity and spiritual vitality of the ideal place of worship and of those who will worship there.*

To us, the New Testament believers, *this vision speaks to us about the importance of God-centered worship.* Bible scholar Warren Wiersbe has compiled *four factors that should constitute our true worship* from the book *'The Best of Tozer'*:

1.   There should be *boundless confidence in the God we worship.* Our concept of God should be clear as we approach His throne of grace.

2.   There should be a *genuine appreciation of the excellency of God.* We should see His greatness as we worship Him.

3.   There should be a *sincere fascination of the beauty of God.* When we try to comprehend the splendor of God, we will be struck with astonished wonder.

4.   Finally, there should be *true adoration in the God we worship.* We will pour out our love and adoration as true praises of God rises up from our hearts.

Let us worship God *only* in the proper way that He desires from us! *"But the hour is coming, and now is, when the true worshipers will worship the Father in spirit and truth; for the Father is seeking such to worship Him. God is Spirit and those who worship Him must worship in spirit and truth."* (John 4:23-24)

SEPTEMBER 9   *Bible Reading: Ezekiel Chapters 43-45*

RADIATING GOD'S GLORY THROUGH OUR LIVES

*Then I heard Him speaking to me from the temple, while a man stood beside me. And He said to me, "Son of man, **this is the place of My throne and the place of the soles of My feet, where I will dwell in the midst of the children of Israel forever. No more shall the house of Israel defile My holy name,** they nor their kings, by their harlotry or with the carcasses of their kings on their high places. Son of man, **describe the temple to the house of Israel that they may be ashamed of their iniquities;** and let them measure the pattern. This is the law of the temple: **The whole area surrounding the mountaintop is most holy. Behold, this is the law of the temple."** (Ezek 43:6-7, 10, 12)*

In a dramatic reversal of the departure of the Lord's glory, Ezekiel saw God's glory returning from the east to dwell once again in His temple. Ezekiel had described how the glory left the old temple (11:22–23), and now he describes how the glory returns and fills the house (43:1–5; 44:4). God said the new temple will be the place where He will *"dwell in the midst of the children of Israel forever."* It will serve as God's permanent dwelling place among His people. The whole area surrounding the mountaintop on which the temple would be built would be most holy. *A true sight of the glory of the Lord makes us ashamed of our iniquities* (v. 10).

Israel's sin brought the destruction of the former temple, and God's mercy will restore the temple *after* Israel's repentance. This vision of a glorious temple was to be declared to the people *so that they would repent of their sins* (43:10). The temple is pivotal to understanding God's message to the people. The temple will be a place of sacrifice and a place where God's glory will dwell (43:1–5). *The beauty and grandeur of the temple mean nothing if God is not present!*

Today, the bodies of God's people are His temple (1 Cor. 6:19–20), and so is His church (Eph. 2:19–22). Just as God has a beautiful plan for His future temple in Jerusalem, so He has a plan for His people individually (Eph. 2:10) and His church collectively. *We are to be a holy temple, dedicated to Him alone, and we are to radiate the glory of God in our lives daily!*

*"Do you not know that **you are the temple of God and that the Spirit of God dwells in you**? If anyone defiles the temple of God, God will destroy him. **For the temple of God is holy, which temple you are.**"* (1 Cor 3:16-17)

SEPTEMBER 10   *Bible Reading: Ezekiel Chapters 46-48*

THE LIFE-GIVING POWER OF THE HOLY SPIRIT

He said to me, "Son of man, have you seen this?" Then he brought me and returned me to the bank of the river. When I returned, there, along the bank of the river, were very many trees on one side and the other. Then he said to me: "This water flows toward the eastern region, goes down into the valley, and enters the sea. When it reaches the sea, its waters are healed. And it shall be that every living thing that moves, wherever the rivers go, will live. There will be a very great multitude of fish, because these waters go there; for they will be healed, and everything will live wherever the river goes." (Ezek 47:6-9)

The final chapters of the book of Ezekiel describe the new land whose major feature will be a life-giving river flowing from the temple (47:1–12). Joel had mentioned this river before Ezekiel's time (Joel 3:18), and Zechariah spoke of it after Israel returned from the Babylonian captivity (Zech. 14:8). Ezekiel saw in a vision a river flowing from the door of the temple, past the altar, through the wall south of the east Gate, and down to the Dead Sea. The waters of the sea will be healed, and fish will abound in it.

This river speaks of the healing and life-giving power of the Holy Spirit of God (see Gen. 2:8–10; John 4:13, 14; 10:10). Apostle John, too, saw the river of the water of life flowing from God's throne (Rev. 22:1). The result of the land's receiving this water is the same in both visions —*the land is healed* (compare vv. 9–12 with Rev. 22:1–3).

What we can understand from this vision is that no matter how deep we want to go into the things of God, the opportunity is there. *It's tragic that too many of us linger in the shallows when we could be enjoying the depths.* This river is also a picture of the blessings that will flow out from God who dwells in His temple. Today God dwells in our bodies (1 Cor. 6:19) and therefore streams of blessing should be flowing to others around us from our lives (John 7:37-39). If we are filled with the Holy Spirit then our lives will bless others as the blessings will overflow to others. *What a challenge for us to meet the conditions that will produce a blessing for others!*

"There is a river whose streams shall make glad the city of God, the holy place of the tabernacle of the Most High. God is in the midst of her, she shall not be moved; God shall help her, just at the break of dawn." (Psalms 46:4-5)

SEPTEMBER 11   *Bible Reading: Daniel Chapters 1-3*

OUR DECISIONS WILL DETERMINE OUR DESTINY

*"But Daniel **purposed in his heart** that he would not defile himself with the portion of the king's delicacies, nor with the wine which he drank; therefore he requested of the chief of the eunuchs that he might not defile himself. God...brought Daniel into the favor and goodwill of the chief of the eunuchs...God gave them knowledge and skill in all literature and wisdom; and Daniel had understanding in all visions and dreams."* (Dan 1:8-9, 17)

Daniel purposed not to eat the king's food which was forbidden to Jews. Such separation is twofold: it is *toward the Lord*, and *away from things that defile*. The results of the ten-day experiment demonstrated God's approval of Daniel's courage and conviction. Even

Nebuchadnezzar found the four Hebrews to be not only healthy, but also wise in giving counsel (v. 19).

There may be three possible reasons why Daniel made the crucial decision not to defile himself with the king's food:

1. The meats provided for the king's table was forbidden by the Jewish law (see Lev. 11).

2. The delicate food would be only to gratify the lust of the flesh (1 Cor. 9:27).

3. The food provided were already consecrated to idols (Acts 15:29).

When Daniel did his part, God did not fail to do His part and made the king's steward greatly respect and admire Daniel. Daniel is distinguished from his companions in his ability to interpret dreams and visions, much as Joseph was in the court of Pharaoh (Gen. 40:8; 41:16). Thus, the obedience of Daniel and his friends to God, and their refusal to compromise their faith in a heathen environment, were rewarded with God's blessing (Deut. 8:3; Matt. 4:4). God's blessing was not just limited to physical well-being, but also included outstanding intellectual development during their three years of Babylonian education.

The success of Daniel's plan was due more to the sovereignty of God in blessing his spiritual commitment than it was to the diet. In times of testing we also need to remain faithful to God. Sometimes this will require:

·   *Wisdom* to seek a creative compromise that would enable us to meet society's expectations without violating our spiritual beliefs (1:8–14)

·   *Courage* to be willing to stand up for our beliefs when no compromise is possible (3:15–18)

·   *Personal discipline* to develop a lifestyle of faithfulness so the right response to a test will come "naturally" (6:10)

Perhaps *in no other area* do we have as great an opportunity to influence people around us as in our ethics and morality in our schools, colleges and workplaces. How we behave on the job tells others everything they need to know about our values and commitments. The question is, are we standing for what is right? *Remember, our decisions will determine our destiny!*

"Do not love the world or the things in the world. If anyone loves the world, the love of the Father is not in him. For all that is in the world—

the lust of the flesh, the lust of the eyes, and the pride of life—is not of the Father but is of the world. And the world is passing away, and the lust of it; but he who does the will of God abides forever." (1 John 2:15-17)

SEPTEMBER 12   *Bible Reading: Daniel Chapters 4-6*

THE IMPORTANCE OF MAINTAINING A DAILY PRAYER LIFE

"Now when Daniel knew that the writing was signed, he went home. And in his upper room, with his windows open toward Jerusalem, he knelt down on his knees three times that day, and prayed and gave thanks before his God, as was his custom since early days." (Dan 6:10)

Daniel was past 80 years of age at this time, yet he was still on his knees thanking God and asking for His guidance and help. Daniel's knowledge of the decree of Darius not only failed to dissuade him from his practice of seeking God's face three times each day, but also created a desire in him to seek God's face immediately. His enemies were correct in assuming that if Daniel was forced to choose between the decree of an earthly king and the eternal word of the King of heaven, he would choose his God (v. 5).

The officers lied when they used the word 'all' (v. 7) for that gave the king the idea that Daniel agreed with them. They conspired against Daniel and went as a group against him *three* times: to get the king to pass the edict (6:6), to watch Daniel pray in his window (6:11), and to make the king enforce his edict (6:15). *But no laws or threats could keep Daniel from his times of prayer!*

We can safely assume that Daniel never knew that he would be miraculously delivered from the jaws of death. He was advanced in years, and there was no reason for him to suppose that God would intervene to spare his life. However, *courage* and *steadfastness in faith* motivated him to continue his walk with God. Daniel knew he had to obey God, no matter what man might command or how much he might stand to lose personally by such actions. He did not increase his prayer out of hypocrisy, nor did he try to conceal it out of fear. *Daniel's steadfastness is a challenge to us to maintain a daily consistent prayer life as well..!!!*

340

*"And who is he who will harm you if you become followers of what is good? But even if you should suffer for righteousness' sake, you are blessed. And do not be afraid of their threats, nor be troubled. But sanctify the Lord God in your hearts, and always be ready to give a defense to everyone who asks you a reason for the hope that is in you, with meekness and fear; having a good conscience, that when they defame you as evildoers, those who revile your good conduct in Christ may be ashamed. **For it is better, if it is the will of God, to suffer for doing good than for doing evil.**"* (1 Peter 3:13-17)

SEPTEMBER 13   *Bible Reading: Daniel Chapters 7-9*

GOD ALWAYS FULFILLS HIS PROPHECIES

"I was watching in the night visions, and behold, One like the Son of Man, coming with the clouds of heaven! He came to the Ancient of Days, and they brought Him near before Him. Then to Him was given dominion and glory and a kingdom that all peoples, nations, and languages should serve Him. His dominion is an everlasting dominion, which shall not pass away, and His kingdom the one which shall not be destroyed." (Dan 7:13-14)

This vision of Daniel in chapter 7 ends with one like the *'Son of Man'* coming before the 'Ancient of Days' to receive an eternal *kingdom* with those of all nations in His service (v. 13b), which is the *kingdom "of our Lord and of His Christ"* (Rev. 11:15). The *'Son of Man'* who came to the *'Ancient of Days'* is the Son of God approaching God the Father who sits as a Judge in court (vv. 10, 26). Here, the Old Testament clearly presents the Father and the Son as two separate persons within the Trinity.

The Lord Jesus Christ is given universal dominion, a kingdom, the one which shall never be superseded (v. 14). His deity is indicated by His coming *"on the clouds of heaven"* (Matt. 24:30; 26:64; Mark 13:26), by the worship that He receives (v. 14), and by the eternity of His kingdom (v. 14; Psalms 2:6–9). The vision depicts the kingdom era or the Millennium (Rev. 21:1–6). The entire vision is explained to Daniel so that he can know the course of world history, culminating in the ultimate triumph of God's kingdom on earth.

In this vision, Daniel saw 'One' like the *"Son of Man,"* indicating that He is not a man in the strict sense, but rather the perfect representation of humanity. Jewish and Christian expositors have identified this individual as the Messiah. The expression *"Son of Man"* is used 69 times in the synoptic Gospels and 12 times in the Gospel of John to refer to Jesus Christ. It is the title Jesus most often used of Himself. Elsewhere in the Old Testament it is only God who comes on the clouds (Ps. 104:3; Isaiah 19:1). Accordingly, the *"Son of Man"* originates in heaven and comes by divine initiative.

The commencement of Christ's everlasting dominion will take place at His second coming (Matt. 24:30; 25:31; Rev. 11:15). Daniel's dream is in part *messianic*; announcing that the *Messiah's coming will inaugurate a new phase of God's rule on Earth.* Christ did this by bringing the kingdom of God into human experience (v. 18), and Christ will one day establish a righteous kingdom that nobody will overthrow! *Remember, God <u>always</u> fulfills His prophecies!*

"Behold, He (Jesus Christ) is coming with clouds, and every eye will see Him, even they who pierced Him. And all the tribes of the earth will mourn because of Him. Even so, Amen." (Rev 1:7)

SEPTEMBER 14   *Bible Reading: Daniel Chapters 10-12*

BE WISE AND SHINE LIKE STARS FOREVER

"And many of those who sleep in the dust of the earth shall awake, some to everlasting life, some to shame and everlasting contempt. Those who are <u>wise</u> shall shine like the brightness of the firmament, and those who turn many to righteousness like the stars forever and ever." (Dan 12:2-3)

Daniel looked into the future and saw *hope* in the midst of death. He described the state of the dead in terms of *"those who sleep"* (v. 2), which is a metaphor. The *"sleep"* of death means that the dead will someday "wake up" from their temporary condition and go on to an eternal state—*"some to everlasting life, some to shame and everlasting contempt"* (12:2).

These verses contain the first explicit teaching of the general resurrection, with everlasting life awaiting the faithful, but eternal punishment for those who reject God (see Matt. 25:46). Those who are wise by obeying the Lord and by leading others to faith and righteousness *will receive honor* from God and *will be resplendent* in eternal glory. They *will glow* like the stars for eternity.

Let's keep in mind that this prophecy gives encouragement to all of God's people in every generation to know that *God is in control* and *will accomplish His purposes in spite of the forces of evil.* No matter what kind of affliction or tribulation God permits us to experience, He is still in control. Let us earnestly seek to win others to righteousness that can only be done by sharing the gospel – *the good news of salvation through Jesus Christ alone!*

*"The fruit of the righteous is a tree of life, and **he who wins souls is <u>wise</u>**."* (Prov 11:30)

Let's be <u>wise</u> and shine like stars forever!

SEPTEMBER 15   *Bible Reading: Hosea Chapters 1-3*

FORGIVENESS CAN SAVE AND TRANSFORM A MARRIAGE

"And it shall be, in that day," says the Lord, *"that you will call Me 'My Husband,' and no longer call Me 'My Master'."* (Hosea 2:16)

Hosea illustrates God's enduring desire and love for His people. The first three chapters, which is Hosea's personal story with his unfaithful wife Gomer, symbolize God's relationship with the unfaithful Israel. In Hosea 2:16, the names 'Ishi' *(My Husband)* and 'Baali' *(My Master)* are significant. The *former* is a *term of affection* and *represents the closest loving relationship*, while the *latter* indicates *servitude and inferiority.*

Just like a gentle husband making sincere attempts to restore his relationship with his wayward wife, God seeks to win Israel back by making romantic overtures and wooing her with tender words of love. God would *"give her back her vineyards"* (v. 15) that had been taken in judgment. Just as Hosea reclaimed his wife, so God will one day *reclaim* His people, *renew* His *"marriage vows,"* and *restore* His people to blessing. *Three specific blessings* will occur *"in that day"* (v. 16) *when God restores His people:*

1. *First, there will be a new relationship* (2:16–17). The people will call God *"my husband,"* not *"my master"*, so there will be a more intimate relationship.

2. *Second, there will be a new covenant* (2:18–20). God will institute a new covenant with His people that will bring universal peace.

3. *Third, there will be a new blessing* (2:21–23). God's promised blessings and fruitfulness will be poured out on the people.

Through the tragic story of Hosea and Gomer, God reveals both the depth and power (a) of His love for Israel and (b) of the marriage bond. God describes His suffering the pain and humiliation of Israel's unfaithfulness; and in obedience to God, Hosea suffers the same pain and humiliation of his own wife's unfaithfulness. But God shows him how the marriage can be saved: *through suffering and forgiveness.*

This is one of the *most profound revelations* about marriage found anywhere in Scripture. Successful marriage is not a relationship of *perfect* people living *perfectly* by *perfect* principles. Rather, marriage is a state in which very imperfect people often hurt and humiliate one another, yet *find the grace to extend forgiveness to one another,* and so allow the redemptive power of God to transform their marriage. Remember, *forgiveness can save and transform a marriage!*

"Let all bitterness, wrath, anger, clamor, and evil speaking be put away from you, with all malice. And be kind to one another, tenderhearted, forgiving one another, just as God in Christ forgave you." (Eph 4:31-32)

SEPTEMBER 16   *Bible Reading: Hosea Chapters 4-6*

COME AND LET US <u>RETURN</u> TO THE LORD

"Come, and let us <u>return</u> to the Lord; for He has torn, but He will heal us; He has stricken, but He will bind us up. After two days He will revive us; on the third day He will raise us up, that we may live in His sight. Let us know, let us pursue the knowledge of the Lord. His going forth is established as the morning; He will come to us like the rain, like the latter and former rain to the earth." (Hosea 6:1-3)

In the above verses, prophet Hosea looks beyond both the Assyrian and Babylonian captivities down to the ultimate day when Israel as a nation will be truly converted (Jer 31:31–34) and God will set up His millennial kingdom over His people and reign for a thousand years. In response to the Assyrian and Babylonian captivity, a remnant will come to this recognition; but in that day the entire nation will come to this realization.

The initial verses (1–3) are Israel's response to God's call to repentance (5:15). At first it seems genuine and heartfelt, but upon closer examination, we see that no sin is specifically confessed. Their repentance is shallow and insincere, which is apparent from the rest of the chapter. True repentance only comes later on when the nation of Israel repudiates its idolatry and acknowledges their need for God's grace.

When God's people truly repent, God is eager to restore His relationship with them. God's restored presence and blessings would be like the rain that waters and renews the earth. The latter rains of Israel came in the spring and caused the plants to *grow*. The former rains came in the autumn and *softened the ground* for plowing and sowing.

Let us understand that the call to return to the Lord is one of the central messages of Hosea (see 2:7; 3:5; 5:4, 15). *True repentance and conversion will bring reconciliation that includes healing of our wounds.* When we come back to God, He brings the dawning of a new day with the refreshing showers. The God who has chastens us will also heal and revive us. *Why do we delay anymore to <u>return</u> to God in <u>humble repentance</u>?*

"<u>Return</u> to Me," says the Lord of hosts, "and I will return to you." (Zech 1:3)

SEPTEMBER 17   *Bible Reading: Hosea Chapters 7-9*

DARE TO BE DIFFERENT BY STANDING APART FOR GOD

"Ephraim has mixed himself among the peoples; Ephraim is a cake unturned. Aliens have devoured his strength, but he does not know it; yes, gray hairs are here and there on him, yet he does not know it." (Hosea 7:8-9)

Israel, addressed in the name of its most prominent tribe Ephraim, was reminded of the mission that God had called it into existence in Gen 12:1–3. Instead, they had mixed themselves among the heathen people by shifting alliances with Egypt, Philistia, Aram, and Assyria, and had adopted their ways. They had much religious activity to show for, but no religious reality.

In this sarcastic metaphor, the people of Israel was compared to an unturned cake because they had refused to turn to the Lord and showed lack of balance. As far as religious activity is concerned, they were overdone. But so far as their attitude and reality towards God was concerned, they were raw. This example fitted Israel's condition perfectly!

Because Israel had entered into foreign alliances and assimilated other cultures, it had lost the distinctions that gave it worth. Their alliances, rather than empowering them, had sapped their strength. The people were *"half-baked"*; there was no depth in their religious experience. The nation was aging, weakened and feeble but did not realize it, and national death would come much sooner than the people realized.

Let's take a valuable lesson from this metaphor concerning Israel. When we truly live as God's children by taking the Scriptures to heart and attempt to live them, we will inevitably come into conflict with the world. We belong to no one but Christ. To be a *true* Christian is to stand apart and yet to remain within – to dare to be different. In order to obey God faithfully, we may need to make changes in our hearts and our lives. Let's stand apart for God by making a change within and declaring a new start today!

"Brethren, I do not count myself to have apprehended; but one thing I do, forgetting those things which are behind and reaching forward to those things which are ahead, I press toward the goal for the prize of the upward call of God in Christ Jesus." (Phil 3:13-14)

SEPTEMBER 18   Bible Reading: Hosea Chapters 10-12

IT'S TIME TO BREAK UP OUR HARDENED HEARTS

*"Sow for yourselves righteousness; reap in mercy; **break up your fallow ground**, for it is time to seek the Lord, till He comes and rains righteousness on you."* (Hosea 10:12)

346

The prophet Hosea calls upon Israel to repentance, reminding them that a decision could not be postponed, and that God's blessings could still be restored. Israel had to reestablish social justice (righteousness) and loyalty (mercy) in the land. The only thing that could prevent God's judgment from falling was repentance and a life of righteousness. The time to come to this repentance and righteousness is now, before the judgment falls. Their repentance will put them into a proper relationship with God, and He can then teach them His ways.

Plowing and planting are the necessary preliminary steps for growing a crop, which eventually sprouts when the rain falls in season. In the same way, repentance would set the stage for restored blessing, which God would eventually rain down on His people. Sowing that which is right and good brings a harvest of blessing from the Lord. Fallow ground is land left uncultivated. When fallow ground is plowed, it produces a particularly abundant harvest, which only God can give (1 Cor. 3:6, 7).

In the above passage, Israel is invited and encouraged to return to God by prayer, repentance, and reformation. *What was wrong with Israel?* They had tried to serve two masters (Hosea 10:1–2), they had lied to God (v. 4), they had worshiped idols (vv. 5–6), and their hearts were hard and needed plowing up (v. 12). They had sowed the wrong seed in the wrong kind of soil and yet expected to reap the right harvest! The *only* hope of escape for Israel would be through repentance and seeking the Lord!

For us, it's no different. It is high time for us to *break up our hardened hearts* by drawing near to God and seeking Him earnestly through repentance. As God's word reminds us: *"God resists the proud, but gives grace to the humble. Therefore **submit to God. Resist the devil and he will flee from you. Draw near to God** and He will draw near to you. **Humble yourselves in the sight of the Lord** and He will lift you up."* (James 4:6-8, 10)

TRUE WISDOM IS TO UNDERSTAND THE WAYS OF GOD

"Who is wise? Let him understand these things. Who is prudent? Let him know them. For the ways of the Lord are right; the righteous walk in them, but transgressors stumble in them." (Hosea 14:9)

Hosea closes his prophecy by emphasizing that wisdom and prudence lie in obedience to the ways of the Lord. This verse constitutes an epilogue to the entire prophecy. Those who are wise and prudent *(who are in right relationship and fellowship with God)* will understand the things written in this prophecy. Those who are transgressors *(who are out of fellowship with God)* will not understand them and will fall in them.

God's ways, His demands and principles, are completely true. Those who are right with God will choose to obey them, but those who are not right with will ignore them and consequently stumble into judgment. Those who were wise would realize the truth of his words and the rightness of the path established by God. The righteous will follow God's path, but the *"rebellious"* will *"stumble"* because of their disobedience.

Thus the key is to know God and His ways, to follow Him and so find righteousness, and to avoid paths that lead to destruction. This epilogue challenges every generation to consider carefully the ways of the Lord that are presented in the Bible (Psalms 1; 18:21; Prov. 10:29). The choices that Israel faced are also set before us: wisdom or folly; discipleship or rebellion; life or death. The wise will "choose life" always! (Deut. 30:19, 20)

"Let us hear the conclusion of the whole matter: fear God and keep His commandments, for this is man's all. For God will bring every work into judgment, including every secret thing, whether good or evil." (Eccl 12:13-14)

Like the wise man in Ecclesiastes, Hosea invites us to hear the conclusion of the whole matter: *"the ways of the Lord are right."*

GOD's PROMISE to POUR OUT HiS SPIRIT upon US

"And it shall come to pass afterward that I will pour out My Spirit on all flesh; your sons and your daughters shall prophesy, your old men shall dream dreams, Your young men shall see visions. And also on My menservants and on My maidservants I will pour out My Spirit in those days." (Joel 2:28-29)

This is the prophecy for which Joel has become most famous in modern days. This prophecy must be considered in the light of its context and in the light of its New Testament usage.

After describing the physical blessings that would come upon his generation if they would repent, Joel describes the spiritual blessings that God would bestow upon His people in the future. This passage was quoted by Peter on the Day of Pentecost (see Acts 2:17–21) to explain the miracle of speaking in tongues. Some Bible scholars suggest that Joel's prophecy was partially fulfilled on the Day of Pentecost. The gift of the Holy Spirit was given, but the signs mentioned in vv. 30–32 will be fulfilled later in connection with the return of Christ in great glory.

We need to note that the words *"pour out"* is derived from the imagery of Israel's heavy winter rains; it speaks here of abundant provision. *"All flesh"* anticipates the inclusion of both Jews and Gentiles in one body in Christ (see Eph. 2:11–3:6). The ministries of the Spirit mentioned here were experienced in the early church (see Acts 11:28; 21:9; 2 Cor. 12:1–4; Rev. 1:1–3). The outpouring of the Spirit and the ministries done through His power will be accomplished without regard to gender, age, or class.

Christians are now experiencing the Holy Spirit in fulfillment of Joel's promise. However, the prophet also describes other events associated with the *"day of the Lord,"* which it appears will not have their ultimate fulfillment until the end times.

The only condition throughout Joel's prophecies is true repentance to the Lord, which involves *turning from sin* on the one hand and *trusting by faith* (with all one's heart) on the other. The Old Testament emphasizes *repentance* (turning) and the New Testament emphasizes *faith* (trusting). Repentance and faith are inseparable. That is why *repentance results in turning to the Lord with all one's heart.*

"Repent, and let every one of you be baptized in the name of Jesus Christ for the remission of sins; and you shall receive the gift of the Holy Spirit. For the promise is to you and to your children, and to all who are afar off, as many as the Lord our God will call." (Acts 2:38-39)

SEPTEMBER 21   *Bible Reading: Amos Chapters 1-3*

REVELATION OF GOD'S WILL IN OUR LIVES

*"Surely the Lord God **does nothing**, unless He reveals His secret to His servants the prophets."* (Amos 3:7)

Israel's sin was intensified because of her position before God. God had specifically chosen Israel among all the peoples of the earth to reveal His glory, but when Israel did not obey God judgment was certain for them. However, God does not bring any calamity *"without revealing his plan to his servants the prophets"*. What Amos was revealing here was: (a) He is a prophet, (b) God has spoken, and (c) God will bring His judgment against Israel. All this would come to pass because the people of Israel did *"not know how to do right."*

The conclusion of Amos was that God in His mercy will do nothing to punish until He has revealed it to His spokesmen the prophets. Amos was blowing the trumpet to warn the people (v. 6) because God had shared His secrets with him (v. 7). In spite of his humble origins, Amos was God's servant.

God does nothing, unless He reveals. The God who acts also reveals Himself and interprets His actions to and through His prophets. God revealed His plans for Sodom and Gomorrah to Abraham (Gen. 18:17; 20:7). Moses, the supreme Old Testament prophet, was called *"the servant of the Lord"* (Deut. 34:5). Subsequent prophets were characterized by the similar phrase, *"My servants the prophets"* (Jer. 7:25; Ezek. 38:17; Dan. 9:10).

In a wider sense, God's will is revealed to all who love God, which it is not to the world (John 15:15; 17:25, 26). Many times in our lives, *God reveals His will to us* through His Word, His prophets, and situations in our lives. When God speaks to us and reveals His will in our lives, let us earnestly attempt to listen to Him and obey His commandments. Otherwise, like Israel, we can expect His judgment to fall upon us in the near future!

"The secret of the Lord is with those who fear Him, and He will show them His covenant." (Psalms 25:14)

SEPTEMBER 22   *Bible Reading: Amos Chapters 4-6*

WE <u>MUST</u> PREPARE OURSELVES TO MEET OUR GOD

"Therefore thus will I do to you, O Israel; because I will do this to you, ***prepare to meet your God, O Israel!*** *For behold, He who forms mountains, and creates the wind, who declares to man what his thought is, and makes the morning darkness, who treads the high places of the earth — the Lord God of hosts is His name."* (Amos 4:12-13)

The consequences of Israel's disobedience were catastrophic. The people had rejected God's ever-increasing warnings. Now they would face God Himself: *"Prepare to meet your God, O Israel."* When God came in judgment, the people would finally understand that He is *"the Lord God Almighty."* From this point on, Amos stressed two key themes: *the coming of God in judgment* and *the covenant name of God* (namely, Yahweh).

God used several means of discipline—drought, famine, crop diseases, locusts, plagues, war, and local catastrophes (v. 11)—and yet the people of Israel did not get the message. They had met with God's disciplines, but the next step was to meet God Himself (v. 12). He was personally coming to judge them.

It was a tragedy that the people of Israel kept living in luxury (vv. 1–3) and carrying out their religious duties (vv. 4–5) while ignoring the call of God. The text *"prepare to meet your God"* is not a command to meet God in the sense of returning to Him. It was too late for this. This was to be a confrontation in which Yahweh would pronounce sentence. The phrase comes from Exodus 19:15–17, where, after three days of sanctification, the people met the Lord at Sinai. Then they met a God who was graciously forging a covenant with them. Now they would meet a God who was coming to judge their covenant disobedience.

However, by application this statement makes a great gospel warning. The evangelist D. L. Moody found *four* things in this text: (a) There is one God; (b) We are accountable to him; (c) We must meet him; (d) We need preparation to meet him (*Notes from My Bible*).

In our comfort and prosperity, we may think that we are immune from God's judgment, but let us always remember that we will be judged by God one day. *Are we prepared to meet our God?* If not, let's prepare ourselves for that greater encounter with God one day!

"For we must all appear before the judgment seat of Christ, that each one may receive the things done in the body, according to what he has done, whether good or bad." (2 Cor 5:10)

SEPTEMBER 23   *Bible Reading: Amos Chapters 7-9*

EXPERIENCING A FAMINE OF GOD'S WORD IN THE FUTURE

"Behold, the days are coming," says the Lord God, "that I will send a famine on the land, not a famine of bread, nor a thirst for water, but of hearing the words of the Lord. They shall wander from sea to sea, and from north to east; they shall run to and fro, seeking the word of the Lord, but shall not find it." (Amos 8:11-12)

The vision of the summer fruit in Amos chapter 8 shows that Israel is ripe for judgment, which will come very soon. One aspect of the judgment will be that people will long to hear the word of the Lord, but it will be withheld from them. Famine and drought (of God's word) will prevail. This curse actually originates from the covenant law (see Deut. 32:20; Hos. 3:4). We see this curse in effect during the period of the judges when sin abounded (Judg. 21:25) and *"the word of the Lord was rare"* (1 Sam. 3:1).

We need to understand that from the beginning, Israel had expressed its contempt for God's Word by trying to mix the worship of God with idolatry. When God sent His prophets, they were not welcomed (see 7:10–13). Now, God will grant Israel's desire. He will not impose His Word on them and they will find that very troubling. They will run everywhere to seek the word of God but will not find it. Their search would be in vain because God would not send them a prophetic word during their time of calamity.

It is very important to remember that God's Word is our spiritual nourishment (Matt. 4:4; 1 Pet. 2:2), and there can be no substitute. When we reject God's Word by refusing to read it and meditate it on a daily basis, a day is coming when God will take away His Word from us, which will leave us hungry and unsatisfied. *Oh, that we may find time to dwell on God's Word today and everyday!*

"Let the word of Christ dwell in you richly in all wisdom, teaching and admonishing one another in psalms and hymns and spiritual songs, singing with grace in your hearts to the Lord." (Col 3:16)

SEPTEMBER 24   *Bible Reading: Obadiah Chapter 1*

GOD WILL FINALLY ESTABLISH HIS KINGDOM

*"But on **Mount Zion** there shall be **deliverance**, and there shall be **holiness**; the house of Jacob shall possess their possessions. The house of Jacob shall be a fire, and the house of Joseph a flame; but the house of Esau shall be stubble; they shall kindle them and devour them, and no survivor shall remain of the house of Esau," for the Lord has spoken. "Then saviors shall come to Mount Zion to judge the mountains of Esau, and **the kingdom shall be the Lord's**."* (Ob 1:17-18, 21)

God's goal in history is the establishment of His kingdom. For Israel this will include the return of the people, the possession of the land, the judgment on Israel's enemies, and the restoration of the kingdom in holiness. The above verses contain the promise of the expansion of God's people in all directions until they regain their ancient territory. God's repeated promise concerning possession of the land (in Gen. 12:7) will have its final fulfillment through God's help!

We should note that *"Mount Zion"* (in v. 17) and *"My holy mountain"* (in v. 16) refer to the same place: **Jerusalem**. The references to the *"house of Jacob"* and the *"house of Joseph"* (in v. 18) signify a **unified Israel**. God intends to rejoin the kingdoms of Israel and Judah as one people again. The closing verse looks forward to that time when the Lord's people will come to mount Zion and judge the mount of Esau during the kingdom age (Dan. 7:27; Rev. 5:10). The emphasis on *"saviors"* (in v. 21) is upon God *the Father* as the Savior (Is. 45:21) and upon God *the Son* as Savior (Acts 4:12). God will be all in all, and His glorious, triumphant people will reign forever with Him!

353

Let us understand that these were Obadiah's last words against all human arrogance, pride, and rebellion. Edom had thought itself indestructible; but the Lord humbled that nation and restored the fallen Israel. Many people are tempted to consider themselves beyond the reach of God. But God will bring them low, just as He will lift those who humble themselves before Him. *And one great day, He will establish His just rule over all…!!!*

"The kingdoms of this world have become the kingdoms of our Lord and of His Christ, and He shall reign forever and ever!" (Rev 11:15)

SEPTEMBER 25   *Bible Reading: Jonah Chapters 1-4*

IT'S A MATTER OF PERSPECTIVE

Then God said to Jonah, "Is it right for you to be angry about the plant?" And he said, "It is right for me to be angry, even to death!" But the Lord said, "You have had pity on the plant for which you have not labored, nor made it grow, which came up in a night and perished in a night. And should I not pity Nineveh, that great city, in which are more than one hundred and twenty thousand persons who cannot discern between their right hand and their left—and much livestock?" (Jonah 4:9-11)

The story of Jonah is truly a story of God's love for even the most unlovable, despicable people on the earth, and the message of Jonah rings out loud and clear: *God cares for the heathen!* God will spare no extreme to get His message to them, even when the messenger is deliberately disobedient. People are of more value than animals, and animals of more value than plants, but the Lord has a concern that extends to all of His creation. The Lord's compassion comes from His character (v. 2; Joel 2:13, 14). We may recall the compassion of Jesus as He looked upon the multitudes (Matt. 9:36; Mark 6:34; 8:2), and His statement in Matt. 10:29 that not a sparrow will fall to the ground apart from the will of the Father. Our care for objects of little significance should remind us of God's great care for things of infinite worth.

If God wanted only to save the city of Nineveh, the book would have ended at chapter 3. But there was still more work to do, for God wanted to save His servant from himself. Jonah was an angry man (vv. 1, 2, 4, 9) who wanted to see Nineveh destroyed. Like the elder brother in the parable of the prodigal son, he stayed outside and vented his bitterness (Luke 15:25–32).

The basic problem was that Jonah was not completely yielded to God. His mind knew God's truth, but he did not do the will of God *"from the heart"* (Eph. 6:6). He obeyed only because he was afraid of what God might do to him. His was not a ministry of love!

In the similar manner, when we are angry with God, *everything in life gets out of perspective*, and we say and do selfish things. Things become more important than people, and comfort more important than ministry. But God is long-suffering and tenderly deals with us to bring us to obey His will.

It is essential in Christian service to be happy with the will of God, and we should be able to say without hesitation: *"I delight to do Your will, O my God, and Your law is within my heart"* (Psalms 40:8).

SEPTEMBER 26   *Bible Reading: Micah Chapters 1-3*

ONE PERSON CAN MAKE ALL THE DIFFERENCE

"But truly I am full of power by the Spirit of the Lord, and of justice and might, to declare to Jacob his transgression and to Israel his sin." (Micah 3:8)

Judah's leadership was corrupt. Civil and religious leaders alike were *"in it for the money,"* as they looked out only for themselves. This could have been a time of great discouragement, but Micah saw it as an opportunity to take a bold stand for the Lord.

In one of the most remarkable contrasts in the entire book, Micah began verse 8 by stating, *"But truly I am. . . ."* Others may have thrown in the towel, but Micah stood firm. He was filled with God's *"power"* that came from the *"Spirit of the Lord."* He was also filled with *"justice and might."* Turning to Judah's leaders, he boldly spoke of their sin and judgment. The leaders, the priests, and the prophets had all perverted what was right for material gain. As a result of their corrupt leadership, Jerusalem would *"become a heap of ruins"* (v. 12).

Thus, unlike the silenced false prophets (vv. 5–7), Micah was divinely empowered (see 1 Cor. 2:13). It was the Lord's Spirit that empowered him to stand up to his generation and boldly point out their sins.

Micah's willingness to stand for what was right changed an entire generation. God held back His judgment because a nation repented in response to Micah's words and deeds. *Remember, one person can make all the difference!* Are you willing to be filled with God's Spirit and be a spokesman for God?

"Knowing this first that no prophecy of Scripture is of any private interpretation, for prophecy never came by the will of man, but holy men of God spoke as they were moved by the Holy Spirit." (2 Peter 1:20-21)

SEPTEMBER 27   *Bible Reading: Micah Chapters 4-7*

<u>THREE</u> ATTRIBUTES THAT GOD REQUIRES FROM US

"He has shown you, O man, what is good; and what does the Lord require of you but to do justly, to love mercy, and to walk humbly with your God?"(Micah 6:8)

In the above verse, the prophet Micah has clearly expressed God's requirement from Israel. God wanted covenant obedience from His people shown in *justice, mercy,* and *humility — three characteristics* that were currently lacking among the people. We can see that God's requirements move in *three dimensions*: outward, inward, and upward.

· *Outwardly*, to *"do justly"* necessitates dealing righteously with one's fellow man.

· *Inwardly*, to *"love mercy"* necessitates having the inward commitment to God's revelation that will manifest itself in a right relationship towards man and God.

· *Upwardly*, to *"walk humbly with your God"* necessitates having a right attitude towards God and a determination to walk in continuous fellowship with Him.

In our lives as well, we can see that our external (outward) dimension is inextricably tied to the internal (the inward and upward) dimension of our lives. How we deal with others is indicative of our inner resolve in being committed to God's plan for our lives by maintaining a right relationship with Him. We will strive to be mission oriented in our lives as we reflect God's love to other people.

Our Lord Jesus Christ was the perfect example of someone who fulfilled Micah 6:8 to the core – He maintained His obedience and loyalty to His Father and became humble even to the death of the cross (Phil. 2:6-8). Through that act of mercy, Jesus did the ultimate justice: *He justified sinners who would believe in His act of sacrifice on their behalf!*

As the representatives of Christ upon this earth, we should promote *reconciliation, justice* and *integrity* in our areas of influence. We should also engage in wholistic mission work by sharing the light of the gospel with the people in darkness and be channels of blessing to everyone in our world. This is the charge that God has given us until that day when Christ will set all things right in the not too distant future (see Rev. 20:11-15).

SEPTEMBER 28   *Bible Reading: Nahum Chapters 1-3*

GOD KNOWS THOSE WHO TRUST IN HIM

*"The Lord is **good**, a stronghold in the day of trouble; and He **knows** those who **trust** in Him."* (Nahum 1:7)

Nahum focused on *three unique aspects* of God's character. *First*, God would destroy Nineveh because of *His justice*. He does *"not leave the guilty unpunished."* His compassion for the people of Judah caused Him to oppose those who oppressed His people. *Second*, God would destroy Nineveh because of *His omnipotence*. *Third*, God would destroy Nineveh because of *His goodness*. He is a refuge for those who look to Him for help in times of trouble.

Jehovah God is intrinsically good; and His goodness is manifested in *two ways*: He protects those who trust, but His enemies will experience destruction. When He punishes, no one can withstand Him. His judgment would sweep like an overflowing flood through Assyria, destroying Nineveh, her capital. Yet He is good to those who trust in Him.

The Assyrians regarded Nineveh as an invincible fortress. Beyond its massive walls, a system of canals, moats, outworks, and armed guards provided strong defenses. But as strong as Nineveh is, this city will be destroyed by a flood (v. 8) and a fire (v. 10). However, God's people will be safe in their refuge, Jehovah God. If people put their trust in God, they will experience Him as good and a defense against trouble.

357

When help is needed God will be their impregnable fortress (Psalms 46:1). *God will be a real stronghold for those who trust in Him!* However, if they follow wickedness, they will experience Him as destruction.

For us who obey God and walk in His footsteps, this verse is the best news of all. Because we know that the Lord is good, we can endure the tribulations of life. In times of trouble and difficulty, we need to focus totally on God's justice, power, and mercy.

*"Truly God is **good** to Israel, to such as are pure in heart."* (Psalms 73:1) *"God is our refuge and strength, a very present help in trouble."* (Psalms 46:1)

SEPTEMBER 29   *Bible Reading: Habakkuk Chapters 1-3*

DIRECTING OUR LIVES TOWARDS GOD'S VISION

Then the Lord answered me and said: "Write the vision and make it plain on tablets, that he may run who reads it. For the vision is yet for an appointed time; but at the end it will speak, and it will not lie. Though it tarries, wait for it; because it will surely come, it will not tarry". (Habakkuk 2:2-3)

During the days of prophet Habakkuk, public notices were engraved in large and clear characters upon clay tablets and openly exhibited in the marketplace. The writings were to be sufficiently large so that one running by could instantly decipher the meaning. If the notice was a warning it would also cause the reader to run quickly to prepare for what was coming.

Bible scholars believe that the vision that Habakkuk was to write down was concerning the fall of Babylon and the restoration of Judah (Daniel 5:30, 31). God guaranteed that what was written would surely come to pass, which was an indispensable test of a true prophet (Deut. 18:21, 22). In fact, the judgment on the Babylonians was fulfilled through Cyrus in 539 B.C - *long after Habakkuk's vision.*

A. J. Pollock says that this verse also refers to the hope of the Christian. When verse 3 is quoted in Hebrews 10:37, the *"it"* (i.e., the vision) becomes *"He"* (i.e., the Lord), who will surely come and will not tarry. So, in the New Testament context, this verse may signify the hope of the Christian, which is *"the Rapture of the Church".*

Let us clearly understand that God knows His plan and is working out all things according to His purpose. We are responsible to study and proclaim His revelation while awaiting its fulfillment. The assurance of fulfillment lies in God Himself, and the fulfillment of the vision would not take any longer than God had planned. Let us direct our lives towards the fulfillment of God vision!

"Therefore do not cast away your confidence, which has great reward. For you have need of endurance, so that after you have done the will of God, you may receive the promise: 'for yet a little while, and He who is coming will come and will not tarry. Now the just shall live by faith; but if anyone draws back, My soul has no pleasure in him.' But we are not of those who draw back to perdition, but of those who believe to the saving of the soul." (Heb 10:35-39)

SEPTEMBER 30   *Bible Reading: Zephaniah Chapters 1-3*

RESTING ON GOD'S POWER, DELIVERENCE AND LOVE

"The Lord your God in your midst, the Mighty One, will save; He will rejoice over you with gladness, He will quiet you with His love, He will rejoice over you with singing." (Zeph 3:17)

In the above verse, prophet Zephaniah describes God's victory and admiration for His redeemed people. As a victorious Redeemer, God will be their Savior. God's love will be seen as deeply felt thoughtfulness and admiration. God's satisfaction with His people will be expressed through His demonstrative singing.

Thus, the future messianic age will be a cause for great joy for the Lord (v. 17) and His people (v. 14). All sources of fear and sorrow will be removed, because the Lord Himself will dwell in their midst (vv. 15, 17). *"Quiet you with His love"* is a beautiful description reminiscent of God's forgiveness, and His refusal to remember man's iniquitous acts (Psalms 32:1, 2; Jer. 31:34; Ezek. 33:16). He will actually rest in His love; there will be no cause in Israel to elicit judgment or rebuke.

The people of God would be called to respond because their deliverance had come. They would take encouragement and strength from the new reality that their God lived among them. The people would rejoice and sing because their discipline is ended, their enemy has been defeated, they are part of the kingdom of God and the Lord Jehovah is ruling over them as their King.

We too can find hope in times of difficulty if we focus on God's power, God's deliverance, and God's love. He is our King (3:15), our Savior (3:16–17a), and our Beloved (3:17b). He will rejoice over us with gladness. This delight is grounded in the character of God, who *"delights in mercy"*.

If we delight in the Lord and obey Him, He delights in us and shares His best with us. If we sin, He will chasten us in love. If we turn to Him in repentance, He will forgive us and restore our joy and peace: *"I will heal their backsliding, I will love them freely"* (Hos. 14:4). *Let us rest on God's power, deliverance and love today!*

"Who is a God like You, pardoning iniquity and passing over the transgression of the remnant of His heritage? He does not retain His anger forever, because He delights in mercy. He will again have compassion on us, and will subdue our iniquities. You will cast all our sins into the depths of the sea." (Micah 7:18-19)

October

Bible Reading: Haggai Chapters 1-2

IT'S TIME TO 'CONSIDER OUR WAYS'

Now therefore, thus says the Lord of hosts: "Consider your ways! You have sown much, and bring in little; you eat, but do not have enough; you drink, but you are not filled with drink; you clothe yourselves, but no one is warm; and he who earns wages, earns wages to put into a bag with holes." Thus says the Lord of hosts: "Consider your ways!" (Hag 1:5-7)

In 520 B.C. the prophet Haggai stood up and rebuked the people of Judah for their laxness toward God. This message was delivered near the end of the summer harvest season. The people assumed *"the time [had] not yet come for the Lord's house to be built,"* even though they had begun the project 16 years earlier (Ezra 3:6–10; 4:4–5, 24). God's house remained in ruins while the people were *"living in paneled houses,"* so God withheld blessing from them. For years their planting had resulted in only small harvests. Their problem was *misplaced priorities*—they put their interests above honoring God. Haggai's solution was simple: *The people were to get right with the Lord and get back to constructing the temple.*

"Consider your ways" in Hebrew is literally, *"set your heart on your ways!"* This command was issued *five times* throughout the course of this prophecy (vv. 5, 7; 2:15, 18-twice). It was a *plea* on the part of God for the people to *take note of what they are doing, and amend their ways accordingly.*

Thus, God was asking the people to take stock of their lives. Though they ate and drank, they never seemed satisfied. Though they put on clothes, they never felt warm. Wage earners constantly felt as though their pockets had holes in them through which their money was lost. Their economic and social hardship was the effect of God's covenant curse on their disobedience (Deut. 11:8-15; 28:29, 38-40; Lev. 26:20). *God had frustrated their efforts because of their lack of concern for His glory!*

Let us always remember that when we plan to give to God *once* we have enough for ourselves will *never* have enough! When we neglect God, we never really improve ourselves. *When we put ourselves first, we lose God's blessing and whatever we spent on ourselves!* However, *when we put God first*, we have the promise of His care. We *never lose* when we put God *first* in our lives!

"But seek first the kingdom of God and His righteousness, and all these things shall be added to you. Therefore do not worry about tomorrow, for tomorrow will worry about its own things." (Matt 6:33-34)

OCTOBER 2   *Bible Reading: Zechariah Chapters 1-3*

CHANGING SELF-RIGHTEOUSNESS TO GOD'S RIGHTEOUSNESS

Then he showed me Joshua the high priest standing before the Angel of the Lord, and Satan standing at his right hand to oppose him. And the Lord said to Satan, "The Lord rebuke you, Satan! The Lord who has chosen Jerusalem rebuke you! Is this not a brand plucked from the fire?" Now Joshua was clothed with filthy garments, and was standing before the Angel. Then He answered and spoke to those who stood before Him, saying, "Take away the filthy garments from him." And to him He said, "See, I have removed your iniquity from you, and I will clothe you with rich robes." (Zech 3:1-4)

In this fourth vision (3:1–10) the interpreting Angel of the Lord shows prophet Zechariah a trial scene in which Joshua, the high priest during the early days of the postexilic period (in Ezra 3:2 he is called *Jeshua*), is standing before God, the Judge. *"Satan"* is the actual Hebrew word in the text and could be translated *"the accuser"* or *"the prosecutor"*.

Joshua's filthy garments represent the pollution of sin, which is the apostasy and infidelity of Israel. Joshua is helpless to cleanse himself, but God removes the sin and then provides His righteousness (Rev. 19:8). These actions symbolize God's restoration of the priesthood and the nation. *Thus this vision discloses the change from self-righteousness to God's righteousness!*

The cleansing of Joshua was not complete with the removal of his sin-soiled garments. God replaced the dirty clothes, dressing Joshua in clean garments that represented the gift of God's righteousness. As sin is removed by the work of Christ, so His righteousness is placed in the believer's account (Rom. 5:18, 19; 2 Cor. 5:21). We are clothed in the garments of Christ's righteousness. The fact that Joshua had no part in his cleansing indicates that this work was totally by God's grace (Eph. 1:7).

Let us understand that Satan is always looking for opportunities to *"accuse"* us before God (Job 1:6–12; 2:1–7; Rev. 12:10). However, we are chosen by God and belong to Him, and Satan cannot condemn us (Rom. 8:31–39). We can actually defeat this accuser through (a) trusting in the finished redemptive work of Jesus Christ, (b) believing in the Word of God completely, and (c) giving our lives in obeying God's commandments. God removes our sin and clothes us with His righteousness because Jesus died for our sins and lives to intercede for us today!

"But now the righteousness of God apart from the law is revealed, being witnessed by the Law and the Prophets, even the righteousness of God, through faith in Jesus Christ, to all and on all who believe." (Romans 3:21-22)

OCTOBER 3   *Bible Reading: Zechariah Chapters 4-6*

IT'S NOT BY MIGHT NOR BY POWER BUT BY HIS SPIRIT

This is the word of the Lord to Zerubbabel: "Not by might nor by power, but by My Spirit," says the Lord of hosts. "Who are you, O great mountain? Before Zerubbabel you shall become a plain!" (Zech 4:6-7)

As governor of Judah, Zerubbabel was ultimately responsible for rebuilding the Temple in Jerusalem, which had began in earnest ten years ago (Ezra 5:1, 2; Hag. 1:14), but this work was currently stalled. It appeared that all his efforts had failed. However, God wanted

Zerubbabel to understand that He (Himself) was his strength and would supply everything that was needed to accomplish the task to which He had called him. Though physical effort and objects were involved in the work, this work was actually spiritual and could be accomplished only through the power of the Holy Spirit. The 'great mountain' mentioned was a figurative reference to the great obstacles the people faced in rebuilding the temple (Ezra 5:3–17).

Even today, God's people are told not to depend on military power and foreign alliances to accomplish their calling (Isaiah 31:1–3; Psalms 20:7–9). Ultimately, brute force is not the way that God accomplishes His work. God's Spirit is the empowering agent of His activity (v. 6). Human energy, creativity, planning, and thinking have value, but they count little without spiritual strength (Ezek. 37:1–14). God's grace can move the biggest mountains (obstacles) one faces, reducing them to easily traveled plains (v. 7). Zerubbabel saw examples of this in his own day when God graciously removed a number of obstructionists who stood in the way of the temple's completion (Ezra 4:1–6:12)

Nations and churches truly prosper, not as a result of their erudition or financial resources, but only because God's power is operative. Let's understand that our weakness is no hindrance to God, nor is our strength an aid to God. God ultimately works out His purposes in our lives by the power of His Spirit (Hos. 1:7; 2 Cor. 4:7, 12:8-9).

"I can do all things through Christ who strengthens me." (Phil 4:13)

OCTOBER 4 *Bible Reading: Zechariah Chapters 7-9*

OBEDIENCE IS <u>BETTER</u> THAN FASTING

Then the word of the Lord of hosts came to me, saying, "Say to all the people of the land, and to the priests: **'When you fasted and mourned** *in the fifth and seventh months during those seventy years,* **did you really fast for Me—for Me?** *When you eat and when you drink, do you not eat and drink for yourselves?* **Should you not have obeyed the words which the Lord proclaimed through the former prophets** *when Jerusalem and the cities around it were inhabited and prosperous, and the South and the Lowland were inhabited?'"* (Zech 7:4-7)

Zechariah chapters 7 and 8 form a division by themselves, dealing with the subject of fasting. A delegation from Bethel came to inquire if they should continue to fast on the anniversary of the fall of Jerusalem. They had been doing this for over seventy years. The answer to the above question is given in four distinct messages (7:4–7; 7:8–14; 8:1–17; and 8:18–23). In this first message, God reminds them that the fast in both the fifth and seventh months had been instituted by themselves, not by Him. Both their fasting and their feasting were for themselves, not for God. Before the destruction of Jerusalem, the former prophets had warned the people that God wanted righteousness and reality rather than rituals. *The fasts were their idea, not God's!*

Prophet Zechariah's answer, like the messages of earlier prophets, shows that God cares more for righteousness than religious forms. Zechariah reminds them that their fasting was intended to be symbolic of changed hearts demonstrated in changed lives. In and of itself their fasting, like their eating and drinking, did not affect God, but only themselves (v. 6).

We see here that God rebuked the false ritualism of the people for the past seventy years (vv. 4–7). God revealed that in neither their fasts nor their feasts has He been pleased, for their motives were wrong. God is never pleased with mere external formalities and conformities. God is a God of realism; and He demands inward reality! The point of this message is: *Obedience is better than fasting. God is pleased by obedience, not by self-imposed fasts!*

Biblical fasting is meant to be time taken from our normal routines of preparing and eating food to express humility and dependence on God during a time of prayer. The fast God wants is not as a ceremony but as a daily way of life. It means showing compassion and mercy and helping the poor and needy. God wants mercy, not sacrifice (Hos. 6:6; Amos 5:21–24; Mic. 6:8; Matt. 15:1–9). This same challenge exists for us today. Attending church, Bible reading, prayers, sharing our faith — as crucial as these are — need to be matched by a lifestyle of obedience to God's word, integrity and Christ-like character, especially in our dealings with others.

*"The fear of the Lord is the beginning of wisdom; a good understanding have all those **who do His commandments**. His praise endures forever."* (Psalms 111:10)

OCTOBER 5   *Bible Reading: Zechariah Chapters 10-12*

KEEPING CHRIST AT THE CENTER OF OUR LIVES

"And I will pour on the house of David and on the inhabitants of Jerusalem the Spirit of grace and supplication; then they will look on Me whom they pierced. Yes, they will mourn for Him as one mourns for his only son, and grieve for Him as one grieves for a firstborn." (Zech 12:10)

Among the prophetical books in the Old Testament, the book of Zechariah ranks high in revealing the coming of Jesus Christ about 500 years before the event. As we closely read this book, we can read about Christ's humanity (6:12), His humility (9:9), His betrayal (11:12-13), His deity (12:8), His crucifixion (12:10), His return (14:4) and His future reign (14:8-21). Zechariah prophesied that the key to Israel's future was the coming Messiah, who will ultimately triumph through struggles and suffering.

This remarkable prophecy about the One Israel pierced (12:10) looks toward a time when Israel will recognize and accept Jesus Christ as its Messiah, whom they had literally pierced with a spear after His death on the cross (John 19:34). God's ultimate deliverance of Jerusalem is rooted in a spiritual renewal, which itself is an act of God's grace. Out of deep conviction and as a result of the action of God's Holy Spirit, the Jewish people will turn in national and individual repentance to accept the One whom they had previously rejected (11:12).

Regarding the nation of Israel, Zechariah foretells their rejection of their Messiah at His First Advent but their regeneration and reception of their Messiah at His Second Advent. The realization of what they have done to their Messiah will cause them to mourn with intense grief for Him, as one mourns for his only son. Godly conviction, as the result of the Holy Spirit's ministry, will bring about godly sorrow in their hearts. When the people of Israel finally see the Messiah (v. 10), they will recognize Him (Matt. 24:30; Rev. 1:7), repent, and be cleansed and forgiven.

Like God's people Israel, we experience many trials and testings; but our Lord Jesus Christ will see us through and share His kingdom and glory with us (Acts 14:22). This is our certain future, so *let us strive to keep Christ at the center of our lives!*

"And this is the will of Him who sent Me (Jesus), that everyone who sees the Son and believes in Him may have everlasting life; and I will raise him up at the last day." (John 6:40)

OCTOBER 6   *Bible Reading: Zechariah Chapters 13-14*

THE <u>GREAT</u> SACRIFICE OF CHRIST, OUR SHEPHERD-SAVIOR

"Awake, O sword, against My Shepherd, against the Man who is My Companion," says the Lord of hosts. "Strike the Shepherd, and the sheep will be scattered" (Zech 13:7)

It should be noted that prophet Zechariah prophesied around 520 B.C. Five centuries later, Jesus cited this prophecy about the striking of the Shepherd as applying to Himself (compare v. 7 with Matt. 26:31–35; Mark 14:27–31; Luke 22:31–34). This verse envisions God's chosen Shepherd-Savior suffering at the hand of God Himself. Jehovah God orders His sword to awake against His only begotten Son – our Lord Jesus Christ. The Good Shepherd was struck at Calvary, and the Jewish sheep have been scattered ever since.

The sword, an instrument of death, is likened to a warrior being roused for action, and is also the symbol of judicial power (Rom. 13:4). Our Lord Jesus Christ took the full brunt of the punishment that was meant for the sins of the whole world, as He indeed was the *"Lamb of God who took away the sins of the world"* (John 1:29)

The term *"My Companion"* is used elsewhere of one who is a near neighbor or close companion (Lev. 6:2; 18:20; 19:15). It suggests a relationship of equality, as Jesus Christ, God's Son enjoyed that relationship from eternal past.

Thus, to save His flock, the Good Shepherd was smitten through suffering and death (Isa. 53:4, 10). Let's remember that the next time we are smitten because of our faith, our Good Shepherd-Savior has silently borne all the sufferings (Matt. 5:38–42; 10:16–26) leaving for us a good example to emulate in our lives!

"For as the sufferings of Christ abound in us, so our consolation also abounds through Christ. Now if we are afflicted, it is for your consolation and salvation, which is effective for enduring the same sufferings which

we also suffer. Or if we are comforted, it is for your consolation and salvation." (2 Cor 1:5-6)

OCTOBER 7   *Bible Reading: Malachi Chapters 1-4*

GOD's PROMISE OF ABUNDANT BLESSING

*"Bring all the tithes into the storehouse, that there may be food in My house, and try Me now in this," says the Lord of hosts, "if I will not open for you the windows of heaven and **pour out for you such blessing that there will not be room enough to receive it."** (Mal 3:10)

Under the Mosaic Law, the Israelites were required to give tithes - a tenth of all their produce and livestock - to God (or, they could redeem it with money and add a fifth part). These tithes were in addition to their numerous offerings, and were an acknowledgment from their part that everything belonged to God and that He was the Giver of all their possessions. However, in prophet Malachi's day, the postexilic Israelites were withholding their tithes and offerings from God (vv. 8–9). Apparently they preferred to keep more for themselves rather than give what God asked. In doing so, they were not only robbing from God, they were in effect robbing from the Levites and the poor!

In the Old Testament, the reward for Israelites for tithing faithfully was in God blessing them with material wealth. If they would be faithful with their tithes, God would bless them with such abundant blessings that there will not be room enough to receive it (v. 10). God would also deliver the Israelites from drought, plague, enemies, and locusts, and make them a blessing in the earth that He had promised their patriarch Abraham (Gen. 12:3).

The New Testament however teaches believers to give systematically, liberally, cheerfully, and proportionately as the Lord has prospered them. But no mention is made of tithing in the New Testament. Rather, the suggestion is that if a Jew living under law gave a tenth, *how much more should a Christian living under grace give!*

Thus our pattern for giving is characterized by *freedom* (2 Cor. 9:6) and *responsible planning* (1 Cor. 16:2). Jesus demands more in terms of *stewardship* than merely the precise compliance with the tithe (Matt. 23:23; Luke 11:42).

The New Testament teaches us to *give substantially to the Lord*. When we do that, our God delights to respond with gracious provision, especially to meet our essential needs (Matt. 6:25-34).

"So let each one give as he purposes in his heart, not grudgingly or of necessity; for God loves a cheerful giver." (2 Cor 9:7)

OCTOBER 8   *Bible Reading: Matthew Chapters 1-3*

REPENTANCE – THE <u>FIRST</u> STEP IN OBEYING GOD

In those days John the Baptist came preaching in the wilderness of Judea, and saying, **"Repent, for the kingdom of heaven is at hand!"** *For this is he who was spoken of by the prophet Isaiah, saying: "The voice of one crying in the wilderness: 'Prepare the way of the Lord; make His paths straight.'"* (Matt 3:1-3)

John the Baptist was six months older than his cousin Jesus Christ (see Luke 1:26, 36). He stepped onto the stage of history to serve as forerunner for the Savior of the world. His dwelling was in the wilderness of Judea, an arid area extending from Jerusalem to the Jordan. John's message was, *"Repent, for the kingdom of heaven is at hand!"* The King would soon appear, but He could not and would not reign over people who clung to their sins. They must change directions, must confess and forsake their sins. God was calling them from the kingdom of darkness to the *'kingdom of heaven'*. The phrase, *'kingdom of heaven'* is peculiar to Matthew and signifies the Messianic earth rule of Jesus Christ, the Son of David.

Repentance was the first command of both John the Baptist and Jesus Christ (4:17). It involves the change of mind and heart in response to the grace of God whereby a person recognizes the futility of his or her human condition apart from God and therefore places faith and trust in God alone for salvation. Let us understand that repentance is not merely being sorrowful. It involves a complete change of attitude regarding God and sin and is often accompanied by a sense of sorrow and a corresponding change in conduct. Such repentance does not arise within man himself, but is the result of God's mercy in leading man to it (Acts 5:31; Rom. 2:4; 2 Tim. 2:25). It involves the very process of conversion whereby we are born again. John's message of repentance was necessary in order to prepare people for the kingdom of heaven which was at hand.

Thus John the Baptist was preparing hearts for the ultimate manifestation of God's reign. In our own context, repentance means hating sin enough to turn away from it. Through repentance, we can change our attitude and mind about God that will in turn change our actions and decisions. We will escape spiritual death by trusting in Jesus, who alone can save us from our sins and eternal death. We confess through godly sorrow, forsake sin and live to honor God.

"He who covers his sins will not prosper, but whoever confesses and forsakes them will have mercy." (Prov 28:13)

OCTOBER 9   *Bible Reading: Matthew Chapters 4-6*

SETTING UP THE RIGHT PRIORITIES FOR OUR LIVES

"Therefore do not worry, saying, 'What shall we eat?' or 'What shall we drink?' or 'What shall we wear?' For after all these things the Gentiles seek. For your heavenly Father knows that you need all these things. **But seek first the kingdom of God and His righteousness, and all these things shall be added to you.** *Therefore do not worry about tomorrow, for tomorrow will worry about its own things. Sufficient for the day is its own trouble."* (Matt 6:31-34)

Through the above passage, our Lord Jesus Christ is teaching us that we should set up the right priorities in our lives by *'putting first things first'*. We should not spend our lives in anxious pursuit of food, drink, and clothing for the future. The world around us is scrambling madly to accumulate material things, and living as if food and clothing were everything to pursue in life.

As God's children, we need to understand that we have a heavenly Father who knows our daily needs. Our God makes the following covenant with us: *"If you will put MY interests first in your life, I will guarantee your future needs. If you seek first MY kingdom and MY righteousness, then I will see that you NEVER lack the necessities of life."* This is God's *"Social Security"* program for us!

Our responsibility is to live for God, trusting Him for our future with unshakable confidence that He will provide everything that we need.

We are called to live one day at a time by focusing only on what is in front of us. We need to simplify our lives, and not worry by being overwhelmed with the life's demands. Worry does not accomplish anything positive but instead makes us miserable with our troubles. We must take things as they come – *one day at a time* – and trust God for the wisdom to respond properly in every situation.

Let us make God's sovereign rule and a right relationship with Him, the highest priority in our lives. Worry is inconsistent with this priority; it doubts the sovereignty or goodness of God and distracts us from the true goals of life. God will meet all our needs when we risk all in Him. Let's aim for total stewardship so that God is in complete control of our lives, and our one desire is to glorify Him alone every day. *This is the secret of living an abundant life free of worries!*

"In the multitude of my anxieties within me, Your comforts delight my soul." (Psalms 94:19)

OCTOBER 10   *Bible Reading: Matthew Chapters 7-9*

BUILDING OUR LIVES ON A SOLID FOUNDATION

"Therefore whoever hears these sayings of Mine, and does them, I will liken him to a wise man who built his house on the rock: and the rain descended, the floods came, and the winds blew and beat on that house; and it did not fall, for it was founded on the rock. But everyone who hears these sayings of Mine, and does not do them, will be like a foolish man who built his house on the sand: and the rain descended, the floods came, and the winds blew and beat on that house; and it fell. And great was its fall." (Matt 7:24-27)

Our Lord Jesus Christ closes His 'Sermon on the Mount' with a parable that drives home the importance of *obedience*. It is not enough to hear these sayings; we must put them into practice. If a person lives according to the principles of this sermon, the world calls him a fool but Jesus calls him a wise man. The world considers a wise man to be someone who lives by sight, who lives for the present, and who lives for self; Jesus calls such a person a fool. Mere religious profession is both unwise and worthless in withstanding the tests of life. Hearing and doing what Jesus said determines success or failure in one's earthly walk.

The key difference in the two houses is not their external appearance. Pharisees and scribes may seem to be as righteous as the heirs of the kingdom. The key in the story is the foundations. The house on the rock pictures a life founded on a proper relationship to Christ (16:18; 1 Cor. 10:4; 1 Pet. 2:4–8). It will stand the test of Christ's judgment, but the house on the sand will fail the test (see 1 Cor. 3:12–15).

It is also legitimate to use the wise and foolish builders to *illustrate the gospel*. The wise man puts his full confidence in the Rock, Christ Jesus, as Lord and Savior. The foolish man refuses to repent and rejects Jesus as his only hope of salvation.

To build our lives on a solid foundation, we need to follow the instructions of Jesus by *both hearing and doing* the things that Jesus has told us (v. 24). Then only we will have safe, solid and significant lives. Building our lives on an unstable foundation like the sifting morals of the present world, worldly permissive culture and the opinions of others will result in total destruction at the times of testing. *By obeying the unwavering truth of God's word will bring stability that is not available anywhere else!*

"But be doers of the word and not hearers only, deceiving yourselves. For if anyone is a hearer of the word and not a doer, he is like a man observing his natural face in a mirror; for he observes himself, goes away, and immediately forgets what kind of man he was. But he who looks into the perfect law of liberty and continues in it, and is not a forgetful hearer but a doer of the work, this one will be blessed in what he does." (James 1:22-25)

OCTOBER 11   *Bible Reading: Matthew Chapters 10-12*

AN OPEN INVITATION TO RECEIVE 'PERFECT' REST

"Come to Me, all you who labor and are heavy laden, and I will give you rest. Take My yoke upon you and learn from Me, for I am gentle and lowly in heart, and you will find rest for your souls. For My yoke is easy and My burden is light." (Matt 11:28-30)

This above passage (vv. 28–30) is peculiar to Matthew's gospel alone. To those burdened by the weariness of the world or, the load of religious legalism, Jesus offered the experience of communion with

Him in which there is rest for the soul. When we are weary in life's struggles, we are invited to 'come' to Him. Believer's Bible Commentary explains that to 'come' means to believe (Acts 16:31); to receive (John 1:12); to eat (John 6:35); to drink (John 7:37); to look (Isa. 45:22); to confess (1 Jn. 4:2); to hear (John 5:24, 25); to enter a door (John 10:9); to open a door (Rev. 3:20); to touch the hem of His garment (Matt. 9:20, 21); and to accept the gift of eternal life through Christ our Lord (Rom. 6:23).

The *rest* that Jesus offers us is unearned and unmerited. This is the *rest of salvation* that comes from realizing that Christ finished the work of redemption on Calvary's cross. It is the *rest of conscience* that follows the realization that the penalty of one's sins has been paid once for all and that God will not demand payment twice.

This does not mean that there are no problems, trials, labor, or heartaches in the Christian life. But it does mean that we do not have to bear them alone. We are yoked with One who gives sufficient grace for every time of need. To serve Him is not bondage but perfect freedom. J. H. Jowett says:

"The fatal mistake for the believer is to seek to bear life's load in a single collar. God never intended a man to carry his burden alone. Christ therefore deals only in yokes! A yoke is a neck harness for two, and the Lord himself pleads to be One of the two. He wants to share the labor of any galling task. The secret of peace and victory in the Christian life is found in putting off the taxing collar of 'self' and accepting the Master's relaxing yoke."

Prayer is the place where burdens change shoulders. Jesus offers to lift our burdens for us. Let us understand that Jesus is the only real solution for our ongoing problems, stress and worry. Today, let us cast our burdens upon Him – for He will sustain us according to His word and give us the 'perfect' rest that we need so badly!

"Cast your burden on the Lord, and He shall sustain you; He shall never permit the righteous to be moved." (Psalms 55:22)

GOD <u>HATES</u> HYPOCRICY IN OUR WORSHIP

"Hypocrites! Well did Isaiah prophesy about you, saying: 'These people draw near to Me with their mouth, and honor Me with their lips, but their heart is far from Me. And in vain they worship Me, teaching as doctrines the commandments of men.' "(Matt 15:7-9)

Our Lord Jesus Christ had harsh words to speak about the scribes and Pharisees from Jerusalem (the religious elite) who tried to find fault against the disciples of Jesus who did not do the ceremonial cleansing before they ate food. Jesus bluntly told them that they were fulfilling the prophecy of Isaiah 29:13: *Therefore the Lord said: "Inasmuch as these people draw near with their mouths and honor Me with their lips, but have removed their hearts far from Me, and their fear toward Me is taught by the commandment of men"* (Isaiah 29:13). Isaiah spoke it of the men of that generation to which he prophesied, yet Christ applies it to these scribes and Pharisees.

These scribes and Pharisees professed to honor God with their lips, but their heart was far from Him. Their worship was worthless because they were giving higher priority to the traditions of men than to the Word of God. *How were the scribes and Pharisees hypocritical in their worship?*

1. They drew close to God through empty words showing to others their spiritual piety as they were the 'professional' worshipers of Israel.

2. Inwardly there was no love towards God; they just made their voices to be heard as a lip service (Isaiah 58:4).

3. Their hearts were far from God even during their motions of worship.

Let us clearly understand that hypocrisy is a contradiction between our words and deeds. We show hypocrisy when we praise and worship God, but our hearts are not in our worship (vv. 5-7). We are eager to listen to God's word, but we do not do what God requires from us (Ezek. 33:31-32). We preach to others only and not to ourselves (Rom. 2:21-23; Psalms 50:16). *God hates hypocrisy in our worship – let us avoid it at all cost!*

"This I say, therefore, and testify in the Lord, that you should no longer walk as the rest of the Gentiles walk, in the futility of their mind, having their understanding darkened, being alienated from the life of God, because of the ignorance that is in them, because of the blindness of their heart; who, being past feeling, have given themselves over to lewdness, to work all uncleanness with greediness." (Eph 4:17-19)

OCTOBER 13   *Bible Reading: Matthew Chapters 16-18*

FORGIVENESS IS 'CHRISTIANITY IN ACTION'

Then Peter came to Him and said, "Lord, how often shall my brother sin against me, and I forgive him? Up to seven times?" Jesus said to him, "I do not say to you, up to seven times, but up to seventy times seven." (Matt 18:21-22)

Peter asked Jesus a sincere question of how often he should forgive a brother who sinned against him. He probably thought he was showing unusual grace by suggesting seven as an outside limit. Actually Peter was being very generous in his willingness to forgive up to seven times. The traditional limit was three times, possibly because of the refrain in Amos 1:3, 6, 9, 11, 13; 2:1, 4, 6. Peter had gone beyond the religious leaders' limit of forgiving an offense three times by suggesting one could be forgiven seven times. However, Jesus raised the level to *"seventy times seven,"* a hyperbole meaning no limits. He did not intend us to understand it as literal 490 times; this was a figurative way of saying *"indefinitely"*, which is that forgiveness really knows no boundaries.

When any brother wrongs us, we should forgive him immediately in our hearts. That will free us from a bitter and wounded spirit. After we have forgiven him in our hearts, we should go to him and rebuke him in love, hoping to lead him to confession. As soon as he apologizes and confesses his sin, we should tell him that he is forgiven. This is God's instruction to us concerning this matter: *"Take heed to yourselves. If your brother sins against you, rebuke him; and if he repents, forgive him. And if he sins against you seven times in a day, and seven times in a day returns to you, saying, 'I repent,' you shall forgive him."* (Luke 17:3-4)

Let us understand that unlimited forgiveness must characterize the true disciple. Jesus asks us to forgive no matter what the attitude of the offender. He means limitless forgiveness (see 1 Cor. 13:4, 5). God has freely forgiven our debt; therefore, we also should practice forgiveness I that liberal fashion. *We are to forgive others because God has forgiven us (Col. 3:13), and He has forgiven us at great cost to Himself!*

"He who cannot forgive breaks the bridge over which he himself must pass." - George Herbert

"And be kind to one another, tenderhearted, forgiving one another, just as God in Christ forgave you." (Eph 4:32)

OCTOBER 14   *Bible Reading: Matthew Chapters 19-21*

LEAD BY SERVING AND SERVE BY LEADING

*Jesus called them to Himself and said, "You know that the rulers of the Gentiles lord it over them, and those who are great exercise authority over them. Yet it shall not be so among you; but **whoever desires to become great among you, let him be your servant. And whoever desires to be first among you let him be your slave** — just as the Son of Man did not come to be served, but to serve, and to give His life a ransom for many."* (Matt 20:25-28)

As Jesus was traveling to Jerusalem to give Himself as a ransom for the sins of the entire humankind, the mother of His two disciples James and John came to Jesus with an unusual request. Knowing full well that Jesus would not turn down any request, she requested that both her sons be given the prime seats, very next to Jesus on both His sides, in the kingdom of God. What she did not realize that this was an impossible request – for God the Father was to be seated on the left hand of Jesus after His resurrection (Romans 8:34b). We can well assume that both John and James and their mother were more preoccupied with status than serving. *They had missed the whole point of Jesus' leadership!*

Jesus then expounds to His disciples His style of leadership that was totally opposite to the worldly leadership. What Jesus wanted from His disciples then and us today is that we 'lead by serving and serve by leading'. The greatest among us must display true 'servant-leadership'. As we *grow* in leadership, our rights, options and privileges should *decrease*.

The term 'ransom' refers to the price paid to deliver someone from slavery or imprisonment. Jesus gave His life a 'ransom' for many. His death satisfied all God's righteous demands against sin. The price of freedom from sin and condemnation was Jesus' life, given for us (1 Pet. 1:18, 19). Since the elect are ransomed from the wrath of God, the ransom was offered to God Himself. Jesus drank the cup of God's wrath (v. 23), not for His own sins, but as the means of ransoming many.

In light of Jesus' own example—particularly in giving up His own life as a *"ransom for many"* (v. 28)—we can observe that 'servant-leadership' means:

· seeing ourselves as called by God to serve/lead others.

· knowing intimately the people we serve/lead.

· caring deeply about the people we serve/lead.

· being willing to sacrifice our own convenience to meet the needs of the people we serve/lead.

Let us clearly understand that in the kingdom of heaven, greatness is manifested by service, and Jesus the perfect example of lowly service. The measure of greatness is not position, power, or prestige; it is service. Jesus came into the world not to be served, but to serve, and to give His life a ransom for many. The whole purpose of the incarnation of Jesus can be summed up in two words—*serve* and *give*. It is amazing to think that the exalted Lord humbled Himself to the manger and to the cross. *His greatness was manifested in the depth of His humiliation…and so it must be for us!*

"Let nothing be done through selfish ambition or conceit, but in lowliness of mind let each esteem others better than himself. Let each of you look out not only for his own interests, but also for the interests of others." (Phil 2:3-4)

OCTOBER 15 *Bible Reading: Matthew Chapters 22-24*

MODELING IN BOTH OUR WORDS AND ACTIONS

Then Jesus spoke to the multitudes and to His disciples, saying: "The scribes and the Pharisees sit in Moses' seat. Therefore whatever they tell you to observe that observe and do, but do not do according to their works; for they say, and do not do." (Matt 23:1-3)

Jesus' final condemnation of the Scribes and Pharisees (the religious super-spiritual people of that time) fills the entire 23rd chapter of Matthew, as He exposes the true hypocrisy of the religious leaders of Israel. Their sitting in Moses' seat represented the synagogue chair which symbolized the origin and authority of their teaching as they taught the Law of Moses. Generally, their teachings were dependable, but their practice was not. Their creed was better than their conduct. It was a case of high talk and low walk. They did not practice what they preached. They made heavy demands (probably extreme interpretations of the letter of the law) on the people, but would not assist anyone in lifting these intolerable loads.

Thus, the Pharisees and Scribes took the Scriptures at face value, so their instructions were to be followed. So, Jesus warned the people of the Pharisees' legalism - their tendency to value their own rules and regulations over the Scriptures. They followed their external laws meticulously and *'appeared'* to be righteous. Yet the people were not to imitate their actions, for although they appeared righteous, their hearts were filled with all kinds of envy, hatred, and malice. Jesus directs His condemnation at hypocritical self-righteousness; full of outward form but devoid of inner spiritual reality.

The Word of God has authority even if the people who teach it lack integrity (vv. 1–3). Our Lord's standard is that we both do and teach His truth (5:17–20). Those who practice hypocrisy erode their character and do untold damage to others. The tragedy is that hypocrisy blinds people (vv. 16–19, 24, 26) so that they cannot see the Lord, themselves, or other people. *Let us be careful that we model our lives both in words and action every day!*

"You are witnesses, and God also, how devoutly and justly and blamelessly we behaved ourselves among you who believe; as you know how we exhorted, and comforted, and charged every one of you, as a

father does his own children, that you would walk worthy of God who calls you into His own kingdom and glory." (1 Thess. 2:10-12)

OCTOBER 16 *Bible Reading: Matthew Chapters 25-28*

GOD WILL HELP US TO FULFILL HIS 'GREAT COMMISSION'

*And Jesus came and spoke to them, saying, "All authority has been given to Me in heaven and on earth. Go therefore and make disciples of all the nations, baptizing them in the name of the Father and of the Son and of the Holy Spirit, teaching them to observe all things that I have commanded you; and lo, **I am with you always**, even to the end of the age." Amen.* (Matt 28:18-20)

In these last verses of the Gospel of Matthew, Jesus was speaking of His authority as the Head of the new creation. Since His death and resurrection, He had authority to give eternal life to all whom God had given to Him (John 17:2). Since He had completed the work of redemption for all humans required as per the law, He had authority as the first-born from the dead: *"that in all things He may have the preeminence"* (Col. 1:15, 18).

As the Head of the new creation, Jesus issued the Great Commission, containing *"standing orders"* for all believers to do before His return, which contains <u>three</u> *'commands'*:

1. *"Go therefore and make disciples of all the nations"*: By preaching the gospel, the disciples were to see others become learners or followers of the Savior—from every nation, tribe, people, and tongue. Discipleship is intended to extend to an international audience, which includes all people groups. The need is not just for truth to be taught but *for transformation to take place in the life of every disciple.*

2. *"Baptize them in the name of the Father and of the Son and of the Holy Spirit"*: In believer's baptism, Christians publicly identify themselves with the Triune Godhead. They acknowledge that God is their Father, that Jesus Christ is their Lord and Savior, and that the Holy Spirit is the One who indwells, empowers, and teaches them. The focus of the Trinitarian baptismal confession is faith in Jesus, who deserves His rightful place along with God the Father and God the Spirit.

379

3. *"Teach them to observe all things that I have commanded you"*:
    This Great Commission goes beyond evangelism – the baptized
    believers must be taught to obey *the commandments of Christ
    found in the New Testament.* The core curriculum for discipleship
    is the life and teachings of Jesus.

Then Jesus *added a promise of His abiding presence* with His disciples
until the end of the age. He will be with us and will see us through.
He will never leave us alone, but will walk with us strengthening,
loving and filling us with faith, hope and love. The *presence of the
Savior* and the *power of the Spirit* (Acts 1:8) are God's twin certainties
that we are to lay hold of and continually keep dear to our hearts as
we serve our risen Lord until He comes. The promise of the abiding
presence of Jesus' ministry throughout the present age lends
comforting assurance for such a daunting task as a worldwide mission.

Let us sense and practice His presence every moment of every day, as
we faithfully obey His command. *For He Himself has said, "I will
never leave you nor forsake you." So we may boldly say: "The Lord is
my helper; I will not fear. What can man do to me?"* (Heb 13:5-6).
God will definitely help us fulfill His Great Commission!

OCTOBER 17   *Bible Reading: Mark Chapters 1-3*

REFOCUSING OUR PRIORITIES EVERYDAY

*Now in the morning, having risen a long while before daylight, He
went out and departed to a solitary place; and there He prayed. And
Simon and those who were with Him searched for Him. When they
found Him, they said to Him, "Everyone is looking for You." But He
said to them, "Let us go into the next towns that I may preach there
also, because for this purpose I have come forth."* (Mark 1:35-38)

Our Lord Jesus was a very busy person after he started his public
ministry, as he was always surrounded by people who wanted to
witness the various miracles that He performed and hear the
wonderful words of wisdom from his mouth. Even after ministering
the whole day, people would still come to him in the evening time
after the sun had set and bring sick and demon possessed people for
healing (v. 32). In fact, he was so much in demand that Mark records

in verse 33: *"and the whole city was gathered together at the door"* where Jesus was. In order to avoid further publicity, Jesus even told the healed individuals (1:43, 3:12) or, the demons (1:34b) not to speak about Him. However, the news that Jesus was a healer spread rapidly, and many sick and demon possessed came to Jesus and He healed them all (v. 32-34).

In the midst of such a busy schedule, Jesus rose up early in the morning before daylight, and went to a *"solitary"* place and spent time communicating to His heavenly Father. *This was the time for Him to prayerfully refocus His priorities.* This is evident due to the fact that when His disciples came to Him and told Him that everyone were looking for Him, Jesus wanted to move on to the other parts of Galilee and reach other people in Judea as well. *This new direction was only due to Jesus being able to refocus His priorities through prayer!*

Jesus saw the need to gain inner refreshment, renewed intimacy with God, and strength for facing the challenges before Him. He opened His ear each morning to receive instructions for the day from God the Father about how He will accomplish His work for that day. *If Jesus felt the need of this early morning quiet time, how much more should we!* Notice too that He prayed when it cost Him something; He rose and went out a long while before daylight. *Prayer should not be a matter of personal convenience but of self-discipline and sacrifice.* Through an early morning prayer, we too can understand what God wants us to do during that day, which in turn will *help us to refocus our priorities every day!*

"The Lord God has given Me the tongue of the learned, that I should know how to speak a word in season to him who is weary. He awakens Me morning by morning, He awakens My ear to hear as the learned. The Lord God has opened My ear; and I was not rebellious, nor did I turn away." (Isaiah 50:4-5)

OCTOBER 18   *Bible Reading: Mark Chapters 4-6*

FAMILIARITY BREEDS CONTEMPT AND UNBELIEF

*But Jesus said to them, "A prophet is not without honor except in his own country, among his own relatives, and in his own house." Now **He*** *could do no mighty work there*, *except that He laid His hands on a few sick people and healed them. And **He marveled because of their unbelief**. Then He went about the villages in a circuit, teaching.* (Mark 6:4-6)

"A prophet is not without honor except in his own country" is a maxim still repeated and still true today. Not only was Jesus rejected by the people of the town and the wider circle of relatives there, but also by His own family (3:31). Perhaps others were jealous of Jesus' popularity and huge following. Their envy even took the form of violence against Christ (see Luke 4:29).

The Nazarenes themselves were a despised people. A popular attitude was: *"Can anything good come out of Nazareth?"* Yet these social outcasts looked down on the Lord Jesus. *What a commentary on the pride and unbelief of the human heart!* Unbelief largely hindered the work of the Savior in Nazareth. He healed a few sick people, but that was all. The unbelief of the people amazed Him. J. G. Miller warns:

Such unbelief as this has immense consequences for evil. It closes the channels of grace and mercy, so that only a trickle gets through to human lives in need.ÿþ

It says that Jesus 'could not' do mighty miracles in his home town. The point was not that Jesus was suddenly lacking in ability to do miracles—He did perform a few there. Rather Jesus found contempt and hardness of heart in the people, which are the opposites of receptivity and faith. Under such circumstances, further disclosure of God's presence in His Messiah was denied. Only here does Mark speak of Jesus as having 'marveled'. Resistance to Him was tragically astounding.

This rejection of Jesus serves as an object lesson for us, as we also experience rejection of our mission to spread the gospel (6:10, 11). Believers today can expect to face the world's rejection as they deliver the message of salvation in Christ. At the same time, let us not become too familiar with God and His teachings that our faith turns into contempt and unbelief like the people in Jesus' hometown!

Beware, brethren, lest there be in any of you an evil heart of unbelief in departing from the living God; but exhort one another daily, while it is called "Today," lest any of you be hardened through the deceitfulness of sin. For we have become partakers of Christ if we hold the beginning of our confidence steadfast to the end, while it is said: "Today, if you will hear His voice, do not harden your hearts as in the rebellion." (Heb 3:12-15)

OCTOBER 19   *Bible Reading: Mark Chapters 7-9*

WHAT 'TRULY' MATTERS COMES OUT FROM OUR HEARTS

*When He had called all the multitude to Himself, He said to them, "Hear Me, everyone, and understand: **There is <u>nothing</u> that enters a man from outside which can defile him; but the things which come out of him, those are the things that defile a man.** If anyone has ears to hear, let him hear!"* (Mark 7:14-16)

Our Lord Jesus Christ made a revolutionary pronouncement that it was not what goes into our mouths that defile us (such as food eaten with unwashed hands). We are not defiled by what goes into us through food (or, physical matter which contains no moral significance). All foods should be considered clean because they do not defile the spirit as do things that are wrong with the heart.

Rather, it's what comes out of our hearts through words and actions contrary to His will that defile us: *evil thoughts, adulteries, fornications, murders, thefts, covetousness, wickedness, deceit, lewdness, an evil eye, blasphemy, pride, and foolishness* (vv. 21-22). If actions, words, or thoughts originate in an evil, rebellious heart, they are certainly contrary to God and His righteousness.

While expounding this passage, Matthew Henry tells us that *only* our wicked thoughts and affections, words and actions defile us. As a corrupt fountain sends forth corrupt streams, so does a corrupt heart send forth corrupt appetites and passions, and all the wicked words and actions that come from them.

So, uncleanness of our hearts is the root of all our problems. The true source of defilement is not a disregard for external rituals or dietary laws, but a polluted heart that plots evil. What 'truly' matters comes out from our hearts! *"If I regard iniquity in my heart, the Lord will not hear."* (Psalms 66:18)

Today, let us ask God to search our hearts and clean us from within! *"Search me, O God, and know my heart; try me, and know my anxieties; and see if there is any wicked way in me, and lead me in the way everlasting."* (Psalms 139:23-24)

BEWARE OF TRUSTING IN UNDERTAIN RICHES

*Then Jesus looked around and said to His disciples, "**How hard it is for those who have riches to enter the kingdom of God!**" And the disciples were astonished at His words. But Jesus answered again and said to them, "**Children, how hard it is for those who trust in riches to enter the kingdom of God! It is easier for a camel to go through the eye of a needle than for a rich man to enter the kingdom of God.**" (Mark 10:23-25)*

In the above passage, Jesus remarked on the difficulty of rich people entering the kingdom of God. The difficulty is not because riches in themselves are evil but because the rich are tempted to depend upon their riches, and may be unable to admit their need of God. The disciples of Jesus were amazed by this remark as they had looked on riches as an indication of God's blessing. Under the Mosaic code, God had promised prosperity to those who obeyed Him. These disciples reasoned that if a rich person couldn't enter the kingdom, then no one else could either!

What can we conclude from the teaching of this passage? It is difficult for rich people to be saved (v. 23) since they tend to love their wealth more than God. They would rather give up God than give up their money, as did the rich young ruler in an earlier incident (vv. 17-22). They put their trust in riches rather than in the Lord. It was true in the Old Testament that riches were a sign of God's favor (example, God blessing King Solomon with riches, 2 Chron. 1:12). However, in the New Testament era this has now changed. Instead of a mark of the Lord's blessing, *riches are a test of a man's devotedness to God!*

Let us understand that our tendency to trust in riches or to be absorbed totally in the pursuit of them makes it very difficult for us to live for God or seek the kingdom of God in our daily lives. Christians who lay up treasures on earth also pay for their disobedience in the lives of their children who depart from God and go after what the world has to offer. Trusting in **uncertain** riches is a dangerous condition for one seeking spiritual life. However, *benevolence with one's finances will be rewarded with true treasure in heaven!*

"Command those who are rich in this present age not to be haughty, nor to trust in __uncertain__ riches but in the living God, who gives us richly all things to enjoy. Let them do good, that they be rich in good works, ready to give, willing to share, storing up for themselves a good foundation for the time to come, that they may lay hold on eternal life." (1 Tim 6:17-19)

OCTOBER 21   *Bible Reading: Mark Chapters 13-16*

DO YOU REALLY __BELIEVE__ IN THE RESURRECTION OF CHRIST?

*"Later He appeared to the eleven as they sat at the table; and **He rebuked their __unbelief__ and hardness of heart, because they __did not believe__ those who had seen Him after He had risen.** And He said to them,* *"Go into all the world and preach the gospel to every creature. He who* **__believes__ and is baptized will be saved; but he who __does not believe__ will be condemned. And these signs will follow __those who believe__**..." (Mark 16:14-17)

In Mark chapter 16, three separate appearances by the resurrected Christ are noted, and in all three the disciples' *unbelief* is highlighted (Mark 16:11, 13, 14). This last appearance to the eleven took place that same Sunday evening (Luke 24:36; John 20:19–24; 1 Cor. 15:5). Although the disciples are referred to as the eleven, only ten were present and Thomas was absent on this occasion. During this appearance, Jesus rebuked His disciples for their refusal to accept the reports of His resurrection from Mary and the others!

Then the disciples were commanded to preach the gospel to the whole creation. The Savior's goal was world evangelization. He purposed to accomplish it with eleven disciples who would literally forsake all to follow Him. There would be *two results* of the preaching: *some would believe, be baptized and be saved; some would disbelieve and be condemned.* In Jesus' commission to preach the gospel (16:15–16), *belief* is outwardly confessed through baptism, and *unbelief* leaves a person condemned in the sight of God.

Let us understand that *belief* is the inward reception of Christ, and baptism is the outward testimony of that belief. What we see in the above passage was that Jesus upbraided these disciples for *not believing* the accounts of eyewitnesses, but He pronounced a blessing on *"those who have not seen and yet have believed"* (John 20:29).

Today, let us truly believe in the resurrection of Christ, and propagate the gospel that originated out of this glorious resurrection! This will be one way we can truly be His disciples!

"For I delivered to you first of all that which I also received: that Christ died for our sins according to the Scriptures, and that He was buried, and that He rose again the third day according to the Scriptures. And if Christ is not risen, then our preaching is empty and your faith is also empty. But now Christ is risen from the dead, and has become the firstfruits of those who have fallen asleep." (1 Cor 15:3-4, 14, 20)

OCTOBER 22   *Bible Reading: Luke Chapters 1-3*

SERVING GOD <u>WITHOUT FEAR</u> IN HOLINESS & RIGHTEOUSNESS

*"Blessed is the Lord God of Israel, for He has visited and redeemed His people, and has raised up a horn of salvation for us in the house of His servant David, as He spoke by the mouth of His holy prophets, who have been since the world began, that we should be saved from our enemies and from the hand of all who hate us, to perform the mercy promised to our fathers and to remember His holy covenant, the oath which He swore to our father Abraham: to grant us that we, being delivered from the hand of our enemies, **might serve Him without fear, in holiness and righteousness before Him all the days of our life."*** (Luke 1:68-75)

The prophecy of Zechariah, found exclusively in these verses, was spoken under the power of the Holy Spirit. His words were filled with messianic importance with references to salvation as God's unchanging covenant with Abraham was literally being fulfilled. It is to be noted that there are no less than sixteen direct allusions to the Old Testament contained in these few verses. Zechariah utters a remarkable prophecy in the form of a song which heralds the coming of the Messiah and His forerunner. This song is called the 'Benedictus' that means *'Praise be'*, and he is singing praises to God for *three specific reasons:*

1. *Praise to God for what He had done* (vv. 68-69). Zechariah realized that the birth of his son, John, indicated the imminence

of the coming of the Messiah. Faith enabled him to say God had already visited and redeemed His people by sending the Redeemer. Jehovah had raised up a *horn of salvation* in the royal house of David. (A *horn* was used to hold the oil for anointing kings; therefore it might mean here a King of salvation from the kingly line of David.)

2. *Praise to God for fulfilling prophecy* (vv. 70-71). The coming of the Messiah had been predicted by the holy prophets since the world began. It would mean salvation from our enemies and safety from our foes.

3. *Praise to God for His faithfulness to His promises* (vv. 72–75). The Lord had made an unconditional covenant of salvation with Abraham (Gen. 12:1-3). This promise was fulfilled by the coming of Abraham's seed, namely, the Lord Jesus Christ. The salvation He brought was both *external* and *internal. Externally*, it meant *deliverance from the hand of our enemies. Internally*, it meant *serving God without fear, in holiness and righteousness.*

What we can apply in our lives today is that God's deliverance from our enemies should result in our *serving God without fear but with holiness and righteousness.* To be holy and righteous is concerned primarily with the *eternal* laws of God. It is *"the divine consecration and inner truth of righteousness"* (Meyer). Let us serve God with reverence in holiness and righteousness and reach out to others as we reflect God's love to others!

*"...that you put off, concerning your former conduct, the old man which grows corrupt according to the deceitful lusts, and **be renewed** in the spirit of your mind, and that you **put on the new man which was created** according to God, **in true righteousness and holiness**."* (Eph 4:22-24)

OCTOBER 23   *Bible Reading: Luke Chapters 4-6*

GOD DESIRES LOVE, MERCY & KINDNESS FROM OUR LIVES!

"But love your enemies, do good, and lend, hoping for nothing in return; and your reward will be great, and you will be sons of the Most High. For He is kind to the unthankful and evil. Therefore be merciful, just as your Father also is merciful." (Luke 6:35-36)

Our Lord Jesus Christ states here that we should *love* our enemies, *do good* and lend, hoping for nothing in return. Such behavior is distinctly Christian and marks us apart from others. This is the way *true* believers manifest themselves to the world as children of God. God is *kind* to the unthankful and the evil people. When we act like God, we show that we have been born of God. To show mercy means *to forgive when it is in our power to avenge.* Our heavenly Father showed us mercy by not giving us the punishment we deserve. In the similar manner, He wants us to *show mercy* to others as well.

Jesus wants our actions to go far beyond what is considered morality by the world, and our standards surpass those of sinners. The practice of loving our enemies was modeled by God Himself. Christian love finds its motivation in God's love for us. Because God does not give or withhold His kindness dependent upon the character of the recipient, so we must be indifferent in our extension of kindness to friends and enemies alike (see Lev. 19:18). Extending the mercy of God into our relationships transforms our behavior into supernatural testimonies. *Mercy* and *grace* are godly character qualities that distinguish believers as genuine children of God (vv. 32–36).

What difference does our faith make in the way we *respond to people in need?* Do we respond to people as God Himself does, with mercy (v. 36)? We need to show *kindness* even to those who wish to do harm to us. Only then will we reflect the heart of the One, who while we were yet enemies, paid the ultimate price to come to our rescue. Our love for Christ is only as real as *our love for our neighbors!*

"Therefore you shall be perfect, just as your Father in heaven is perfect." (Matt 5:48)

OCTOBER 24   Bible Reading: Luke Chapters 7-9

SALVATION IS FREE BUT DISCIPLESHIP IS COSTLY!

*Then He (Jesus) said to them all, "If anyone desires to come after Me, **let him deny himself, and take up his cross <u>daily</u>, and follow Me.** For whoever desires to save his life will lose it, but whoever loses his life for My sake will save it. For what profit is it to a man if he gains the whole world, and is himself destroyed or lost?"* (Luke 9:23-25)

In the above passage, our Lord Jesus invites His disciples to follow Him *by denying themselves* and *taking up their 'own' crosses on a daily basis*. To deny self means *willingly to renounce any so-called right to plan or choose*, and *to recognize His lordship in every area of life*. To take up the cross means *to deliberately choose the kind of life Jesus lived*. This involves bearing the opposition of loved ones, bearing the reproach of the world, forsaking family, houses, lands and the comforts of this life, putting complete dependence on God, obeying the guidance of the Holy Spirit, proclaiming an unpopular gospel message, taking a pathway of loneliness, bearing organized attacks from established religious leaders, suffering for righteousness' sake, suffering slander and shame, pouring out our lives for others, and dying to self and to the world.

But it also involves *laying hold of life that is everlasting*! It means finding at last the reason for our existence, and our eternal reward. We instinctively recoil from a life of cross-bearing. Our minds are reluctant to believe that this could be God's will for us. Yet the words of Christ *"If anyone desires to come after Me"* mean that *nobody is excused!*

The Romans required a condemned criminal to carry the crossbeam to his place of execution. Luke adds the word 'daily' to the Lord's requirement of cross-bearing, indicating a *progressive and continuous renouncing of one's natural self-centeredness* (v. 23). Jesus affirms that one must be prepared even to die if he would be a follower of Christ. To take up the cross means to *renounce selfish ambition; it is a death to a whole way of life.*

Since Jesus bore the cross for us, we should be willing to bear our own crosses on a daily basis. We should have a *strong personal relationship with God* – a relationship born of faith in the work of Jesus at the cross. We should be willing to sacrifice everything for the privilege of proclaiming Him in our daily lives. Let us remember that what is gained in Christ far outweighs all that is lost for Christ. *Salvation is free but discipleship is costly!*

"I have been crucified with Christ; it is no longer I who live, but Christ lives in me; and the life which I now live in the flesh I live by faith in the Son of God, who loved me and gave Himself for me." (Gal 2:20)

DON'T BE DISTRACTED WITH 'GOOD' ACTIVITIES

*But **Martha was distracted with much serving**, and she approached Him and said, "Lord, do You not care that my sister has left me to serve alone? Therefore tell her to help me." And Jesus answered and said to her, "Martha, Martha, you are worried and troubled about many things. But one thing is needed, and **Mary has chosen that good part**, which will not be taken away from her." (Luke 10:40-42)*

When Jesus visited the home of Martha and Mary, we see that Mary sat at Jesus' feet and heard His word, while Martha became distracted by her preparations for her beloved Rabbi (vv. 39-40). Martha's complaint to Jesus indicates that she was irritated that her sister was not helping her. Jesus' tender reply is evident in the double address of *'Martha, Martha'* (6:46; 8:24; 13:34; 22:31) as He observed that Martha was anxiety-ridden over ordinary matters. On the other hand, Mary was a silent example. She said nothing, but did what was right by devoting herself to Jesus' teaching. Jesus valued Mary's affection above Martha's service!

Based upon this incident, Charles R. Erdman writes: *"While the Master does appreciate all that we undertake for Him, He knows that our first need is to sit at His feet and learn His will; then in our tasks we shall be calm and peaceful and kindly".*

The lesson to be learned from this true story is that *we must choose our relationship with God over anything else.* C. S. Lewis has one remarked, *"You can't get second things by putting them first; you can get second things only by putting first things first".* The *first thing* above everything else is *our relationship with God.* There is nothing wrong with serving in His vineyard but we must take time to sit at the feet of Jesus and hear His Word. It is important to serve God and serve others, but it is even more important to delight God by spending quality time with Him alone!

Like Martha, we are called on to strike a balance between faithful, diligent service in our day-to-day responsibilities, and a constant attitude of dependence on the Lord by maintaining close relationship with Him. *Are we so busy serving Him that we have no time to love Him and listen to Him?*

"One thing I have desired of the Lord, that will I seek: that I may dwell in the house of the Lord all the days of my life, to behold the beauty of the Lord, and to inquire in His temple." (Psalms 27:4)

OCTOBER 26   *Bible Reading: Luke Chapters 13-15*

GOD STILL 'REJOICES' OVER A SINNER WHO REPENTS

*"I say to you that likewise **there will be more joy in heaven over one sinner who repents** than over ninety-nine just persons who need no repentance...Likewise, I say to you, **there is joy in the presence of the angels of God over one sinner who repents...It was right that we should make merry and be glad, for your brother was dead and is alive again, and was lost and is found."*** (Luke 15:7, 10, 32)

Jesus told three parables in Luke 15 to correct the Pharisees' misconception about God, and in answer to their question as to why He welcomed sinners and ate with them. Through these parables, Jesus shared His Father's heart in rejoicing when any sinner repents and turns to Him.

The literary art and message of these three parables are beautifully intertwined. The ratio of ninety-nine sheep to one, nine coins to one, and one son to one focuses in each case on the one recovered. *Rejoicing occurs in each case.* In the first story those who rejoice are all in heaven. In the second, rejoicing is found in the company of the angels. In the third, the father is the leader of the party, celebrating the return of his wayward son. The lost sheep was located in the wilderness; the woman's coin was lost inside the house; and the younger son was lost outside the house.

The *key point* of these three parables is the *joy of God when the lost is recovered.* God's joy is to forgive and restore. In each story something is lost in increasing value: a sheep, a coin and a son. In each case, the lost object is found and produces rejoicing. The sheep is innocently lost, the coin carelessly lost, but the son willfully lost. The percentage of loss grows in each case from one out of a hundred, to one out of ten, to one out of two.

The three parables is a moving portrayal of a loving God's persistence in seeking out the lost, and of human perversity in resenting such grace, which exceeds our natural understanding. Each parable records the anguish of loosing, the effort of searching and the joy of finding! The 'sinner' who humbles himself and confesses his lost condition brings joy to the heart of God.

Jesus wants us never to forget God's concern for the *'lost'* sinner who has no relation with Him. He loves sinners and actively seeks them; His joy is great when they turn to Him. God views every sinner with compassion as a lost but loved son. He longs for each one to return to Him. Let us be God's messengers in seeking the *'lost'* and lead them to restore their relationship with God. God truly 'rejoices' over a sinner who repents!

"The Lord your God in your midst, The Mighty One, will save; He will rejoice over you with gladness, He will quiet you with His love, He will rejoice over you with singing." (Zephaniah 3:17)

OCTOBER 27 *Bible Reading: Luke Chapters 16-18*

HUMILITY *ALWAYS* COMES BEFORE EXALTATION

"For everyone who exalts himself will be humbled, and he who humbles himself will be exalted." (Luke 18:14)

Our Lord Jesus spoke the parable of the Pharisee and the tax collector (vv. 9–14) to people who prided themselves on being righteous, and who despised all others as inferior. He reminded them that it is this spirit of self-humiliation and repentance that is acceptable to God. *God exalts the humble, but He humbles those who exalt themselves!*

Although the Pharisee went through the motions of prayer, he was really not speaking to God. He was so proud of himself that he started off his prayer with a comparison: *"God, I thank you that I am not like other men"*. Instead of comparing himself with God's perfect standard and seeing how sinful he really was, he compared himself with others in the community and prided himself on being better.

The tax collector was a striking contrast. Standing before God, he sensed his own utter unworthiness. He did not think of himself as one sinner among many, but as the sinner who was unworthy of anything from God. This man shows us the path to true identity. It is based on honesty about ourselves and becoming like Christ!

Thus, Jesus identified the contrast between the Pharisee and the tax collector as one between pride and humility, between those who exalt and those who humble themselves. God will bring down the proud and will exalt the humble. The Pharisee relied on his own merits, not having discovered that no human righteousness is sufficient before a God who demands perfection (Matt. 5:48). The tax collector relied on God's mercy and found it.

True prayer should humble us and make us love others more. We should be like children coming to a Father when we pray. Let us remember that humility *always* comes before exaltation!

Likewise you younger people, submit yourselves to your elders. Yes, all of you be submissive to one another, and be clothed with humility, for "God resists the proud, but gives grace to the humble". Therefore humble yourselves under the mighty hand of God, that He may exalt you in due time, casting all your care upon Him, for He cares for you." (1 Peter 5:5-7)

OCTOBER 28   *Bible Reading: Luke Chapters 19-21*

SEEKING TO SAVE THOSE WHO ARE LOST

"Today salvation has come to this house, because he also is a son of Abraham; for the Son of Man has come to seek and to save that which was lost" (Luke 19:9-10)

In the above passage Jesus announced that salvation had come to the house of Zacchaeus, because he was a son of Abraham. Salvation did not come just because Zacchaeus was a Jew by birth but because he exercised the same kind of faith in God as Abraham. Later on, Apostle Paul uses *"son of Abraham"* to refer to those *who share the faith of Abraham.* Previously, he may have been a physical son of Abraham, but by his repentance he has become a spiritual son, and his entire household shared in Abraham's blessings.

Zacchaeus may have been a higher-ranking "publican" rather than an ordinary tax collector. Either way, he would have been despised by the citizens of Jericho. This account describes how a sinner becomes a son. Zacchaeus behaved as one with a heart touched by God. His faith was demonstrated in his repentance and his restitution of funds according to the Law, which demanded repayment plus 20 percent (Lev. 6:5; Num. 5:7). Let us understand that *righteous obedience is an evidence of saving faith*!

Zacchaeus is a good example of a man whose riches did not prevent him from coming to Christ. But like so many today, what he needed was someone to explain the way of salvation to him. Jesus came to him, sought him, and saved him. Though He was surrounded by a great crowd of people, Jesus took time for individuals, and He even saw a man up on a tree!

We can learn *four things* from this passage of Jesus' encounter with Zacchaeus in Luke 19:1-10:

1. We should *see the need of God's love* in everyone we encounter during our life journey.

2. We should *never discount the ministry to individuals,* as they may be instrumental in attracting many more to Christ (e.g. Zacchaeus in Luke 19 or the Samaritan Woman in John 4)

3. We should *seek to find lost people* in our area of influence, try to know them personally and share the gospel with them.

4. We should *move further in these relationships* and make them our friends, like Jesus did with Zacchaeus (v. 5)

"Sow for yourselves righteousness; reap in mercy; break up your fallow ground, for it is time to seek the Lord, till He comes and rains righteousness on you." (Hosea 10:12)

OCTOBER 29　　　　　*Bible Reading: Luke Chapters 22-24*

CHRIST'S RESURRECTION DEMANDS A RESPONSE FROM US

*Then He said to them, "These are the words which I spoke to you while I was still with you, that all things must be fulfilled which were written in the Law of Moses and the Prophets and the Psalms concerning Me." And He opened their understanding, that they might comprehend the Scriptures. Then He said to them, "**Thus it is written, and thus it was necessary** for the Christ to suffer and to rise from the dead the third day, and that **repentance and remission of sins should be preached in His name to all nations**, beginning at Jerusalem. And you are witnesses of these things."* (Luke 24:44-48)

This is a summary of the teachings of Jesus between His resurrection and His ascension. Jesus explained to His disciples that His resurrection was the fulfillment of His own words to them. *Had He not told them that all the Old Testament prophecies concerning Him had to be fulfilled?* The *Law of Moses*, the *Prophets* and the *Psalms* were the three major divisions of the Old Testament and comprise the entire Old Testament. *What was the burden of the Old Testament prophecies concerning Christ?* They were:

1. *That He must suffer* (Psalm 22:1–21; Isa. 53:1–9)

2. *That He must rise again from the dead the third day* (Ps. 16:10; Jonah 1:17; Hosea 6:2)

3. *That repentance and remission of sins should be preached in His name to all nations, beginning at Jerusalem.*

Then, Jesus summarized the mission of the disciples as preaching repentance, calling people to turn from their own selfish ways to Christ, the One who had died for them. From the start, a relationship to Christ carries with it the privilege and responsibility to proclaim the gospel.

In His perfect holiness of life, Jesus reflects compassion for sin-stained and suffering mankind—brokenhearted, sick, mistreated, and bereaved. Our fulfillment of the Great Commission requires such a worldwide scope in ministering compassion and human concern. Jesus' style—sensitive and touchable—is a summons to His followers to speedily answer His command and to answer with His compassion. No geographic boundary, no sin barrier, no ethnic, political, or economic partisan interest is ever to restrict our reach or penetration with the gospel.

God opens our eyes (v. 31) and opens our understanding (v. 45) so that when He opens the Scriptures to us (vv. 27, 32), we may open our mouths and tell others about Him (v. 48). Jesus gives us the commission, the power, and the message. *There is no reason to be silent!* Jesus gives us the privilege and responsibility of telling the good news about His provision of forgiveness and eternal life to all who will listen. *Will we respond to the resurrection of Jesus and share the wonderful gospel with others in our lives!*

GRACE AND TRUTH CAME THROUGH JESUS CHRIST

*"And the Word became flesh and dwelt among us, and we beheld His glory, the glory as of the only begotten of the Father, full of grace and truth. John bore witness of Him and cried out, saying, this was He of whom I said, 'He who comes after me is preferred before me, for He was before me.' And of His fullness we have all received, and grace for grace. For the law was given through Moses, but **grace and truth came through Jesus Christ.**" (John 1:14-17)*

The Word became flesh when Jesus was born as a Baby in the manger at Bethlehem. He had always existed as the Son of God with the Father in heaven, but now chose to come into the world in a human body. Jesus dwelt among us as He *"pitched His tent"* here. His body was the tent in which He lived among men for 33 ½ years. God stooped to our level when He came to this earth, and this led to His greatest accomplishment among all – bridging the gap between the infinite God and finite man. *Hallelujah!*

Jesus Christ was truly human during His earthly existence: He was tired and thirsty (4:6, 7); He wept (11:35); He was troubled in spirit (12:27; 13:21); and He died (19:30). Without becoming less than God (Phil. 2:5–11), Jesus took upon Himself complete human nature. At His incarnation, God did not become man; He became God-Man.

Jesus Christ was full of grace and truth. Jesus came to this world to be *God's grace* – something that we did not deserve as we had sinned and deserved punishment. Grace is God's unmerited favor toward sinners for their salvation. It was God's grace upon us that Jesus humbled Himself to connect with us in our weakness. Jesus also came to be the *Truth* (John 14:6) to bring us back to God as He came to save us from our sins (Matt. 1:21). Grace was evident in the Old Testament (Gen. 6:8; Ex. 34:6), but not in the *fullness* that we experience in Jesus Christ. *God met us at our point of need in the Person of Jesus Christ, including all His power and provision!*

Taking on human limitations, our Lord Jesus Christ did countless acts of compassion to accommodate us in our weakness. To be channels of His blessings, let us allow the love of Jesus Christ *expressed overtly through grace and truth* flow through us into the lives of others!

"For by grace you have been saved through faith, and that not of yourselves; it is the gift of God, not of works, lest anyone should boast." (Eph 2:8-9)

OCTOBER 31   *Bible Reading: John Chapters 4-6*

TRUE WORSHIP = WORSHIPPING GOD IN 'SPIRIT' AND 'TRUTH'

"But the hour is coming, and now is, when **the true worshipers will worship the Father in spirit and truth;** *for the Father is seeking such to worship Him.* **God is Spirit and those who worship Him must worship in spirit and truth."** (John 4:23-24)

When our Lord Jesus encountered the Samaritan woman at the well in Sychar, He addressed the issue of lasting satisfaction. First, He established a common point of reference (water, v. 7), then aroused her curiosity on spiritual matters (vv. 9-14) that resulted in directly confronting her sins (immoral lifestyle, vv. 16-19). However, Jesus centered His conversation on the *main issue – worship* (vv. 21-24), and finally revealed Himself as the *Messiah – the object of worship* (vv. 25-26).

Jesus clearly revealed to the Samaritan woman that, with His coming, God no longer had a certain place on earth for worship. All who believe on the Lord Jesus can worship God at any time and in any place. The Jewish people had reduced worship to outward forms and ceremonies. On the other hand, the Samaritans worshiped what they did not know; they had created their own religion. Jesus was actually rebuking both Jews and Samaritans when He stated that worship must be *'in spirit and truth'*!

The emphasis lies on Spirit as God's essence as He is free from the limitations of time and space. *True worship* is thus not confined to a place but is rather an action of the heart. John gives three descriptions of God. He is *Spirit* (John 4:24), *love* (1 John 4:8), and *light* (1 John 1:5). God is a spiritual being who is invisible and without a body; He is a divine person who reveals Himself in perfect intellect, emotion, and will. No idols and no images need assist us in worship. *True worship* means that *a believer enters the presence of God by faith* (in keeping with the truth of God's revealed Word) *and there worships Him!*

Thus, Jesus makes worship a *matter of the heart*. Worship must be *in truth*, that is, *transparent, sincere, and according to biblical mandates*. Truth is what is in harmony with the nature and will of God. The issue is not where a person worships, but *how* and *whom*. Jesus Himself is *"The Truth"* (John 14:6), so *true worship is specifically the worship of God through His Son Jesus Christ.*

"Who shall not fear You, O Lord, and glorify Your name? For You alone are holy. For all nations shall come and worship before You, for Your judgments have been manifested." (Rev 15:4)

NOVEMBER 1 *Bible Reading: John Chapters 7-9*

'TRUE' VISION AND 'TRUE' BLINDNESS

And Jesus said, "For judgment I have come into this world, that those who do not see may see, and that those who see may be made blind." Then some of the Pharisees who were with Him heard these words, and said to Him, "Are we blind also?" Jesus said to them, "If you were blind, you would have no sin; but now you say, 'We see.' Therefore your sin remains." (John 9:39-41)

John chapter 9 ends with an insightful *two-fold purpose statement of Jesus' ministry. He came to heal the blind, and to blind those who claimed they could see* (v. 39). The blind were those who were willing to recognize their need for His help. Those who claimed they could see were the self-righteous who, because of their refusal to believe, would remain unforgiven and be judged guilty for their sins.

In this passage, Jesus brings to light the impact of His coming: *those who falsely imagine they have special insight into the things of God become blind opponents of God's ways*, and *those who seem less informed are able to see when the Spirit of God opens their eyes and leads them to faith.*

Jesus did not come into the world to execute judgment, and at first glance this verse seems to contradict John 3:17, *"For God did not send His Son into the world to condemn the world..."* But there is no real conflict. The purpose of Christ's coming into the world was not to judge but to save. However, judgment is the inevitable result for all who fail to receive Him. The preaching of the gospel has *two effects.*

399

Those who admit that they do not see are given sight. But those who insist that they can see perfectly, without the Lord Jesus, are confirmed in their blindness.

The First Coming of Christ did not bring in the Last Judgment, but He confronted people with the obligation to decide for or against Him (Matt. 12:30; Luke 11:23). In the light of the revelation of the gospel, let us truly 'see' what Christ has already accomplished for us, and live a life pleasing Him alone as His 'Children of Light'!

"But God, who is rich in mercy, because of His great love with which He loved us, even when we were dead in trespasses, made us alive together with Christ (by grace you have been saved), and raised us up together, and made us sit together in the heavenly places in Christ Jesus." (Eph 2:4-6)

NOVEMBER 2 *Bible Reading: John Chapters 10-12*

DYING TO SELF IS THE SECRET OF FRUITFULNESS

"Most assuredly, I say to you, unless a grain of wheat falls into the ground and dies, it remains alone; but if it dies, it produces much grain. He who loves his life will lose it, and he who hates his life in this world will keep it for eternal life." (John 12:24-25)

This is a powerful illustration of Christian discipleship. A grain of wheat that is not sown in the ground remains alone. This grain of wheat must die before it can reproduce itself and be fruitful.

Christ used this to illustrate His own death, which resulted in a rich spiritual harvest after His death and resurrection. He referred to Himself as a grain (or kernel) of wheat. If He did not die, He would abide alone. He would enjoy the glories of heaven by Himself; there would be no saved sinners there to share His glory. But if He died, He would provide a way of salvation by which many might be saved.

The same applies to us, as T. G. Ragland says: *"If we refuse to be corns of wheat—falling into the ground, and dying; if we will neither sacrifice prospects, nor risk character, and property, and health; nor, when we are called, relinquish home, and break family ties, for Christ's sake; then we shall abide alone. But if we wish to be fruitful, we must follow our Blessed Lord Himself, by becoming a corn of wheat, and dying; then we shall bring forth much fruit.ÿþ"*

Many people in this world think that the important things in life are food, clothing, and pleasure. They live for these things. But in thus loving their lives, they fail to realize that *the soul is more important than the body*. By neglecting their soul's welfare, they lose their lives. On the other hand, there are those who count all things loss for Christ. To serve Him, they forego things highly prized among men. These are the people who will keep their lives for eternal life. *To hate one's life means to love Christ more than one loves his own interests!*

Hating our lives involve serving Christ. We must individually establish our own priorities. We cannot give ourselves fully to this life and yet be committed to the life to come. There are *three things* we can learn from this illustration:

1. We should be willing to die to ourselves and to the world in order to be fruitful.
2. We should give more importance to the things of God than seeking our own pleasures.
3. We should be willing to serve God and follow the direction that He shows in our lives.

"But seek first the kingdom of God and His righteousness, and all these things shall be added to you." (Matt 6:33)

NOVEMBER 3   *Bible Reading: John Chapters 13-15*

ABIDING IN CHRIST FOR 'GREATER' FRUITFULNESS

*"I am the true vine, and My Father is the vinedresser. Every branch in Me that does not bear fruit He takes away; and every branch that bears fruit He prunes, that it may bear more fruit. **Abide in Me**, and I in you. As the branch cannot bear fruit of itself, unless it abides in the vine, neither can you, unless you abide in Me. I am the vine, you are the branches. He who abides in Me, and I in him, bears much fruit; for without Me you can do nothing. By this My Father is glorified, that you bear much fruit; so you will be My disciples."* (John 15:1-2, 4-5, 8)

This is the seventh and final of the great *"I am"* statements of Jesus in the Gospel of John. Here, Jesus explains the divine-human relationships by the analogy of a grapevine. Jesus is like the main vine. The disciples are compared with branches. God, the Father tends the branches like a gardener.

401

In the Old Testament, the nation of Israel was depicted as a vine planted by Jehovah. The Jews believed that because they were the descendants of Abraham, they were connected to God. But Israel proved to be unfaithful and unfruitful, so the Lord Jesus now presented Himself as the *True Vine*, the perfect fulfillment of all the other types and shadows.

A vine branch has one purpose only—*to bear fruit*. It will bear fruit as long as it abides in the vine. A branch abides in a vine by drawing all its life and nourishment from the vine. The point of the allegory is that Jesus' purpose in the believer's life is to produce fruit (v. 5). Fruit is mentioned eight times in this chapter and a progression is seen: *"fruit"* (v. 2a), *"more fruit"* (v. 2b), and *"much fruit"* (vv. 5, 8). In order to be a fruitful Christian, we must learn to depend on Christ and let the power and Spirit of Christ flow through our lives. *The key to spiritual fruitfulness is abiding in fellowship with Christ!*

Just as a real vine must be cleaned from insects, mildew, and fungus, we must be cleaned from worldly things that cling to us through God's Word. In our daily walk, we should stay in intimate fellowship with God through prayer, reading and obeying His Word, having fellowship with God's people, and being continually conscious of our union with God. *The only way we can bear the fruit of a Christ-like character is by living in touch with Christ moment-by-moment!*

Thus, our *total continued dependence* on Christ is the *only way* to grow in Christian character and our witness before others. This is also the *only way* we can *bear much fruit* in our lives!

"But the fruit of the Spirit is love, joy, peace, longsuffering, kindness, goodness, faithfulness, gentleness, self-control. Against such there is no law. And those who are Christ's have crucified the flesh with its passions and desires." (Gal 5:22-24)

NOVEMBER 4   *Bible Reading: John Chapters 16-18*

'UNITY' IS ESSENTIAL FOR 'ALL' BELIEVERS

*"I do not pray for these alone, but also for those who will believe in Me through their word; **that they all may be one**, as You, Father, are in Me, and I in You; **that they also may be one in Us**, that the world may believe that You sent Me. And the glory which You gave Me I have*

given them, that they may be one just as We are one: I in them, and You in Me; **that they may be made perfect in one,** *and that the world may know that You have sent Me, and have loved them as You have loved Me."* (John 17:20-23)

In John chapter 17, Jesus Christ our eternal High Priest prayed for Himself (vs. 1–5); for His current disciples (vs. 6–19); and for His entire future church and believers (vs. 20–26). We can boldly say, *"Jesus prayed for me over 1900 years ago"*! *What specifically did Jesus pray that should happen among us?*

Jesus prayed for unity among believers in fellowship for witness-bearing (vv. 20–23). He prayed that believers might be *one* in exhibiting the character of God. This is what would cause the world to believe that God had sent Jesus. This is the unity which makes the world say, *"We see Christ in those Christians as God the Father was seen in Christ."* Through our unity, the world will not only realize that Jesus was God the Son, but that believers are loved by God just as Christ was loved by God. *The loving relationship of believers to each other is the greatest witness to Jesus Christ!*

Jesus also prayed for unity among believers in their future glory (vv. 24–26). The Father had manifested Himself through the Son, and now the Son manifests Himself through His followers. This looks forward to the time when believers will receive their glorified bodies. We do not have this glory yet and we will not receive it until our Savior returns to take us to heaven (Rev 1:12–18). *It will be manifested to the world when Christ returns to set up His kingdom on earth!*

Just as it was the prayer and intense desire of Jesus that all believers should be united, *we should take the mantle of responsibility* and *actively strive to promote unity in the body of Christ.* This will help the world to believe that God has sent His only begotten Son Jesus into this world. We should *get along with other believers* as we spread the *sweet aroma of Christ's love* to others. We should *love and serve one another* (John 13:34-35; Matt. 20:20-28), and *never sow discord among believers* as this is one of the seven things that God hates (Prov. 6:19).

"I (Paul), therefore, the prisoner of the Lord, beseech you to walk worthy of the calling with which you were called, with all lowliness and gentleness, with longsuffering, bearing with one another in love, **endeavoring to keep the unity of the Spirit ÿþÿþin the bond of peace. There is one body and one Spirit, just as you were called in one hope**

of your calling; one Lord, one faith, one baptism; one God and Father of all, who is above all, and through all, and in you all." (Eph 4:1-6)

NOVEMBER 5   *Bible Reading: John Chapters 19-21*

DO WE LOVE ANYTHING/ ANYBODY MORE THAN JESUS?

So when they had eaten breakfast, Jesus said to Simon Peter, "Simon, son of Jonah, do you love Me more than these?" (John 21:15)

In this passage, the underlying lesson is that *love for Jesus* is the *only* acceptable motive for serving Him. Just as Peter had *denied* the Lord *thrice*, so he *was given three opportunities to confess Him*. The most important thing in ministry is *to love Jesus totally* - for *all* ministries flows out from *that love*!

This intimate interview was probably conducted within the hearing of the other six disciples. Peter had publicly professed his loyalty before the Crucifixion and Jesus wants the other disciples to understand Peter's restoration. The point of the entire dialogue is to question *not the extent of Peter's love for the Master, but the nature of his love.* Jesus wanted to impress upon Peter the *diverse responsibilities* ("feed" and "tend") and the *tenderness* (for "sheep" and "lambs") demanded by his love for Jesus. It is possible to construe the question posed by Jesus in several ways: *"Do you love Me more than these others love Me?"*; *"Do you love Me more than you love these others?"*; and *"Do you love Me more than you love these nets and fish?"*

Never rebuking Peter for his replies, Jesus *repeatedly commissioned him* for the pastoral ministry of God's people. The grace of God had recovered a fallen disciple, one who was later *greatly used by God to win many people to Christ* (Acts 2–5; 10–11) and who later wrote two general epistles. When Peter wrote to his fellow elders (1 Pet. 5:1, 2), he urged them to *"shepherd the flock of God"* apparently having taken to heart the words of Jesus, and called Jesus the *"Chief Shepherd"* (1 Pet. 5:4).

As we meditate on the three repeated questions that Jesus asked Peter after His resurrection, we need to ask ourselves this question: "What do I love more than Jesus?" It may be something innocent or harmless or something seemingly good like food, hobbies, work, etc. We need to realize that Jesus demands our first love over everything else. *Let us be careful to love Jesus more than anything or anyone in our lives!*

Let us always remember the following words of Jesus: *"He who loves father or mother more than Me is not worthy of Me. And he who loves son or daughter more than Me is not worthy of Me."* (Matt 10:37)

NOVEMBER 6   *Bible Reading: Acts Chapters 1-3*

POWER TO BE A WITNESS TO JESUS CHRIST

"But you shall receive power when the Holy Spirit has come upon you; and you shall be witnesses to Me in Jerusalem, and in all Judea and Samaria, and to the end of the earth." (Acts 1:8)

Acts 1:8 is the key verse of the book of Acts, serving as an inspired outline of its contents. The disciples of Jesus were now to give their attention to worldwide witness. God's Spirit would empower them as they executed their purpose. Starting from Jerusalem, the apostles' witness would radiate farther and farther, as ripples do when a stone lands in a placid pool of water. But first they must receive power— the power of the Holy Spirit, which would be indispensable for Christian witness!

Let us understand God's strategy of Christian witness:

1. The witness was to *begin* in *Jerusalem*, a meaningful prearrangement of the *grace of God*. This was the very city where our Lord Jesus was crucified, and it was first to receive the call to repentance and faith in Him.

2. Then *Judea*, the southern section of Palestine with its strong Jewish population, and with Jerusalem as its chief city.

3. Then *Samaria*, the region in the center of Palestine, with its hated, half-breed population with whom the Jews had no dealings.

4. Then the *end of the then-known world—the Gentile countries*, which had until now been outside the fold of Christ's impact.

The Book of Acts follows this strategy. The Jerusalem witness (chapter 2) gives in miniature form God's worldwide ministry: the "Jews … from every nation" (2:5) who heard and believed carried the message far and wide. In the rest of Acts the gospel spreads to Jerusalem (3:1–

8:1), to Judea and Samaria up to Antioch of Syria (8:1–12:25), and to the ends of the earth (13:1–28:31).

The power promised was not force or political authority but meant *ability* or *capacity*. The ability had more to do with *being* than doing. Evangelism is a *process*, not just an event. It involves a *total lifestyle*, not just occasional efforts. The power *came from without*, not from within. The believers were to *look for supernatural ability* from the Spirit to make them effective in gospel presentation. The believers were to *be witnesses to Christ*, not to themselves. They *were to make disciples* not to themselves but *to the risen Lord* (Matt. 28:18–20).

Let us note that Jesus commanded His disciples to be His witness and to tell others about Him regardless of the consequences. Church tradition tells us that all but one of the eleven apostles who heard this promise became martyrs (John died in exile). God empowered His disciples to be faithful witnesses even when they faced the most vehement opposition. That same power for witnessing is available to us today. Our task is not to convince people, but *to testify of the truth of the gospel. Let us be effective witnesses of God driven by the power of the Holy Spirit in our known world today!*

*"For I am not ashamed of the **gospel of Christ**, for it is the **power of God to salvation for everyone who believes**, for the Jew first and also for the Greek. **For in it the righteousness of God is revealed from faith to faith**; as it is written, "The just shall live by faith."* (Romans 1:16-17)

NOVEMBER 7   *Bible Reading: Acts Chapters 4-6*

THREE CHARACTERISTICS OF AN EFFECTIVE CHURCH

*"Now the multitude of those who believed were of one heart and one soul; neither did anyone say that any of the things he possessed was his own, but they had all things in common. And with **great power** the apostles gave witness to the resurrection of the Lord Jesus. And **great grace** was upon them all. **Nor was there anyone among them who lacked**; for all who were possessors of lands or houses sold them, and brought the proceeds of the things that were sold, and laid them at the apostles' feet; and they distributed to each as anyone had need."* (Acts 4:32-35)

The church that was formed on the day of Pentecost was greatly effective in their known world. The core reason for such effectiveness was that this Spirit-filled community was united ("of one heart and of one soul") with bonds of love. We can see *three remarkable characteristics* in this church that should be evident in any church that wants to be effective in the community:

1. ***Great Power (v. 33a):*** The *'great power'* is translated from the Greek word *"Dunamis"* that means energy, power, might, great force, great ability, and strength. There was a mysterious power connected with lives that were totally dedicated to the Lord due to dramatic transformations. This was the norm for the Spirit-filled and Spirit-led church, and God gave their testimony and the gospel they shared remarkable attractiveness and force (Romans 1:16).

2. ***Great Grace (v. 33b):*** The power in the witness of the believers was their love and grace for one another in witnessing and living (see Luke 2:40). The word *"grace"* as used in this text refers to *"operations of the power of God"* (Acts 11:23). Just as God through His mercy has saved us by His grace, so that grace is manifested in great dynamic where the Holy Spirit is at work in our lives.

3. ***Great Provision (v. 34a):*** One of the key characteristics of the first church was its lack of selfishness. The love of the believers towards Christ and one another manifested itself in giving. These believers were extraordinarily generous and responded to each other with gracious, Christ-like compassion. Such behavior was one powerful result of the outpouring of the Spirit (2:1–4), and this was Christian charity in its finest display.ÿþ If we, too, are filled with the Spirit of Christ, then we should also respond to the needs of people with the love of Christ!

The 1st century church has laid for us the above three characteristics to emulate – let our lives, actions and words show our love being poured out to the people around us. *"But this I say: He who sows sparingly will also reap sparingly, and he who sows bountifully will also reap bountifully. So let each one give as he purposes in his heart, not grudgingly or of necessity; for **God loves a cheerful giver. And God is able to make all grace abound toward you,** that you, **always having all sufficiency in all things, may have an abundance for every good work.**"* (2 Cor 9:6-8)

EXPERIENCING GOD IN THE MIDST OF OUR PROBLEMS

*When they heard these things they were cut to the heart, and they gnashed at him with their teeth. **But he, being full of the Holy Spirit, gazed into heaven and saw the glory of God, and Jesus standing at the right hand of God, and said, "Look! I see the heavens opened and the Son of Man standing at the right hand of God!"** And they stoned Stephen **as he was calling on God** and saying, **"Lord Jesus, receive my spirit."** Then he knelt down and cried out with a loud voice, **"Lord, do not charge them with this sin."** And when he had said this, **he fell asleep.** (Acts 7:54-56, 59-60)*

Stephen, the first martyr of the Christian church died the *"death of the righteous"* (Num. 23:10b). To die the death of the righteous, he first had to *live* the life of the righteous. Stephen comes to the limelight when he gets selected as one of the seven men to serve in the daily food distribution, and was described as a man *"full of wisdom"* (Acts 6:3), *"full of the Holy Spirit"* (6:3, 5), *"full of faith"* (6:5, 8), *"full of power"* (6:8), and one who *"did great wonders and signs among the people"* (6:8). His lifestyle was so profound that the people *"were not able to resist the wisdom and the Spirit by which he spoke"* (6:10), and he was presented before the Sanhedrin being falsely accused for having spoken *"blasphemous words against Moses and God"* (6:11).

However, Stephen responded by giving one of the most profound sermons ever recorded in the Bible through the power of the Holy Spirit (7:2-53). He did not mince his words as he accused the high priests, elders and the scribes of resisting the Holy Spirit (v. 51), persecuting the prophets (v. 52) and even killing Jesus through betrayal (v. 52). As soon as Stephen bore public testimony to seeing the heavens opened, the mob refused to listen to him further; they cried fiercely, charged upon him, dragged him outside the city walls and stoned him to death.

The name Stephen means *"a crown,"* and he won the crown of life because he was faithful unto death (Rev. 2:10). Stephen prayed two times during his death in a manner very similar to our Lord Jesus Christ:

- Stephen prayed, *"Lord Jesus, receive my spirit"* (v. 59). Jesus had prayed, *"Father, into Your hands I commit My spirit"* (Luke 23:46).
- Stephen prayed, *"Lord, do not charge them with this sin"* (v. 60). Jesus had prayed, *"Father, forgive them, for they do not know what they do"* (Luke 23:34).

What this suggests to us is that Stephen had been *"transformed into the same image from glory to glory, just as by the Spirit of the Lord"* (2 Cor. 3:18). When the men of Israel were at their worst, Stephen was at his best. He interceded to the Lord God of heaven for those who persecuted him. Even in death his concern was for their eternal life. Stephen is a good model for us of someone who *experienced God in the midst of his problems.* Let us also seek God like Stephen and be heavenly minded in the midst of our earthly troubles!

"If then you were raised with Christ, seek those things which are above, where Christ is, sitting at the right hand of God. Set your mind on things above, not on things on the earth." (Col 3:1-2)

NOVEMBER 9   *Bible Reading: Acts Chapters 10-12*

THE VISIBLE MARKS OF A 'TRUE' CHRISTIAN

*"So it was that for a whole year they assembled with the church and taught a great many people. **And the disciples were first called Christians in Antioch.**"* (Acts 11:26)

Christianity is ranked as the largest religion in the world today with approximately 2 billion adherents, and 33% of the world's population is considered to be 'Christian'. According to World Christian Encyclopedia (2001), there are approximately *38,000* Christian denominations in the world. Of the 2 billion Christians in the world today, 648 million (11% of the world's population) are 'Evangelical' Christians. Evangelicals have grown from *only 3 million* in AD 1500 to *648 million* worldwide, *with 54% being Non-Whites.*

Today in America, about 75% of adults identify themselves as 'Christian', while there are more than 1500 different Christian faith groups in America. We need to probe a bit further, and get a clear understanding about who can be referred to as a 'Christian', and what are the visible marks of a 'true' Christian - strictly based from biblical standards only.

The name 'Christian' means *'adherent to Christ'* or, *'one who sticks to Christ'*. From our biblical passage today, we can understand that the name 'Christian' was first given to the disciples in Antioch by others who noted their behavior being similar to that of their teacher Jesus Christ. There are *two things* that defined the early believers or followers of Christ:

1. They talked and preached the gospel and the resurrection of Christ to others (v. 20) with the objective of witnessing to them based on the directive of Acts 1:8.

2. They taught scriptures to the believers who assembled in the church (v. 26) with the intention of making them disciples based on the 'Great Commission' described in Matt. 28:19-20.

Even though the name 'Christian' was first directed at the followers of Jesus in scorn, these believers embraced this name as a badge of honor and as a mark of allegiance to Jesus. The question that we are facing today is: *"Are we living lives that are worthy of the name 'Christian'?"* In order to truly identify ourselves with the name of our Lord Jesus Christ, we should display love to one and all and reach out to them as acts of compassion. To unbelievers, we should witness and speak the gospel, to believers, we should disciple them by teaching them what Jesus has taught us already. We should impact others *in both word and deed*s as the disciples did to their neighbors in Antioch!

Let us *truly obey* the 'new' commandment that our Lord Jesus Christ has given us: *"A new commandment I give to you, that you love one another; as I have loved you, that you also love one another. By this all will know that you are My disciples, if you have love for one another."* (John 13:34-35)

NOVEMBER 10   *Bible Reading: Acts Chapters 13-15*

ENTERING GOD'S KINGDOM THROUGH TRIBULATIONS

*And when they had preached the gospel to that city and made many disciples, they returned to Lystra, Iconium, and Antioch, strengthening the souls of the disciples, exhorting them to continue in the faith, and saying, **"We must through many tribulations enter the kingdom of God."*** (Acts 14:21-22)

In the above passage, we read that Paul and Barnabas *"**returned** to Lystra, Iconium, and Antioch"*. Their purpose at this time was to *"follow-up"* on their initial ministries in those cities. They were not satisfied just to preach the gospel and bringing people to the saving knowledge of Jesus. They wanted to build up the believers in their most holy faith, especially by teaching them the truth of the church and its importance in God's program in the world. Erdman points out: *"A proper missionary program has as its aim the establishing on the field of self-governing, self-sustaining, self-propagating churches. This was ever the purpose and the practice of Paul."*

Two things can be noted here. *First*, the exact nature of their follow-up work was *strengthening the souls of the disciples and establishing the Christians in the faith by instructing them from the word of God.* Paul described the process in Colossians 1:28, 29: *"We warn everyone we meet, and we teach everyone we can, all that we know about him, so that, if possible, we may bring every man up to his full maturity in Christ Jesus. This is what I am working at all the time, with all the strength that God gives me"* (JBP).

Second, they exhorted them to continue in the faith, an exhortation especially timely in view of the widespread persecution then prevalent. With this exhortation went a reminder that they must through many tribulations enter the kingdom of God. This refers to the kingdom of God in its future aspect (or, heaven), when believers will share Christ's glory. A person enters the kingdom of God in the first place through the new birth. Persecutions and tribulations do not have any saving value. However, those who enter the kingdom of God by faith at the present time are promised that the pathway to future glory is filled with tribulations. *"If indeed we suffer with Him, that we may also be glorified together"* (Rom. 8:17b).

What we can understand is that *it is important to continually grow in Christian life.* This process of growth will bring us through continued troubles and sufferings to enter heaven eventually. Earth is a land of trials, while heaven is the land of joy. Much of our life is getting through sufferings that are inevitable in this world.

Let is persevere through them as our *"will to persevere is often the difference between failure and success."* (David Sarnoff). Let us bear our troubles *joyfully* remembering what Jesus has told us: *"In the world you will have tribulation; but be of good cheer, I have overcome the world."* (John 16:33b)

OFFERING A 'SUPERNATURAL' RESPONSE TO OUR PROBLEMS & PAIN

*"Then the multitude rose up together against them; and the magistrates tore off their clothes and commanded them to be beaten with rods. And when they had **laid many stripes on them**, they **threw them into prison**, commanding the jailer to keep them securely. Having received such a charge, he **put them into the inner prison** and **fastened their feet in the stocks. But at midnight Paul and Silas were praying and singing hymns to God, and the prisoners were listening to them.**"* (Acts 16:22-25)

After being forbidden by the Holy Spirit to preach the word in Asia (v. 6) and Bithynia (v. 7), Apostle Paul got a *'Macedonian Call'* through a vision in which a man from Macedonia pleaded to Paul to go there and help them (v. 9). Taking this as a confirmation from God to redirect his ministry, Paul started for Macedonia with Silas (v. 10), and reached Philippi where God opened Lydia's heart (vv. 12-15). In due time, Paul delivered a demonized slave girl (vv. 16-18) and as a reward, both Paul and Silas were beaten up badly with rods and thrown into the inner prison with shackles of chains on their feet (vv. 19-24).

When Paul and Silas experienced this injustice and mistreatment, instead of moaning and grumbling, they *displayed their faith in God* by praying and singing praises loudly at the midnight hour (v. 25). Such unusual behavior opened the ears of the unbelieving prisoners and the jailer. God intervened through a great earthquake, opening the prison doors, and loosening everyone's chains so that all the prisoners could escape immediately (v. 26).

However, Paul and Silas *showed their integrity* by not trying to escape even when the opportunity was there. Even the other prisoners were so moved that they did not escape. God then intervened spiritually by opening the jailer's heart so that in the wee hours of the morning, he and his family got saved and baptized (vv. 27-32). It was due to Paul and Silas' supernatural response to their problem and pain that an entire household came to know the Savior (vv. 33-34).

Let us understand that sometimes *our disappointments*, problems and pain may be *God's appointments* to touch other people's lives. God can turn our *obstacles* into wonderful *opportunities* to display His glory and power. When we experience delays, changes in our well-laid plans and abrupt re-directions, it is possible that God may be leading us to do something different for Him in order to achieve His purposes through our lives. *Our inconveniences may actually be God's divine appointments!* Like Paul and Silas, *let us offer supernatural responses to our problems & pain!*

*"And we know that **all things** work together **for good** to those who **love God**, to those who are the **called according to His purpose**."* (Romans 8:28)

NOVEMBER 12   *Bible Reading: Acts Chapters 19-21*

IT IS IMPORTANT FOR BELIEVERS TO RECEIVE THE HOLY SPIRIT

*And it happened, while Apollos was at Corinth, that Paul, having passed through the upper regions, came to Ephesus. And finding some **disciples** he said to them, **"Did you receive the Holy Spirit when you believed?"** So they said to him, "We have not so much as heard whether there is a Holy Spirit."…And **when Paul had laid hands on them, the Holy Spirit came upon them, and they spoke with tongues and prophesied.** Now the men were about twelve in all.* (Acts 19:1-2, 5-7)

When Paul visited Ephesus, he met twelve men who professed to be disciples. As he talked with them, he realized that their knowledge of the Christian faith was very imperfect and defective. He wondered if they had ever really received the Holy Spirit as believers. The thought of this verse is not that the reception of the Holy Spirit is a work of grace which follows salvation. As soon as a sinner trusts the Savior, he receives the Holy Spirit.

However, these disciples did not know was that the Holy Spirit had already been given to the Church on the Day of Pentecost. They did not know that Christ had died, had been buried, and had risen from the dead and ascended back to heaven, and that He had sent the Holy Spirit. As followers of John the Baptist, these believers had not been instructed about the coming of the Spirit. Paul explained all this to them. Then these disciples were baptized in the name of the

Lord Jesus as a public acknowledgment that they have accepted Jesus Christ as Lord.

We see that Apostle Paul then laid his hands on them, and they received the Holy Spirit (vv. 6, 7). This is the *fourth* time in Acts when the Holy Spirit was given. The *first* was on the Day of Pentecost (2:1–4), and *involved the Jews primarily*. The *second* was when the Spirit was *given to the Samaritans* through the laying on of the hands of Peter and John (8:14–17). The *third* time was at the *household of the Gentile* Cornelius in Joppa (10:44- 45; 11:15–17). It is to be noted that the order of events leading up to the reception of the Holy Spirit was different in each case. Here in Acts 19 the order is: *faith – rebaptism - laying on of the Apostle's hands - reception of the Holy Spirit*. When the disciples of John received the Holy Spirit they spoke with tongues and prophesied.

The moment we believe on the Lord Jesus Christ, we are indwelt by the Holy Spirit; we are sealed by the Spirit; and we receive the earnest of the Spirit. It is the Holy Spirit who convicts us of sin, convinces us of Christ, and comes into our hearts to abide forever. However, there is no denying that the Holy Spirit comes on believers in a sovereign manner through a separate experience, empowering them for special ministries, giving them great boldness in the faith, and pouring out upon them a passion for souls. Let us truly understand the importance for us, *as believers*, to *receive* (v. 2) and *be filled* (Eph. 5:18) by the Holy Spirit as our everyday experience!

Brethren, do not be children in understanding; however, in malice be babes, but in understanding be mature. In the law it is written: "With men of other tongues and other lips I will speak to this people; and yet, for all that, they will not hear Me," says the Lord. Therefore tongues are for a sign, not to those who believe but to unbelievers. (1 Cor 14:20-22)

NOVEMBER 13   *Bible Reading: Acts Chapters 22-24*

MAINTAIN A CLEAR CONSCIENCE BEFORE GOD AND PEOPLE

"But this I confess to you, that according to the Way which they call a sect, so I worship the God of my fathers, believing all things which are written in the Law and in the Prophets. I have hope in God, which they

*themselves also accept, that there will be a resurrection of the dead, both of the just and the unjust. This being so, **I myself always strive to have a conscience without offense toward God and men.***" (Acts 24:14-16)

Apostle Paul's defense before Governor Felix was *threefold*: his *life*, his *faith* and his *service* to his nation. In his spirited defense, Paul did not deny the third charge that he was a ringleader of the sect of the Nazarenes. But what he did say was that in this capacity *he served the God of the Jews*, believing all things which are written in the Old Testament. He shared the expectation of all orthodox Jews, especially the Pharisees, that *there would be a resurrection of the dead, both of the just and the unjust,* and this was his conviction and source of comfort.

In the light of this coming resurrection, Paul earnestly tried to preserve an unclouded relationship with God and with his fellow men at all times, and emphasized the importance of having a conscience void of offense toward God and man (vs. 16). *Having a clear conscience was vital to his preparation for spiritual warfare!*

God has given us a conscience that brings guilt in our hearts when we do wrong. Romans 2:15 tells is that our conscience either accuses or excuses us for our actions. For the obedient follower of Christ, care for the conscience is an important way to maintain a moral compass in our lives. We should freely and regularly confess our sins before God, turn away from it and make restitutions as a way of our lifestyle (1 John 1:9; Lev. 6:2-5). Apostle Paul modeled a well-maintained conscience in his lifestyle (v. 16), and *we should also always earnestly attempt to keep our conscience clear through confession and repentance!*

*"Beloved, **if our heart does not condemn us, we have confidence toward God**. And whatever we ask we receive from Him, because we keep His commandments and do those things that are pleasing in His sight."* (1 John 3:21-22)

UNDERSTANDING THE SCOPE OF OUR COMMISSION

And He said, 'I am Jesus, whom you are persecuting. But rise and stand on your feet; for I have appeared to you for this purpose, to make you a minister and a witness both of the things which you have seen and of the things which I will yet reveal to you. I will deliver you from the Jewish people, as well as from the Gentiles, to whom I now send you, **to open their eyes, in order to turn them from darkness to light, and from the power of Satan to God, that they may receive forgiveness of sins and an inheritance among those who are sanctified by faith in Me.'** *(Acts 26:15-18)*

Apostle Paul's experience on the road to Damascus (9:1–19) was so important to him that he recounted it twice, once before the Jewish crowd in Jerusalem (22:6–16), and again before this mainly pagan audience in Caesarea. Here Paul gives a condensed summary of the commission which was given him by the risen Lord Jesus Christ. He had had this special revelation of Christ in glory because he was appointed to be a servant of the Lord and a witness of all he had seen that day along with all the great truths of the Christian faith.

Paul was sent especially to the Gentiles to open their eyes, in order to turn them from darkness to light and from the power of Satan to God. Through faith in the Lord Jesus, they would receive forgiveness of sins and an inheritance among those who are sanctified. H. K. Downie shows how verse 18 reveals *four things what the gospel does in the lives of people*:

1. It relieves from darkness.
2. It releases from the power of Satan.
3. It remits sins.
4. It restores a lost inheritance.

Paul understood Christ's commissioning to mean that the Gentiles' salvation depended on his presenting the gospel to them. No wonder he felt as though he was charged with a debt to the Gentiles (Rom. 1:14). These people were not saved prior to the hearing of the gospel; they needed to hear the message of salvation from one like Paul.

Paul was totally committed to his call to spread the gospel and establish churches throughout the known world. The gospel itself is forever the same, but as Christ's followers we are called to shape our message to fit our various audiences. Let us understand the scope of our commission, which is similar to Paul, and make sincere attempts to preach the gospel to the lost people around us and also send others with our prayers and financial support!

*For there is no distinction between Jew and Greek, for the same Lord over all is rich to all who call upon Him. For "**whoever calls on the name of the Lord shall be saved**." How then shall they call on Him in whom they have not believed? And how shall they believe in Him of whom they have not heard? And how shall they hear without a preacher? And how shall they preach unless they are sent? As it is written: "How beautiful are the feet of those who preach the gospel of peace, who bring glad tidings of good things!" (Romans 10:12-15)*

NOVEMBER 15 *Bible Reading: Romans Chapters 1-3*

NO MORE EXCUSES FOR IGNORING GOD

*"For the wrath of God is revealed from heaven against all ungodliness and unrighteousness of men, who **suppress the truth** in unrighteousness, because what may be known of God is manifest in them, for God has shown it to them. For since the creation of the world His invisible attributes are **clearly seen**, being **understood** by the things that are made, even His eternal power and Godhead, **so that they are without excuse**." (Romans 1:18-20)*

Ever since the creation of the world, two invisible characteristics of God have been on display for all to see: *His eternal power* and *His divinity* (or Godhead). The argument here is clear: *Creation demands a Creator. Design demands a Designer.* By looking up at the sun, moon, and stars, anyone can know there is a God who has created them. God has revealed Himself to heathen as well *through His creation*, so they are condemned for *being unfaithful* to what they could know about God.

The argument from *cause and effect* is one logical argument for the existence of God. The Scripture identifies that *"cause"* as the *creative power of God* (Gen. 1:1). In looking at the created world, every person should see abundant evidence of God's existence and power. *'Natural revelation'*, discussed in 1:19–20, refers to what everyone knows about God because of *what He has revealed about Himself in nature*. What He has revealed about Himself in Scripture is *'Special Revelation'*. *Natural revelation* makes people responsible to respond to their Creator in worship and submission, but it does not give sufficient information for them to experience salvation. *That is why everyone needs to hear the gospel!*

God has revealed Himself to us primarily in *four* different ways:

1.   *In Nature* (see Psalms 19:1)

2.   *In History* (e.g. Israel, Jews, Jesus Christ, etc.)

3.   *Through Scriptures* (Written Word of God)

4.   *Through His Holy Spirit* (who guides us to ALL truth)

We have no more excuses for ignoring God any longer. Let us turn to God – for He alone is the answer for all our needs!

*"Truly, these times of ignorance God overlooked, but **now commands all men everywhere to repent**, because He has appointed a day on which He will judge the world in righteousness by the Man whom He has ordained. He has given assurance of this to all by raising Him from the dead."* (Acts 17:30-31)

NOVEMBER 16   *Bible Reading: Romans Chapters 4-6*

WHAT IS THE 'REAL' SIGNIFICANCE OF WATER BAPTISM?

*"How shall we who died to sin live any longer in it? Or do you not know that as many of us as were baptized into Christ Jesus were **baptized into His death**? Therefore we were buried with Him through baptism into death, that just as Christ was raised from the dead by the glory of the Father, even so **we also should walk in newness of life**. For if we have been **united together in the likeness of His death**, certainly **we also shall be in the likeness of His resurrection**..."* (Romans 6:2-5)

In ancient times, baptism was an act to identify with a particular group. The word 'baptism' comes from the Greek word *'baptizo'* which means to dip, immerse or submerge. In the Jewish culture, baptism was a rite of passage for a Gentile who converted into Judaism. It was a purification rite of the washing away the old life of pagan thinking and embracing Jehovah as the One True God. It was John the Baptist who introduced baptism by inviting both Jews and Gentiles to the baptism of repentance in order to get right with God.

A Christian baptism or believer's baptism is associated with a confession of faith and repentance of sins just like an ancient soldier's oath of loyalty. It is a public confession and witness of the inward faith in the death and resurrection of Jesus Christ. It is associated with both repentance (Acts 2:38) and discipleship (Matthew 28:19), and indicates our union with Jesus Christ as we identify with His death, burial and resurrection.

For us who have died to the world and in Christ, the death of one way of life means that we have a new glorious normal reality so that we can walk in the 'newness of life'. Through baptism, we put on Christ (Gal. 3:27). *To be in Christ through baptism is to share in His life, in His death, and in His resurrection.* This is the real significance of baptism!

Jesus answered, "Most assuredly, I say to you, unless one is born of water and the Spirit, he cannot enter the kingdom of God." (John 3:5)

NOVEMBER 17   *Bible Reading: Romans Chapters 7-9*

GETTING A BETTER PERSPECTIVE OF OUR LIFE PROBLEMS

*"And we know that **all things work together for good to those who love God, to those who are the called according to His purpose.** For whom He foreknew, He also predestined to be conformed to the image of His Son, that He might be the firstborn among many brethren. Moreover whom He predestined, these He also called; whom He called, these He also justified; and whom He justified, these He also glorified."* (Romans 8:28-30)

Through this passage, Apostle Paul gives us an astounding truth - *whatever God permits to come into our lives is designed to conform us to the image of His Son!* Our lives are controlled by our wonderful God who has a wonderful plan for our lives. The next two verses give us a better understanding about God's divine program for our lives:

First of all, God *foreknew* us in *eternity past* (v. 29). God's foreknowledge has a purpose and insures our eventual repentance and belief in Jesus Christ. In due time, God has *called* us in *recent past* when we heard the gospel call (v. 30). When we responded to God's call, repented from our sins and accepted Jesus as our Lord and Savior, God *justified* us (declared us to be righteous). One day, we shall be *glorified* and reign with Christ! This is one of the strongest passages in the New Testament on the eternal security of the believer (John 6:37).

In the midst of our life problems, God wants to make us aware that He is working on every detail of our lives to the end established in His eternal purposes. This gives us a better perspective with regards to the many problems that trouble us many times. We need to understand that these problems are meant to develop us so that we can better understand God's purpose for our lives.

How can we make this passage work for us as we face tough, troubling times? Let us *affirm our trust in God's presence* that is with us always until the end of our lives. Let us *align our goals with God's purposes*, which are much greater than our wildest imagination. Let us *accept the reliability of God's promises*, which are more precious that anything we have in our possession.

"Beloved, now we are children of God; and it has not yet been revealed what we shall be, but we know that when He is revealed, we shall be like Him, for we shall see Him as He is. And everyone who has this hope in Him purifies himself, just as He is pure." (1 John 3:2-3)

NOVEMBER 18   *Bible Reading: Romans Chapters 10-12*

HOW SHOULD CHRISTIANS REACT TO EVIL?

"Repay no one evil for evil. Have regard for good things in the sight of all men. If it is possible, as much as depends on you, live peaceably with all men. Beloved, do not avenge yourselves, but rather give place to wrath; for it is written, 'Vengeance is Mine, I will repay,' says the Lord. Therefore 'if your enemy is hungry, feed him; if he is thirsty, give him a drink; for in so doing you will heap coals of fire on his head.' **Do not be overcome by evil, but overcome evil with good.***"* (Romans 12:17-21)

Repaying evil for evil is a common practice in this world. However, this delight in vengeance should have no place our lives if we are to be Christ-like. We must resist the tendency to avenge wrongs that are done to us. Vengeance is God's prerogative, and He will repay at the proper time and in the proper manner (Deut. 32:35). Lenski writes the following on this subject: *"God has long ago settled the whole matter about exacting justice from wrongdoers. Not one of them will escape. Perfect justice will be done in every case and will be done perfectly. If any of us interfered, it would be the height of presumption.ÿþ"*

Actually Christianity goes beyond non-resistance to *active benevolence*, and attempts to convert enemies by love. *"To heap live coals on a person's head"* means to *"make him ashamed of his hostility by surprising him with unconventional kindness."* The great African-American scientist, George Washington Carver, once said, *"I will never let another man ruin my life by making me hate him."* As a Christian believer he would not allow evil to conquer him!

Evil may tend to make us feel powerless. However, Apostle Paul instructs us that we should *'hate evil'* (v. 9), *'not repay evil with evil'* (v. 17) and *'not be overcome by evil'* (v. 21a). We should instead let the goodness of God shine through our lives, and overcome evil with good just as light overcomes darkness. We can be confident in the *providence of God* and the *certainty of His judgment.*

As Christian believers, we must resist the impulse to retaliate but rather we should promote our sanctification by doing good to those who do evil to us. Through this attitude we exhibit our life of transformation before a watching world. This can be done only through the phenomenal power of God's love in our lives. If we let God have His way, He will even use our enemies to build us and make us more like Christ!

"Finally, all of you be of one mind, having compassion for one another; love as brothers, be tenderhearted, be courteous; **not returning evil for evil or reviling for reviling, but on the contrary blessing,** *knowing that you were called to this, that you may inherit a blessing."* (1 Peter 3:8-9)

NOVEMBER 19   *Bible Reading: Romans Chapters 13-16*

LOVE IS THE ULTIMATE FULFILLMENT OF GOD'S LAW

Owe no one anything except to love one another, for **he who loves another has fulfilled the law.** *For the commandments, "You shall not commit adultery," "You shall not murder," "You shall not steal," "You shall not bear false witness," "You shall not covet," and if there is any other commandment, are all summed up in this saying, namely, "You shall love your neighbor as yourself." Love does no harm to a neighbor; therefore* **love is the fulfillment of the law.** (Romans 13:8-10)

In the above passage, Apostle Paul tells the Roman believers that it is their privilege to fulfill God's law by loving others. They should subjugate their beliefs/convictions to the *'law of love'* for *love truly fulfills the law* by leading everyone to peace and mutual edification.

Love is a debt that is never paid in full considering the fact how much Jesus has loved us and given His own life for us. *Love is the final summary of God's moral laws.* If we truly understood and completely followed the command to love one another, we would fulfill every social duty and would especially observe those commandments that are most fundamental in human relations (v. 9).

There are *two kinds* of debts: those *with the lender's consent* and *those without his consent.* It is the second kind of outstanding debt that Paul refers here as our obligation to love (agapç), which signifies a *deep, unselfish, superhuman affection for others.* This love *manifests itself in giving*, and generally in *sacrificial giving.* Thus, God so loved the world that He gave His only begotten Son (John 3:16), and Christ loved the church and gave Himself for her (Eph. 5:25).

Love is primarily a matter of the 'will' rather than 'emotions'. The fact that we are *commanded* to love indicates that it is something we can choose to do, and it can only be exhibited by the power of the indwelling Holy Spirit. *Love enables us to perfectly fulfill all our obligations*, whether to the state, to the citizens, or to God. Love for God and for our neighbors is our *highest motive for obedience* and the *ultimate fulfillment of God's law!*

If you really fulfill the royal law according to the Scripture, "You shall love your neighbor as yourself," you do well. (James 2:8) *For all the law is fulfilled in one word, even in this: "You shall love your neighbor as yourself." (Gal 5:14)*

NOVEMBER 20   *Bible Reading: 1 Corinthians Chapters 1-3*

FACING OUR 'ULTIMATE PERFORMANCE REVIEW'

"For no other foundation can anyone lay than that which is laid, which is Jesus Christ. Now if anyone builds on this foundation with gold, silver, precious stones, wood, hay, straw, each one's work will become clear; for the Day will declare it, because it will be revealed by fire; and the fire will test each one's work, of what sort it is. If anyone's work which he has built on it endures, he will receive a reward. If anyone's work is burned, he will suffer loss; but he himself will be saved, yet so as through fire." (1 Cor 3:11-15)

Apostle Paul describes in this passage the *ultimate performance review* that we will face one day when we stand before God and when He evaluates the worth of our lives on the earth. He uses the image of metal being purified in a refining fire (vv. 13–15). God's fire will burn away the worthless impurities, leaving only what is valuable.

Of the six types of materials mentioned, three are combustible and three are incombustible. Our service that has brought glory to God and blessing to people like teaching sound doctrine, living lives of fidelity to the truth, leading converts to spiritual maturity, etc. are comparable to gold, silver, and precious stones that will not be consumed by the fire, but actually be purified and increase in value. On the other hand, our work that has brought dishonor to God like providing inadequate/unsound teaching or compromising the truth by demonstrating a life-style that fails to model it, will be consumed by the fire and nothing will remain.

An interesting thought in connection with this verse is that the Word of God is sometimes likened to fire (Isa. 5:24, Jer. 23:29). The same Word of God which will test our service at the Judgment Seat of Christ is available to us now. If we are building in accordance with the teachings of the Bible, then our work will stand the test in that final judgment day!

The question to ask ourselves today is - *when the smoke clears on that day what will be left of our lives to display?* Let us build our lives on commodities that will stand the test of God's judgment. Let us give priority to things of lasting value every day. Let us live only for His glory!

"And behold, I am coming quickly, and My reward is with Me, **to give to everyone according to his work.** *I am the Alpha and the Omega, the Beginning and the End, the First and the Last."* (Rev 22:12-13)

NOVEMBER 21   *Bible Reading: 1 Corinthians Chapters 4-6*

KEEPING OUR BODIES HOLY AS 'TEMPLES' OF THE HOLY SPIRIT

"Flee sexual immorality. Every sin that a man does is outside the body, but he who commits sexual immorality sins against his own body. Or **do you not know that your body is the temple of the Holy Spirit who is in you,** *whom you have from God, and you are not your own? For you were bought at a price; therefore glorify God in your body and in your spirit, which are God's."* (1 Cor 6:18-20)

In the above passage, Apostle Paul warns us to *run away from sexual immorality* just as Joseph ran away when he was tempted to sin by Potiphar's wife (Gen. 39:1-12). Most sins have no direct effect on our bodies, but we reap the consequence of sexual immorality in our own bodies. For example, many of the recently discovered diseases (in most cases) like HIV AIDS and other venereal diseases are direct after effects of unrestrained sexual immorality. Sexual immorality truly has far-reaching effects along with great spiritual significance and social complications.

The *solemn truth* that we need to comprehend is that our bodies are *'temples of the Holy Spirit'*. We belong to God both *by creation* (when He had created us) and *by redemption* (when He had bought us back through His sacrificial death on the Cross with the price of His own precious blood). We should honor and care for our bodies as the very sanctuaries of God so that other people may *clearly see* that we belong to God alone!

What a special privilege it is for our bodies to be God's spiritual dwelling place! This reality has huge ramifications. God's residence in our bodies should transform us to live in such a way that brings glory to God. Our relationships, the way we serve our employers, the way we use our money, the way we treat our enemies and every other faucet of our lives should reflect the wonderful reality that God resides in our hearts. *Let that difference show!*

"I beseech you therefore, brethren, by the mercies of God, that you **present your bodies a living sacrifice, holy, acceptable to God,** *which is your reasonable service. And do not be conformed to this world, but be transformed by the renewing of your mind, that you may prove what is that good and acceptable and perfect will of God."* (Romans 12:1-2)

NOVEMBER 22 *Bible Reading: 1 Corinthians Chapters 7-9*

RUNNING FOR THE IMPERISHABLE CROWN

"Do you not know that those who run in a race all run, but one receives the prize? **Run in such a way that you may obtain it.** *And everyone who competes for the prize is* **temperate** *in all things. Now they do it to obtain a perishable crown, but we for an imperishable crown. Therefore I run thus:* **not with uncertainty.** *Thus I fight: not as one who beats the air. But I* **discipline my body** *and bring it into subjection, lest, when I have preached to others, I myself should become disqualified."* (1 Cor 9:24-27)

The Isthmian Games took place in a town near Corinth every two or three years and were second only to the Olympic Games in importance. Paul used these contests to illustrate how we should live the Christian life. In the above passage, Apostle Paul is encouraging us that we should all run in such a way that we may obtain the imperishable crown. How do we run this race of life and get the reward at the end? Below are *three things* to consider:

1. *Run purposefully keeping our end in mind:* Our Christian life is like a race in which we all have to run to be winners. It demands determination, a definiteness of purpose and a clear understanding of *"the race that is set before us, looking unto Jesus, the author and finisher of our faith"*. (Heb 12:1-2)

2. *Practice self-control & self-discipline:* In our Christian life race, we must practice self-mastery over our wants and desires. The

word 'temperate' (v. 25) carries the meaning of 'self-control' practiced by athletes who train to win. In order to do that they restrict themselves in all things: their diet, their activities, their associations, and probably even their friendships. One way of practicing self-control is by following this statement: *"All things are lawful for me, but all things are not helpful. All things are lawful for me, but I will not be brought under the power of any."* (1 Cor 6:12)

3. *Be faithful until the end*: Even when there are many reversals in life, we should keep on running. We should run faithfully spurred on with the knowledge that we are running to honor our King and we will receive the imperishable crown from Him. Greater than winning any prize will be hearing our beloved Master telling us: *"Well done Son/Daughter, you have done your part"*.

Today, let us be willing to set aside our self & selfish interests and focus towards our primary goal in life: to *obtain the imperishable crown* at the end of our life journey!

*"Not that I have already attained, or am already perfected; but **I press on**, that I may lay hold of that for which Christ Jesus has also laid hold of me. Brethren, I do not count myself to have apprehended; but one thing I do, forgetting those things which are behind and reaching forward to those things which are ahead, **I press toward the goal for the prize of the upward call of God in Christ Jesus.**"* (Phil 3:12-14)

NOVEMBER 23   *Bible Reading: 1 Corinthians Chapters 10-12*

WHY SHOULD WE OBSERVE THE LORD'S SUPPER?

"For as often as you eat this bread and drink this cup, you proclaim the Lord's death till He comes. Therefore whoever eats this bread or drinks this cup of the Lord in an unworthy manner will be guilty of the body and blood of the Lord. But let a man examine himself, and so let him eat of the bread and drink of the cup" (1 Cor 11:26-28)

On the night that our Lord Jesus was betrayed by one of His disciples, He took bread and gave thanks for it. Since the bread was typical of His body, Jesus was, in effect, thanking God that He had been given a human body in which He might come and die for the sins of the world. For us to partake of the bread is to remember how Jesus had allowed His body to be beaten and bruised for our sins. When Jesus took the cup after supper, He said that it was the *new* covenant which was ratified and sealed by His own blood (Heb 9:12). The foundation of this *new* covenant was laid through the cross. We receive all the benefits that were promised in this *new* covenant (Jeremiah 31:31–34; Hebrews 8:10–12) when we trust in the atoning death of our Lord Jesus Christ on our behalf.

The Lord's Supper is a memorial service left for us as we gather together as believer-priests to proclaim the Lord's death until He comes. It is designed to symbolize and communicate *seven distinct truths*:

1. *It is a memorial to remind us of the atonement of Christ* (vv. 24, 25)

2. *It signifies our fellowship as believers being part of Christ's body* (v. 18)

3. *It is an occasion to pause, reflect and examine our walk with Christ* (v. 28)

4. *It is an occasion to thank God for our salvation* (v. 24)

5. *It stands as a witness to Christ's death on our behalf* (v. 26)

6. *It is an occasion to celebrate our blessed hope that we have in Christ* (v. 26)

7. *It is an occasion to worship Christ for His finished work of atonement* (v. 26)

The Lord's Supper has a *past reference* to Christ's death. It has a *present reference* to our corporate participation in Him through faith. It has a *future reference* in that it is a pledge of His return. It encourages us to be faithful in our daily walk and in our expectation. This service of worship is a distinctive sacrament instituted for the church, and to be observed until our Lord Jesus Christ comes back. The ultimate realization of the Lord's Supper will be when we will one day celebrate the grand 'Marriage Supper of the Lamb' in New Jerusalem.

Let us be glad and rejoice and give Him glory, for the marriage of the Lamb has come, and His wife has made herself ready." And to her it was granted to be arrayed in fine linen, clean and bright, for the fine linen is the righteous acts of the saints. Then he said to me, "Write:

'Blessed are those who are called to the marriage supper of the Lamb!'"
And he said to me, "These are the true sayings of God." (Rev 19:7-9)

NOVEMBER 24   *Bible Reading: 1 Corinthians Chapters 13-16*

IT'S ALL ABOUT LOVE

"Love suffers long and is kind; love does not envy; love does not parade itself, is not puffed up; does not behave rudely, does not seek its own, is not provoked, thinks no evil; does not rejoice in iniquity, but rejoices in the truth; bears all things, believes all things, hopes all things, endures all things. Love never fails...And now abide faith, hope, love, these three; but the greatest of these is love." (1 Cor 13:4-8, 13)

To the Corinthian believers who were impatient, discontented, envious, inflated, selfish, unmindful of the feelings and interests of others, suspicious and resentful, Apostle Paul writes this beautiful treatise on love, which stands out as a literary gem of the New Testament. The believers had spiritual gifts, but they lacked spiritual graces and needed to be reminded why love is so important in the Christian life.

The attributes of true agape love is not described by feelings but in action items, listed below:

- Does not rival for attention ("envy")
- Does not brag on itself ("parade")
- Does not inflate its self-view ("puffed up")
- Does not tread on another's feelings ("rude")
- Does not take another's things ("seek its own")
- Does not take offense easily ("provoked")
- Does not keep a record of wrongs suffered ("no evil")
- Does not make unrighteousness its object of rejoicing ("rejoice in iniquity")
- Does celebrate others' achievements in righteousness ("rejoices in the truth")
- Does keep all things in confidence ("bears all things")
- Does know what God can do ("believes all things")
- Does hold out holy ambitions for others to achieve ("hopes all things")
- Does survive under every condition ("endures all things")

Love is the greatest of the graces because it is most useful to others. It is not self-centered but others-centered. Its clearest expression can be seen on Golgotha's hill. This is the kind of love that God shows to us. Love alone is eternal, for God is love (1 John 4:8). D. L. Moody has once said: *"God hates the great things in which love is not the motive power; but He delights in the little things that are prompted by a feeling of love."*

If we practice love, it will save us from the misuse of gifts and from the strife and divisions that have arisen as a result of their abuse. We can grow in love through the following *three ways:*

1. *Ponder God's love in Christ* as we reflect on how Jesus gave His life for us.

2. *Pray for the love of God* by asking God to give an understanding of His love and to teach us how to live that love in our relationships.

3. *Practice the love of God* by giving ourselves to love others. As the love of God grows in us, His love will flow out to others around us as well.

If someone says, "I love God," and hates his brother, he is a liar; for he who does not love his brother whom he has seen, how can he love God whom he has not seen? And this commandment we have from Him: that he who loves God must love his brother also. (1 John 4:20-21)

NOVEMBER 25   *Bible Reading: 2 Corinthians Chapters 1-3*

GOD <u>ALWAYS</u> LEADS US IN TRIUMPH IN CHRIST

*"Now thanks be to God **who always leads us in triumph in Christ**, and through us diffuses the fragrance of His knowledge in every place. For we are to God the fragrance of Christ among those who are being saved and among those who are perishing. To the one we are the aroma of death leading to death, and to the other the aroma of life leading to life."* (2 Cor 2:14-16)

Calvary was the mighty display of the victory that Christ had won for humankind. In the above passage, Apostle Paul regarded himself as a signal trophy of God's victorious power in Christ. His Almighty

429

Conqueror was leading him about, through all the cities of the Greek and Roman world, as an illustrious example of His power at once to subdue and to save.

In the above passage, Paul borrows a figure from the triumphal processions of Roman conquerors. Returning home after glorious victories, they would lead their captives along the streets of the capital. So Paul pictures the Lord Jesus marching as a conqueror from Troas to Macedonia, and leading His apostle in His train. *Wherever the Lord goes, through His servants, there is victory!* We have *five promises* from God about how He gives us victory:

1. God gives us victory *over the evil influences of people* (Psalms 44:5)

2. God gives us victory *over the power of the enemy* (Luke 10:19)

3. God gives us victory *over severe afflictions* (Romans 8:35)

4. God gives us victory *over worldly attractions* (1 John 5:4)

5. God will give us victory *over Satan ultimately* (Rev. 15:2)

We must grasp Paul's perspective on the unfailing success of God's work in the world today, and of those of us who participate in it. We must see our lives in the light of God's word and avoid discouragement because of the *apparent* failure of many of our activities. *Christ has conquered, and we are privileged to march in His triumphal procession!* Let us give our heartfelt thanks to God who *always* lead us in triumph *in* Christ!

"Yet in all these things <u>we are more than conquerors</u> through Him who loved us." (Romans 8:37)

NOVEMBER 26 *Bible Reading: 2 Corinthians Chapters 4-6*

CARRYING <u>TREASURE</u> IN OUR EARTHEN VESSELS

*"For we do not preach ourselves, but Christ Jesus the Lord, and ourselves your bondservants for Jesus' sake. For it is the God who commanded light to shine out of darkness, who has shone in our hearts to give the light of the knowledge of the glory of God in the face of Jesus Christ. **But we have this treasure in earthen vessels** that the excellence of the power may be of God and not of us."* (2 Cor 4:5-7)

In the above passage, Apostle Paul compares the conversion of a sinner to the entrance of light at the dawn of creation where God, who had commanded light to shine out of darkness (Gen. 1:3), has now *Himself* shone in our hearts. The material creation in Genesis began with light and so also does the spiritual creation when we are *'born again'* through the light of the gospel.

In ancient times it was a common practice to bury treasures inside clay jars. As these treasures were enclosed in earthen vessels, so the indwelling Christ lives within our earthly bodies. Jesus Christ, the *'Light of the World'* (John 8:12) came into our hearts when we accepted Him as our Lord and Savior. In doing so, *God has given us a wonderful treasure in our earthen vessels*, which is Christ *in us, the hope of glory* (Col. 1:27), and the salvation offered to those believing in His name (John 3:16). God does not shine in our hearts simply to give us this knowledge, but rather that through us this knowledge might shine to others. *We are not just the terminals of God's blessing but His channels and reflectors of His light!*

Now, in our frail human bodies we are carrying a treasure within us that will guide others to their heavenly destiny. This treasure is the *'glorious message of the gospel'*. Why has God planned that this treasure should be in earthen vessels? The answer is so that the excellence of the power may be of God and not of us. All the praise and glory must go to the Creator (God) and not the creature (humans).

One interesting comparison can be found in the book of Judges (chapter 7) where Gideon equipped his army of 300 men with trumpets, empty pitchers, and lamps within the pitchers. At the appointed signal, his men were to blow their trumpets and break the pitchers. When the pitchers were broken, the lamps shone out in brilliance. This terrified the enemy and they were defeated. Just as in Gideon's case the light only shone forth when the pitchers were broken, so it is in connection with the gospel. *Only when our human instruments (earthen vessels) are broken and yielded to the Lord can the gospel light shine forth through us in all its magnificence!*

By God's grace and power, let us live in *such a way* so that others can see Jesus living through us. Let us be living and shining vessels carrying of the glorious gospel of Jesus Christ every day!

"You are the light of the world. A city that is set on a hill cannot be hidden. Nor do they light a lamp and put it under a basket, but on a

lampstand, and it gives light to all who are in the house. Let your light so shine before men, that they may see your good works and glorify your Father in heaven." (Matt 5:14-16)

NOVEMBER 27   *Bible Reading: 2 Corinthians Chapters 7-9*

GOD LOVES A <u>CHEERFUL</u> GIVER

*"But this I say: He who sows sparingly will also reap sparingly, and he who sows bountifully will also reap bountifully. So let each one give as he purposes in his heart, not grudgingly or of necessity; for **God loves a cheerful giver**. And God is able to make all grace abound toward you, that you, always having all sufficiency in all things, may have an abundance for every good work."* (2 Cor 9:6-8)

In this key New Testament passage on giving, Apostle Paul appealed to the Corinthian believers to give to their needy brethren by citing the good example of their neighbor Christians (8:1–7). He then focused on the *supreme motive for giving - Jesus Christ's gift of Himself for needy people* (8:8–15), and explained the arrangements for collecting and delivering their gift (8:16–24) and his own plans to visit Corinth soon (9:1–5). He concluded by reviewing several benefits of generous giving: *the more we give, the more we will benefit* (9:6–15).

God loves a *cheerful giver* because *giving is the language of love*. *"God so loved that He gave!"* (John 3:16). *Does God really need our money?* No, the cattle on a thousand hills belong to Him, and if He needed anything, He would not tell us (Psalms 50:10–12). But *our heart's attitude is what is important to God*. He loves to see us so filled with the joy of the Lord that we want to share what we have for God's kingdom!

The *formula for giving* is found in 1 Cor. 16:2 where *three principles* can be seen:

1.   Our giving should be **regular**, *"on the first day of the week"*

2.   Our giving should be **systematic**, *"let each one of you lay something aside"*

3.   Our giving should be **proportionate** (to our income), *"as he may prosper"*

We should give *as an act of worship with preparation, purpose, and joy.* Then God will supply us with resources so that we will not only have a sufficiency ourselves, but so that we will be able to share what we have with others, and thus have abundance for every good work (v. 8). God will meet *all our needs* when we give sacrificially to God's kingdom (Phil. 4:19; Prov. 11:24-25). We will then enjoy *physical/material blessings* (Prov. 19:17; Isaiah 58:8; Psalms 41:1-3); *spiritual blessings* (v. 9-10; Acts 10:4, 44, 47); and *eternal blessings* (1 Tim. 6:18-19).

Let us also understand that *we cannot give our substance until we first give ourselves* (v. 5). When we belong to the Lord, we start looking for opportunities to give instead of excuses not to give. We are constant recipients of God's generous grace. God promises that if we will give of ourselves, He'll enable us to have an abundance of resources for the work to which He has called us (v. 8).

*"I beseech you therefore, brethren, by the mercies of God, that **you present your bodies a living sacrifice, holy, acceptable to God, which is your reasonable service.** And do not be conformed to this world, but be transformed by the renewing of your mind, that you may prove what is that good and acceptable and perfect will of God."* (Romans 12:1-2)

NOVEMBER 28   *Bible Reading: 2 Corinthians Chapters 10-13*

GOD'S STRENGTH IS MADE 'PERFECT' IN OUR WEAKNESS

*"And lest I should be exalted above measure by the abundance of the revelations, a thorn in the flesh was given to me, a messenger of Satan to buffet me, lest I be exalted above measure. Concerning this thing I pleaded with the Lord three times that it might depart from me. And He said to me, "My grace is sufficient for you, **for My strength is made perfect in weakness.**" Therefore most gladly I will rather boast in my infirmities, that the power of Christ may rest upon me. Therefore I take pleasure in infirmities, in reproaches, in needs, in persecutions, in distresses, for Christ's sake. **For when I am weak, then I am strong.**"* (2 Cor 12:7-10)

Our world prizes *strength* - the *physical strength* of athletes, the *financial strength* of companies, the *political strength* of office-holders, and the *military strength* of armies. But Apostle Paul put a new twist on our notion of *strength*: **God's strength is made perfect (complete, mature) in our weakness**. Our trials will remain but will always be accompanied by the enduring grace of God, when we put our trust on Him. *God's grace will be sufficient for what we may face in our lives!*

Despite human weaknesses, God's grace attains His purposes in a fallen world. When believers are without strength and look to God (v. 8), He provides power by His grace. This promise from God no doubt gave Paul strength and encouragement in subsequent sufferings. Paul's spiritual view was so clear that he could see his sufferings as reasons for rejoicing, because he knew that in them all of Christ's power was at work. In Paul's weaknesses, Christ's power was made more apparent to others. It would bring praise to the only One who deserved it!

Let us understand that both natural weakness and supernatural power are constantly at work in us, as they were in Paul and in Jesus. *The greater we sense our weakness, the more we can sense God's power.* Our success does not depend on our natural abilities but on God's power working in and through us. *Human weakness can be a profound blessing if it results in our depending more on God and less on self!*

In God's kingdom, greatness comes when we are willing to assume positions of weakness (Matt. 20:26). Weakness thus has a way of making us rely on God far more than our strengths do. It is when we are conscious of our own weakness and nothingness that we depend on the power of God. And it is only when we are thus cast on Him in complete dependence that His power is manifested to us, and *we are truly strong*!

"I can do all things through **Christ who strengthens me**." (Phil 4:13)

NOVEMBER 29   *Bible Reading: Galatians Chapters 1-3*

ARE WE 'TRULY' CRUCIFIED WITH CHRIST?

*"For I through the law died to the law that I might live to God. **I have been crucified with Christ**; it is no longer I who live, but Christ lives in me; and the life which I now live in the flesh I live by faith in the Son of God, who loved me and gave Himself for me."* (Gal 2:19-20)

The penalty for breaking the law is death (Rom. 6:23). As sinners by birth we have broken the law, so we are condemned to die. But Christ paid the penalty of the broken law for us by dying in our place. The only way we can now live for God is by being dead to the law. Apostle Paul died to the law in the death of Christ; he was crucified with Christ (v. 20), for he was united to Christ who died in his place (3:13; Rom. 4:25; 5:6). So too, he was raised with Christ and lived in relation to God (Col. 2:12; 3:1).

We also identify with Christ in His death to the Mosaic Law (Rom. 7:6). Our lives are no longer self-efforts in keeping the law, but our lives are empowered by the indwelling Spirit of Christ. Jesus did not die for us in order that we might go on living our lives as we choose. He died for us so that from now on He might be able to live His life in us. We now live by continual dependence on Christ, by yielding to Him and by allowing Him to live His life in us.

When we put our trust in Christ by accepting Him as our Lord and Savior, and publicly identifying ourselves with Christ through water baptism, God identifies us with His Son not only in the present and future but also in the past. Thus we can boldly say, *"When Christ died, I died. When Christ arose from the grave, I arose to newness of life. My old self-centered life died when I died with Christ. His Spirit-directed life began in me when I arose with Christ." Therefore in this sense our new lives are really a manifestation of the life of Christ!*

Let us always remember that the power of sin has died in us – no more self-centeredness and harboring greed, lust, pride or bitterness. We now live by faith in the Son of God, who has died for us and has given His life for us. We are crucified with Christ, and He has control over our lives now. *Have you ever turned your life over to the Lord Jesus with the prayer that His life might be manifest in your body? Are we 'truly' crucified with Christ?*

*"Now then, we are ambassadors for Christ, as though God were pleading through us: we implore you on Christ's behalf, **be reconciled to God**. For He made Him who knew no sin to be sin for us, that **we might become the righteousness of God in Him**."* (2 Cor 5:20-21)

NOVEMBER 30   *Bible Reading: Galatians Chapters 4-6*

THE MEANING OF 'TRUE' FREEDOM IN CHRIST

Stand fast therefore in the **liberty** *by which* **Christ has made us free,** *and do not be entangled again with a yoke of bondage. For you, brethren,* **have been called to liberty;** *only do not use liberty as an opportunity for the flesh, but* **through love serve one another.** *For all the law is fulfilled in one word, even in this: "You shall love your neighbor as yourself." But if you bite and devour one another, beware lest you be consumed by one another! I say then:* **Walk in the Spirit,** *and you shall not fulfill the lust of the flesh.* (Gal 5:1, 13-16)

Freedom is the prevailing cry of the world today. Yet even though Scripture speaks of a liberty that Christ offers (Gal. 5:1–12), some people resist Christianity as itself an obstacle to freedom.

What is the meaning of 'true' freedom in Christ? It is *not* the removal of moral restraints, but *the freedom to serve one another in love.* The gospel exchanges the oppressive bondage of legalism for the higher bondage of love. Liberty is freedom from exterior rule as we are no longer ruled by the law but by the Holy Spirit ruling from our hearts. A. T. Pierson says:

"True freedom is found only in obedience to proper restraint. A river finds liberty to flow, only between banks: without these it would only spread out into a slimy, stagnant pool. Planets, uncontrolled by law, would only bring wreck to themselves and to the universe. The same law which fences us in, fences others out; the restraints which regulate our liberty also insure and protect it. It is not control, but the right kind of control, and a cheerful obedience which make the free man.ÿþ"

We must daily walk and live in the Holy Spirit (v. 16) by the following:

1. We must believe that the Holy Spirit is within us, having been sent by God into our hearts (4:6).

2. In every spiritual confrontation we must yield to the Holy Spirit completely (v. 13).

3. We must depend on the Holy Spirit for help that will enable us to live a God-pleasing life (v. 5).

436

4. We should anticipate the effects of the Holy Spirit's help in our daily lives as we will not carry out the strong desires of our sinful nature (v 16).

Our freedom in Christ is costly, for it did cost Jesus His own life. In Jesus we stand free as the yoke of the law has been removed (Acts 15:6–11). Freedom brings with it the responsibility to serve as we use the faith God has given us to work through love in serving others (v. 6b). *Love motivates us to fulfill the law of God* (Rom. 13:8–14).

Are we walking in the Spirit? Are we experiencing 'true' freedom in Christ? Let us understand that as we yield to the Holy Spirit, the life of Christ manifests in our actions as we yield the fruit of the Spirit. Walking each moment by faith in God's word under the Spirit's control assures absolute victory over the desires of our sinful nature. *True Christian freedom is Christ-like freedom!*

"Therefore if the Son makes you free, you shall be free indeed." (John 8:36)

$\mathcal{D}ecember$

Bible Reading: Ephesians Chapters 1-3

UNDERSTANDING THE 'DIMENSIONS' OF GOD'S LOVE

*"For this reason I bow my knees to the Father of our Lord Jesus Christ, from whom the whole family in heaven and earth is named, that He would grant you, according to the riches of His glory, to be strengthened with might through His Spirit in the inner man, that Christ may dwell in your hearts through faith; that you, **being rooted and grounded in love, may be able to comprehend with all the saints what is the width and length and depth and height— to know the love of Christ which passes knowledge**; that you may be filled with all the fullness of God."* (Eph 3:14-19)

In the above passage, Apostle Paul is praying to God that we may be able to understand and appreciate God's love for us (v. 17). God loved us so much that He delivered His only begotten Son Jesus Christ for us (Rom. 8:32). The only permanent solution to the problem of sins that surface in our lives is to replace them with the love of God. The more we are filled with God's love, the less there is room for anything else in our lives.

The way that we can be rooted and grounded in God's love is through Jesus Christ who dwells in our hearts through faith, by which we are filled with the fullness of God (v. 19). At the same time, *we should be able to comprehend the width, length, depth and height of God's love*:

·   **Width** *of God's love*: Encompasses the entire world (John 3:16)
·   **Length** *of God's love*: Forever, through all generations (1 Cor. 13:8; Eph. 3:21)

438

- **Depth** *of God's love*: Even down to the cross at Calvary (Phil. 2:8)
- **Height** *of God's love*: Even up to heaven, our final destination (1 John 3:1-2)

The *width* of God's love (2:11-18) refers to the wideness of God's grace in saving Jews and Gentiles, and then incorporating them into the church. The *length* of God's love (1:4) extends from eternity past to eternity future. We were chosen in Christ before the foundation of the world (1:4). As to the *depth* of God's love, we were sunk in a pit of unspeakable sin (2:1-3) and degradation from where Christ picked us up and gave us a new lease of life (Psalms 40:1-3). The *height* of God's love can be seen from the fact that we have not only been raised up with Christ, but also enthroned in Him in heaven to share His glory forever (2:6).

Thus, Apostle Paul desired that we would apprehend the love of Christ, even though a fuller comprehension of that love is impossible because it is beyond our wildest imagination. *Instead, let us appreciate Christ's love by loving other people genuinely even as He has loved us! "This is My commandment, that **you love one another** as I have loved you. Greater love has no one than this, than to lay down one's life for his friends. You are My friends if you do whatever I command you." (John 15: 12-14)

DECEMBER 2   *Bible Reading: Ephesians Chapters 4-6*

IS THERE ANY AGE-LIMIT FOR HONORING OUR PARENTS?

Children, obey your parents in the Lord, for this is right. "Honor your father and mother," which is the first commandment with promise: "that it may be well with you and you may live long on the earth." (Eph 6:1-3)

As Apostle Paul about to end his letter to the church of Ephesus, he veers away from giving general doctrinal directions to the believers as a whole, and targets specific relationships: husband-wife (5:22-33), children-parents (6:1-3), fathers-children (6:4), and servant-masters (6:5-9). Among these relationships, children-parents relationship has been affected greatly by a lifestyle that promotes a more casual and friendly approach. Many children do not respect or honor parents any more, which may be due to many relevant factors.

However, when we examine the Bible, God has clearly established some critical rules in this relationship that does not change in our post-modern age and times. Children should obey their parents 'in the Lord' and 'honor their parents' without any restrictions. This is so important for God that He has purposely included this relationship (unlike the others mentioned above) in the 'Ten Commandments' and added a promise of longevity for obedience. Apostle Paul has quoted this commandment as he has also commanded all children to obey and respect their parents...always.

In the book 'The Gift of Blessing', Gary Smalley and John Trent write the following:

"When Paul tells us to honor our parents, he is telling us that they are worthy of high value and respect. Some people treat their parents as if they are a layer of dust on a table. Dust weighs almost nothing and can be swept away with a brush of the hand. Dust is a nuisance and an eyesore that clouds any real beauty the table might have. Paul tells us that such an attitude should not be a part of how any child views his or her parents, and for good reason. If we fail to honor our parents, we not only do what is wrong and dishonor God, but we also literally drain ourselves of life!"

So, is there any age-limit for honoring parents? In a recent devotion of 'Our Daily Bread' (dated Nov 11, 2011), the author (Dennis Fisher) has emphasized that there is no age-limit for honoring our parents:

*"For **young children**, this means obeying parents. For **teenagers**, it indicates showing respect for Mom and Dad even if you think you know more than they do. For **young adults**, this means including your parents in your life. And for **those in middle-age and beyond**, it means making sure that parents are cared for as they move into old age or their health declines".*

Let us strive to honor our parents all our lives as God desires, knowing that their days are numbered on this earth. As one New Testament commentary says that to honor parents is to *"treat him/her with the deference, respect, reverence, kindness, courtesy, and obedience which his/her station in life...demands!"*

'PRESSING ON' TOWARDS OUR GOAL BY FOCUSING ON CHRIST

*"Not that I have already attained, or am already perfected; but **I press on**, that I may lay hold of that for which Christ Jesus has also laid hold of me. Brethren, I do not count myself to have apprehended; but one thing I do, forgetting those things which are behind and reaching forward to those things which are ahead, **I press toward the goal for the prize of the upward call of God in Christ Jesus.**"* (Phil 3:12-14)

In the above passage, Apostle Paul exhorts us that we must focus and prioritize on what matters most in our eternal future. We must not be distracted by lesser things that try to grab our attention every day. Rather, we must be focused on *"one thing"* which is a lifetime pursuit of becoming more like Jesus Christ, our ultimate model. God has already predestined us to be confirmed to the image of His Son Jesus Christ (Romans 8:29), and that is where we should focus all our energy during our lifetime.

We have a choice every day: either to look back at our failures, our disappointments, our struggles or to move forward by shedding every sin and weight that pulls us back in the race set before us (Heb. 12:1). As we move forward, we should focus our sight on our Lord Jesus Christ who has already set Himself as an example before us. He is both the author and finisher of our faith (Heb. 12:2). Jesus truly is *"the prize of the upward call of God"* (v. 14*). Let us seek to be shaped in the image of Christ as we look forward to spending eternity with Him!*

Our *"upward call of God in Christ Jesus"* includes all the purposes that God had in mind in saving us. It includes salvation, conformity to Christ, a home in heaven, and numerous other spiritual blessings. Let us remember that *our goal* would be to *finish our life's journey fulfilling God's purposes for us.* The prize awaiting us would be the *crown of righteousness* which God has already prepared for us!

This is what Apostle Paul tells us about himself towards the close of his life's journey: *"For I am already being poured out as a drink offering, and the time of my departure is at hand. I have fought the good fight, **I have finished the race**, I have kept the faith. Finally, **there is laid up for me the crown of righteousness**, which the Lord, the righteous Judge,* *will give to me on that Day, and not to me only but also to all who have loved His appearing."* (2 Tim 4:6-8)

DECEMBER 4   *Bible Reading: Colossians Chapters 1-4*

SEEKING 'ONLY' THINGS THAT 'REALLY MATTER

"If then you were raised with Christ, seek those things which are above, where Christ is, sitting at the right hand of God. Set your mind on things above, not on things on the earth. For you died, and your life is hidden with Christ in God. When Christ who is our life appears, then you also will appear with Him in glory." (Col 3:1-4)

In the above passage, Apostle Paul exhorts us to set our minds on heavenly things that *'really matter'*. When we have our minds fixed on *heaven* and our eyes fixed on *Jesus*, then naturally we will hold loosely the things that are on the earth. We will then be always reminded that *"we have died to sin and to the world, and our lives are now hidden with Christ in God"*. We will not be anxious when bad things happen in our lives. Just like an object lying at the bottom of the ocean is unruffled by the storms and the tumultuous waves on the surface, our frustrations will turn into songs of praise when we have put our confidence on the 'Rock of Ages'!

What are the things we should seek that 'really matter'? They include obtaining a deeper knowledge of Christ, having a closer fellowship with Him, experiencing His resurrection power in our daily living, being victorious over sin (Col. 3:5–11), developing our godly virtues (vv. 12–17), fulfilling our domestic and social responsibilities (3:18–4:1), having an effective prayer life (4:2) and be fruitful in witnessing to others (4:3–6).

As a child of God, we have said goodbye to our former way of life, and have entered upon a completely new life of the risen Lord Jesus Christ. So, we should view things not as they appear to our natural eyes but only in reference to their importance to God and to eternity. A. T. Robertson writes:

"The baptized life means that the Christian is seeking heaven and is thinking heaven. His feet are upon the earth, but his head is with the stars. He is living like a citizen of heaven here on earth."ӱþ

Let us continually discipline ourselves to focus on eternal realities, instead of the temporal realities of this earth since our lives are no longer dictated by this world but are hidden with Christ. *Let us set your mind on things that 'really matter', and seek to experience all that we have in Christ!*

DECEMBER 5   *Bible Reading: 1 Thessalonians Chapters 1-3*

ROLE OF THE CHURCH IN SPREADING THE GOSPEL

*"For our gospel did not come to you in word only, but also in power, and in the Holy Spirit and in much assurance, as you know what kind of men we were among you for your sake. **And you became followers of us and of the Lord**, having received the word in much affliction, with joy of the Holy Spirit, so that **you became examples to all in Macedonia and Achaia who believe. For from you the word of the Lord has sounded forth, not only in Macedonia and Achaia, but also in every place. Your faith toward God has gone out, so that we do not need to say anything."* (1 Thess 1:5-8)

In the above passage, Apostle Paul is commending the church in Thessalonica for their exemplary living and effective witness, as they conveyed the gospel most effectively by example and also by word-of-mouth. In a way, the believers in church of Thessalonica were practicing 'show-and-tell'. They were 'showing' to their unbelieving world of their extraordinary faith in Christ, and also sharing the living gospel through words. Thus, the Thessalonians became model Christians and they are good example for us to emulate.

The gospel of the Lord Jesus Christ is God's great plan for bringing people into a living relationship with Him. It is sobering to think that people are supposed to be able to see Christ in us. We should be able to say with Paul, *"Imitate me, just as I also imitate Christ"* (1 Cor. 11:1). We are intended to be channels of our blessings to others who do not know Christ. God shines in our hearts so that the light might shine out to others (2 Cor. 4:6). As we focus on Jesus, we will reflect His image to others (2 Cor. 3:18).

Sharing our faith is a combination of spontaneous conversation about God and premeditated ideas about the gospel. The following is a set of practical steps (Courtesy: The Open Bible) to take in witnessing for Christ:

1.   *Regularly talk about God.* Sprinkle your ordinary conversation with occasional references to God's activity in your life. It is much easier to share your faith when your friends know God is an integral part of your affairs.

2.   *Prepare your testimony.* Learn to describe your pre-Christian life, your encounter with Christ, and subsequent changes in your life in fewer than five minutes. If you became a Christian as a child, focus on the impact Christ has had on your adult life.

3.   *Learn a brief summary of the gospel.* It will be good to learn a condensed version of the gospel, for example: Four Spiritual Laws, Roman Road of Salvation, etc.

For I am not ashamed of the gospel of Christ, for it is the power of God to salvation for everyone who believes, for the Jew first and also for the Greek. For in it the righteousness of God is revealed from faith to faith; as it is written, "The just shall live by faith." (Romans 1:16-17)

DECEMBER 6   *Bible Reading: 1 Thessalonians Chapters 4-5*

JESUS CHRIST is COMING SOON - ARE YOU READY?

"For the Lord Himself will descend from heaven with a shout, with the voice of an archangel, and with the trumpet of God. And the dead in Christ will rise first. Then we who are alive and remain shall be caught up together with them in the clouds to meet the Lord in the air. And thus we shall always be with the Lord. Therefore comfort one another with these words." (1 Thess 4:16-18)

Just as the Old Testament foretold the first coming of Jesus through the prophets, Apostle Paul clearly states that Jesus Christ Himself is coming back the second time. The following observations can be made about the above verses:

· This is a message of comfort *for born-again believers* today.

· This event could happen at *any time in the near future.*

· Christ is coming down from heaven for *His bride - the church.*

· The church will be escorted by Christ to heaven after this event.

The exact order of events at Christ's coming is given for our benefit. It will begin with *a shout*, with *the voice of an archangel*, and with the *trumpet of God*. Some Bible scholars feel that *the shout* is the voice of the Lord Jesus Himself which raises the dead (John 5:25; 11:43, 44). The *voice of an archangel* may be to summon the angels as a military escort to accompany the Lord and His saints through enemy territory back to heaven (Luke 16:22). The *trumpet of God* is the same as the last trumpet (1 Cor. 15:52) that calls the saints to their eternal blessing.

The *air* is Satan's sphere (Eph. 2:2), so this is a triumphal gathering in open defiance of the devil right in his own stronghold. The bodies of the *dead in Christ* will rise first. Then the *living righteous believers* will be caught up together with them in the clouds to meet the Lord Jesus in mid air. This event is also described by the word *"Rapture"* (a snatching away).

The *Rapture* is thus the first phase of Christ's return, involving every righteous Christian alive at that time, as they will be caught up to meet Christ in the clouds instantaneously receiving glorified bodies. All those who have died *"in Christ"* will be resurrected as well. Then, we shall be forever with the Lord! What a glorious *'blessed hope'* we have, so let us comfort one another with this truth. Let us seriously prepare ourselves for this great event, *for Jesus is coming sooner than we anticipate!*

"Watch therefore, for you do not know what hour your Lord is coming. But know this that if the master of the house had known what hour the thief would come, he would have watched and not allowed his house to be broken into. Therefore **you also be ready, for the Son of Man is coming at an hour you do not expect.***" (Matt 24:42-44)

DECEMBER 7   *Bible Reading: 2 Thessalonians Chapters 1-3*

IDLENESS IS THE DEVIL'S PLAYGROUND

"For you yourselves know how you ought to follow us, for we were not disorderly among you; nor did we eat anyone's bread free of charge, but worked with labor and toil night and day, that we might not be a burden to any of you, not because we do not have authority, but to make ourselves an example of how you should follow us. For even when we

were with you, we commanded you this: **If anyone will not work, neither shall he eat.** *For we hear that there are some who walk among you in a disorderly manner, not working at all, but are busybodies. Now those who are such we command and exhort through our Lord Jesus Christ that they* **work in quietness and eat their own bread.**" (2 Thess 3:7-12)

Apostle Paul made tents in order to provide for his needs whenever this became necessary on his missionary journeys (Acts 18:1-3). He did not abandon his tent-making work even though he was expecting Christ to come back at any moment (1 Thess. 4:17a). No one could accuse Paul of planting himself in someone's home and eating the food which someone else's toil had earned. He earned his own living while he was preaching the gospel. This meant long days and weary nights, but Paul was determined that he would not be a burden to anyone!

The teaching that Christ could return at any moment had led some of the believers in Thessalonica into idleness. They had quit their jobs and were simply waiting for Him to come. After giving his own example, Apostle Paul makes a general statement: *If a person will not work, he/she should not eat!* This statement applies to those *unwilling to work,* <u>not</u> to those *unable to work.* Let us understand that *idleness breeds sin.* Those who are disorderly, not working at all, become busybodies, causing trouble and division in the church.

Paul's example also bears upon the reputation of churches and ministries today. *Is there any reason why modern Christian leaders shouldn't at least consider doing as Paul did—earning a living outside the ministry to support their basic needs?* Dorothy L. Sayers has made the following statement:

"Work is not primarily a thing one does to live, but the thing one lives to do. It is, or should be, the full expression of the worker's faculties, the thing in which he finds spiritual, mental and bodily satisfaction, and the medium in which he offers himself to God."

We are thus commanded and exhorted by Apostle Paul to work with the best of our ability and earn our own living to take care of our own needs. *This is a good testimony that glorifies God!*

"And whatever you do, do it heartily, as to the Lord and not to men, knowing that from the Lord you will receive the reward of the inheritance; for you serve the Lord Christ." (Col 3:23-24) *"Let him who*

stole steal no longer, but rather let him labor, working with his hands what is good, that he may have something to give him who has need." (Eph 4:28)

DECEMBER 8   *Bible Reading: 1 Timothy Chapters 1-3*

WE ARE RESPONSIBLE TO PRAY FOR OUR LEADERS

"Therefore I exhort first of all that supplications, prayers, intercessions, and giving of thanks be made for all men, for kings and all who are in authority, that we may lead a quiet and peaceable life in all godliness and reverence. For this is good and acceptable in the sight of God our Savior, who desires all men to be saved and to come to the knowledge of the truth." (1 Tim 2:1-4)

Prayer moves the hand that governs the world. Prayer is both a *privilege* and an *obligation*: it is a *privilege* for us to have audience with the Almighty God, and it is an *obligation* for we are debtors to all with reference to the good news of salvation (Romans 1:14). Apostle Paul lists *four* aspects of prayer—*supplications, prayers, intercessions,* and *giving of thanks,* which the Believer's Bible Commentary has distinguished as follows:

· *Supplication* is the *earnest pleading* of *specific requests and needs.*
· *Prayers* cover all kinds of our *reverent approaches to God.*
· *Intercessions* are those forms of petition in which we address God on behalf of others.
· *Giving of thanks* describes prayer in which we rehearse the grace and kindness of our Lord, and pour out our hearts in gratitude to Him.

Thus, we should be *humble, worshipful, trustful,* and *thankful* when we pray. In the above passage, in particular Apostle Paul is exhorting his spiritual son Timothy that he is responsible to pray for his leaders – *whether political, government, spiritual, work-related, etc.* – anyone who is an authority figure. The reasons for that are because authorities are *ordained of God* (Rom. 13:1), and they are *ministers of God to us for good* (Rom. 13:4).

This instruction takes special meaning when we remember that Apostle Paul wrote this letter in the days of Nero. The terrible persecutions which were inflicted on the Christians by this wicked ruler did not affect the fact that Christians should pray for their government leaders. The reason Apostle Paul gives is that we may lead a quiet and peaceable life in all godliness and reverence (v. 2).

It is for *our own good* that our government should be stable and that the country be preserved from revolution, civil war, turmoil, and anarchy. We must pray for those who are in authority over us if we wish to reap the benefits of good government, which is a prized gift from God for the church's welfare and advancement of the gospel. This prayer is good and acceptable in the sight of God as well (v. 3).

To influence our leaders for God, we need to intercede on their behalf before God. God is the ultimate Sovereign. He is in control, and our prayers affect decisions at the highest level. God hears the prayers of the righteous (Prov. 15:29), and God will turn the leader's heart as He wishes as an answer to our prayers, as read in Prov. 21:1: *"The king's heart is in the hand of the Lord, like the rivers of water; He turns it wherever He wishes."*

DECEMBER 9 *Bible Reading: 1 Timothy Chapters 4-6*

WHAT IS BETTER THAN PHYSICAL EXERCISES?

"But reject profane and old wives' fables, and exercise yourself toward godliness. **For bodily exercise profits a little, but godliness is profitable for all things**, *having promise of the life that now is and of that which is to come. This is a faithful saying and worthy of all acceptance."* (1 Tim 4:7-9)

In this passage, Apostle Paul compares Christian service to an athletic regimen as he speaks of doing exercises that has godliness as its end result. Instead of wasting time on useless myths, we should exercise our minds, intellect and will power towards attaining godliness. Such exercise involves reading and studying the Bible, prayer, meditation, obeying God's Word daily, fellowshipping with other believers, and other acts of Christian service. Stock says, *"There is no such thing as drifting into godliness; the 'stream of tendency' is against us."* There must be exercise and effort from our part!

Paul compares two kinds of exercises: *'physical exercises'* and *'exercises to attain godliness'*. Physical exercise has certain values for our bodies, but these values are limited and of short duration. Godliness, on the other hand, is good for our spirit, soul, and body, and is not only for our time on earth but for eternity as well. Godliness yields the greatest joy in this life, and it holds the promise of great rewards in eternity.

Let us understand that *discipline in godliness affects both our present and future lives.* Let us put *at least* as much effort into our spiritual lives as we do in our recreation and hobbies – this will make such a great difference! Physical exercise is important, but spiritual exercise is even more essential. *Both discipline and devotion are needed to make a winning athlete and an effective Christian!*

"Therefore I run thus: not with uncertainty. Thus I fight: not as one who beats the air. But I discipline my body and bring it into subjection, lest, when I have preached to others, I myself should become disqualified." (1 Cor 9:26-27)

DECEMBER 10   *Bible Reading: 2 Timothy Chapters 1-4*

HOW CAN WE GET APPROVAL FROM GOD?

"Be diligent to **present yourself approved to God**, *a worker who does not need to be ashamed, rightly dividing the word of truth."* (2 Tim 2:15)

Apostle Paul is counseling his beloved spiritual son Timothy (1:2) to be *"diligent"* (which implies constant earnest effort) to get God's approval since that is what matters most. Approval means one has been put to the test and measures up, thus winning the approval of the person testing him/her. Timothy's efforts should involve a total effort of his mind, emotion, and will. Apostle Paul counsels Timothy that he should make earnest efforts to properly interpret the Word of God.

Truth defines the nature of Scripture. It is a beacon of truth in the darkness of all kinds of falsehoods. As a teacher of the Bible, Timothy should make every effort to handle God's Word accurately. Failure to do so will ultimately lead to divine judgment (see James 3:1).

In the Greek Old Testament, the word *"rightly dividing"* is used in Prov. 3:6; 11:5 to depict God's provision of a straight path for the righteous. This is used by a skilled craftsman cutting something straight. Paul encouraged Timothy to handle the word of truth in a straight way, like a road that goes straight to its goal, without being turned aside by useless debates. All of the Word of God is true. There are no contradictions when rightly laid out. We cannot add to nor take away anything from God's Word (Rev 22:19).

For us, this exhortation means that we should take time to study the Bible diligently while prayerfully asking guidance from the Holy Spirit to reveal the truth that God has intended through His Word. It also means that we should teach the truth directly and correctly. We need to *apply ourselves* first to study God's Word and then *apply His Word* in our daily living. *That is how we can get God's approval.*

"For the word of God is living and powerful, and sharper than any two-edged sword, piercing even to the division of soul and spirit, and of joints and marrow, and is a discerner of the thoughts and intents of the heart." (Heb 4:12)

December 11   *Bible Reading: Titus Chapters 1-3*

LEARN TO MAINTAIN 'GOOD WORKS'

*"This is a faithful saying, and these things I want you to affirm constantly, that **those who have believed in God should be careful to maintain good works.** These things are good and profitable to men. **And let our people also learn to maintain good works,** to meet urgent needs, that they may not be unfruitful."* (Titus 3:8, 14)

A major theme in this letter of Apostle Paul to Titus is *good works* (1:16; 2:7, 14; 3:1, 8, 14). Paul is emphasizing that what he has written (vv. 4–8) is a trustworthy statement, one that is central to the Christian faith. These things are good and profitable, and emphasize the *practical benefit of good works. People who are busy for the Lord do not have time for useless arguments!*

Titus was to teach the other Christians to show hospitality, to care for the sick and afflicted, and to be generous toward those who were in need. Instead of working merely to meet their own needs and wants, they should have the distinctly Christian vision of earning money in order to share with the less privileged (Eph. 4:28b). This would save them from the misery of selfishness and the tragedy of a wasted, unfruitful life.

A recurring theme throughout the New Testament is that *believers should live up to their holy calling.* They should continue being sanctified (Heb. 10:14, 23–26). Justification is solely a gift from God, but we will be rewarded according to what we do on this earth (Rev. 22:12). What a tragedy it will be for some to stand ashamed at Christ's return (1 John 2:28). *How much better it will be to abound in good works which the Holy Spirit empowered us to do!*

"The night is far spent, the day is at hand. Therefore let us cast off the works of darkness, and let us put on the armor of light. Let us walk properly, as in the day, not in revelry and drunkenness, not in lewdness and lust, not in strife and envy. But put on the Lord Jesus Christ, and make no provision for the flesh, to fulfill its lusts." (Romans 13:12-14)

DECEMBER 12   *Bible Reading: Philemon Chapter 1*

UNDERSTANDING THE DEPTH OF GOD'S LOVE

"Therefore, though I might be very bold in Christ to command you what is fitting, yet for love's sake I rather appeal to you—being such a one as Paul, the aged, and now also a prisoner of Jesus Christ— I appeal to you for my son Onesimus, whom I have begotten while in my chains, who once was unprofitable to you, but now is profitable to you and to me." (Philemon 1:8-11)

The background of Apostle Paul's letter from his prison to Philemon is to ask for a favor through an appeal. Philemon's slave, Onesimus stole from his master and ran away to Rome where he had an encounter with Paul. Paul led Onesimus to the saving knowledge of Jesus, so this runaway slave became a Christian believer. How should Paul deal with Onesimus now? Should he allow him to stay in Rome knowing that he has offended both his master Philemon and God in stealing and running away?

Instead, Paul writes a very personal letter to his *"beloved friend and fellow laborer"* (v. 1) on behalf of Onesimus requesting that Philemon receive Onesimus back as a beloved brother and no longer as a slave (v. 15). He would pay for any loss from his personal account (vv. 18-19).

The name Onesimus means *'profitable'*. But when he ran away, Philemon was probably tempted to call him a worthless rascal. Paul says, in effect, *"Yes, he was useless as far as you were concerned, but now he is useful to you and to me."* The slave who was returning to Philemon was a better slave than the one who had run away!

We can understand the depth of God's love through this moving story. On the cross, Jesus paid the price of our sins because He loved us so much. *"For when we were still without strength, in due time Christ died for the ungodly. For scarcely for a righteous man will one die; yet perhaps for a good man someone would even dare to die. But God demonstrates His own love toward us, in that while we were still sinners, Christ died for us."* (Romans 5:6-8)

How can we repay the love of God? Only through obeying God's commandments, for this is what Jesus told when He was on earth: *"If you love Me, keep My commandments."* (John 14:15)

DECEMBER 13   *Bible Reading: Hebrews Chapters 1-3*

THERE'S SOMETHING THAT WE NEED TO DO 'TODAY'

*"Beware, brethren, lest there be in any of you an evil heart of unbelief in departing from the living God; but **exhort one another daily, while it is called "Today,"** lest any of you be hardened through the deceitfulness of sin. For we have become partakers of Christ if we hold the beginning of our confidence steadfast to the end, while it is said: "Today, if you **will hear His voice, do not harden your hearts as in the rebellion."*** (Heb 3:12-15)

The above passage gives us an important application drawn for us from Israel's experience from Psalm 95:7, 8, most of who hardened their hearts and rebelled against God and the leaders God had placed over them. The way to avoid this is through mutual exhortation. Especially in days of difficulty and distress, we should be daily urging others not to go back on their Christian commitments.

Let us understand that serious losses are awaiting unbelieving believers who refuse to listen to God and hardens their hearts deliberately. People with hard hearts know the truth but resist it and refuse to obey it. They know that God chastens disobedient children, but they almost defy God to act. They think they can sin and get away with it. The first step toward a hard heart is neglect of the Word of God (Heb. 2:1–4), not taking it seriously. It is either *"hearing"* or *"hardening."*

Christ saves completely those who come to God through Him (7:25), but we must guard our own and each other's endurance by encouraging one another as the author does throughout this letter (13:22). This is an important stronghold to resist the temptation of sin, the world and Satan. Constant encouragement in the midst of a caring fellowship will help believers remain faithful to God.

The writer of Hebrews tells us that **there is something we need to do today and everyday of our lives** – we need to exhort others and receive exhortation from others based on God's Word *on a daily basis.* The great benefit from this is that our hearts will not become hardened through sinning before God on a constant basis. Through mutual exhortation only we can remain true to God and His Holy Word!

*"Let us hold fast the confession of our hope without wavering, for He who promised is faithful. And let us consider one another in order to stir up love and good works, not forsaking the assembling of ourselves together, as is the manner of some, **but exhorting one another, and so much the more** as you see the Day approaching."* (Heb 10:23-25)

DECEMBER 14   *Bible Reading: Hebrews Chapters 4-6*

JESUS CHRIST IS OUR 'COMPASSIONATE' HIGH PRIEST TODAY

"Seeing then that we have a great High Priest who has passed through the heavens, Jesus the Son of God, let us hold fast our confession. For we do not have a High Priest who cannot sympathize with our weaknesses, but was in all points tempted as we are, yet without sin. Let us therefore come boldly to the throne of grace that we may obtain mercy and find grace to help in time of need." (Heb 4:14-16)

The writer of Hebrews has already introduced Jesus Christ as our great High Priest earlier as follows: *"Therefore, holy brethren, partakers of the heavenly calling, consider the Apostle and High Priest of our confession, Christ Jesus"* (Heb 3:1). He is our great High Priest who is seated in His heavenly throne on the right hand of God the Father (Rom. 8:34). He was both human (Jesus) and divine (Christ), who can truly sympathize and empathize with us even though He was the sinless perfection who *knew no sin* (2 Cor. 5:21), who *committed no sin* (1 Pet. 2:22), and *no sin was seen in Him* (1 John 3:5).

Our state of total transparency before a sinless and sympathetic God ought to encourage us to come boldly before Him, seeking *mercy* and *grace*. *Mercy* refers to the remission and removal of our sins the punishment of which *we do deserve*, while *grace* refers to us receiving spiritual gifts the blessings *we don't deserve*.

God's throne has now become to us a *'throne of grace'* through the mediation of our High Priest at God's right hand (Heb 8:1; 12:2). We approach this *throne of grace, not of judgment*, obtaining *mercy for the past* and *grace for the present and future*. Our confidence to approach Him boldly is based on the knowledge that *He died to save us* and that *He lives to keep us*. He will welcome us with open arms when we go to Him in prayer.

Only Christianity provides such boldness for sinful men before a holy God, and that boldness is possible only because of our High Priest, Jesus Christ. The sobering thought of our complete exposure before God draws us to the merciful High Priest who, having been tempted can help us in our weakness. He *lives to intercede for us* (7:25) and *to help us to do His will* (13:20–21).

"And now, little children, abide in Him, that when He appears, we may have confidence and not be ashamed before Him at His coming." (1 John 2:28)

DECEMBER 15   *Bible Reading: Hebrews Chapters 7-9*

ARE WE 'EAGERLY' WAITING FOR CHRIST TO RETURN?

*"And as it is appointed for men to die once, but after this the judgment, so Christ was offered once to bear the sins of many. To those who **eagerly** wait for Him He will appear a second time, apart from sin, for salvation."* (Heb 9:27-28)

The writer of Hebrews presents a contrast between the Old and the New Covenant in the above passage. Under the Old Covenant, the law condemned sinners to die and face the judgment. However under the New Covenant Christ, as God's 'perfect sacrifice', was offered once to bear all the sins of humankind. He finished that work at the cross, but will come to take us to His home in heaven. This will be the culmination of our salvation; we will receive glorified bodies and be forever beyond the reach of sin.

The expression, those who 'eagerly' wait for Him, is a description of all *true* believers who belong to Christ (1 Cor. 15:23) - who are *"the dead in Christ"* and *"we who are alive and remain"* (1 Thess. 4:16, 17). Hebrews 9:24–28 mentions three appearances of Jesus Christ: a *past appearance for our salvation* (v. 26), a *present appearance for our sanctification* (v. 24), and a *future appearance for our glorification* (v. 28). This may be described further as follows:

1. *Jesus has appeared* (v. 26). This refers to the first time when He came to earth to save us from the *penalty* of sin (the past tense of salvation).
2. *Jesus now appears* (v. 24). This refers to His present ministry to save us from the *power* of sin (the present tense of salvation).
3. *Jesus will appear* (v. 28). This speaks of His imminent return when He will save us from the *presence* of sin (the future tense of salvation).

Jesus Christ appeared on earth once to accomplish His atoning work (v. 26). Then He entered *"into heaven,"* opening the way for our access to God (v. 24). One day He will reappear to consummate our salvation.

Are we eagerly waiting and looking forward for our Lord Jesus Christ to return? Are we maintaining a steady relationship with God on a day-to-day basis? Are we seeking God's interest and His kingdom first before anything in our lives? *If not*, let us make a new commitment to God's kingdom values, and give Him the top priority in our daily living!

*"Beloved, now we are children of God; and it has not yet been revealed what we shall be, but we know that when He is revealed, we shall be like Him, **for we shall see Him as He is**. And everyone who has this hope in Him purifies himself, just as He is pure."* (1 John 3:2-3)

DECEMBER 16   *Bible Reading: Hebrews Chapters 10-13*

SEEING OUR FUTURE THROUGH EYES OF FAITH

*"These all died in faith, not having received the promises, but **having seen them afar off** were assured of them, embraced them and confessed that they were strangers and pilgrims on the earth. For those who say such things declare plainly that they seek a homeland. And truly if they had called to mind that country from which they had come out, they would have had opportunity to return. But now they desire a better, that is, a heavenly country. Therefore God is not ashamed to be called their God, for He has prepared a city for them."* (Heb 11:13-16)

D. L. Moody has once said that *"faith makes all things possible; love makes all things easy."* The people referred in the above passage were Abraham, Isaac, Jacob, and Sarah (vv. 8, 9, 11), who all died before taking possession of the land of *Canaan* that God had promised them (Gen. 12:1-3). They did not live to see the fulfillment of the divine promises. However, they endured in their faith until the end knowing that this world was temporary, that their eternal home would be with God. Finally, they died believing God would fulfill His promises to them eventually one day.

It is interesting to note that these patriarchs were seeking a *'heavenly'* homeland. This is rather remarkable since most of the promises made by God had to do with material blessings on this earth. But they had a *heavenly hope* that enabled them to treat this world as a foreign country. This spirit of pilgrimage is especially pleasing to God, as Darby writes, *"He is not ashamed to be called the God of those whose heart and portion are in heaven."* God had prepared a city for them, and there they would find rest, satisfaction and perfect peace.

In the same way, we should not abandon our hope in the promises of God. Even though we do not see the outcome of today's struggles, *by faith let us see our future* and the fact that we are going to our heavenly home where we will live with our beloved Lord and Savior Jesus forever! Let us remain faithful to our heavenly calling until the very end of our earthly existence!

Remember, for over 2000 years Jesus is preparing a heavenly habitation for us to inhabit one day, and these are His own words of reassurance: *"Let not your heart be troubled; you believe in God, believe*

456

also in Me. In My Father's house are many mansions; if it were not so, I would have told you. I go to prepare a place for you. And if I go and prepare a place for you, I will come again and receive you to Myself; that where I am, there you may be also." (John 14:1-3)

DECEMBER 17   *Bible Reading: James Chapters 1-3*

UNDERSTANDING THE TRUTH ABOUT 'HEAVENLY' WISDOM

*"Who is **wise** and understanding among you? Let him show by good conduct that his works are done in the meekness of wisdom. But **the wisdom that is from above** is first pure, then peaceable, gentle, willing to yield, full of mercy and good fruits, without partiality and without hypocrisy."* (James 3:13, 17)

The *'heavenly' wisdom* of which James speaks is practical and relational that is evidenced by godly attitudes and actions. He exhorts believers to demonstrate their faith through works and demonstrate their wisdom by godly living. The outward sign of *'heavenly' wisdom* is a gentle and humble spirit. Our Lord Jesus was meek and lowly in heart (Matt. 11:29). Therefore, all who are *truly wise* will have the hallmark of genuine humility!

'Heavenly' wisdom that comes from God has the *following characteristics*:

- It is *pure* in thoughts, words, deeds, spirit, body, doctrine, practice, faith and morals.
- It is *peaceable* and will love to maintain peace in every situation without sacrificing purity.
- It is *gentle*, courteous and respectful of the feelings of others.
- It is *willing to yield*, open to reason and ready to give in when truth requires it.
- It is *full of mercy* to those who are in the wrong, and anxious to help them find the right way.
- It is *full of good fruits* by being compassionate and kind.
- It is *without partiality* and does not produce favoritism.
- It is *without hypocrisy* by being sincere and genuine.

James says that *'heavenly' wisdom* is necessary in a teacher. The teacher must exhibit a meek and practical application of the truth. One cannot teach what one does not live. The wisdom that comes from God is *first* pure, *then* promotes peace, and *finally* ends in righteousness (vv. 17, 18). Through the heavenly wisdom we have the ability to view life from God's perspective along with mental perception and comprehension that God will bestow upon us.

Is there bitterness in our hearts or envy? Are we speaking from God's wisdom or the wisdom of the world? Are we peacemakers or troublemakers? If your hearts are right before God, He will use ours words to produce the right kind of fruit in our lives. Our outward behavior will reflect if we are wise as we control our tongues and place our minds deliberately under the authority of God in order to let God control us. Let us ask God in faith to grant us heavenly wisdom today!

"If any of you lacks wisdom, let him ask of God, who gives to all liberally and without reproach, and it will be given to him. But let him ask in faith, with no doubting, for he who doubts is like a wave of the sea driven and tossed by the wind." (James 1:5-6)

DECEMBER 18   *Bible Reading: James Chapters 4-5*

DO <u>NOT</u> MAKE ANY PLANS <u>WITHOUT</u> GOD

Come now, you who say, "Today or tomorrow we will go to such and such a city, spend a year there, buy and sell, and make a profit"; whereas you do not know what will happen tomorrow. For what is your life? It is even a vapor that appears for a little time and then vanishes away. Instead you ought to say, "If the Lord wills, we shall live and do this or that." But now you boast in your arrogance. All such boasting is evil. (James 4:13-16)

In approximately thirteen days, we are going to step into a new year. It is a common trend to make 'New Year Resolutions' that will list our plans for the New Year. Usually in churches, believers will get an occasion to say their testimonies during the 'Watch Night Service' on December 31st night, and barring few exceptions, believers will publicly declare what they plan to do during the New Year. All of us have hopes, dreams, and plans, and the Bible *never* discourages us from looking to the future with bright expectation!

However, in the above passage Apostle James specifically exhorts us that we should *not* make any plans apart from God and boast about them. Since we have absolute no control over our lives or over the events that may happen in our lives, we should *never* boast about our short-range and long-range plans without God in the equation. Let us not forget the parable of the rich fool (Luke 12:13–21) who boasted about his future business plans not knowing that he would die that same night, and would see none of his grandiose plans getting fulfilled. Let us *never* boast about our future as we read in Proverbs 27:1 as follows: *"Do not boast about tomorrow, for you do not know what a day may bring forth."*

Our lives and our future are in God's control. His thoughts and ways are much higher than our thoughts and ways as God Himself tells us: *"For My thoughts are not your thoughts, nor are your ways My ways,"* says the Lord. *"For as the heavens are higher than the earth, so are My ways higher than your ways, and My thoughts than your thoughts"* (Isaiah 55:8-9). So, even if we make any plans for our future, let us ensure that they are written using a chalk or pencil asking ourselves the following question: *"What if?"* and let God have the eraser!

Let us *always* remember that God should be consulted in all our plans, and they should be made *according to His will* and *based on His Word*. We should live and speak in the realization that our destinies are in *His* control. We should say, *"If the Lord wills, we shall live and do this or that."* Omitting God from our future plans is not merely bad planning; *it is sin*. We should *only* make plans in conscious dependence on God, recognizing His sovereign control over our lives. Let all our future plans be only according to God's will and purposes. We can be confident that God has *only* good thoughts and plans about us and our future!

"For I know the thoughts that I think toward you, says the Lord, thoughts of peace and not of evil, to give you a future and a hope." (Jer 29:11)

DECEMBER 19   *Bible Reading: 1 Peter Chapters 1-3*

FOUR POSITIVE ATTITUDES TO LIVE A GODLY LIFE

Therefore gird up the loins of your mind, be sober, and rest your hope fully upon the grace that is to be brought to you at the revelation of Jesus Christ; as obedient children, not conforming yourselves to the former lusts, as in your ignorance; but as He who called you is holy, you also be holy in all your conduct, because it is written, "Be holy, for I am holy." (1 Peter 1:13-16)

Apostle Peter wanted his readers to live joyfully in the midst of sufferings, so he outlined their major responsibilities to God, to other believers, and to the world. In this passage, Peter encouraged his readers to adopt *four positive attitudes* to live a godly life, which are as follows:

1. *Control the imaginations in our minds*: We need to prepare for vigorous and sustained spiritual exertion as we *"fasten our belts"* or *"roll up our sleeves"*. As we go into a hostile world, we should avoid panic and distraction, but instead be poised and stable in our minds. In order to do that we should maintain personal discipline in our thought patterns as we use spiritually sound judgment in all our decisions.

2. *Trust in God with our hearts*: We need to rest our hope fully on the grace of God brought to us through the revelation of Jesus Christ as we put our trust in Him. The fact that Jesus is coming back is a compelling motive for us to endure through the storms and tribulations of life as we lean upon His grace.

3. *Obey God's Word in our actions*: As obedient children, we should not indulge in the sins which characterized us in our former lives. Through obedience to God's word, we should pattern our lives after Christ whose name we bear.

4. *Be holy in our lives and conduct*: Just as Israel was set apart by God from the surrounding nations to be holy, so also are we set apart from sin to the service of God (2:9; Lev. 19:2). Our standard and motivation for holiness is the *absolute moral perfection of God Himself* (v. 16; Matt. 5:48; Eph. 5:1). We are empowered to live holy lives by the Holy Spirit who lives in us. We are to live

dedicated totally to God and separated totally from the sins of this world.

"I beseech you therefore, brethren, by the mercies of God, that you present your bodies a living sacrifice, holy, acceptable to God, which is your reasonable service. And do not be conformed to this world, but be transformed by the renewing of your mind, that you may prove what is that good and acceptable and perfect will of God." (Romans 12:1-2)

DECEMBER 20   *Bible Reading: 1 Peter Chapters 4-5*

TRANSFERRING <u>ALL</u> OUR WORRIES TO GOD

Likewise you younger people, submit yourselves to your elders. Yes, all of you be submissive to one another, and be clothed with humility, for "God resists the proud, but gives grace to the humble." Therefore humble yourselves under the mighty hand of God, that He may exalt you in due time, **casting all your care upon Him, for He cares for you.** (1 Peter 5:5-7)

Corrie Ten Boom has remarked once like this: *"Worry does not empty tomorrow of its sorrow; it empties today of its strength"*. Today's world can be described with three words: *hurry, worry* and *bury*. Worry is like a rocking chair, it gives us something to do, but it doesn't get us anywhere. Many people these days seem to have been infected with GAD (Generalized Anxiety Disorder) a condition marked with a perpetual state of worry about most aspects of their lives.

Our Lord Jesus Christ has expressly counseled us that we should not worry about what we will eat, drink, wear or generally about the future, for God, our Heavenly Father, knows that we need all these things and will take care of us (Matt. 6:25-34, esp. v. 32b). Instead, Jesus invites us to go to Him for rest for our souls (Matt. 11:28-30). Many years ago, King David has echoed the same thought as he expressed these words: *"Cast your burden on the Lord, and He shall sustain you; He shall never permit the righteous to be moved."* (Psalms 55:22)

Worry is *unnecessary*; there is no need for us to bear the burdens when God is willing and able to bear them for us. Worry is *futile*; it hasn't solved a problem yet. Worry is *sin*. A preacher once said: "**Worry is sin** because **it denies the wisdom of God**; it says that He doesn't *know what He's doing.* **It denies the love of God**; *it says He does not care. And* **it denies the power of God**; *it says that He isn't able to deliver me from whatever is causing me to worry."*

In the above passage, Apostle Peter has suggested that *we should transfer all our worries to God, for He cares for us* as our Heavenly Father. Many times Satan uses discouragement as an effective tool against us to pull us down to a state of stress and depression. It is at these times that we should clothe ourselves with the joy of the Lord, which will be our strength and help us to overcome all our worries. The way we can transfer all our worries and care upon God is to go to Him in prayer!

"Be anxious for nothing, but in everything by prayer and supplication, with thanksgiving, let your requests be made known to God; and the peace of God, which surpasses all understanding, will guard your hearts and minds through Christ Jesus." (Phil 4:6-7)

DECEMBER 21   *Bible Reading: 2 Peter Chapters 1-3*

GROWING IN THE GRACE AND KNOWLEDGE OF JESUS CHRIST

"You therefore, beloved, since you know this beforehand, beware lest you also fall from your own steadfastness, being led away with the error of the wicked; but **grow in the grace and knowledge of our Lord and Savior Jesus Christ.** *To Him be the glory both now and forever. Amen."* (2 Peter 3:17-18)

Apostle Peter, the chief Apostle and a close disciple of the Lord Jesus, wrote two general epistles (letters) to all the believers living during his time and beyond. While his *first letter* was a warning about trials *from without* (persecution), his *second letter* was a warning about trials *from within* (heresy). Peter warns everyone to be careful and avoid shortsightedness (1:2-11), guard against false teachers (2:1-22), and in general, be vigilant against personal complacency that would lead to a lazy faith.

As Peter was acutely aware of his impending death (1:14), he wrote some memorable words as he concluded his final letter. He counseled us that we should 'grow in the grace and knowledge of our Lord and Savior Jesus Christ' (v. 18b). 'Grace' is the practical demonstration of the fruit of the Spirit. Growth in grace is not increased head knowledge

462

or tireless activity; it is *increasing likeness to the Lord Jesus. 'Knowledge'* means *getting to know God through His Word.* Growth in knowledge means *increasing study of and subjection to His words, works, and ways.*

We need to grow in our actual, personal knowledge of Jesus Christ as such knowledge is our *greatest protection* against false teachings. This knowledge is the ever-deepening experience of Christ and understanding of His truth that should characterize the entire course of our lives as well.

Our spiritual growth will only happen when our faith is cultivated. We can only do that as we meditate on the word of God (Psalm 119:97-104) as the blessed Holy Spirit will remind us about our areas for personal growth and improvement. Along with that, small group studies and active involvement in a local church will help us to remember the vital truth required for our spiritual growth.

Let us remember that we have a responsibility to appropriate our spiritual resources and grow daily *"till we all come to the unity of the faith and of the knowledge of the Son of God, to a perfect man, to the measure of the stature of the fullness of Christ"* (Eph 4:13).

DECEMBER 22   *Bible Reading: 1 John Chapters 1-3*

LOVING THE 'WORLD' IS A SIN AGAINST GOD

"Do not love the world or the things in the world. If anyone loves the world, the love of the Father is not in him. For all that is in the world— the lust of the flesh, the lust of the eyes, and the pride of life—is not of the Father but is of the world. And the world is passing away, and the lust of it; but he who does the will of God abides forever." (1 John 2:15-17)

In the above passage, the term 'world' does not refer to the universe created by God but the community of sinful humanity that possesses a spirit of rebellion against God under the dominion of Satan (1 John 5:19). In this sense, the 'world' is the satanic system opposing Christ's kingdom on this earth. We are plainly warned not to love the 'world' or the things that are in the 'world' since our love for the world is not compatible with our love for God.

All that the 'world' has to offer may be described as the *lust of the flesh* (sinful sensual pleasures), the *lust of the eyes* (covetousness or materialism), and the *pride of life* (being proud about ourselves). The *lust of the flesh* refers to such sensual bodily appetites as proceed from within our evil nature. The *lust of the eyes* applies to such evil desires as may arise from what we see. The *pride of life* is an unholy ambition for self-display and self-glory. These three areas of appeal were presented to Eve, who gave in (Gen. 3:6) and to Jesus Christ, who overcame through the Word of God (Matt. 4:1–11). We should also depend on the Word of God to defeat temptation in our lives.

Living for this 'world' is like rearranging the deck chairs on the Titanic that will sink soon. This 'world' is passing away so there is no point in living for this world alone. To be consumed with this life is to be unprepared for the next. What a tragedy to invest our resources in what will not last. But we will abide forever when we do the will of God as this will deliver us from the temptation of passing things.

Let us be careful that nothing breaches our spiritual defense. We cannot afford to let down our guard anytime, but need to be alert to what entices us today. A lapse opens the door to sin, which in turn may develop into a sinful habit that will eventually cause us to drift from God. Let us pray this simple prayer today: *"Search me, O God, and know my heart; try me, and know my anxieties; and see if there is any wicked way in me, and lead me in the way everlasting."* (Psalms 139:23-24)

DECEMBER 23   *Bible Reading: 1 John Chapters 4-5*

KNOWING GOD THROUGH 'LOVING ONE ANOTHER'

*"**Beloved, let us love one another**, for love is of God; and everyone who loves is born of God and knows God. He who does not love does not know God, for God is love. In this the love of God was manifested toward us, that God has sent His only begotten Son into the world, that we might live through Him. In this is love, not that we loved God, but that He loved us and sent His Son to be the propitiation for our sins. Beloved, if God so loved us, **we also ought to love one another**."* (1 John 4:7-11)

In the above passage, Apostle John spelled out the nature of the love demanded from every believer. We are to love as a response to God's own love and to His loving activity. The love of God the Father for *"His only begotten Son"* (v. 9) is the source of the love that binds the fellowship of believers together as a family. By giving us His Son, God the Father introduced us to the perfect love and eternal life that the Father and the Son have always enjoyed.

We must emulate God's *'agape'* love by *loving one another* (vv. 7, 11, 12) since we are *"born of God"*. God provides both the source (v. 9) and example (v. 11) of our love for others that is an integral part of our relationship with God (v. 12). While we have never seen God (v. 12a, John 1:18), we can see that God's love is evident in the work of Christ (v. 9) and in our love for others (v. 12).

Apostle John explains the manifestation of God's love in *three tenses*. In the *past*, it was manifested to us as sinners in the gift of His only begotten Son (4:9–11). In the *present*, it is manifested to us as saints in His dwelling in us (4:12–16). In the *future*, it will be manifested to us in giving us boldness in the Day of Judgment.

God loved us by sending His Son Jesus Christ as the *'propitiation'* (satisfaction) for our sins. How can we personify God's love in our lives?

- Just like God personifies love (4:8, 16), we should reflect God's love in our world (4:7)
- Just like God loved us (4:19), we should love God by keeping His commands (4:18, 19; 5:3)
- Just like God gave up His Son for us (4:9, 10), we should give ourselves and our substance for others (3:17; 4:11)
- Just like Christ laid down His life for us (3:16), we should also lay down our lives for others (3:16)

Thus, we can show that we are God's children *through our sacrificial attitudes and actions for others*. Our love for others makes God's love real and visible to them so we can better witness to them about Christ. It also makes God real and personal to us thus enabling us to *'know'* God better. Let us seek to experience God's love in your heart by sharing it with others!

If someone says, "I love God," and hates his brother, he is a liar; for he who does not love his brother whom he has seen, how can he love God whom he has not seen? And this commandment we have from Him: that **he who loves God must love his brother also.** (1 John 4:20-21)

PROSPER IN ALL THINGS, BUT 'WALK IN TRUTH'

*"Beloved, I pray that you may prosper in all things and be in health, just as your soul prospers. For I rejoiced greatly when brethren came and testified of the truth that is in you, just as you **walk in the truth**. I have no greater joy than to hear that my children **walk in truth**." (3 John 1:2-4)*

In the above passage, Apostle John is wishing his beloved Gaius that his physical health might correspond to his spiritual vigor. Gaius was clearly a dear friend of Apostle John. His physical health and prosperity was as important to John as his spiritual health. So, John prays that the temporal prosperity and physical health of Gaius will be commensurate with his spiritual status. This prayer gives us a warrant for praying for the physical, the material, and the spiritual well-being of others; and also provides us with a model of intercession.

The reason for John's prayer was because he had heard from others that Gaius's lifestyle was consistent with the *truth*. *Truth* here refers to the *'body of truth'* given to the church through the apostles and prophets, that is, *according to God's Word, the revelation of His truth*. Gaius walked according to the God's Word rather than the ways of the world. He could have been a disciple of John's or simply a younger believer.

The importance of doctrinal integrity and *truth* is evident in John's affirmation that nothing brought greater joy to him than to know that his *spiritual* children *walk in truth*. What a thrill it is to see our *spiritual* children going on for the Lord, from grace to grace. This emphasizes the importance of follow-up work in all our evangelistic endeavors.

We should not only hold the *truth*, but allow the *truth* to hold us. People would rather see a sermon than hear one. People could see the truth in Gaius because he loved it and walked in obedience to it, and that brought great joy to John. May every Christian parent can echo this and even make it a daily prayer!

*"I rejoiced greatly that I have found some of your children **walking in truth**, as we received commandment from the Father." (2 John 1:4)*

Bible Reading: Revelation Chapters 1-3

HAVE WE LEFT OUR 'FIRST LOVE'?

*"To the angel of the **church of Ephesus** write, 'These things says He who holds the seven stars in His right hand, who walks in the midst of the seven golden lampstands:...**Nevertheless I have this against you, that you have left your first love.** Remember therefore from where you have fallen; repent and do the first works, or else I will come to you quickly and remove your lampstand from its place—unless you repent.'"* (Rev 2:1, 4-5)

When Apostle John started writing the 'revelation of Jesus Christ' while on exile in the island of Patmos (1:9), he was commissioned to write *'the things he saw, the things that are and the things that will take place'* (1:19). Among *'the things that are'*, the Lord Jesus wanted to speak about the *true* condition of the seven churches in Asia (1:11b) and *exhort* them to *overcome* their liability in order to receive the reward that Jesus would give them one day.

The church of Ephesus was started by Apostle Paul in A.D. 53 (Acts 19:1-10) who stayed there for three years in order to warn the believers *'night and day with tears'* (Acts 20:31). This church further enjoyed the ministries of Priscilla/Aquila, Apollos and Timothy (1 Tim. 1:3). In fact, they were fervent in their faith and love as evidenced from Paul's writing to them from his prison cell in about A.D. 62 (Eph. 1:15-16). We can also note that Apostle John continued as an Elder in that church in Ephesus and wrote three epistles (1, 2, 3 John) that centered on *love*. However, about thirty years later, God revealed their *true* current state – *'they had left their first love'*.

Why is love so important to God? The best answer to this is because God's essence is love: *God IS love* (1 John 4:8b). Love is *greater than anything else in our lives* and *it never fails* (1 Cor. 13). Love is the *core objective* of the *new* (John 13:34) and the *great* (Matt. 22:36-40) commandment that Jesus has given us. We *lie* to God when we say that we *love* God and *hate* other people (1 John 4:20). God expects us to love Him and other people as His children!

What is meant by first love? Jeremiah 2:2 describes it beautifully as follows: *'thus says the Lord: "I remember you, the kindness of your youth, **the love of your betrothal**, when you went after Me in the wilderness, in a land not sown."* It is that *fervent, passionate love* felt by either an engaged or newly wedded couple. The wise man Agur finds it too wonderful to explain it as he describes it as *'the way of a man with a virgin'* (Prov. 30:19). This is the kind of love Jesus has for us and expects us to have in return.

However, *many of us have left our 'first love'*. We had it at one stage of our life journey, but when we examine ourselves today we will soon realize that we have *'left our first love'* somewhere along the way. We have *lost our fervency in worship* that displays our love to God and we are lukewarm (Rev. 3:15-16) in our relationship with God. We *fail to obey the commands* that Jesus has given us (John 14:15). We are hyper-critical on the faults of other people, as we disregard what Apostle Peter has told us: *'and above all things have fervent love for one another, for "love will cover a multitude of sins"'* (1 Peter 4:8). Our lack-luster love is a fulfillment of the end-time prophecy (Matt. 24:12) as well.

Ask yourself this question: *Have I left my 'first love'?* On this Christmas Day that reflects God passionate love for humankind (by giving up His only begotten Son to this world to live among us and die as our substitute: John 3:16), let us renew our commitment to truly love God and people fervently and passionately ('first love') – *for God expects nothing lesser than this from our lives!*

DECEMBER 26   *Bible Reading: Revelation Chapters 4-6*

'THE LION OF JUDAH' BECAME 'THE SACRIFICIAL LAMB' FOR US

*'So I wept much, because no one was found worthy to open and read the scroll, or to look at it. But one of the elders said to me, "Do not weep. Behold, **the Lion of the tribe of Judah**, the Root of David, has prevailed to open the scroll and to loose its seven seals." And I looked, and behold, in the midst of the throne and of the four living creatures, and in the midst of the elders, stood a **Lamb as though it had been slain**, having seven horns and seven eyes, which are the seven Spirits of God sent out into all the earth. Then He came and took the scroll out of the right hand of Him who sat on the throne'.* (Rev 5:4-7)

In the above passage we see the consummation of God's *twofold purpose* in history: *to reclaim His kingdom* and *to redeem His people*. This *twofold victory* over Satan was first predicted in Genesis 3:15 and then covenanted to Abraham in the promise of a land and a Seed (see Gen. 12:1-3, Deut. 30:1-5, 2 Sam. 7:12-16). What we can visualize through the pages of this last prophetical book is how God will finally fulfill His *ultimate purpose* that He has planned before time began!

When Apostle John wept much as it appeared that no one was found worthy to open the scroll containing God's revelation, one of the elders comforted John with the glad news that Jesus, the Lion of the tribe of Judah, was qualified to open the scroll, break the seals, and thus release the judgments.

In Revelation, our Lord Jesus Christ is presented both as the sacrificial Lamb for the world (Redeemer, see John 1:29) and Lion of Judah (Ruler, see Gen. 49:10). At His First Coming, He was the Lamb for the *ultimate sacrifice* and became our *Savior*. At His Second Coming, He will be the Lion, *our Ruler and Judge*. Christ has the right to judge, possess, and rule the earth because of His submission to the death of the Cross (Phil. 2:8–11).

Apostle John further saw God the Father on the throne and the Lamb coming and taking the scroll out of His right hand, symbolizing a *transfer of authority* from the Father to the Son to reveal the future and to execute judgment. This transfer precipitated an outpouring of praise for the Lamb because it signaled that Christ would begin judging in response to the prayers of believers throughout history (v. 8). As Lamb, Jesus offers salvation to everyone who will believe in Him; as Lion, one day He will judge all those who reject Him.

Let us understand that *Jesus Christ, who had ultimate power and authority became the sacrificial Lamb for the ultimate sacrifice for our sins.* Let us sincerely thank Him today for paying the *ultimate price* of our redemption!

"Knowing that you were not redeemed with corruptible things, like silver or gold, from your aimless conduct received by tradition from your fathers, but with the precious blood of Christ, as of a lamb without blemish and without spot." (1 Peter 1:18-19)

DECEMBER 27   *Bible Reading: Revelation Chapters 7-9*

SEVEN 'BLESSINGS' FROM GOD FOR FAITHFULNESS

"Therefore they are before the throne of God, and serve Him day and night in His temple. And He who sits on the throne will dwell among

them. They shall neither hunger anymore nor thirst anymore; the sun shall not strike them, nor any heat; for the Lamb who is in the midst of the throne will shepherd them and lead them to living fountains of waters. And God will wipe away every tear from their eyes." (Rev 7:15-17)

In his vision, Apostle John sees a great multitude of Gentiles from among all the different parts of the world, who were converted during the Great Tribulation, arrayed in white and standing before the throne (v. 9). This great multitude appears in white robes displaying their purity and carries palm branches in their hands symbolic of their final victory. Their earthly trials are now over. John is informed by one of the elders that these people had come out of the Great Tribulation and their robes have been washed in the blood of the Lamb (v. 14).

Faith in Christ had made these redeemed Gentiles both holy and righteous. These redeemed saints will receive *seven wonderful blessings* as a reward for their faithfulness:

1. *Blessing of Proximity to God:* "*Therefore they are before the throne of God*" (v: 15a). They would be stationed right before the throne where they can see Him forever.

2. *Blessing of Unending Service to God:* "*And serve Him day and night in His temple*" (v: 15b). 'To serve' indicates priestly service before the Lord (1:6; 5:10).

3. *Blessing of Close Fellowship with God:* "*He who sits on the throne will dwell among them*" (v: 15c). The majority in the multitude had not seen Christ when He dwelt among Jews (John 1:14) but now God will 'tabernacle' among them in heaven.

4. *Blessing of Total Satisfaction:* "*They shall neither hunger nor thirst anymore*" (v: 16a). Christ will give them the 'bread of life' (John 6:33, 35, 48, 51) and 'living water' (John 4:10; 7:38) that will totally satisfy them.

5. *Blessing of Total Security:* "*The sun shall not strike them, nor any heat*" (v: 16b). Just like Jehovah went before the Israelites by day in a pillar of cloud to lead the way and by night in a pillar of fire to give them light (Exodus 13:21-22), He will provide them total security in heaven.

6. *Blessing of Accurate Guidance: "For the Lamb who is in the midst of the throne will shepherd them and lead them to fountains of the waters of life"* (v: 17a). Jesus will fulfill His role as the Good Shepherd (Psalms 23; John 10) as He will guide them continually for eternity.

7. *Blessing of the Fullness of Joy: "God will wipe away every tear from their eyes"* (v: 17b). Earthly sorrows will be over, as God will Himself wipe away every tear of grief. Instead, the following observation by the Psalmist will become a reality: *"In Your presence is fullness of joy; at Your right hand are pleasures forevermore."* (Psalms 16:11)

Let us endeavor to live righteously before God and other people. The only way to gain entry into heaven, God's Kingdom, is to be born again (John 3:5) by accepting Jesus Christ as our Lord and Savior. It also involves us staying true to God and being faithful to the upward call of Jesus Christ all the days of lives.

DECEMBER 28   *Bible Reading: Revelation Chapters 10-12*

THREE WAYS TO OVERCOME THE POWER OF SATAN

Then I heard a loud voice saying in heaven, "Now salvation, and strength, and the kingdom of our God, and the power of His Christ have come, for the accuser of our brethren, who accused them before our God day and night, has been cast down. **And they overcame him by the blood of the Lamb and by the word of their testimony, and they did not love their lives to the death.***" (Rev 12:10-11)*

The announcement that *"salvation, and strength, and the kingdom of our God and the power of His Christ have come"* (v. 10) celebrates Christ's resurrection victory over Satan and the beginning of the New Covenant age (see Col. 2:15; Heb. 2:14). Satan is called *"the accuser of our brethren"* (v. 10), and he was able to accuse God's people before the throne of God (see Job 1–2; Zech. 3:1) until the death of Christ. Now, because of the atonement that Christ has obtained for His children, Satan has now lost *all* grounds for accusation!

"What then shall we say to these things? If God is for us, who can be against us? He who did not spare His own Son, but delivered Him up

for us all, how shall He not with Him also freely give us all things? Who shall bring a charge against God's elect? It is God who justifies. Who is he who condemns? It is Christ who died, and furthermore is also risen, who is even at the right hand of God, who also makes intercession for us." (Romans 8:31-34)

Satan's activity is now limited to the earthly level as he seeks to accuse our consciences against ourselves and seeks to bring us under self-condemnation. In response to such attacks from Satan, we should *plead the accomplishments of the blood of the Lamb* (v. 11). This constitutes *the defensive part* of our spiritual warfare. The *word of our testimony* (evangelism) is our *offensive warfare*. The fact that we are prepared to die demonstrates that *our victory is measured in faithful martyrdom*.

Thus, there are *'three ways'* to overcome the power of Satan in our lives: (1) the blood of the Lamb (which justifies us before our Holy God), (2) the word of our testimony (being a 'faithful' witness) to the work and grace of God, and (3) our willingness to be martyred (not loving our lives) for our faith.

With Christ's victory over Satan, we can maintain our confession of faith in Him and thereby share in His victory. With our sins blotted out and our declaration of Jesus' redemptive work in our lives, we can silence the accusations of Satan. His accusing voice of condemnation and guilt has already been swallowed up in the triumph of Calvary. Let us boldly declare our abiding faith in the accomplished work of the Cross. Let us constantly participate in Jesus' ultimate victory by overcoming Satan by the power of the blood of Jesus and our steady confession of faith in Christ's triumph!

DECEMBER 29   *Bible Reading: Revelation Chapters 13-15*

BLESSED ARE THOSE WHO 'DIE' IN JESUS CHRIST

*Here is the patience of the saints; here are those who keep the commandments of God and the faith of Jesus. Then I heard a voice from heaven saying to me, "Write: **'Blessed are the dead who die in the Lord from now on.'"** "Yes," says the Spirit, "that they may rest from their labors, and their works follow them."* (Rev 14:12-13)

In the above passage Apostle John receives special instruction regarding those who die in Christ. These born-again sanctified believers in Christ, who *patiently* with endurance keep His commandments and faith in very difficult times, will receive a special divine blessing. They will be blessed through rest, resurrection and reigning with Christ during the Millennium (20:4–6).

The word *'blessed'* mentioned in this passage is the second of the seven *'beatitudes'* in the book of Revelation (see 1:3; 16:15; 19:9; 20:6; 22:7, 14). We are *'blessed'* to die in Christ (2 Cor 5:6, 8) mainly due to the following *three reasons*:

1. We die in a state of vital union with Christ and will be with Him forever.
2. We rest from all sin, temptation, sorrow, and persecution.
3. Our good deeds remain on the earth while we receive heavenly rewards for our services and sufferings.

Spiritual rest is available to anyone who comes to Jesus Christ in faith (see Matt. 11:28). Godly believers who die will rest from their labors and their good works will be remembered and rewarded (see 1 Tim. 5:25). It would indeed be a blessing for the believers who live during the Great Tribulation to die as martyrs as they would be at rest beyond the grave and God would then reward their faithful deeds.

Let us understand that everything we do for Christ and in His name for others will be richly rewarded—every kindness, sacrificial gift, prayer, and word of testimony. Let us determine to live for Christ, so that we can die in Christ, and be counted among the *'blessed'* in Christ!

"For to me, to live is Christ, and to die is gain. But if I live on in the flesh, this will mean fruit from my labor; yet what I shall choose I cannot tell. For I am hard pressed between the two, having a desire to depart and be with Christ, which is far better." (Phil 1:21-23)

DECEMBER 30 *Bible Reading: Revelation Chapters 16-18*

ARE 'WE' <u>AMONG</u> THE 'CALLED', 'CHOSEN' AND 'FAITHFUL'?

"The ten horns which you saw are ten kings who have received no kingdom as yet, but they receive authority for one hour as kings with the beast. These are of one mind, and they will give their power and

authority to the beast. *These will make war with the Lamb, and the Lamb will overcome them, for He is Lord of lords and King of kings; and **those who are with Him are called, chosen, and faithful**.*" (Rev 17:12-14)

The above passage speaks about an evil empire that fights against the Lord Jesus when He returns to earth at the end of the Tribulation with His followers. This empire consists of ten government leaders who unanimously surrender their military power, political authority and national sovereignty to the beast. The purpose of Satan through the beast and this ten-nation confederation is to establish an invincible kingdom that Christ cannot overcome when He returns.

However, this war will result in victory for the Lamb (Jesus Christ) and His redeemed children (not angels), and *two reasons can be ascribed for this victory*:

1. *The character of the Lamb*: Christ is *"King of kings and Lord of lords"*. He has supreme dominion and power over all things both by His nature and by His office. All the powers of earth and hell will bow to His authority.

2. *The character of Christ's followers*: These redeemed people are *"called, chosen, and faithful"*. They are called out by commission to this warfare; they are chosen and fitted for it, and they will be faithful in their allegiance to Christ.

The question for us today is: are we among the *"called, chosen, and faithful"* that will be in the Lord's army? Let us examine these terms in detail:

- **We have been *"called"***: God calls only those He has *predestined* (Romans 8:30), and *"not many mighty, not many noble, are called"* (1 Cor 1:26). His calling is *irrevocable* (Romans 11:29). God has called us *"into the fellowship of His Son, Jesus Christ our Lord"* (1 Cor 1:9), *"not according to our works, but according to His own purpose and grace which was given to us"* (2 Tim 1:9).

- **We have been *"chosen"***: *"Many are called, but few are chosen"* (Matt 22:14). We did not choose God, but *He chose us* so that we should go and bear fruit and our fruit should remain (John 15:16). We *"are a chosen generation"* to *"proclaim the praises of Him who called us out of darkness into His marvelous light"* (1 Peter 2:9).

- **We should remain *"faithful"***: We should be faithful in small things, and we will be then faithful in greater aspects of our lives

(Luke 16:10). We should be faithful until our death and God will reward us with *"the crown of life"* (Rev 2:10).

Let Apostle Paul's proclamation towards the end of his life become our guiding principle as well: *"I have fought the good fight, I have finished the race, I have kept the faith. Finally, there is laid up for me the crown of righteousness, which the Lord, the righteous Judge, will give to me on that Day, and not to me only but also to all who have loved His appearing."* (2 Tim 4:7-8)

DECEMBER 31   *Bible Reading: Revelation Chapters 19-22*

IS YOUR NAME WRITTEN IN THE LAMB'S 'BOOK OF LIFE'?

"Then I saw a great white throne and Him who sat on it, from whose face the earth and the heaven fled away. And there was found no place for them. And I saw the dead, small and great, standing before God, and books were opened. And another book was opened, which is the **Book of Life***. And the dead were judged according to their works, by the things which were written in the books.* **And anyone not found written in the Book of Life was cast into the lake of fire.***"* (Rev 20:11-12, 15)

In this passage, Apostle John viewed another terrifying scene in his vision. The *"great white throne"* is God's throne in heaven. John saw earth and heaven flee from God's presence, which indicates that we have come to the end of God's dealings with this earth. The dead ones standing before this throne are the *unsaved of all ages* who are now resurrected and judged. They come from all classes and groups of humanity. The *"books"* contain a *record of their deeds*. The *"book of life"* contains the *names of God's elect*.

This judgment closes the millennial period and opens the age to come in God's eternal kingdom. It is the greatest of all judgments because it encompasses all the wicked from the beginning of man's history. Jesus Christ is the one sitting on the great white throne, fulfilling John 5:22. Those who are judged are lost because they refused God's salvation in Christ by grace through faith. *Their doom is the second and final death!*

God will condemn those raised to face this judgment because of their works, including failure to believe in Jesus Christ (see John 6:29).

Only God's elect, those whose names are written in the Book of Life, will escape the lake of fire. The rejection of the eternal gospel results in eternal condemnation (14:6, 7). An eternal separation is now made between those who have *"life"* and those who have *"death"* (Dan. 12:2; John 5:29).

Let us understand that this judgment involves only the lost and follows the second resurrection, which is the resurrection to condemnation. Sinners who rejected Christ will face Him and hear Him say, *"Depart from Me!"* (Matt. 7:23; 25:41). This solemn scene ought to move us to ask ourselves this question: *"Is my name written in the Lamb's Book of Life?"* If we have accepted Jesus Christ as our Lord and Savior, and we are living in obedience to His commandments, we will not have to face the *"great white throne"* judgment. We should also *pray for the lost people around us* and *witness to them* so that they will not have to face this final judgment as well.

"For God so loved the world that He gave His only begotten Son, that whoever believes in Him should not perish but have everlasting life. For God did not send His Son into the world to condemn the world, but that the world through Him might be saved. He who believes in Him is not condemned; but he who does not believe is condemned already, because he has not believed in the name of the only begotten Son of God." (John 3:16-18)

CPSIA information can be obtained at www.ICGtesting.com
Printed in the USA
LVOW05s2348280214

375592LV00034B/1787/P